Sunset

Western Garden Annual

2004 EDITION

By the Editors of *Sunset Magazine* and Sunset Books

Creeping thyme grows between flagstone pavers
in this entry garden featured on page 258.

Sunset Publishing Corporation ■ Menlo Park, California

STEVEN GUNTHER

'Hachiya' and 'Fuyu' persimmons, page 325

The Century Progresses

Like its ten predecessors, this *Western Garden Annual* gathers together the entire body of gardening and outdoor living material presented in the previous year's issues of *Sunset Magazine.* In each of the 12 chapters—one for each month of 2003—you will find all garden-related information compiled from all regional editions of the magazine.

Each chapter opens with the month's Garden Guide mini-articles: a potpourri of short pieces on plants, tools, innovations, and events relevant to that month or to the gardening period just ahead. Next, the Garden Checklists, one for each magazine region, highlight the appropriate garden activities. Alluringly illustrated feature articles conclude the chapter's offerings.

Throughout these pages, plant performance and gardening activities are keyed to numbered climate zones; 24 of these zones are contained in the contiguous Western states, while an additional 5 cover Alaska and Hawaii. All zones are mapped and fully described in the seventh edition (2001) of the *Sunset Western Garden Book.*

SUNSET BOOKS

VP, General Manager
Richard A. Smeby
VP, Editorial Director
Bob Doyle
Production Director
Lory Day
Director of Operations
Rosann Sutherland
Sales Development Director
Linda Barker
Executive Editor
Bridget Biscotti Bradley
Art Director
Vasken Guiragossian

STAFF FOR THIS BOOK

Managing Editor
Suzanne Normand Eyre
Contributing Editors
Philip Edinger
Helen Sweetland
Indexer
Pamela Evans
Production Coordinator
Danielle Javier

Front cover: *Chrysanthemum.*
Photographer: Thomas J. Story.

Back cover: One of the gardens selected for *Sunset*'s 2003 Garden Design awards.
Photographer: Saxon Holt.

First printing: February 2004
Copyright © 2004 Sunset Publishing Corporation, Menlo Park, CA 94025.
First edition. All rights reserved, including the right of reproduction in whole or in part in any form.

ISSN 1073-5089
Hardcover edition: ISBN 0-376-03911-6
Softcover edition: ISBN 0-376-03912-4
Printed in the United States.

SUNSET PUBLISHING CORPORATION

Senior Vice President
Kevin Lynch
VP, Publisher
Tom Marshall
VP, Administration and Manufacturing
Lorinda Reichert
VP, Marketing Director
Beth Whiteley
VP, Consumer Marketing Director
Christina Olsen
VP, General Manager
Mark Okean
VP, Editor-in-Chief, Sunset Magazine
Katie Tamony
Executive Editor
Carol Hoffman
Creative Director
Paul Donald
Managing Editor
Alan J. Phinney
Art Director
James H. McCann
Senior Editor, Gardening
Kathleen Norris Brenzel
Senior Editor
Richards E. Bushnell
Designers
Dennis W. Leong
Laura H. Martin
Keith Whitney

All material in this book originally appeared in the 2003 issues of *Sunset Magazine.*

Sunset Western Garden Annual was produced by Sunset Books. If you have comments or suggestions, please let us hear from you. Write us at:
Sunset Books
Garden Book Editorial
80 Willow Road
Menlo Park, CA 94025
or visit our website at
www.sunset.com

Contents

CLAIRE COLEMAN

THIS PLANTING IN PALM DESERT was among the first in the area to feature showy drifts of Southwest native species such as brittlebush, bunny ears cactus, and deer grass. For more on this garden, see page 326.

Outdoor Living...Western Style

Given the West's spectacular scenery and varied topography, it's no wonder Westerners zestfully embrace the out-of-doors and all that it offers. Nowhere is this more evident than in Western attitudes toward the garden. As long ago as 1955, seminal California landscape designer Thomas Church proclaimed his credo "Gardens Are for People"; and in the years since, *Sunset* has been the foremost proponent of the garden as extended living space.

In the 2003 gardening year encapsulated between these covers, the outdoor living message resonates boldly and in great variety. The 2003 Western Garden Design Award–winning entries, announced in February, feature people-friendly designs to suit a cross section of modern situations, with an emphasis on the garden as an outdoor living room and recreation space. A subtheme, reflecting our growing numbers and shrinking lots, was designing for privacy and optimal use of space.

Other months highlighted design responses to specific outdoor living needs: a garden for children and pets, a garden room composed of varied culinary plants, a garden as entertainment venue, and several front-yard makeovers that rescued that space from public property and converted it to private use. Even the dreaded narrow side yard was remodeled into a place to enjoy rather than avoid.

But of course a garden must be interesting enough, and well enough grown, to entice. And *Sunset*—as usual—rose to the occasion with timely features on all facets of gardening, from plant selection to maintenance. September, in fact, tackled the totality of landscaping in four distinct Western regions: Northwest, California, High Country, and Desert. For each region you'll find its climatic characteristics and challenges, design tips for gardens attuned to the region, star plant performers, and illustrated planting pointers.

In keeping with the Western embrace of elements from diverse cultures, April revealed how to adapt that most English of creations—the cottage garden—to climates throughout the West. Later, July instructed daring gardeners how to obtain more garden color. . . from paint! And at the nuts-and-bolts, dirty-fingernails level, the spring months advised on drought-fighting techniques, how to remodel around mature trees, and how to employ landscape fabrics for mulch, shade, and protection.

But a garden is not a garden without plants, and intrepid *Sunset* reporters made sure that plant aficionados had plenty of new material to ponder. For the legions of rose lovers, the year kicked off with a feature on landscaping with roses, naming the best varieties for the various Western climates; October countered with a garden devoted to ornamental grasses. Other notable plant profiles included witch hazels, *Euphorbia characias wulfenii,* gerberas, drought-tolerant zinnias, spuria irises, compact lavenders, amazingly varied evergreen conifers, and the vast world of poppies. For Southern California and desert dwellers, July featured a signature regional plant: the palm. In prime planting time—November—the emphasis was on good choices for growing beneath native oaks and a feature on the best really fast-growing trees.

For readers who garden to eat, a cornucopia of articles presented new plants and fresh techniques: a dwarf avocado, truly dwarf citrus trees, lemon grass, vegetable varieties for small spaces and containers, the best fruits for the high desert around Las Vegas, tepee-trained tomatoes, and how to grow your own mixed salad greens.

Updates to container gardening included features on plant combinations to attract nectar-seeking birds, bees, and butterflies; plants to stock containers for all-year beauty; how to create flower-packed hanging baskets; and a stellar choice for desert containers: tough-as-nails agave.

If the range of 2003 topics appears diverse, even scattered, it has succeeded in capturing Western openness to new ideas from everywhere. Although Western gardening varies from region to region, in every corner of the West, the spirit is global.

MINIATURE WATER PLANTS fill these ceramic cache pots to create a serene, green tabletop garden. For more ideas on indoor mini-landscapes, see pages 24–27.

THOMAS J. STORY

January

2003 All-America Selections

Since 1932, the All-America Selections program has been introducing exceptional plants that have proved themselves in trial gardens across the country. This year, a dozen flowers and vegetables are making their debut. Here are four selections (three are shown at right) that excelled in *Sunset's* garden in Menlo Park, California. They were all grown in full sun.

Rudbeckia hirta 'Prairie Sun' (top). Unlike other black-eyed Susans, 'Prairie Sun' has pale green centers surrounded by 3- to 6-inch-wide daisies. Petals are golden near the center, fading to butter yellow at the tips. A single plant, 2 to 3 feet tall, bears as many as 20 blooms at a time. The flowers are great for cutting.

'Papaya Pear' summer squash (bottom right). Shaped like a Hawaiian papaya, this squash has brilliant yellow skin. Harvest fruits when they're about 3 inches across, before large seeds form. The white flesh has a mild flavor; try it steamed or stir-fried. At just 2 feet tall by 2½ feet wide, this plant is a compact choice for small gardens.

Agastache foeniculum 'Golden Jubilee' (bottom left). With lavender flower spikes set against fragrant chartreuse leaves, this hyssop looks stunning in large containers. The plant reaches 3½ feet tall with a spread of 10 to 12 inches and flower spikes up to 3 inches long.

Dianthus 'Corona Cherry Magic' (not pictured) bears mounds of frilly, 2-inch-wide flowers with variable bicolor patterns of deep cherry red and pale rose pink.

Look for these plants at garden centers and nurseries this spring, or order seeds from **Park Seed Company** *(www. parkseed.com or 800/845-3369).* Visit *www.all-americaselections.org* to see all the 2003 winners. —*Julie Chai*

Agave stars in this pot

Finding a beautiful year-round container plant that can stand up to harsh desert climates is often a serious challenge. If you want that plant to coexist with a changing cast of seasonal annuals, you're left with a very short list of candidates. A top pick for Tucson landscape designer Jeffrey Trent is octopus agave *(A. vilmoriniana)*.

Trent selected this agave with twisty 2- to 3-inch-wide leaves as the focal point of a container at the entryway to the La Paz Foundation. To suit the charity's circa-1900 building, Trent chose a cast-iron urn typical of that era. To avoid changing all the plants every season, he elected to use one bold permanent feature—the octopus agave—underplanted with annuals that can be easily popped in and out of the urn. In the cool-season arrangement shown above,

blue lobelia and white sweet alyssum skirt the agave; later, trailing lantana or portulaca will take their place. "The hot, wet soil in this container would rot out most succulents, but octopus agave is incredibly tolerant," says Trent.

In the ground, octopus agave spreads slowly to 6 feet across. But in a generous container, it will stay a manageable size for several years. This agave is cold-hardy in the low and intermediate deserts, but it needs frost protection in the high desert. It will grow in full sun or partial shade. —*Sharon Cohoon*

Tune in your very own weather report

A new generation of high-tech instruments makes it easier to track the weather outside your home, while you're cozy and dry inside. With this wireless technology, there are no cables to install. Instead, a remote sensor placed outdoors transmits a radio signal to a monitor inside your house, which shows the data on a liquid crystal display. These instruments accurately measure a variety of atmospheric conditions, from air temperature to rainfall.

There are several battery-powered devices priced from $30 to $100 that measure outdoor and indoor temperatures and humidity; some record barometric pressure as well. Rain gauges are sold separately (self-emptying models cost $60 to $80). Wind sensors are sold as part of complete wireless weather stations ($400 to $1,000).

Most remote sensors can transmit data 80 or 90 feet, but walls and other obstructions can sharply reduce their range. For the most accurate readings, mount the sensor within unobstructed sight of a monitor that's positioned just inside a window.

Look for these instruments at garden and nature shops, or order from Weather Shop (www.weathershop.com or 800/949-8434) or Wind & Weather (www.windandweather. com or 800/922-9463).

—*Jim McCausland*

Two-in-one tool sharpener

Until now, gardeners usually needed at least two sharpeners to keep the blades of their tools honed—one for axes, hatchets, and other tools that have a double-sided edge; and the other for large garden shears, hoes, shovels, and lawn mowers with a single sharp edge. But a new device called the Axe & Tool Sharpener is equipped with two

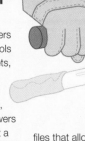

Position sharpener's small pointed file on the blade, then grasp the handle as shown and pull it toward you.

files that allow you to easily and quickly sharpen tools of either type.

One file on the sturdy orange plastic handle has two edges made of diamond-sharpened carbide. When the sharpener is pulled firmly across a double-sided blade, it hones both sides of the tool at once. The other file has only one sharpening edge. All tools should be clamped securely (with the blade up) in a vise before they are filed.

The Axe & Tool Sharpener is available at some Home Depot stores and, for $12 (plus shipping), from Creative Sales Co. (www.supersharpener.com).

—*Lauren Bonar Swezey*

Classy combo

Covered with tiny flowers and resistant to frost and rain, members of the heath *(Erica)* clan rank among the most beautiful winter-blooming plants. Pop some in a pot this month and they'll bloom until spring.

For the rectangular terra-cotta container shown at right, we planted eight *Erica* x *darleyensis* 'Kramer's Red' from 4-inch pots, plus one *Chamaecyparis lawsoniana* 'Treasure' (a dwarf, gold-leafed form of Port Orford cedar) from a 1-gallon nursery can.

Most readily available commercial potting mixes do a good job of supplying the slightly acid soil and proper drainage that heaths need to thrive. If you mix controlled-release fertilizer into the soil when planting, all you'll have to do during the first several months is water them.

The heaths and the dwarf *Chamaecyparis* thrive in full sun on the mild western side of the Cascades. On the eastern side, they need partial shade in summer and protection from hard freezes in winter. (These also do well in California's coastal Sunset zones 15 through 17.)

—J.M.

Red-flowered heather billows around dwarf Port Orford cedar.

Terra-cotta pot, lion statue, and container with *giglio* (fleur-de-lis) detail, at ColleZione.

Timeless terra-cotta

If you long for the craftsmanship of handmade Italian terra-cotta pottery but a trip to Italy is not in your future, visit ColleZione, a new specialty shop in Menlo Park. Here you'll find peach-hued pieces in a range of styles and sizes, from urns to olive jars, all handcrafted by artisans in Tuscany and Umbria.

"We love to bring such fine craftsmanship to the United States," says MaryAnn Mullen, who runs the store with husband Ron van Thiel. Everything in the 1,100-square-foot showroom is made using traditional materials and techniques, many of which bear their creators' handprints. "For us, design and quality equal value," Mullen says.

10–4 Wed–Sat. 43485 Edison Way, Menlo Park; www.collezioneusa.com or (650) 327-1342. —J. C.

The white queue

'Mme Alfred Carrière' may be a dowager—she was introduced in 1879—but in the West's low elevations where winter temperatures don't drop below 10°, this venerable noisette is still one of the best white climbing roses around. Madame's main asset is her flowers. They're creamy white tinged with pink, moderately large but not oversize, loose and casual rather than formal, and blessed with a strong tea-rose fragrance. Madame is generous too: she pumps out these sweet blossoms well into fall. Like most noisettes, this rose has a weak neck. However, nodding is an asset in a climber; it makes the blooms easy to see.

This rose's foliage is mostly disease-resistant. But Lynne Blackman's coastal garden, shown here, is quite shady, so mildew is a recurring problem. "'Mme

Noisette roses, like this white climber in Del Mar, are perfect for small arbors.

Alfred Carrière' is worth the nuisance," she says, "because there's no other white climber quite like her."

To find this beauty, try a rose specialist like **Burkard Nurseries** in Pasadena *(www.burkards.com or 626/796-4355)*, or contact a mail-order source such as **Vintage Gardens** *(www.vintagegardens. com or 707/829-2035)* or **Roses Unlimited** *(www.rosesunlimiteddownroot.com or 864/ 682-7673). —S.C.*

Garden art

Stephen Block's business, collecting and selling garden ornaments, began at a swap meet. Not finding containers for potted plants that suited his taste, Block started tracking down vintage pots. "Then," he says, "I just kept going." Today, Inner Gardens takes up a 10,000-square-foot warehouse and is filled with beautifully aged pots, urns, balustrades, garden furniture, and other *objets du jardin* that Block has collected from Europe, Asia, and elsewhere.

Though the Inner Gardens has always been open to the public, until recently it has been mostly a trade secret. Now, to be more accessible to everyone, the store

is open on Saturdays. One caveat: patina comes with a price. You could find the perfect urn to use as a garden focal point or a Bauer jar to give to a dear friend, but don't expect the

store's elaborate offerings to bear discount price tags.
Inner Gardens: *8:30–5 Mon–Fri, 10–3 Sat. 6050 W. Jefferson Blvd., Los Angeles; (310) 838-8378. —S. C.*

Winged cherubs and glazed pots at this garden-art supplier have the patina of age.

OPPOSITE: THOMAS J. STORY (3); JIM McCAUSLAND; RIGHT: STEVEN GUNTHER (2)

Clippings

THE BEST TOOLS. Japanese blades are considered to be some of the sharpest and best in the world. Hida Tool & Hardware imports high-quality garden tools, as well as woodworking tools and kitchen knives, directly from Japan. Order by mail or visit its Berkeley California store *(9–5 Mon–Sat; 1333 San Pablo Ave.; www. hidatool.com, 800/443-5512, or 510/524-3700).*

NEW RESOURCE. American Soil Products, Magic Gardens Nursery, and the Urban Farmer Store recently teamed up to open Garden Source Central in Richmond, California—a one-stop garden and landscaping center for both home gardeners and professionals. The 8½-acre site sells landscaping stone, soil, plants, and irrigation and lighting supplies. Classes are offered Saturdays. *2121 San Joaquin St.; www.gardensourcecentral. com or (510) 528-8221.*

WILDFLOWER PLANT GUIDE. The Lady Bird Johnson Wildflower Center and eNature.com have joined together to offer online native plant guides. *www.enature.com; click on "Native Plants" under "Field Guides."*

PEST PATROL. If deer, gophers, ground squirrels, rabbits, or roof rats are a problem in your neighborhood, get help from *Wildlife Pest Control Around Gardens and Homes,* a useful booklet from the University of California, Division of Agriculture and Natural Resources. The authors, Terrell P. Salmon and Robert E. Lickliter, give sound advice on how to reduce or eliminate damage from these creatures and other nuisances in a practical and environmentally acceptable manner. *$17, plus tax and shipping. http://anrcatalog.ucdavis.edu or (510) 642-2431 (ask for publication 21385).*

Let nature decorate your garden in winter

Some savvy gardeners refrain from the autumn tradition of pruning their herbaceous perennials to the ground. Instead, they leave the plants standing. These faded mementos of last season's glory have an austere beauty, especially when they're flocked with snow, as in the Denver garden shown above. In addition, the plants' dried seed heads and stalks provide food and shelter for wild birds. Gardeners who follow this practice wait until late winter or early spring to cut back perennials.

Here are some that display especially attractive form or color in winter. Consider adding one or more to your shopping list as you plan next year's garden.

- Bronze fennel (*Foeniculum vulgare* 'Purpurascens' or 'Smokey')
- Joe pye weed (*Eupatorium purpureum*)
- Mullein (*Verbascum* species)
- Ornamental grasses, particularly *Miscanthus* species
- Russian sage (*Perovskia*)
- *Sedum* 'Autumn Joy'
- Statice (*Limonium* species)
- Yarrow (*Achillea* species; pictured above)

—*Dick Bushnell*

Salmon-friendly gardening

If you live on or near the waterways that drain into Puget Sound, your gardening practices have a direct impact on salmon. A well-planned and properly maintained garden can make life a little easier for fish. To that end, Seattle Public Utilities has developed a Salmon Friendly Gardens website. The site's recommendations also can be applied by gardeners who live along any Northwest waterway where salmon swim. *www.cityofseattle.net/util/rescons/plantnaturally/salmonfriendly.htm*

Six practices to follow

1. **Amend your soil with compost.** Its organic matter filters out pollutants and absorbs rainfall, reducing storm runoff.

2. **Choose the right plants, reconsider the lawn.** The website offers a list of plants—many of them Northwest natives—that work well in a variety of habitats. Reduce the size of your lawn or remove it. Lawns tend to be chemical intensive, resulting in runoff that pollutes surface water.

3. **Water wisely.** Choose unthirsty plants. Use soaker hoses or drip irrigation to reduce water consumption and runoff.

4. **Go natural.** Apply organic or controlled-release fertilizers and the least-toxic pest controls.

5. **Redirect rainwater.** Lay down porous paving materials such as gravel to absorb rain and decrease runoff.

6. **Protect shorelines.** Plant a buffer of trees, shrubs, and ground covers to prevent erosion and provide shade and shelter for salmon. —*J. M.*

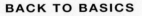

BACK TO BASICS

How to plant a bare-root rose:

1. **Unwrap and shake** organic matter from roots.

2. **Prune off** broken roots and canes.

3. **Immerse the roots** in a bucket of water for a few hours.

4. **Dig a planting hole** 2 feet wide and 1 foot deep. If your soil contains a lot of clay or sand, mix in 1 cubic foot of compost.

5. **Make a 10-inch-tall cone of soil** in the middle of the hole, center the rose over it, and spread out its roots.

6. **Fill hole with soil;** keep the graft (the thickened area at the stem base) above ground level. Water well and rock the rose back and forth to settle it in. Add more soil if necessary. —*L.B.S.*

WHAT TO DO IN YOUR GARDEN IN JANUARY

PLANNING AND PLANTING

☐ DISPLAY MOTH ORCHIDS. Moth orchids *(Phalaenopsis)* are at peak bloom in winter. Buy plants with at least four true leaves and one or two well-budded stalks. Place them in a bright east- or north-facing window and you'll have bloom for months.

☐ ORDER SEEDS. Regional seed suppliers carry flowers and vegetables that are proven winners in the Northwest. Call for catalogs or visit the websites of these companies: Nichols Garden Nursery *(www.nicholsgardennursery.com or 541/928-9280)*, Territorial Seed Company *(www.territorial-seed. com or 541/942-9547)*, and West Coast Seeds *(www.westcoastseeds. com or 604/952-8820)*.

☐ SET OUT BARE-ROOT PLANTS. *Sunset* climate zones 4–7: Plant bare-root berries, fruit and shade trees, grapes, perennial vegetables, roses, and other ornamental shrubs. Two Northwest growers offer a vast selection of fruits: One Green World *(www.onegreenworld.com or 877/ 353-4028)* and Raintree Nursery *(www.raintreenursery.com or 360/ 496-6400)*. In zones 1–3: Once bare-root stock arrives, you can plant when air and soil temperatures are above freezing.

☐ START HARDY FLOWERS. In a coldframe or greenhouse, sow seeds of aster, calendula, delphinium, English daisy, hellebore, pansy, Shasta daisy, veronica, and viola. Transplant seedlings into the garden about a month before the average date of last spring frost in your area.

☐ WINTER-FLOWERING SHRUBS. Zones 4–7: Shop nurseries for blooming specimens of ornamental filberts *(Corylus* species), *Garrya elliptica,* sarcococca, sasanqua camellias, wintersweet *(Chimonanthus praecox)*, and a wide array of witch hazels *(Hamamelis* species and hybrids).

MAINTENANCE

☐ APPLY DORMANT OIL. On a mild, dry day, spray leafless fruit trees and roses with horticultural oil to smother overwintering insect eggs and larvae.

☐ FEED ASPARAGUS, RHUBARB. To encourage these perennials to produce abundant spring crops, top-dress plants with a 2-inch layer of composted manure.

☐ FIGHT SLUGS. During rainy or mild weather, slugs come out. Handpick when you see them, or set out bait.

☐ PRUNE FRUIT TREES. Zones 4–7: Cut out dead, diseased, and injured branches, then remove closely parallel, rubbing, or crossing branches. Finally, prune for shape, always working from the bottom of the tree to the top, and from the inside out. In zones 1–3, wait until after the weather turns mild.

☐ PRUNE ROSES. Zones 4–7: Cut back hybrid tea roses to the most vigorous three to five canes, removing any diseased or injured ones. Prune landscape roses to shape. In zones 1–3, wait until April. ◆

WHAT TO DO IN YOUR GARDEN IN JANUARY

PLANTING

☐ BERRIES AND VEGETABLES. *Sunset* climate zones 7–9, 14–17: Bare-root artichokes, asparagus, blackberries, grapes, raspberries, and strawberries are available at nurseries this month.

☐ INSTANT COLOR. Zones 7–9, 14–17: To chase away the winter blues, buy 4-inch pots of instant color (smaller plants will not grow much until spring) and design a colorful potted arrangement for the front porch or patio. Look for calendula, candytuft, cineraria, dianthus, English daisy, English and fairy primroses, Iceland poppy, pansy, snapdragon, stock, and viola.

☐ ORCHIDS. Nurseries and florists stock a number of blooming orchids this month. Liven up your living room with orchids such as *Cattleya*, miniature cymbidium, moth orchid *(Phalaenopsis), Oncidium,* or pansy orchid *(Miltonia).* All need bright light indoors and cool temperatures to prolong bloom. Move cymbidiums outdoors when bloom is over (protect from frost). For a large selection of orchids, order from Cal-Orchid *(www.calorchid. com or 805/967-1312)* or Santa Barbara Orchid Estate *(www.sborchid. com or 800/553-3387).*

Sunset
CLIMATE ZONES
- Mountain (1–2)
- Valley (7–9)
- Inland (14)
- Coastal (15–17)

☐ ORDER SEEDS. This is a good time to thumb through catalogs and search the Web for fun new varieties. Well-stocked Western seed companies include Nichols Garden Nursery *(www.nicholsgardennursery. com or 541/928-9280),* Ornamental Edibles *(www.ornamentaledibles. com or 408/929-7333),* Redwood City Seed Company *(www.batnet. com/rwc-seed* or *650/325-7333),* Renee's Garden *(www.reneesgarden. com or 888/880-7228),* Seeds of Change *(www.seedsofchange.com or 888/762-7333),* and Territorial Seed Company *(www.territorialseed. com or 541/942-9547).*

☐ SMALL MAPLES. Small to moderate-size maples make handsome trees for home gardens. The following maples grow in zones 2, 7–9, 14–17. *Acer truncatum* (also grows in zone 1): Deeply lobed 4-inch-wide leaves start out purplish red, change to green in summer, and turn orange to maroon in fall. Grows to 25 feet or taller. Japanese maple *(A. palmatum):* Many varieties to choose from, including ones with deeply cut leaves or variegated foliage. Heights range from 7 to 20 feet. Paperbark maple *(A. griseum):* Leaves are dark green above, silvery below. Foliage turns brilliant red in fall. Reddish bark peels away in thin sheets. Grows to 25 feet tall.

MAINTENANCE

☐ FEED CITRUS. Zones 7–9, 14–17: Fertilize citrus trees six to eight weeks before they bloom, following package directions. Citrus trees are heavy nitrogen feeders, so Fremont-based wholesale citrus nursery Four Winds Growers *(www.fourwindsgrowers.com)* recommends a fertilizer with a nitrogen, phosphorous, and potassium ratio of 2:1:1. The nursery also suggests slow-release granular fertilizer rather than fertilizer stakes because granules can be distributed more evenly to the rootball, while stakes stay in one spot.

☐ PRUNE HYDRANGEAS. Zones 7–9, 14–17: Cut back stems that have bloomed to 12 inches. To produce fewer but larger flowers next spring, also reduce the number of stems by trimming some of them to the base of the plant. For more numerous medium-size blooms, retain more stems. ◆

WHAT TO DO IN YOUR GARDEN IN JANUARY

PLANTING

☐ **ANNUALS.** It's not too late to plant pansies, Iceland poppies, or other winter annuals, especially along the coast. In the low desert (*Sunset* climate zone 13), set out petunias.

☐ **BARE-ROOT PLANTS.** Stone fruit trees are at peak supply in nurseries (for the best varieties, consult the *Western Garden Book* or the California Rare Fruit Growers' website: *www.crfg.org*). You'll also find cane berries, grape and kiwi vines, perennial vegetables like asparagus, and, of course, roses. (For suggestions on good landscaping roses, see page 18.)

☐ **SUCCULENTS.** Winter-blooming succulents are a fresh way to liven up a dreary winter garden, and they look particularly at home in Mediterranean-style landscapes. Look for flowering aloes, *Echeveria,* and kalanchoe.

☐ **SUMMER BULBS.** Plant calla lilies, canna, crocosmia, dahlia, gladiolus, lilies, *Nerine, Tigridia,* and other summer bulbs at the same time you set out your cool-season annuals.

☐ **WINTER VEGETABLES.** Germination will be slow, but it's still possible to start cool-season crops from seed, especially lettuces and other leafy greens. Onions, peas, and radishes are other possibilities. You can also plant broccoli, brussels sprouts, and cabbage seedlings.

MAINTENANCE

☐ **COLLECT RAINWATER.** Set out containers to catch the rain; use the water to irrigate houseplants.

☐ **FERTILIZE SELECTIVELY.** In frost-free coastal areas, feed citrus this month. Farther inland, wait until February. Feed staghorn ferns with a high-nitrogen liquid fertilizer. Renew mulch on camellias and azaleas, and gently work cottonseed meal into top 2 inches of soil. Cool-season annuals and emerging bulbs benefit from fertilizing now.

☐ **PRUNE DECIDUOUS FRUIT TREES.** Deciduous fruit trees should be cut back before new leaf buds begin to form, but the amount of trimming differs for each type. Before starting, consult a pruning reference book or the CRFG website listed under "Bare-root Plants."

☐ **PRUNE ROSES.** Remove dead, damaged, or crossing branches first, then prune all the remaining canes by one-half to one-third, cutting back each cane to just above an outward-facing bud.

PEST AND DISEASE CONTROL

☐ **APPLY DORMANT SPRAY.** After pruning, spray roses with horticultural oil to smother overwintering insects. To control peach leaf curl on deciduous fruit trees, spray with fixed copper or lime sulfur mixed with horticultural oil (follow label directions). Don't use lime sulfur on apricots. Spray branches, crotches, and trunks of trees, plus the ground beneath the drip line.

☐ **CONTROL CAMELLIA BLIGHT.** If your camellias are plagued with petal blight, place shade cloth under the shrubs to catch decaying blossoms and make them easier to gather and discard. This will help break the blight cycle and improve next year's flower crop.

☐ **MANAGE WEEDS.** Replenish mulch in vegetables and flower beds and around trees and shrubs to minimize weed germination. ◆

WHAT TO DO IN YOUR GARDEN IN JANUARY

PLANNING & PLANTING

☐ BUY ANNUAL FLOWER SEEDS. Order packets now for the best selection. Good drought-tolerant choices include amaranth, arroyo lupine, breadbox poppy, California desert bluebells, clary sage, desert marigold, flower-of-an-hour, larkspur, love-in-a-mist, white prickly poppy, Mexican gold poppy, mountain phlox, portulaca, purple aster, Tahoka daisy, tansy scorpionflower, and snow-on-the-mountain. Two seed sources are Plants of the Southwest *(www.plantsofthesouthwest. com or 800/788-7333)* and Select Seeds Co. *(www.selectseeds.com or 860/684-9310).*

☐ SOW HARDY PERENNIALS. Seeds of most hardy perennials—including bleeding heart, butterfly weed, columbine, delphinium, liatris, and penstemon—require a period of chilling to germinate. Start seeds now in soil-filled pots and place them outdoors but out of direct sun. Keep the soil moist, and whenever snow is available, pile it on the pots. After six weeks of chilling, bring pots into a greenhouse or set them on a sunny windowsill to sprout. When seedlings have two sets of true leaves, transplant them into individual containers. Continue growing plants indoors until spring, then plant them in the garden.

☐ START A JOURNAL. A notebook-style engagement calendar is a handy place to keep records of the gardening year. Jot down what is planted when and where, weather information, disease and insect problems, successes and failures.

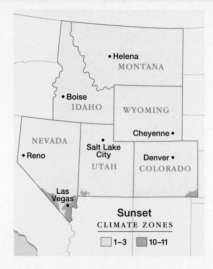

Sunset
CLIMATE ZONES
☐ 1–3 ☐ 10–11

☐ ADD WINTER COLOR. Even without leaves, many deciduous shrubs and trees display bright fruits or bark. For red or orange berries or other fruits, consider cotoneaster, crabapple, hawthorn, pyracantha, silver buffaloberry, and sumac. For colored bark or twigs, try beauty bush, corkscrew willow, mountain mahogany, Mormon tea, and redtwig and yellowtwig dogwood. Note now which of these would fit your landscape so you'll remember to add them in the spring.

MAINTENANCE

☐ MULCH BEDS. Pile discarded Christmas-tree boughs and evergreen prunings on top of perennial, bulb, and shrub beds. Hay, straw, and pine needles also work.

☐ PRUNE FIREBLIGHT-DAMAGED TREES. Fireblight is a bacterial disease that most commonly attacks apple and crabapple trees, but it also can bother cotoneaster, hawthorn, mountain ash, pear, pyracantha, quince, and serviceberry. New spring growth on affected branches wilts and appears scorched. Pruning in winter when the bacteria is dormant helps prevent the spread of this disease. Remove all blighted branches—look for sunken cankers 4 to 6 inches below surface of infected wood. Dispose of prunings.

☐ WATCH FOR FROST-HEAVED PLANTS. When soil freezes and thaws in recurrent cycles, it can heave shallow-rooted perennials right out of the ground. If this happens, add soil around plants to cover any exposed roots.

☐ WATER. Dry winter conditions can seriously dehydrate plants. When snow or rain has not fallen for several weeks and the top 3 to 4 inches of ground are dry, thoroughly water permanent plantings with a soaker hose. Water at midday when the temperature is above freezing and the soil surface is not frozen solid. —*Marcia Tatroe*

WHAT TO DO IN YOUR GARDEN IN JANUARY

PLANTING

☐ BARE-ROOT FRUIT TREES. *Sunset* climate zones 11–13 (Las Vegas, Tucson, Phoenix): Select low-chill varieties of apples ('Anna' and 'Dorsett Golden'), apricots ('Castlebrite' and 'Katy'), peaches ('Desertgold' and 'Tropic Snow'), and plums ('Santa Rosa' and 'Satsuma').

☐ BARE-ROOT ROSES. Zones 11–13: Set out bare-root plants, especially varieties that tolerate the Southwest's alkaline soil and other harsh conditions. Exceptional choices include 'Adelaide Hoodless' shrub rose with bright red semi-double flowers, 'Father Hugo's Rose' *(Rosa hugonis)* with pale yellow single flowers, 'Morden Blush' shrub rose with fragrant double flowers that fade from pale pink to ivory, and 'Nearly Wild' floribunda rose with aromatic pink flowers. For more on roses, see page 18.

☐ COOL-SEASON FLOWERS. Zones 10–11: Set out transplants of bachelor's button, calendula, sweet pea, and violet. Zones 12–13: Sow seeds of nasturtium and stock. Set out transplants of calendula, pansy, petunia, sweet alyssum, and sweet pea.

☐ HERBS. Zones 11–13: Sow seeds of cilantro, dill, and parsley.

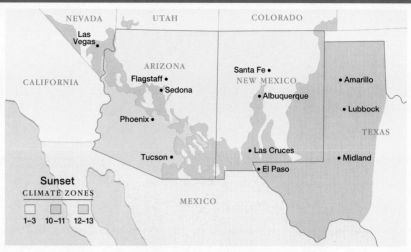

☐ VEGETABLES. All zones: Start seeds of eggplant, pepper, and tomato indoors for transplanting in 8–10 weeks. For tomatoes, try 'Bloody Butcher', 'Christmas Grapes', 'Jaune Flamme', and 'White Wonder', all available from Burpee at *www.burpee.com* or *(800) 888-1447*. Another good choice is 'Punta Banda' from Native Seeds/SEARCH at *www.nativeseeds.org* or *(520) 622-5561*. Zones 1A–3B (Flagstaff, Taos, Santa Fe): By month's end, start squash indoors; try 'Veracruz Pepita' from Native Seeds/SEARCH (see above). Zone 10 (Albuquerque): Start melons indoors for transplanting in early April; try 'Malali' and 'Verona' watermelons from Seeds of Change at *www.seedsofchange.com* or *(888) 762-7333*. Set out asparagus root crowns and artichoke transplants. Zones 11–13: Sow seeds of arugula, carrots, mesclun mixes, and radishes. Set out asparagus root crowns and transplants of broccoli, brussels sprouts, cabbage, cauliflower, kohlrabi, and lettuce.

MAINTENANCE

☐ CONTROL INSECTS. Small holes and damaged leaf edges on annual flowers and vegetable plants are often caused by cabbage loopers or other small caterpillars. Inspect plants frequently and remove these pests by hand. Gray aphids infest cabbages and other leaf crops. Blast them off plants with a strong jet of water, or drench infested plants with a solution of 1 tablespoon of dishwashing liquid mixed with 1 gallon of water.

☐ IRRIGATE. If dry weather persists, deep-water conifers and other evergreen trees and shrubs once a month. —*Kim Nelson*

Landscaping with roses

Fresh ways to grow these garden favorites

By Lauren Bonar Swezey

A hedge of white shrub roses along a white picket fence, a climbing rose cloaked in red blooms at the back of a hot-colored flower border, coral ground cover roses spilling over a stone retaining wall: these are ways gardeners incorporate roses into the landscape today—boldly, and with savvy attention to bloom color and growth habit.

Among the many long-blooming, easy-care roses now available are types that are superbly suited to landscape use. Small, compact types are excellent edgings along walkways or in narrow beds; they also look good in containers. Low spreaders are ideal as ground covers. More upright varieties are handsome in shrub borders or, planted 3 or 4 feet apart, as an informal hedge. Climbers dress up arching trellises, obelisks, or fences. On page 22, we recommend landscape roses to get you started.

There's always room for roses—no matter what their habits—in any landscape. "Roses fit any style of garden, from casual English cottage to Mediterranean to formal," says Tom Carruth of Weeks Roses in Upland, California.

All you have to do is make sure their flower or foliage colors work together, as rose fancier Heidi Tanner does in her garden in Pleasanton, California, pictured on page 20. Tanner fills her garden with roses for nearly nonstop color. She arranges them in color themes, using red and orange roses to spice up hot-color borders, and apricots, blushes, and whites in her "quiet garden."

'Polka' climbs over a metal arbor in Helene Henderson's garden in Los Angeles. Opposite: 'Royal Sunset' decorates a pillar.

Position the roses where they'll deliver maximum effect, as another rose fancier, Sheri Workman, does in her Fountain Valley, California, garden. Workman grows 'Abraham Darby', a lanky-stemmed David Austin shrub rose, against the wall at the back of a 2-foot-wide border and allows it to arch across the border toward the path. "The plant is so huge in my mild climate that it grows into a fountain," she says. "The blooms are right in your nose when you walk by."

For maximum color impact, you can pair roses with annuals or perennials, as Workman does. Other ornamentals help hide the roses' "ugly legs" and give the garden a filled-in look, she says.

The dormant season (from January to March, depending on climate) is the prime time to set out bare-root plants such as roses.

Choosing the right varieties

Before you shop for roses, it helps to know which varieties grow best in your climate. We list some suggestions on page 22. For other ideas:

Visit public rose gardens. Many local botanical gardens and parks display roses suitable to your climate. To find them, check the American Rose Society's website (*www.ars.org*).

Rose care

To succeed at landscaping with roses, follow these guidelines for planting, care, and maintenance.

Plant in a spot that gets at least six hours of full sun per day and plenty of air circulation. If soil is not fast-draining, grow roses in raised beds.

Amend the soil by mixing compost into the planting hole.

Mulch after planting with compost or other organic matter to a depth of 1 to 3 inches (avoid mounding it around the rose canes).

Water often enough to keep the soil moist, but not soggy, to a depth of 16 to 18 inches (check water penetration to make sure you're watering long enough).

Fertilize after main (dormant-season) pruning and again after each bloom flush (or per package directions).

Prune off old flowers when they fade. Trim back surrounding plants as needed so they won't engulf the rose bushes.

Control pests and diseases with non-chemical methods or low-toxicity chemicals and by choosing varieties that resist disease. *Aphids and mites:* Rinse off with a strong stream of water, or spray plants with insecticidal soap or horticultural oil. *Black spot and rust:* Avoid overhead irrigation, prune off and discard infected foliage, and pick up fallen leaves. *Powdery mildew:* Prune off infected leaves.

Pink and coral roses create layers of blooms around Steve and Heidi Tanner's patio. Top: 'Mary Rose'.

'Sally Holmes' makes a hedge in Judy Oliphant's garden. Below: 'Eden' frames an entry in Shirle McConnor's garden. Both gardens are in Rancho Santa Fe, California.

Ask a rosarian. E-mail your questions to a consulting rosarian in your region. On the ARS website, click on "Ask Us," then "CR by Geographical Area."

Contact local rose societies. Some rose societies have websites that offer lists of roses adapted to specific climates. You can locate some of these lists by going to the ARS website and clicking on "ARS Societies."

What to plant with roses

Roses look best when they're planted among other landscape plants. While low-growing perennials are perfect for hiding bare canes, taller ones—delphinium, for instance—are best planted behind or to the side of a shrubby rose, or in front of a climber. Here are our favorite companions.

Low plants to grow beneath roses. Agapanthus (dwarf), arabis, basket-of-gold, brachyscome, campanula, candytuft, catmint, coreopsis, dianthus, dusty miller, erigeron, feverfew, geraniums (species types), heuchera, lamb's ears, licorice plant, nemesia, scabiosa, sweet alyssum, thyme, verbena (ground-cover types), yarrow.

Tall or spiky plants for contrast. Alstroemeria, bearded iris, canna, delphinium, *Verbena bonariensis*.

Shrubby or clumping partners. Japanese barberry (with red or gold foliage), lavender, ornamental grasses, Russian sage, santolina, summer phlox, *Veronica* 'Sunny Border Blue'.

Which to plant?

If you can't find the roses listed here at your local nursery, check the mail-order sources below. In mild climates, some vigorous shrub roses grow as climbers (as noted). The shrub rose list includes floribundas; use these types in borders and informal hedges. Plant climbers against fences or trellises, ground cover roses on slopes as edgings. (The latter stay below 2½ ft. tall, except where noted.) *Hardy above 7,000 feet. **Compiled with the help of Eve Reshetnik-Brawner, Harlequin's Gardens Nursery, Boulder, CO.

SHRUB ROSES

Mild climates	Hot climates	Cold climates**	Foggy coasts
'Amber Queen' (golden amber)	'Amber Queen' (golden amber)	'Abraham Darby' (orange pink)	'Abraham Darby' (orange pink)
'Amber Waves' (apricot and yellow)	'Angel Face' (lavender)	'Adelaide Hoodless' (deep pink)	'Amber Queen' (golden amber)
'Betty Boop' (yellow with bright red edge)	'Apricot Nectar' (soft apricot)	'Bonica' (pink)	'Apricot Nectar' (soft apricot)
'Bonica' (pink)	'Belle Story' (soft pink and yellow)	'Carefree Beauty' (pink)	'Bonica' (pink)
'Easy Going' (peachy yellow)	'Cathedral' (apricot)	'Darlow's Enigma' (white)	'Brass Band' (orange and yellow)
'Hot Cocoa' (brown orange)	'Cherish' (orange pink)	'Frau Dagmar Hartopp'* (single pink)	'Evelyn' (apricot yellow)
'Iceberg' (white)	'Circus' (yellow with pink, orange, and red)	'Golden Wings' (single light yellow)	'Iceberg' (white)
'Knock Out' (raspberry red)	'Europeana' (crimson red)	'Gourmet Popcorn' (white)	'Intrigue' (plum purple)
'Livin' Easy' (apricot orange)	'Hot 'n' Spicy' (orange red)	'Harison's Yellow'	'Mary Rose' (medium pink)
'Playboy' (yellow, orange, and cerise)	'Iceberg' (white)	'Linda Campbell' (bright red)	'Sally Holmes' (or climber; single white)
'Sally Holmes' (or climber; single white)	'Origami' (pink blend)	'Mary Rose' (medium pink)	'Scentimental' (red and white)
'Scentimental' (red and white)	'Redgold' (gold edged with vermilion)	'Morden Blush'* (light pink)	'Simplicity' (pink)
'Sexy Rexy' (pink)	'Sally Holmes' (or climber; single white)	'Pink Meidiland'	'Singin' in the Rain' (apricot gold)
'Simplicity' (pink)	'Showbiz' (red)	'The Alexandra Rose' (single coppery pink with yellow center)	'Sun Flare' (lemon yellow)
'Trumpeter' (red orange)	'Sun Flare' (lemon yellow)	'Thérèse Bugnet'* (lilac pink)	'Trumpeter' (red orange)

CLIMBERS

Mild climates	Hot climates	Cold climates**	Foggy coasts
'Altissimo' (single red)	'Altissimo' (single red)	'Dortmund' (single red with white eye)	'Altissimo' (single red)
'Berries 'n' Cream' (pink and creamy white)	'America' (coral pink)	'Henry Kelsey'* (red)	'America' (coral pink)
'Cl Cécile Brünner' (pale pink)	'Blaze' (red)	'John Cabot'* (rosy pink)	'Cl Iceberg' (white)
'Cl Iceberg' (white)	'Candy Cane' (deep pink)	'New Dawn' (light pink)	'Eden' (pink with cream)
'Dortmund' (single red with white eye)	'Cl Iceberg' (white)	'William Baffin'* (strawberry pink)	'Phyllis Bide' (yellow and apricot)
'Eden' (pink with cream)	'Cl Queen Elizabeth' (medium pink)		'Sombreuil' (creamy white)
'Fourth of July' (red and white)	'Don Juan' (deep red)		
'Jeanne Lajoie' (medium pink)	'Dream Weaver' (pink)		
'Joseph's Coat' (red, pink, orange, and yellow)	'Dublin Bay' (red)		
'Polka' (apricot and peach)	'Golden Showers' (yellow)		
'Royal Sunset' (orange apricot)	'Jeanne Lajoie' (candy pink)		
'Sombreuil' (creamy white)	'Joseph's Coat' (red, pink, orange, and yellow)		
'Spice So Nice' (apricot orange with yellow center)	'Lace Cascade' (white)		
	'Meg' (pink)		
	'Royal Sunset' (orange apricot)		

Bright red 'Don Juan'

GROUND COVERS

All climates

'Alba Meidiland' (white)	'Monticello' (warm pink)
'Aspen' (yellow)	'Pebble Beach' (medium pink)
'Fire Meidiland' (dark red)	'Red Meidiland'
'Flower Carpet' (pink, red, white, or yellow)	'Sea Foam' (white)
'Fuchsia Meidiland' (mauve pink)	'Sun Runner' (yellow)
'Magic Carpet' (lavender pink)	'Tumbling Waters' (white)
'Magic Meidiland' (medium pink)	'Versailles Palace' (rich coral)

Where to buy roses by mail

Arena Roses: www.arenaroses.com or (888) 466-7434.

David Austin Roses: www.davidaustinroses.com or (800) 328-8893.

Edmunds' Roses: www.edmundsroses.com or (888) 481-7673 (in Portland area, 503/682-1476).

Heirloom Roses: www.heirloomroses.com or (503) 583-1576.

High Country Roses: www.highcountryroses.com or (800) 552-2082.

Jackson & Perkins: www.jacksonandperkins.com or (800) 292-4769.

Regan Nursery: www.regannursery.com or (510) 797-3222.

Wayside Gardens: www.waysidegardens.com or (800) 845-1124. ◆

BOB WIGAND

'Orange Beauty' glows in the sun. The stems of 'Winter Beauty' are cloaked with inch-long petals (below).

Bewitching hazel

This winter-blooming shrub smells as good as it looks

In late winter, blossoms resembling colorful shreds of coconut cover the leafless branches of hybrid witch hazel *(Hamamelis* x *intermedia)*. Endowed with a clean, strong fragrance that carries well in cold air, these flowers may be the most exotic blooms in the winter garden.

Just as surely as its flowers win over most gardeners, this shrub's name puzzles them. The moniker's origin dates to America's colonial days when dowsers—or water witches—used divining rods to locate underground water for wells. Dowsers used branches of native *Hamamelis,* which settlers called "witch hazel."

Later on, explorers found other witch hazels in Asia: Japanese witch hazel *(H. japonica)* and Chinese witch hazel *(H. mollis). H.* x *intermedia* claims both of these species as parents and has superior fragrance and flower colors. Of the hybrid varieties, the best red is 'Diane'; the best oranges are 'Jelena' and 'Winter Beauty'; and the best yellows are 'Arnold Promise', which has the strongest scent, and 'Sunburst'. These hybrids grow into large shrubs, reaching 12 to 15 feet tall and as wide. Prune only to guide growth and use the cuttings for winter bouquets.

Witch hazel grows in mild parts of the West *(Sunset* climate zones 3–7 and 15–17). Blooming plants are

commonly sold in nurseries at this time of year. Buy them in full flower and plant in a place that has good drainage and filtered shade or full sun. You can mail-order plants from Gossler Farms Nursery *(www. gosslerfarms.com or 541/746-3922)* or Greer Gardens *(www.greergardens. com or 800/548-0111).*

—*Jim McCausland*

Serene
greens

Six easy ways to create miniature indoor landscapes

By Kathleen N. Brenzel with Jil Peters and Mary Jo Bowling
Photographs by Thomas J. Story

The scent of grass, a hint of blooms, the shimmer of a placid pool: all bring tranquility to a garden. You can re-create their ambience indoors with the ideas pictured here. Shop for mosses and dichondra at nurseries, orchids and wheatgrass at markets. Keep plants in bright, indirect light, away from heat sources.

Moss boxes. Copper trays contain Irish moss and Scotch moss. They don't have drain holes but work well for temporary display (2–3 weeks). Irrigate about once a week and drain excess water by turning each tray upside down over a sink (with one hand over the moss to keep it in place). Or drill drain holes in the bottom and display trays on pavers or plastic. For a similar effect, substitute wood boxes. *Copper trays: 6¼ inches square by 1½ inches tall; $9 each from Smith & Hawken (800/981-9888).*

Mini bogs. Miniature water plants fill these ceramic cache pots. The largest pot ($5\frac{1}{2}$ in. diameter, 5 in. tall) features a dwarf papyrus (submerged in its nursery pot) and duckweed. The midsize pot ($4\frac{1}{2}$ in. diameter, 4 in. tall) holds frogbit with duckweed (both are invasive; keep them away from natural waters). The small pot ($2\frac{1}{2}$ by $2\frac{1}{2}$ in.) contains duckweed.

Tabletop pool. A shallow serving dish (about 12 by 16 in.) becomes a reflecting pool when you add a camellia clipping with a bamboo stake to hold it upright. *Sunset's* Bud Stuckey made the stake from a 16-inch-long, 2-inch-diameter piece of bamboo, which he sliced in thirds with a table saw; the stake is the center cut.

Pond in glass. A water hyacinth floats in a glass vase, which shows off the plant's delicate roots. If you can't find floating water plants at your nursery (or if you don't have access to a pond from which to borrow one), gently place a fluffy-petaled bloom, such as a camellia or a rose, atop the water.

Turf cubes. Dichondra, a ground cover often used outdoors between pavers, fills two of these 4-inch-square terra-cotta pots; wheatgrass fills the middle container. We used four dichondra plants from sixpacks in each of the two end pots; the center one holds a clump of wheatgrass from a single 4-inch nursery pot.

Garden in a tray. Irish moss and Scotch moss combine with lady's slipper orchids *(Paphiopedilum)* to form the illusion of a garden. A copper tray catches drips from terra-cotta pots with soft earth-tone glazes. *Copper tray: 14 inches square; $26 from Smith & Hawken (800/981-9888). Terra-cotta pots: $16–$50 from Bluestone Main (707/765-2024).* ◆

THIS SIMPLE YET ELEGANT GARDEN in Danville, California, was a winner in the "Renovation" category in our 2003 Western Garden Design Awards. You'll find all 15 winners—and plenty of inspiration—beginning on page 43.

February

Flower-bed cymbidiums

When people told Jim Hitchner that he couldn't grow cymbidiums in the ground, he set out to prove them wrong. For years, Jim and his wife, June, had been growing these hardy orchids in containers, amassing more potted cymbidiums than they had room for. When they ran out of space for containers, they began setting their plants in flower beds.

Starting with a small plot, Jim began to plant his cymbidiums as described below (we've simplified his method where possible). He set them right among other ornamentals—alstroemeria, camellia, and Japanese maple—to help maintain humidity.

For continuous bloom from mid-September through mid-June, the Hitchners chose varieties with different bloom cycles. Their flower-bed cymbidiums seem to bloom more profusely and stand up to temperatures ranging from 26° to 101° much better than those in pots. —*Julie Chai*

This cymbidium's fleshy petals stand out like golden butterfly wings. Flower stems (left) arch out amid grassy foliage in shade.

Planting tips

1. For a cymbidium in a 10-inch pot, dig a planting hole about 14 inches deep and 20 inches across in well-drained soil. If you garden in heavy clay soil, dig a 3-foot-deep hole.

2. Line the hole with plastic sheeting to keep surrounding soil in place. Leave gaps or cut small holes in the sheeting for drainage.

3. In the hole, build a cone of ¾-inch pebbles (you'll need 90 to 100 pounds per hole) as illustrated. For a

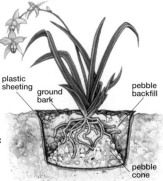

3-foot hole, first pour a 20-inch-deep layer of larger (3- to 8-inch) rocks in the bottom, then build the cone of pebbles on top of it.

4. Remove the plant from its pot, shake the loose bark from its roots, and position it atop the cone so its roots fall loosely around the pebbles.

5. Use pebbles to fill in the hole up to 1 inch below the plant's previous soil line.

6. Top the pebbles with a 1-inch layer of large bark chips to retain moisture.

7. Irrigate once or twice a week after planting. After bloom, use a timed-release fertilizer every three months.

8. Stake plant stems as needed; at the end of the season, trim spent foliage.

Clipping

WATER-WISE JOURNAL

Born in Colorado in the early 1980s, the Xeriscape movement has gathered momentum as a result of the severe drought that continues to have an impact on communities around the state. Whether you're already a believer in xeriscaping or are converting to a water-thrifty garden, you'll find practical support in the *Xeriscape Maintenance Journal: Evidence of Care, Volume II* (Colorado WaterWise Council, Denver, 2003; $9.95; 303/628-6159), edited by David Winger. This 56-page paperback is designed as a workbook to steer you through the gardening year. For each month, there's an illustrated calendar, a checklist of tasks, a feature on plants or maintenance (watering trees during drought, for example), plus a page to jot notes.

—*Dick Bushnell*

Rosy outlook in Colorado

To revitalize her small front garden and create an inviting entry in Denver, Georgie Pelsue cleared out existing shrubs, such as overgrown juniper, and replaced them with a raised bed filled with colorful roses and cheery perennials.

First, Pelsue had a landscape design firm build a 10-inch-tall dry-laid flagstone wall to frame the bed. After filling the 11- by 13-foot area with a mixture of topsoil, peat moss, and manure, she planted mounds of snow-in-summer *(Cerastium tomentosum)* and yellow-flowered ice plant so that they would tumble over the wall. 'Elijah Blue'

fescue and spiky miniature iris add foliar texture just behind. Five columnar Colorado blue spruce *(Picea pungens glauca)* form a soft backdrop.

But the real stars of the show are the 29 hybrid tea and floribunda roses that Pelsue managed to squeeze into the space. "I have a small yard, so I wanted a bold splash of color," she says.

You can plant bare-root roses as soon as the ground is workable. Or wait until temperatures rise in midspring, then set out container-grown roses from a nursery.

—*J.C.*

Pictorial guide to alpine plants

Hike above the tree line almost anywhere in western North America and you're bound to see tiny clumps of flowers clinging tenaciously to arid scree-covered slopes. These are America's native alpine plants. When Graham Nicholls, a British nurseryman specializing in alpines, came to the United States to see these magnificent plants in the wild, he was surprised that no one had written a book about them yet. So he did, and quite successfully too—*Alpine Plants of North America: An Encyclopedia of Mountain Flowers from the Rockies to Alaska* (Timber Press, Portland, 2002; $50; www.timberpress.

com or 800/327-5680).

Covering some 650 species, the 344-page volume is organized as a pictorial encyclopedia of plants that grow in the West's alpine areas from the southern Rockies to Alaska's Brooks Range. Color photographs show the jewel-like beauty of these plants, such as *Silene hookeri bolanderi* (shown at left). Rock gardeners will appreciate Nicholls's instructions for cultivating everything from *Aquilegia* to *Zauschneria*.

—*Jim McCausland*

Cactus plus poppies

If you buy a cactus from Plants for the Southwest this month, it's likely to come with a free bonus—a poppy seedling. Gene Joseph, one of the owners of this Tucson-based specialty nursery, tried overseeding his cactus pots with wildflower seeds as an experiment several years ago. He found that most wildflowers needed too much water to be compatible with cactus—except for Mexican gold poppy *(Eschscholzia mexicana)*. Once its seeds germinate, the poppies can co-exist with cactus on the same water regimen, says Joseph.

You can seed cactus pots with *E. mexicana* anytime from mid-October through December, he says. Seeds sown on top of decorative rock mulch

will drop through. Water lightly—just enough to keep the surface moist—until seeds germinate. Then water normally (approximately every two weeks). When the poppies finish blooming and have spilled their seed, pull out the dead plant material. Na-

ture takes over from there. Joseph has seeded *E. mexicana* only once and has had poppies every spring since.

Plants for the Southwest: 9–5 Wed–Sat. 50 E. Blacklidge, Tucson; www.lithops.com or (520) 628-8773.
—Sharon Cohoon

'Dorsett Golden' apples have sweet flesh. 'Flame' seedless grapes (right) taste good fresh or dried as raisins.

Winning fruits in Las Vegas

Five years ago, the Master Gardeners of Southern Nevada started a fruit tree orchard on a 1-acre site near Las Vegas. Ever since then, a corps of 15 volunteers has carefully maintained the orchard's 450 fruit trees using organic gardening practices. They have also amassed a wealth of information that can be of great help to desert gardeners, especially those in Nevada's Clark County (*Sunset* climate zone 11) who want to grow fruits successfully in their own yards. The following varieties are recommended by the master gardeners, based on the trees' performance and productivity in the trial orchard. February is a good month to plant bare-root fruit trees and grapevines; peak harvest months are listed.

APPLES. 'Anna': Large fruit with sweet flesh; August harvest. Plant with 'Dorsett Golden' for cross-pollination.

'Pink Lady': Medium-size fruit with sweet-tart flesh, good fresh or cooked; August. Plant with 'Granny Smith' for cross-pollination.

APRICOTS. 'Blenheim': Medium fruit has very sweet flavor, excellent for drying; late July.

'Gold Kist': Medium fruit has good flavor, bears large crop; early July.

NECTARINES. 'Arctic Star': Medium fruit with sweet white flesh; mid-June.

'Desert Dawn': Medium fruit has excellent flavor; May.

PEACHES. 'Fairtime': Large freestone fruit with sweet white flesh; September.

'Summerset': Large freestone fruit has yellow flesh with excellent flavor; September.

PEARS. 'Hood': Large fruit with sweet flesh; August.

'Kieffer': Medium fruit is excellent for cooking and canning; August.

PLUMS. 'Elephant Heart': Medium fruit with sweet flesh; July.

'Sugar': Small fruit with sweet flesh; July.

Other recommendations

FIGS. 'Black Mission', 'Kadota'.
GRAPES. 'Fantasy', 'Flame', 'Perlette', 'Thompson'.
PERSIMMONS. 'Fuyu', 'Hachiya'.
PLUOTS. 'Dapple Dandy', 'Flavor Supreme'.

These fruit trees may be ordered through local nurseries.
—Liz Hartley

A pergola casts shade across the front entry, while berm plantings screen the patio from the street.

Front-yard facelift

Reshaping a typical tract-house landscape converted this Phoenix yard into a welcoming hacienda. When Tyler Gerdes and Harald Spohr moved into their home, the front yard was downright barren (see photo at right). Though the front entrance enjoyed cool northern exposure and offered a wonderful view of nearby Stony Mountain, there was no sitting area from which to enjoy either. "It was just a space you walked through in order to get indoors," Gerdes recalls.

Fortunately, Gerdes had seen plenty of more inviting entryways through his work as a landscape maintenance supervisor, so he knew some strategies to remedy the situa-

tion. First he removed a privacy wall and a walkway that made an uninteresting beeline from the sidewalk to the front door. Then he poured a colored, salted concrete slab in front of the house to make a patio. Over it, he erected a 9- by 32-foot pergola of stained fir posts and beams. The patio provides ample seating, and the pergola casts the filtered shade suited to Gerdes's potted plants.

Gerdes reshaped the formerly flat yard into a series of gentle berms (the tallest one shields the patio) and installed a curving walkway (see photo above). He planted the berms with an assortment of Southwest natives, including blue yucca *(Y. rigida),* brittle-

BEFORE

bush *(Encelia farinosa),* indigo bush *(Dalea pulchra),* and palo brea *(Cercidium praecox),* plus a few non-native perennials like yellow-flowered angelita daisy *(Tetraneuris acaulis).* A small lawn of Bermuda grass sweeps across the yard to the berm screening the patio.

"Before the renovation, we didn't use the front yard at all," says Gerdes. "Now, except for maybe August, we're out there every day."

—*S.C.*

NORM PLATE (1)

Bromeliads, including urn plants with showy pink bracts, can bloom for months in a bright room.

PAUL BOUSQUET

Visit the queen of flower shops

Find houseplants and other treasures in Denver

Established in 1911, City Flo- ral Greenhouse and Garden Center is the dowager queen of Denver's commercial green- houses. Yet this sprawling com- plex, located east of downtown, always provides plant shoppers with a sensuous excursion. This is especially true in the dead of winter, when blossoms perfume the balmy air and the kaleido- scopic array of plants stands in lush contrast to the cold, drab outdoor scene.

As you wander through the nine greenhouses, you'll see everything from aquatic plants to cactus. The selection of flow- ering plants changes with the season: look for bromeliads and cyclamen in heart-throbbing hues of red and pink for Valen- tine's Day, along with daffodils, hyacinths, lilies, and tulips in bright Easter-egg shades. Fresh- cut flowers are also sold.

When the weather warms up outside, City Floral offers a vast selection of seasonal bedding plants: annual and perennial flowers, vegetables, and herbs. The center also stocks contain- ers, potting soil, and acces- sories ranging from gloves and tools to wind chimes.

9–5 Mon–Sat, 10–5 Sun. 1440 Kearney St., 1/2 block south of Colfax Ave. (look for the tall yellow chimney); www. cityfloralgreenhouse.com or (303) 399-1177. —Colleen Smith

Gnarled Harry Lauder's walking stick (top left, behind spreading white fir) and blue-needled weeping Atlantic cedar (far right) frame an entry arbor.

Fresh ideas at Seattle's big show

"Take your basic Northwest green garden. Add blue, lots of blue. Blue foliage, flowers, pots, and gate. Too much blue? In Seattle? I don't think so." That's how landscape designer Mike Jeppesen of Sammamish Landscape *(360/435-3769)* describes the Blue Garden (shown above) he designed for display last year at the Northwest Flower & Garden Show in Seattle. A gold-medal winner, the garden, with pots designed by Tina Dixon of Plants à la Carte, was filled with good ideas, which I jotted down in my notebook: "Glazed blue pot filled with purple sage. Woolly thyme and 'Curly Girl' rue edge the path." Like many avid gardeners in the Northwest, I find the show to be a virtual supermarket of ideas.

If you're planning to attend this year's five-day show in late February, here's how to get the most from your visit.

• Carry a notebook and a camera with a flash for recording ideas and plant names, plus a tote bag for collecting designers' brochures.

• View each display garden from several angles, then focus on the details that strike you.

The annual show features around 30 display gardens, plus hundreds of vendors offering everything from garden books to greenhouses. Once again, *Sunset* will sponsor a free seminar series with more than 100 presentations by horticultural experts.

For information, contact the. Washington State Convention Center, Seventh Ave. and Pike St.; www.gardenshow.com or (800) 229-6311.

—*Kathleen N. Brenzel*

LEFT: PADDY WALES; TOP: DAVID McDONALD

This trellis holds four vines—gourds, mini pumpkins, morning glory, and scarlet runner beans.

Insects, up close

If there's one book that changes the way you garden this season, it may well be Eric Grissell's "gnat's-eye level" tour of the insect world, *Insects and Gardens: In Pursuit of a Garden Ecology* (Timber Press, Portland, 2001; $30; www.timberpress.com or 503/227-2878). Carll Good-pasture's extraordinary illustrative photos are from the same vantage point. This book's prose and images were lauded with two Garden Globe Awards from the Garden Writers Association last year.

Grissell's prose is as entertaining as it is informative. In describing how insects dispose of dead matter, he notes: "There is one heck of an assortment of insects tidying up your garden at no cost to you, and 99 percent of the time you don't even know it."

According to Grissell, a garden that suffers from aphids, scale, or other insect pests is simply a garden that's out of balance and needs more predators like ladybugs and lacewings. One of the best ways to attract such beneficial insects, he writes, is to have something in flower most of the year.—S. C.

Flowering tepee

Watching vines spring up from seed and shoot for the sky is one of the joys of summer. To grow them, you first need to rig up a support. Lynne Blackman's version of the classic tepee, pictured at left, is perfect. Made from four pieces of timber bamboo loosely bound together with braided grapevine, both of which were harvested from her Del Mar garden, it goes up in minutes. She used floral wire in a few places to bind the grapevine to the poles. Eight-foot bamboo poles from a nursery, lashed together at the top with garden twine, work fine too. Sow seeds for vining annuals around the base; leave an opening for the tepee entrance. Then keep soil moist until the seeds germinate. —*S. C.*

Uprooting weeds

Eliminating deeply rooted weeds takes a long, strong tool like the Diggit2 (pictured at right). Created by Seattle-area gardener Elena Shemeta and her son Paul

after years of using an old tent stake to pull up weeds, this foot-long tool has a sturdy, daggerlike 8-inch blade made of stainless steel that won't bend in tough soils or rust. The soft handle provides a comfortable grip, and its bright yellow color makes it hard

to lose. The blade's center channel also works for sowing seeds, digging bulb holes, and transplanting seedlings; inch and centimeter notches along its edges make it useful for spacing plants.

$15 plus shipping when ordered directly from Shemeta. To order, call (425) 454-0125. —J. C.

Burgundy foliage of *Loropetalum* (foreground) and Eastern redbud enhances the effect of chartreuse *Euphorbia*.

An overture to spring

Euphorbia's chartreuse flowers open the season

If there's not much going on in your garden right now, one plant could solve the problem: *Euphorbia characias wulfenii.* The succulent lights up the Grace Kallam Perennial Garden at the Arboretum of Los Angeles County in the photograph above.

E. c. wulfenii puts out its big poufs of chartreuse flowers (bracts, really) in late winter, just when you need a jolt of color. The impressive display persists for months. When bracts finally fade, cut off the stems at the base. By then the new shoots that will produce next year's flowers will have emerged.

This Mediterranean native's lime green flowers, blue-green leaves, and strong sculptural shape complement a wide range of plants. But to really make the plant shine, add burgundy. In the Kallam Garden, Eastern redbud *(Cercis canandensis)* 'Forest Pansy' and low-growing *Loropetalum chinense* 'Razzleberri'

provide that boost. Berberis, flax, nandina, and 'Zwartkop' aeonium would also work.

E. c. wulfenii is drought-tolerant but doesn't object to regular watering. It prefers full sun but can take some shade. Its only flaws are its milky sap, which can irritate your skin, and its habit of reseeding a bit too generously.

If you can't find *E. c. wulfenii* at your nursery, ask to have it ordered for you from a wholesale grower. *Grace Kallam Perennial Garden, 301 N. Baldwin Ave., Arcadia; www. arboretum.org or (626) 821-3222.*

—S.C.

WHAT TO DO IN YOUR GARDEN IN FEBRUARY

PLANTING

☐ **BARE-ROOT STOCK.** Zones 4–7, 17: Often displayed in bundles and usually with roots sunk into damp sawdust or sand, bare-root stock cuts across all plant categories. Among edibles, look for asparagus, blackberries, raspberries, rhubarb, and strawberries. Among ornamentals, look for all kinds of shade trees, flowering trees, vines, roses, and shrubs. In zones 1–3, plant as soon as bare-root stock is available and on a day when air and soil temperatures are above freezing.

☐ **EARLY VEGETABLES.** Zones 4–7, 17: Seeds of peas and spinach will both germinate in cool soil, but peas do best if you presprout seeds in damp paper towels. Plant in raised beds, which drain well and warm up faster than heavier garden soil.

☐ **ENGLISH PRIMROSE.** Acaulis primroses usually have a single flower per stem, while polyanthus types have multiple flowers growing from a single strong stem. Use acaulis primroses in sheltered locations (on a covered porch or windowsill) and more weather-resistant polyanthus types in outdoor beds.

☐ **HARDY ANNUALS.** Direct-sow calendula, English daisy, godetia, pansy, many kinds of poppy (including California and Iceland types), snapdragon, and viola. Or buy seedlings now for bloom next month and beyond.

☐ **SWEET PEAS.** Start seeds of flowering sweet peas indoors in 4-inch pots. Transplant seedlings into the garden in March or April.

☐ **WINTER-BLOOMING TREES, SHRUBS.** This month you can buy and plant containerized English holly for bright berries; *Sarcococca* for tiny, fragrant winter flowers; camellias, heaths, Japanese andromeda, and rhododendrons for showier, mostly unscented blooms; and heavenly bamboo for red winter leaves. Among deciduous plants with February flowers, try 'Autumnalis' cherry, Cornelian cherry *(Cornus mas),* corylopsis, forsythia, *Prunus blireiana,* Japanese flowering apricot *(P. mume),* viburnums, wintersweet, and witch hazel. Hazelnuts, pussywillows, and silktassel *(Garrya)* all make a great winter show with elegant hanging catkins.

MAINTENANCE

☐ **CARE FOR HOUSEPLANTS.** Feed flowering houseplants such as moth orchids and African violets, but wait until spring growth begins to fertilize foliage plants. Prune off yellowing leaves and cut back plants that are getting leggy to force regrowth from lower on the plant. Palms are the exception; if you cut their tops off, they die.

☐ **PRUNE ROSES.** Zones 4–7: Cut out dead, injured, or diseased canes, and all suckers. Then prune hybrid teas for shape. Select the three to five strongest canes and cut them back by about a third, nipping the cane off just above a strong, outward-facing bud. In zones 1–3, wait to prune until just before new growth begins (you can tell by looking at the swelling buds). ◆

WHAT TO DO IN YOUR GARDEN IN FEBRUARY

PLANTING

☐ GLADIOLUS. Zones 7–9, 14–17: Explore your local garden centers for new, unusual types. Or order three gorgeous new varieties from Dutch Gardens: 'Ice Cream' (white and soft yellow blossoms), 'Mon Amour' (butter yellow and pale pink flowers), or 'Sophie' (pure white blooms). Dutch Gardens: *www.dutchgardens.com or (800) 818-3861.*

☐ PEPPERS. Zones 7–9, 14–17: Spice up your vegetable beds with different types of peppers. If you prefer mild varieties, try sweet 'Cubanelle'. For more heat, plant mildly hot 'Elephant's Trunk'. If you like to play with fire, you'll love super-hot 'Tepín'. Start seeds indoors this month; transplant seedlings into larger pots when they reach 2 inches tall. When plants reach 4 to 6 inches tall and nighttime temperatures are above 50°, plant outdoors in rich soil. Seeds are available from the Redwood City Seed Company *(www. ecoseeds.com or 650/325-7333).* Another good source for pepper seeds is Territorial Seed Company, *(www.territorialseed.com or 541/ 942-9547).*

☐ PERENNIAL VALENTINE. Zones 7–9, 14–17: Instead of chocolates or a bouquet, why not give your loved one a gift that will last throughout the seasons? Choose a plant such as an azalea, a hydrangea, or a miniature rose that can be planted in the ground after bloom. Or select a spring bloomer like delphinium, forget-me-nots, or violets that can go into the ground right away.

Sunset
CLIMATE ZONES

☐ Mountain (1–2)
☐ Valley (7–9)
☐ Inland (14)
☐ Coastal (15–17)

MAINTENANCE

☐ HARVEST CITRUS. Zones 7–9, 14–17: Most citrus varieties are at peak flavor now (lemons are harvested year-round). Before picking large quantities, taste one fruit to make sure it's sweet (ripening time varies from year to year, depending on the weather). Harvest as needed, but get fruit off the tree before it dries out or loses flavor, usually within two to three months.

☐ REPLANT CYMBIDIUMS. Zones 7–9, 14–17: If your cymbidium orchids are outgrowing their containers or the bark has decomposed, it's time to replant them. Do this between mid-February and early July. Remove old bark, cut off dead roots, and discard soft or rotted bulbs. Repot the entire plant into a larger container. Or divide it into groups of three to five bulbs (with leaves), then repot each cluster in a medium-size container filled with bark or cymbidium mix. In mild, frost-free climates (zone 17), try planting cymbidiums directly in the ground (see article on page 30).

☐ SPRAY FOR PEACH LEAF CURL. Zones 7–9, 14–17: In mid- to late February when buds are beginning to swell, but before any green foliage appears, apply a dormant spray of lime sulfur to prevent peach leaf curl—a fungus that distorts leaves and destroys the fruit on peach and nectarine trees. Use it with a spreader-sticker to improve coverage; do not spray when rain is predicted within 36 hours.

PEST CONTROL

☐ CONTROL SLUGS AND SNAILS. Zones 7–9, 14–17: As nighttime temperatures rise, snails and slugs become more active and can quickly devour favorite plants. At night, handpick and discard these pests. Or get rid of snails and slugs by using a beer trap, strips of copper tape around containers, or commercial bait such as Sluggo that won't harm people or pets. ◆

WHAT TO DO IN YOUR GARDEN IN FEBRUARY

PLANTING

☐ BARE-ROOT PLANTS. It's not too late to plant bare-root roses, fruit trees, berries, and grapes. But shop carefully: quality and selection dwindle as the temperatures warm up. If you're considering adding a low-chill peach, 'Bonita', 'Red Baron', and 'Saturn' are good choices. All three cultivars have been high scorers in taste tests at the University of California South Coast Research & Extension Center in Irvine.

☐ COOL-SEASON VEGETABLES. In coastal (*Sunset* climate zones 22–24), inland (zones 18–21), and high-desert (11) gardens, continue to seed beets, carrots, celery, chard, chives, collards, endive, fennel, kale, leeks, lettuce, mustards, onions, parsley, peas, potatoes, radish, spinach, and turnips. For a fast crop, try a micro greens mix, which you harvest when plants are only a few inches high. If you like a little bite in your salads, Micro Greens Spicy Mix from Botanical Interests of Broomfield, Colorado *(www.gardentrails.com)*, is a great seed blend of cress, mustards, and radish.

☐ PERENNIAL WILDFLOWERS. In the low desert (zone 13), plant coreopsis, desert marigold, evening primrose, penstemon, and salvia.

☐ SUMMER VEGETABLES. Zone 13: plant eggplant, peppers, tomatoes, and other warm-season vegetables late this month. But be prepared to protect them with row covers or hot caps if a late frost threatens.

☐ WINTER COLOR. Coastal and inland gardeners can fill in bare spots with calendula, cineraria, Iceland poppy, nemesia, pansy, primrose, schizanthus, snapdragons, stock, or sweet peas. If the soil is too soggy, plant in containers.

MAINTENANCE

☐ DETHATCH WARM-SEASON GRASSES. Early spring is a good time to dethatch Bermuda, Kikuyu, St. Augustine, and other warm-season grasses. Mow lawn as low as possible before starting. Then rent a dethatcher (a vertical cutter or vertical mower) and make several crisscrossing passes across the lawn to loosen the interlocking runners that hold the thatch in place. Dethatching works best on damp but not soggy soil. Rake up and dispose of loose thatch; don't compost.

☐ DRAIN STANDING WATER. If plants are standing in pools of water, dig small, temporary trenches to let the water flow away. Or scoop out excess water with a shovel.

☐ SPRING FEEDING. Feed ground covers, shrubs, perennials, trees, and other permanent plants with a slow-release fertilizer such as bonemeal, cottonseed meal, or well-rotted manure to provide gradual nutrition through the season. Or, if preferred, scatter a granular complete fertilizer and water well. If you're within 10 miles of the coast, also feed citrus and avocado. Cool-season lawns, like tall fescue, should be fertilized as well.

PEST & DISEASE CONTROL

☐ APPLY DORMANT SPRAY. While deciduous fruit trees are still leafless, spray them with horticultural oil to smother overwintering insect pests such as scale, mites, and aphids. For fungal diseases such as peach leaf curl, add lime sulfur or fixed copper to the oil, following package directions. Spray the branches, crotches, trunk, and ground beneath the tree out to the drip line. ◆

WHAT TO DO IN YOUR GARDEN IN FEBRUARY

PLANNING AND PLANTING

☐ ORDER PLANTS. For a good selection of drought-resistant plants, check out the catalog offerings of these regional sources. Agua Fria Nursery of Santa Fe *(505/983-4831)* specializes in difficult-to-find perennials, Western wildflowers, and trees and shrubs, including many that don't require any supplemental watering after they become established. Great Basin Natives of Holden, Utah *(www.greatbasinnatives.com or 435/795-2303),* carries a wide selection of native plants.

☐ PLANT BARE-ROOT VEGETABLES. As soon as the soil can be worked, plant bare-root asparagus, horseradish, Jerusalem artichokes, and rhubarb. Choose a sunny location and dig in several inches of compost and a handful of balanced fertilizer before planting. Johnny's Selected Seeds of Winslow, Maine *(www.johnnyseeds.com or 207/437-4301),* offers an extra-early Jerusalem artichoke called 'Stampede'. Nourse Farms of South Deerfield, Massachusetts *(www.noursefarms.com or 413/665-2658),* sells many varieties of asparagus, horseradish, and rhubarb.

☐ PLANT LILIES. Lily bulbs can go into the ground as soon as the soil has thawed. Many garden centers stock lilies at this time. Or order bulbs from the Lily Garden in Vancouver, Washington *(360/253-6273).*

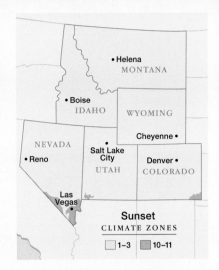

Sunset
CLIMATE ZONES
☐ 1–3 ☐ 10–11

☐ START AN INDOOR HERB GARDEN. Plant several kinds of herbs together in a wide, shallow pot, or grow them individually in 4- to 6-inch pots. Chives, marjoram, mint, oregano, parsley, sage, tarragon, and thyme are good choices for a sunny kitchen windowsill. Snip and use the herbs during their indoor stay. In spring, set the pots outdoors or transplant into the ground.

☐ START COOL-SEASON CROPS. Indoors or in a greenhouse, start seeds of cool-season vegetables, including broccoli, brussels sprouts, cabbage, cauliflower, kale, kohlrabi, and Swiss chard for transplanting into the garden in April. Botanical Interests of Broomfield, Colorado *(www.gardentrails.com),* offers seeds of heirloom vegetables; try 'Italian Sprouting' or 'Raab' broccoli, 'Nero' or 'Russian Red' kale, or 'Fordhook Giant' or 'Italian White Rib' Swiss chard.

MAINTENANCE

☐ CONTROL WHITEFLIES. Before bringing a new houseplant home, inspect the undersides of leaves for winged adult whiteflies and their pinhead-size larvae, both of which suck the sap from plants and excrete messy "honeydew." Whiteflies are resistant to most pesticides, but repeated applications of neem oil, a botanical pesticide, will kill larvae and adults. Yellow sticky traps are also effective.

☐ PREVENT CROCUS DAMAGE. As crocus come into bloom, stop sparrows and finches from shredding their delicate blossoms by placing foil pinwheels every few feet among the flowers. The flashing foil frightens away birds.

☐ SPRAY DORMANT PLANTS. Apply dormant oil on deciduous fruit and ornamental trees and shrubs to kill overwintering insects. Thoroughly wet all surfaces, including the undersides of leaves and branches. Dormant oil is not recommended for blue spruce because it may discolor the needles. With evergreens, test the spray's effect on a small, inconspicuous area before treating the entire plant.
—*Marcia Tatroe*

WHAT TO DO IN YOUR GARDEN IN FEBRUARY

PLANTING

☐ **BARE-ROOT FRUITS.** Zone 10 (Albuquerque): Plant apples, apricots, berries, grapes, peaches, and pears. Zones 11–13 (Las Vegas, Tucson, Phoenix): Plant bare-root or container-grown grapes (see page 32 for recommendations).

☐ **HERBS.** Zones 11–13: Outdoors, sow seeds of chives, cilantro, dill, and parsley. Indoors, start basil seeds now for transplanting in late March. Set out transplants of marjoram, oregano, sage, and thyme.

☐ **PERENNIALS.** Zones 11–13: For spring and summer color and year-round texture, plant blackfoot daisy *(Melampodium leucanthum),* desert marigold *(Baileya multiradiata),* desert milkweed *(Asclepias subulata),* evening primrose *(Oenothera* species), lantana, paper daisy *(Psilostrophe cooperi),* penstemon, and salvia.

☐ **SPRING COLOR.** Zones 12, 13: Set out transplants of calendula, dianthus, English primrose, larkspur, stock, and viola.

☐ **VEGETABLES.** Zone 10: Indoors or in a coldframe, start seeds of broccoli, cabbage, cauliflower, and salad greens for transplanting in eight weeks. Outdoors, direct-sow seeds of kale, onions, and peas. Zones 11–13: Indoors, start seeds of eggplant, pepper, and tomatoes for transplanting at the end of March. Outdoors, direct-sow seeds of beets, carrots, chard, kohlrabi, melons, onions, radishes, salad greens, spinach, and turnips.

MAINTENANCE

☐ **AMEND SOIL.** Before sowing or transplanting new crops into planting beds or containers, dig in compost and well-rotted manure to improve the soil texture and fertility and enhance water retention.

☐ **CARE FOR CITRUS.** Undersized fruit with dry, shriveled flesh indicates inadequate watering. To eliminate this problem, irrigate to a depth of 3 feet every two to three weeks. Yellow leaves with green veins suggest an iron deficiency, which is easily corrected with an application of chelated iron.

☐ **FERTILIZE.** To foster rapid spring growth and improve fruit and flower development, apply a high-nitrogen fertilizer in granular form over the root zones of citrus trees. Apply a fertilizer with a complete formula (20-20-20, for example) to grapes, other deciduous fruits, and roses. Water before and immediately after you apply fertilizer to avoid burning plants and to wash the nutrients down to the roots.

☐ **USE WATER WISELY.** Harvest rainwater and snowmelt by placing plastic barrels under roof downspouts. Learn about recycling gray water—the water you have used for bathing, dishwashing, and laundry—in your garden. New Mexico State University Cooperative Extension Service offers helpful information on the Internet *(http://cahe.nmsu.edu/pubs/_m/ m-106.html). —Kim Nelson*

**Great gardens
in 5 categories**

· Outdoor living
· Small space
· Renovation
· Regional
· Details

Our 2003
Western Garden
Design Awards

15 winners offer planting, paving,
and problem-solving inspiration

By Lauren Bonar Swezey

As the winners in *Sunset's* contest prove, a garden with a great design not only presents plants beautifully, it extends a home into the outdoors and expresses its owner's taste and personality. Our panel of six judges (see page 53) selected the best gardens from several hundred entries submitted by landscape architects and designers across the West. Each garden is ripe with ideas you can use.

A park of one's own

Beverly Hills. More than 200 trees turned this formerly barren lot into a woodland. "The transformation from bare lot to verdant forest is amazing," one juror remarked. "That's why we love plants."

The goal for designers Mia Lehrer, Esther Margulies, and Sara Fairchild was to screen the neighborhood from the large contemporary home. In the process, they created the illusion that the house had been built in a park.

An irregular stone path meanders through the grounds, connecting the various gardens: a square thicket containing nine crape myrtles in rows of three; a circular fountain surrounded by tulip trees (*Liriodendron tulipifera* 'Arnold'); and an amphitheater with a firepit. Bands of blue fescue ornamental grass interspersed with sections of lawn are among the most striking elements. This garden is all about fabulous textures, one juror noted.

DESIGN: Mia Lehrer + Associates, Los Angeles *(213/384-3844)*

"The transformation from bare lot to verdant forest is amazing."

A square stone wall frames nine 'Natchez White' crape myrtles. Surrounding it are bands of blue fescue ornamental grass interspersed with lawn. The view at left shows the thicket from a distance.

Strap-leafed sansevieria grows indoors and out. Above, concrete and gravel stairs zigzag down the slope.

Winding ways

Santa Monica Canyon, CA.
Gardening on an incline is always a challenge. But finding usable space on tilted ground for growing herbs and vegetables and for dining and outdoor living is a true accomplishment.

The first challenge for the Dry Design team—Maria Denegri, John Jennings, Sasha Tarnopolsky, and Jerry Williams—was to develop more garden area while providing easy access around the property. Switchback paths and "zipper" stairs (a series of zigzagging 6-foot squares that mimic the paving grid below it) connect terraces up and down the slope. To expand the areas where the hillside falls away, Dry Design added decks made of sustainable wood. Bold succulents span the front entry and can be viewed from high windows, strengthening the indoor-outdoor relationship.

Jurors were particularly excited by the beautifully crafted and well-organized spaces. "It looks like a garden that would be fun to walk through," noted one juror.

DESIGN: Dry Design, Los Angeles *(323/954-9084 ext. 22).* The firm also won in Renovation category for Jennifer and Patrick Choi's Los Angeles garden.

Fabric awning shades a dining courtyard. Bougainvillea is a vivid backdrop for fountain (right) and urn (page 43).

Patio pleasures

Paradise Valley, AZ. It takes amazing vision to transform a crumbling, almost lifeless garden into a series of vibrant outdoor rooms that become both gathering spaces and exterior focal points.

Landscape architect Steve Martino met the challenge by opening up the indoor/outdoor views with large sliding glass doors, cutting back light-blocking overhangs, creating a series of terraces around the house, and using vivid color on the surrounding walls and fountains.

In front, bold desert plants frame the taupe walls. Inside those walls is a courtyard alive with color and the sound of water splashing from a fountain. Lights both overhead and around the periphery make the courtyard magical at night.

The living room looks south to an intensely colored wall fountain, which underscores a mountaintop view while it obscures the neighbor's roof. To the west, a dining terrace opens up to an arroyo and offers glimpses of the desert. "The change to the garden is so dramatic," a juror remarked. "The dazzling spaces look very livable."
DESIGN: Steve Martino & Associates, Phoenix *(602/957-6150)*

Steps lead down to a new sunken lawn. At right, a bubbling urn is a focal point.

A house within a garden

Santa Monica. Elevation changes within a landscape can present both challenges and opportunities. Before Bill and Debbi Wisher remodeled their Southern California garden, the ground sloped down to the house from the garage at the back of their property. There were no plants to screen the yard from the street, and passersby could easily see over the 5-foot wall.

But landscape architect Pamela Palmer and landscape designer Miriam Rainville were able to completely transform the garden into what Palmer calls "a house within a garden," a private backyard retreat suitable for entertaining or relaxing. They carved out a 16-by 27-foot rectangle of soil in the center of the existing lawn, then added retaining walls around three sides to maintain the original level.

On one side of the garden, the designers created an intimate flagstone terrace backed by a thick screen of podocarpus trees. On the street side is a lush perennial-and-shrub garden accented by a bubbling urn, with black bamboo and king palms behind it to provide privacy from the street.

Extending directly off the house at the same level as the lawn is a new dining area for small gatherings. "Now the garden works for one person or 50 people," Palmer says. "It's a great use of a small space," noted a juror. "The sunken area makes the garden feel much more extensive."
DESIGN: Artecho Architecture and Landscape Architecture, Venice, CA *(310/399-4794)*

SMALL SPACE ▲

Geometry lesson

Santa Cruz, CA. It didn't take long for landscape architect Michael Bliss to realize that Alison and Gary Macbeth's bold, brightly colored house called for a garden with strong features.

Bliss chose a "highly geometric" layout, right down to the paving patterns. In the backyard, a concrete patio that wraps around the home gives way to squares of concrete with lawn between them. A large adjoining square of flagstone connects the patio to a "moat" (a straight-sided dry streambed), which carries away excess water caused by an existing drainage problem.

The plant material is equally dramatic, colorful, and particularly suited to the garden's Mediterranean climate. In the front yard, purple hop bush and kangaroo paw reflect the rusty colors of the home. At the back of the house, low-maintenance plants such as euphorbia, lavender, and ornamental grasses give the garden its casual feel. "The designer did an outstanding job of integrating the paving and plants," a juror observed. "It has a seamless flow."

DESIGN: Bliss Design, Soquel, CA *(831/476-2702)*

Rust-colored kangaroo paw and New Zealand flax complement the house. Concrete squares interconnect with the lawn in the backyard (above left).

Lush plantings, marble tiles, and a stair-stepped water channel accent this courtyard.

◄ SMALL SPACE

Beautifully crafted

San Francisco. If *Casablanca* had ended differently, Bergman and Bogart might have lived happily ever after in a Moroccan-style courtyard like this one. You can easily picture the star-crossed lovers embracing in this lush, romantic garden.

Designer Stephen Suzman took advantage of the courtyard's wind-protected site to offer a warm, secluded retreat for entertaining or relaxing. Marble-capped seat walls and hand-painted tile benches provide the perfect places to linger. Trickling water from a wall fountain flows through a stair-stepped runnel (water channel) into the patio below to provide soothing sound.

A huge mayten tree shades the courtyard. Planted beneath it, and in the matching raised bed across the runnel, is a collection of bold and textural plants such as abutilon, acanthus, agapanthus, and Tasmanian tree fern. Dozens of pots filled with foliage and flowers decorate the seat wall and patio.

Several jurors described the courtyard as "beautifully constructed" and "elegant." Every one of them could imagine spending time there.

DESIGN: Suzman Design Associates, San Francisco *(415/252-0111)*

An arbor-shaded slate patio, edged with raised planters, offers a cozy setting for outdoor dining. A wooden walkway (right) leads to the side yard.

MARION BRENNER; ABOVE: THOMAS J. STORY (2)

◄ SMALL SPACE

Less is more

Walnut Creek, CA. As homes grow larger and fill more of their lots, gardens are getting smaller and smaller. Landscape designers try to make every inch count. The suburban garden of David Brewster and Alvey Halloway is a perfect example of how to make the most of a small yard.

Using complementary paving materials to define each space, landscape architects Stefan Thuilot and Joseph Huettl transformed a very narrow side yard into a slate patio, gravel potting area, and a small lawn that wraps around the end of the house. Wooden walkways set flush with the patio act as bridges between the various garden areas.

A raised bed that runs the length of the patio is filled with a variety of blooming plants and foliage to help soften the tall fence. A striking two-tiered fountain provides a focal point from inside the house. Overhead, white wisteria trained on a sturdy arbor provides shade. "The arbor brings the garden down to a human scale," a juror noted.

"The materials flow together," said another impressed juror. "It's such a good example of how to work with a long, narrow space."

DESIGN: Huettl-Thuilot Associates, Lafayette, CA *(925/937-6400)*

◄ RENOVATION

Simply elegant

Danville, CA. Jack and Shelley Bays wanted a garden with variety, seasonal color, and plenty of foliage to soften stark walls.

Landscape architect Mathew Henning and landscape designer Heather Anderson provided a simple yet elegant solution for the small property by removing a lawn and developing a series of garden rooms that are visually appealing from indoors and out.

Outside the living room, a tired-looking Mexican fountain and tile patio were replaced with refined gray slate. A small pond filled with iris and water lilies adds a handsome focal point from indoors. Surrounding the patio is a low stone wall that doubles as party seating. In spring, flowering spiraea and coral bells bloom behind it. A semicircle of 'Akebono' flowering cherries softens the neighbors' wall and shades the patio in summer.

"It's such a sophisticated solution," one juror remarked.

DESIGN: Henning/Anderson, Oakland, CA *(510/531-3095)*

Pink blooms of 'Akebono' flowering cherries are echoed by underplanted coral bells.

A stacked stone wall surrounds a Zen-like spa garden and complements the thick native forest around it.

TOP: PROVIDED BY J. B. MCCARTHY OF NOBLE DESIGN STUDIO; BOTTOM: SAXON HOLT

REGIONAL ▶
Mountain refuge

Aspen, CO. It's difficult to improve on nature when you're already surrounded by native woodlands. That's why this casual retreat particularly impressed jurors. "It's like a wonderful sanctuary scooped out of the forest," a juror observed. "The stone wall and spruce trees form a striking transition between the manmade and natural landscape." Even more remarkable is the fact that the site began as a barren lot stripped of plants.

The design—a collaborative effort between owners Dick Gallun and Judy MacGregor, designers J. B. McCarthy and Ace Lane, and foreman Manuel Duran—evolved as the garden took shape. The sunken terrace grew from a need for more privacy from a nearby pedestrian path. The clean, simple approach came from the owners' appreciation for Japanese gardens.

A dry-stacked stone retaining wall, made of native sandstone and accented by large moss-covered boulders, defines this outdoor living area. Within its walls, a flagstone terrace and spa are connected by two gravel-covered terraces. Around them, rocks and shrubs are carefully positioned to achieve the simple overall mood. As several jurors remarked, anyone would immediately feel at peace here.

DESIGN: Noble Design Studio, Carbondale, CO *(970/963-7027)*

REGIONAL ▶
Gentle touch

Glen Ellen, CA. Perched on a hill overlooking the Sonoma Valley, this elegant landscape rests gently on its oak-studded lot. "You definitely know it's in California," a juror observed of the regionally appropriate landscape. "The oaks, the grassland, the clean lines of the pool area … such restraint!"

The owners asked designer Stephen Suzman to create a landscape that appeared as if it were part of nature. That meant disturbing the ½-acre landscaped area as little as possible and incorporating materials from the land.

Stone used in walls that separate the native grasslands from the pool area were gathered on the property. Native brodiaea bulbs disrupted during construction were transplanted to another part of the garden.

Although the steel-and-concrete pergola next to the pool was built for this project, its cast-concrete pillars were distressed to make them look old, and its steel lath was allowed to rust in a nearby field for several months before it was installed.

Pacific Coast iris, sword fern, and other native plants enhance the natural areas. Around the house is a mix of edibles (persimmon, grapes) and old-fashioned plants like wisteria that suggests a restored ranch garden. "Its simplicity magnifies the beauty of the surrounding land," a juror noted.

DESIGN: Suzman Design Associates, San Francisco *(415/252-0111)*

A grass-edged rectangular pool reflects native oak woodlands.

"The beautiful textures and colors make a graceful transition."

A flagstone-covered retaining wall sets off perennials (white Santa Barbara daisy, red penstemon, purple lavender) and grasses. Stairs meander up the hillside (below).

Open to change

Lafayette, CA. Nestled at the base of a steep hillside with gorgeous views of Northern California's rolling hills, Brian and Cristen Godfrey's charming small-space garden feels perfectly matched to its surroundings. But just a few years ago, much of the land was overrun with a carpet of scraggly junipers 3 feet deep. A huge fir tree growing up through the junipers blocked much of the view. The only connection to the open space was a set of wooden steps that went straight up the hill.

Stefan Thuilot and Joseph Huettl made some dramatic changes. First they stripped the hillside of juniper and cut down the fir tree to improve the views. They also rerouted the stairs to make them more inviting and becoming. The new steps gently curve up the slope, leading the eye to the hills beyond.

Below the hill, a new flagstone-covered retaining wall expands the outdoor living area. An old, rotting deck was replaced with a handsome concrete-and-flagstone patio. A smaller deck was added off the bedroom, along with a new French door that improved access to the deck.

The hillside was replanted with an exciting palette of vibrant, California-appropriate plants,

THIS PAGE: SAXON HOLT; OPPOSITE: NORM PLATE

Steps lead from the dining patio to a gathering spot with fireplace and seat wall. Cactus thrive in pots (below).

including California fescue, carex, catmint, coral bells, erigeron, 'Garnet' penstemon, lavender, Mexican bush sage, 'Morning Light' miscanthus, rosemary, and species geraniums. "The beautiful textures and colors make such a graceful transition to the open space," observed a juror. All of the jurors agreed that it was an amazing transformation.

DESIGN: Huettl-Thuilot Associates, Lafayette, CA *(925/937-6400)*

Living on the edge

Tucson. Residing in the desert has many advantages, including year-round outdoor living and the ability to grow a wonderful diversity of plants. Owners Barbara Gutek and Geza Bottlik appreciate all the desert has to offer, including the many birds that visit their property. So when they hired Jeffrey Trent to design their desert-edge garden, they requested that it be suitable for entertaining both friends and wildlife.

The garden, which slopes away from the house, was parceled into a series of terraces to maximize the usable area. The upper terrace—with its outdoor kitchen, dining patio, and seat wall—is the main entertaining area. Surrounding it are many colorful native and desert-adapted plants that provide creatures with food and shelter. A small pond in the back welcomes visiting birds.

An intimate gathering spot on the middle terrace has a built-in fireplace edged with a low seat wall; square cutouts in the wall frame views of the desert.

The lowest and most intimate terrace—screened by an existing California pepper tree—is re-served for a spa. "It's a wonderful series of spaces for outdoor living," noted a juror. "The subdued colors and gentle transitions to the desert make the garden very unobtrusive."

DESIGN: Natural Order Inc., Tucson *(520/792-9274)*

"The rusted steel gives the
garden a warm, cozy feel."

Richly colored rusted
steel is used in place
of wood throughout
the garden. A 2-inch-
thick steel plate
edges a raised bed
(above right).

DETAILS ▶

A path worth reading

Tiburon, CA. Visitors would never guess that the elegant walkway leading to Judith Thompson and Cindy Brooks's front door contains a hidden message: stones, arranged in gravel like braille dots, spell out the poem "The Passionate Shepherd to His Love" by Christopher Marlowe.

It's like a special secret between friends, says designer Topher Delaney.

DESIGN: T. Delaney Inc./Seam Studio, San Francisco *(415/621-9899)*. The firm also won in Small Space category for a children's garden in San Francisco.

In a walkway lined with callas, clusters of stones are arranged like braille dots.

◀DETAILS

Perfect materials

Palo Alto. Sometimes, remodeling a house presents opportunities. This recent remodel relocated a master bedroom to the front of the house, producing a need for more privacy from the street. Landscape architect Gary Strang's solution was to create an intimate courtyard.

He built a low fence made from teaklike ipe, with concrete masonry unit columns topped by a wood-and-steel trellis. The cleverly crafted structure provides privacy without completely blocking the view. The reed grass's feathery flower plumes add screening while softening hard lines. "It's wonderfully crisp and clean," the jurors agreed.

DESIGN: GLS Architecture/ Landscape Architecture, San Francisco *(415/285-3614)* ◆

◀DETAILS

Steeled to perfection

Yountville, CA. In any garden, details make the difference between a good landscape and a great one. In Steven and Kimberly Cook's garden, designed by Jack Chandler, an unusual collection of rusted steel elements—including an arbor, retaining walls, light fixtures, and sculptures—creates a bold statement. "The rusted steel gives the garden a warm, cozy feel," remarked a juror. "It's not at all cold or industrial-looking."

Chandler, who makes furniture and sculptures in addition to designing landscapes, had used scrap steel in his work for years. But this was his first attempt to use it throughout the garden in place of wood or other materials. In spite of the logistical challenges (the 2-inch-thick steel plates used as retaining walls required a crane to set them in place), the use of steel was very successful. Fortunately, the expense of the crane was offset by the low cost of the salvaged materials, which should last many years longer than wood.

DESIGN: Jack Chandler & Associates, Yountville, CA *(707/944-8352)*

Slats of ipe wood create an attractive courtyard fence. Tall reed grass is a soft counterpoint in front.

This year's jury
(from left to right)

Christine Ten Eyck, ASLA
Ten Eyck Landscape Architects
Phoenix

Scott Woodcock, ASLA
The Berger Partnership
Seattle

Lauren Bonar Swezey
Director, Western Garden Design Awards Program,
Sunset

Bernard Trainor, APLD, MSGD
Bernard Trainor Design Associates
Royal Oaks, CA

Pamela Burton, ASLA
Pamela Burton & Company
Santa Monica

Kathleen N. Brenzel
Senior Garden Editor, *Sunset*

STEVEN GUNTHER

A PAIR OF 'LADY BANKS' ROSES meets over a vintage Mexican gate at the entry to this Carefree, Arizona, garden. For details on this spectacular desert climber, see page 58.

March

Hot-colored nasturtiums accent cream-fringed herbs.

Triple-pleasure herb pot

Variegated forms of culinary herbs offer three sensuous pleasures: fragrance, flavor, and multicolored foliage. You can magnify their effect by combining several kinds in a single container, as Robin Cushman did here for the sunny entry of her home in Eugene, Oregon.

Cushman filled a 20-inch-diameter terracotta pot with fast-draining soil mix. She paired plants with creamy yellow variegations to unite her design. Large leaves of comfrey (*Symphytum* x *uplandicum* 'Variegatum') get the center position, while the stems of pineapple mint (*Mentha suaveolens* 'Variegata') rise behind. On the left side, tiny leaves of sweet marjoram (*Origanum majorana* 'White Anniversary') contrast with the round, gold-splashed leaves of Alaska Series nasturtiums, whose edible flowers add a peppery accent to salads. Trailing among the nasturtiums is Cuban oregano (*Plectranthus amboinicus* 'Variegatus'), whose cream-fringed leaves play off the pale lilac flowers of 'English Wedgewood' thyme. —*Mary-Kate Mackey*

More herbs with showy leaves

To create your own combinations, look in nurseries for other herbs with variegated foliage, such as the following.

Golden apple mint (*Mentha* x *gracilis*)

Golden oregano (*Origanum vulgare* 'Aureum' or 'Aureum Crispum')

Golden sage (*Salvia officinalis* 'Aurea' or 'Icterina')

Lemon thyme (*Thymus* x *citriodorus* 'Aureus' or 'Argenteus', with gold- and silver-splashed leaves, respectively, or 'Doone Valley' with yellow-spotted leaves)

Rosmarinus officinalis 'Golden Rain' (also sold as 'Joyce DeBaggio'), with gold-edged leaves

Scented geraniums such as *Pelargonium* x *fragrans* 'Creamy Nutmeg' or *P. crispum* 'Variegatum', both of which have white-fringed leaves

ROBIN CUSHMAN

Wildflowers in Tucson

I f you live in Tucson, you don't have to drive beyond city limits to see a great wildflower show. The "front yard" of the Nature Conservancy field office at 1510 East Fort Lowell Road is a blaze of desert marigolds, poppies, and owl's clover every spring. But don't just admire it from your car. Park and explore. The strip of wild-flowers out front is only the beginning; the collection of Sonoran and Chihuahuan desert plants continues all the way around the building and into the central courtyard. To fully appreciate what you're seeing, pick up the conservancy's descriptive brochure at the front desk before you take the self-guided tour.

The conservancy staff is justifiably proud of their "garden," which is how they think of the grounds. Though Tucson landscape architect John Chinnock did the design, staff members provided a lot of input. They also do most of the maintenance themselves.

For more information about the Conservancy, call (520) 622-3861.
—Sharon Cohoon

Drifts of rosy-purple owl's-clover and desert marigolds (left) stop traffic outside the Nature Conservancy office in Tucson.

A laurel with fragrant flowers

In early spring, Texas mountain laurel *(Sophora secundiflora)* explodes into bloom, perfuming the air with the sweet scent of grape soda. Clusters of bright purple flowers cling to the branches for several weeks before giving way to cream-colored pods that resemble strands of giant pearls when they mature. It's best to clip off the pods; eventually they open to expose bright red seeds, which are poisonous. Clipping also increases the likelihood of a second bloom.

Native to Texas, New Mexico, and northern Mexico, Texas mountain laurel, or mescal bean as it is sometimes called, can be grown in *Sunset* climate zones 8–16 and 18–24. This slow-growing evergreen shrub or tree reaches 15 to 25 feet tall and 10 to 15 feet wide. The species bears 4- to 6-inch-long leaves composed of glossy, bright green leaflets. The variety 'Silver Peso' bears silvery green foliage.

Use Texas mountain laurel alone as a focal point, or plant it in groups of three to five. It can also be used as a screen when planted 6 to 8 feet apart.

To compensate for its slow growth, start with larger plants (from 5- or 15-gallon containers). Once established, Texas mountain laurel survives on rainfall and even during drought requires only monthly irrigation. In spring and summer, small caterpillars devour new growth; control them by handpicking or with regular applications of the biological pesticide *Bacillus thuringiensis* (Bt).
—Kim Nelson

Flower clusters are 4 to 8 inches long.

Queen of desert roses

They told Marimarie Konicek not to plant a climbing rose at the entry to her garden in Carefree, Arizona. "Your soil's too poor. That wall will get too hot," they warned. But, as shown on page 54, Konicek ignored their advice. She's a knowledgeable gardener, a member of the Garden Club of America, and she knows her roses. There was one rose, she knew, that would be up to the challenge: *Rosa banksiae* 'Lutea', fondly known as Lady Banks' rose.

It's one of the very best roses for desert areas with mild winters and very hot summers. Although it's hardy to −15°, it is superbly adapted to handle heat. For one thing, *R. b.* 'Lutea' is an early bloomer, putting on its big show of double yellow blossoms in March, shortly after winter rains. When the weather turns scorching, Lady Banks' rose goes semidormant but continues clinging to her small, leathery green leaves. Those leaves, incidentally, are very disease-proof and unattractive to aphids. This climber is also nearly thornless—a virtue especially when planted near a passageway, as shown on page 54.

Lady Banks' has performed beyond Konicek's expectations. This rose is supposed to be a once-a-year bloomer, but her two plants often produce a second round of flowers. Though not as spectacular as the spring display, it's "a nice bonus all the same," she says.

Look for Lady Banks' rose at nurseries. There are also white-flowered forms, such as *R. b.* 'Alba Plena'. Or you can order from Antique Rose Emporium *(www.weareroses. com or 800/441-0002).* —S.C.

Ranunculus and more

If you drive Interstate 5 between Orange County and San Diego anytime in the spring, you can't help but notice the hillside of vibrant-colored ranunculus glowing in the sun near Palomar Airport Road. But if you haven't taken that exit to the Flower Fields recently, you're missing a lot. This working ranch and tourist attraction has added new features.

Among them is the Chance Garden, a floral labyrinth. Designed by Gary Lang, it's part of the Color Project, a program that commissions artists to create works using flowers as their primary medium. Also worth checking out are the All-America Rose Selections test garden, the Walk-of-Fame rose garden (featuring every AARS winner since 1940), and several theme gardens.

Feeling inspired? There's also a new Armstrong Garden Center on the premises, where you can buy the plants you see. You can purchase cut ranunculus flowers too.

Open daily, Mar 1–May 11. 9–5 through Apr 5, 9–6 thereafter; $7. www. theflowerfields.com or (760) 431-0352.
—S.C.

Gopher-proof garden beds

After trying every nontoxic gopher eradication method she knew of and having no success, Renee Shepherd—owner of Renee's Garden Seeds—tried lining her garden beds with hardware cloth to protect seedlings. It worked.

First, Shepherd's trial garden manager, Arlene Kozimbo, dug a trench 18 inches deep and 4 feet wide. Then she lined the bottoms and sides with pieces of ½-inch-mesh hardware cloth, making sure that a few inches of the wire mesh protruded above soil level. She "sewed" together the pieces by overlapping the edges, lacing them together with strong floral wire, then tying off the ends.

Above soil level, Kozimbo framed the beds with redwood 2-by-4s on edge to create a short wall that deters gophers from climbing into beds aboveground. She used a staple gun (you could substitute poultry nails) to secure the hardware cloth to the boards, spacing staples no more than 2 inches apart. Kozimbo placed metal stakes 6 feet apart to hold the boards in place. She then filled the beds with soil for planting. —*Julie Chai*

Ground covers, shrubs, and trees form a multilayered landscape of color and texture.

Rocky Mountain Mediterranean

This drought-tolerant garden looks lush all season long

The red tile roof, rose-tinted stucco, and sun-drenched garden suggest Tuscany. But the landscape that wraps around the home of La Verne and Byron Akers of Colorado Springs is decidedly Rocky Mountain. Because the property is exposed to unrelenting sunshine and desiccating wind, landscape architect Fawn Bell, also of Colorado Springs, chose tough, drought-tolerant plants rather than lawn for the front yard.

Masses of ground covers and shrubs create a sense of lushness and volume on this very narrow lot. Two small trees—a bristlecone pine and thornless cockspur hawthorn—screen the windows from the street. 'Broadmoor' junipers carpet the foreground. The earth tones of the plants connect this landscape with neighboring vistas of red sand-

stone formations and juniper forests. Bell's design won first prize for residential Xeriscape in a competition sponsored by the Colorado Springs water department.

During the growing season, something is always in bloom. Beneath the front window, a row of Scotch broom (*Cytisus scoparius* 'Lena') becomes a haze of yellow in spring, providing a backdrop for the sweetly fragrant, pink flowers of dwarf Korean lilacs. In early summer, the silvery foliage of snow-in-summer is smothered with white blossoms. Pink 'Bonica' roses, planted near the house to protect them from the elements, bloom from May through hard frost. Apache plume *(Fallugia paradoxa)*, a native shrub with white roselike blossoms and fluffy pink seed heads,

Fuzzy flower heads cloak Apache plume in spring and summer.

serves as a billowy foil to the roses. Later in the season, blue mist *(Caryopteris* x *clandonensis)* and violet-blue Russian sage carry on the show. Despite its lush looks, this landscape requires little maintenance—only occasional tidying—and infrequent irrigation to supplement rainfall. —*Marcia Tatroe*

Lavender blooms in drifts along the retaining walls. Tough plants like pink-flowered orchid rockrose (*Cistus*, below right) and agaves add color punch in spring.

Mediterranean charmer

This award-winning garden makes the most of texture, scent, and color

Some landscape remodels are subtle. Others completely change the character of a property. Take Patrick and Jennifer Choi's California garden, for instance—a winner of *Sunset's* 2003 Western Garden Design Awards in the renovation category. Before the remodel, the garden was formal, consisting of lawn and roses. Now it's relaxed and softly flowing, with plants chosen not only for durability and ease of maintenance but also for color, texture, and fragrance.

"The use of elegant but simple landscape materials and casual plants was a brilliant choice," noted an impressed juror, one of *Sunset's* panel of six landscape professionals who judged the entries.

When the Chois bought the property, their main objectives for the garden were to provide play areas for their children and to create screening for the house. Landscape architects Sasha Tarnopolsky and Jerry Williams developed terraces to retain the yard's gentle slope and form level areas for lawn and planting beds. In a nod to the formality of the 1920s brick house, the designers delineated the beds with sinuous lines of myrtle shrubs. They softened the walls' straight lines with sweeps of echium, lavender, ornamental grasses, rockrose, and other unthirsty native and Mediterranean plants. "It's a formal parterre with a twist," explains Tarnopolsky.

Each area of the garden has a theme. There's a fragrance garden, iris walk, kitchen garden, secret garden, thyme walk, and wild garden—and within each area is a fountain,

bench, or other focal point to help define the space. An existing Chinese elm and new native oaks and California sycamores planted from 24- to 48-inch boxes help give the garden a mature look.

DESIGN: Dry Design, Los Angeles (323/954-9084)

—*Lauren Bonar Swezey*

New lilies with long vase life

Oriental lilies like 'Casablanca' have traditionally been considered the aristocrats of the lily family. Yet they had a reputation for being touchy in the garden and sometimes too strongly scented to enjoy indoors.

Now, the new breed of OT, or "orienpet," lilies—hybrids between Oriental and trumpet lilies—have changed all that. They have the look of their Oriental mother, combined with the trouble-free performance of their trumpet father. OT lilies' fragrance is sweet but not heavy. About a dozen kinds of OT hybrids are available, virtually all of them with flowers in variations of yellow and white. They reach 4 to 5 feet tall, but need no staking. Each stem supports seven or eight 10-inch-wide blossoms. The cut flowers last up to a month in the vase.

Long-lived OT lilies cost about $10 per bulb. A good mail-order source is B&D Lilies *(www.lilybulb.com or 360/765-4341)*. *—Jim McCausland*

'Conca d'Or' lilies reach 5 feet tall.

Vision in blue (or white)

Of the hundreds of different campanulas in the world, few are prettier than the charming European hybrid, pictured at left, that has recently appeared in florists and nurseries.

This double-flowered campanula is an amazing bloomer. Plants cover themselves with 1/4- to 1/3-inch-wide flowers of periwinkle blue or pure white that resemble tiny roses. Indoors in bright light, the blooms continue opening over a four-week period.

Although this campanula is often sold as a gift plant, it's actually a tough little ground cover (4 inches tall, 12 inches wide) that grows outdoors in most Western climates except the desert. Plant it in full sun (part shade in hot climates) and in well-drained soil. Keep the soil evenly moist but not wet. Once acclimated to the garden, bloom time is from summer into fall.

The blue-flowered variety is most commonly available; the white one is generally offered during late fall and early winter. Plants are usually sold in 4-inch pots, which cost about $7 each.
—*L.B.S.*

'Wonder Bells Blue' campanula

BOTTOM: THOMAS J. STORY; TOP: JIM McCAUSLAND

From rosemary rings (below) to coleus "trees" (far right), topiary plants come in a vast array of styles at Rabbit Shadow Farm.

Devoted to topiary in Colorado

The horticultural art of topiary dates back at least 2,000 years, to when the ancient Romans cut bushes and trees into ornamental shapes. Over the centuries, topiary has grown in and out of fashion. Today it seems to be enjoying a resurgence in popularity.

One of America's largest cultivators of topiary plants is Rabbit Shadow Farm in Loveland, Colorado. Inside the firm's 30,000-square-foot greenhouse, about 200 varieties of plants— African mallow, Chinese jasmine,

coleus, ivy, lavender, rosemary, and thyme among them—are pruned and trained into traditional topiary shapes, including cones, globes, hearts, and wreaths.

Owned by Jeff and Kristy Sorenson, a brother and sister team, the company supplies wholesalers in 37 states, but it also welcomes drop-in customers for retail sales. Prices range from $9 to $50 for plants in 3- to 10-inch pots, all of which come with care instructions. Most of the plants are frost tender, so they must be grown

indoors during cold weather.

The Sorensons steer beginners toward more forgiving species, such as coleus. A shop at the entrance stocks an assortment of containers suited for topiary. You can also buy container gardens combining herbal topiary.

9–6 Mon–Sat, 10–4 Sun. From I-25 in Loveland, take exit 255 and drive west about 2¹/₂ miles to 2880 E. State 402. For more information or to request a mail-order plant list, call (800) 850-5531 or (970) 667-5531.
—*Colleen Smith*

BACK TO BASICS

Feeding tulips

Tulips benefit from a feeding right after bloom as new bulbs are forming. This is true whether you live in a cold climate where Darwin and other hybrid tulips rebloom for several years, or in a mild climate where you can grow species types (*Tulipa bakeri* 'Lilac Wonder', for instance) that come back year after year. Dutch growers use a 12-10-18 formulation, but any balanced fertilizer (such as 12-12-12) will do. Wait until foliage turns yellow to remove it.
—*L. B. S.*

Sowing fine seeds

Some seeds, like those of parsley, Shirley poppies, and violas, can be difficult to sow evenly because they're so fine. Try this method to make the process easier.

1. Pour loose, fast-draining potting soil into a 4-inch plastic nursery pot.
2. Mix seeds with a small amount of fine sand in a plastic bag. shake well.
3. Fold a small piece of paper in half and put some of the seed-sand mixture in the crease. Lightly tap the paper over soil to distribute the seeds.
4. Mist lightly with a spray bottle of water. —*J. C.*

WHAT TO DO IN YOUR GARDEN IN MARCH

PLANTING

☐ CAMELLIAS. *Sunset* climates zones 4–7: As winter-flowering *Camellia sasanqua* types finish blooming, spring-flowering *C. japonica* varieties are starting. Nurseries carry both kinds now. *C. sasanqua* resists camellia petal blight, while *C. japonica* is susceptible to this disease.

☐ COOL-SEASON CROPS. Zones 4–7: Plant bare-root stock of perennial vegetables, including artichokes, asparagus, horseradish, and rhubarb. Sow seeds of beets, carrots, peas, and spinach directly in the ground. Set out seedlings of broccoli, brussels sprouts, cabbage, cauliflower, Chinese cabbage, chives, kale, kohlrabi, leeks, lettuce, onions, and Swiss chard, as well as garlic cloves and seed potatoes.

☐ HARDY PERENNIALS. Sow seeds of hardy kinds such as delphinium, rockcress, and veronica directly in the ground.

☐ LAWNS. Sow grass seed or lay sod before month's end. Prepare the area by tilling the top 6 to 8 inches of soil, level it with a roller, then lay the sod or rake in seed and reroll. Keep the soil moist until grass is growing strongly.

☐ TREES, SHRUBS. Zones 1–3: You can still plant bare-root stock of many deciduous trees and shrubs. Zones 4–7: Set out container-grown flowering trees including Cornelian cherry *(Cornus mas),* flowering cherries and plums *(Prunus* species), saucer and star magnolias *(M. soulangeana* and *M. stellata),* plus flowering shrubs such as forsythia, *Pieris japonica,* and quince.

☐ SUMMER VEGGIES. Indoors, start seeds of warm-season crops, including cilantro, cucumbers, eggplant, melons, peppers, and tomatoes. They'll be ready for transplanting into the garden in May.

MAINTENANCE

☐ CONTROL SLUGS. Every time you see a snail or slug, eliminate it by handpicking. For broader control, apply bait formulated with iron phosphate or methaldehyde.

☐ DIVIDE PERENNIALS. Zones 4–7: Divide summer- and fall-flowering perennials such as asters, chrysanthemums, and Shasta daisies. Use a spade or shovel to dig up clumps and cut the root mass into quarters, then replant. In zones 1–3, wait until April to do this job.

☐ FEED LAWNS. Zones 4–7: Apply ½ pound of actual nitrogen per 1,000 square feet of turf.

☐ PRUNE CLEMATIS. Zones 4–7: Cut back both summer- and fall-flowering clematis to the strongest stems now, then scratch fertilizer in around the base of the plant. In zones 1–3, prune after danger of hard frost is past. Prune spring-flowering kinds after bloom. ◆

WHAT TO DO IN YOUR GARDEN IN MARCH

PLANTING

☐ DWARF CITRUS. *Sunset* climate zones 7–9, 14–17: If you garden in a small area, consider one of these dwarf citrus, which grow only 6 to 8 feet tall (unless noted). Try 'Dwarf Bearss Seedless' lime, 'Dwarf Campbell' Valencia orange, 'Dwarf Lisbon' lemon (8 to 12 feet tall), 'Dwarf Redblush' grapefruit (8 to 12 feet tall), 'Dwarf Washington Navel' orange, or 'Nagami' kumquat.

☐ FLOWER SEEDS. Zones 7–9, 14–17: Easy-to-grow choices include alyssum, bishop's lace *(Ammi majus),* cosmos, gloriosa daisy, marigold, purple coneflower, spider flower, and sunflower. Start seeds soon either by sowing them directly in the ground (the easiest method) or by planting them in containers and then transplanting them into the ground at the seedling stage. Zones 1 and 2: Start seeds indoors six to eight weeks before last frost.

☐ NEW FRAGRANT ROSES. Try one of these 2003 introductions for their strongly fragrant flowers. New from David Austin Roses *(www.davidaustinroses.com or 800/328-8893):* 'Alnwick Castle' (shrub, pink), 'Benjamin Britten' (shrub, orange-red), and 'The Mayflower' (shrub, deep pink). New from Jackson & Perkins *(www.jacksonandperkins.com or 877/456-8800):* 'Bella'roma' (hybrid tea, pale yellow edged with pink) and 'Flirtatious' (floribunda, cream with pink and yellow).

• Eureka
• Redding
CALIFORNIA
NEVADA
• Mendocino
Santa Rosa
• Sacramento
Sunset
CLIMATE ZONES
• San Francisco
• San Jose
☐ Mountain (1–2)
☐ Valley (7–9)
☐ Inland (14)
☐ Coastal (15–17)
• Fresno
• Monterey

☐ PERENNIALS. Zones 7–9, 14–17: Shop for perennials such as 'Powis Castle' artemisia, coreopsis, *Diascia* (coral, pink, or purple), gaillardia, *Gaura lindheimeri* 'Siskiyou Pink' (it doesn't reseed readily like the species), purple-leaf heuchera, ornamental oregano, penstemon, perennial foxglove *(Digitalis* x *mertonensis),* salvia, Santa Barbara daisy, and wallflower.

☐ SUMMER BULBS. Zones 7–9, 14–17: Calla, canna, dahlia, gladiolus, lilies, and tigridia bulbs are available at nurseries. Plant in well-drained soil or containers (for canna, use only dwarf types in containers); mix a balanced fertilizer into the soil before planting. If you can't find what you're looking for, try Dutch Gardens *(www.dutchgardens.com or 800/818-3861)* or Van Bourgondien *(www.dutchbulbs.com or 800/622-9997).*

MAINTENANCE

☐ AMEND SOIL. Zones 7–9, 14–17: Before planting, amend soil with compost, ground bark, or other organic material. This will increase water retention in sandy soil, decrease it in heavy clay soil, and improve the texture of both kinds. If you use ground bark or another wood product, make sure it has been nitrogen stabilized (read the label or ask the supplier); otherwise, the mulch will retard plant growth. If it hasn't been stabilized, add a nitrogen fertilizer at planting time.

☐ FEED LAWNS. Zones 7–9, 14–17: Feed bent, blue, fescue, and rye grasses now with a high-nitrogen lawn fertilizer (try one of the new organic ones available at many nurseries), according to directions. ◆

WHAT TO DO IN YOUR GARDEN IN MARCH

PLANTING

☐ HERBS. Plant chives, parsley, rosemary, sage, savory, sorrel, tarragon, and thyme. Sow seeds of arugula, chervil, cilantro, and dill.

☐ PERENNIALS. Nurseries are well stocked with blooming perennials now, and early spring is a fine planting time. Reliable choices include alstroemeria, coral bells, delphinium, dianthus, geranium, nemesia, penstemon, salvia, scabiosa, and yarrow. Coreopsis is another good option, especially the new burgundy 'Limerock Ruby' and pink and white 'Sweet Dreams'. Don't forget foliage plants like *Helichrysum,* lamb's ears, and santolina.

☐ RABBIT-RESISTANT PLANTS. Rabbits will eat just about anything. But they dislike highly aromatic plants like artemisia, lavender, marigold, mint, rosemary, santolina, scented geranium, and society garlic. Other unappealing choices: *Agastache,* euphorbia, lantana, milkweed *(Asclepias),* nasturtium, penstemon, and *Zauschneria.*

☐ SUMMER BULBS. Plant caladium, callas, cannas, dahlias, gladiolus, tigridia, tuberous begonias, and watsonia. When planting gladiolus, don't plant them all at once, suggests Walter Andersen Nursery in San Diego. Plant the first row in the back of the bed. Then, two or three weeks later, plant another row 12 to 16 inches in front of it.

Repeat with a third row a few weeks later and, if you have space, a fourth. The back row of glads will start blooming first; when they're starting to fade, they'll be hidden by the second row, which will be up and ready to flower.

MAINTENANCE

☐ ACIDIFY HYDRANGEAS. If you want to keep blue-flowered hydrangeas blue, the soil needs to be acidified before the shrubs form flowers. Apply aluminum sulfate, often packaged expressly for hydrangeas, following label directions.

☐ FERTILIZE. Almost everything in your garden will appreciate a boost of nitrogen this month. Feed fruit and ornamental trees, ground covers, shrubs, perennials, and annuals that have been in the ground at least six weeks. Also fertilize turf grass, container plants, and houseplants. Wait until after bloom to feed camellias; then give them an acidic fertilizer, like cottonseed meal.

☐ SPRAY OLIVES. If you don't want trees to form fruit, spray with a product like Fruit Eliminator when flowers start to open. You may need to spray several times.

PEST CONTROL

☐ CONTROL APHIDS. Strip aphids from plants by hand. (Wear thin disposable rubber gloves if you're squeamish.) Or dislodge them with a strong blast of water from a hose.

☐ MANAGE SNAILS. To reduce their numbers, handpick—you'll find them hiding in strap-leafed plants like agapanthus and daylilies during daylight hours. Or trap them under slightly raised pieces of wood. Protect citrus trees by circling their trunks with copper bands. Used around the perimeter of raised beds, the bands can also protect vegetables and annuals. ◆

WHAT TO DO IN YOUR GARDEN IN MARCH

PLANNING AND PLANTING

☐ PLANT GRAPES. Dormant vines are available now and can be planted as soon as the soil is workable. Choose hardy varieties such as 'Beta', 'Concord', 'Golden Muscat', 'Interlaken', 'Lakemont', 'Suffolk Red', and 'Valiant'. Two good mail-order sources are Raintree Nursery *(www.raintreenursery. com or 360/496-6400)* and St. Lawrence Nurseries *(www.sln. potsdam.ny.us or 315/265-6739)*.

☐ SEEK XERISCAPE AID ONLINE. For guidance on converting your landscape to a water-thrifty Xeriscape, visit these websites: *www. ext.colostate.edu/ptlk/1904.html* or *www.xeriscape.org*

☐ SOW COOL-SEASON VEGETABLES. If you didn't prepare planting beds last fall, dig several inches of well-rotted manure or compost into the soil as soon as it is workable. Then sow seeds of beets, carrots, endive, kohlrabi, lettuce, onions, parsnips, peas, radishes, spinach, Swiss chard, and turnips.

☐ SOW MESCLUN SALAD MIX. Mesclun greens take as few as 25 days from sowing to harvest. Sow seeds in good garden soil. Thin seedlings when they're 2 inches tall; use thinnings in salads and continue harvesting all season.

Sunset
CLIMATE ZONES
☐ 1–3   ☐ 10–11

Each seed firm creates its own mesclun mixes. Look on nursery seed racks for one of these blends from Botanical Interests *(800/486-2647 or www.gardentrails.com)*: Micro Greens Mild Mix, Micro Greens Spicy Mix, or Q's Special Mesclun Mix.

☐ SOW WILDFLOWERS. Scatter seeds of wildflowers directly over the ground where you want them to grow. Among drought-tolerant flowers that germinate best in cold, moist soil are annual coreopsis *(C. tinctoria)*, California desert bluebells *(Phacelia campanularia)*, mountain phlox *(Linanthus grandiflorus)*, Tahoka daisy *(Aster tanacetifolius)*, and Texas bluebonnet *(Lupinus texensis)*. Seeds of these plants are available from Plants of the Southwest *(www. plantsofthesouthwest.com or 800/ 788-7333)*.

☐ TRANSPLANT ROSES. While they're still dormant, transplant rosebushes that are too large for their site or are not blooming well because of too much shade. Cut the canes back to 2 to 3 feet, then dig deeply around the plant to extract as many roots as possible. When choosing a new site, consider the east or north side of the house, where roses will be more protected from freeze-thaw cycles in winter. Position roses far enough from the house walls that they receive 3 to 5 hours of direct sunlight daily.

FLORICULTURE

☐ CUT BRANCHES FOR FORCING. Using sharp pruners, cut budding branches of bridal wreath spiraea, flowering quince, forsythia, honeysuckle, pussywillow, and serviceberry. Place the stems in a bucket of lukewarm water with a pinch of sugar and a drop of chlorine bleach, then put the container in a cool, sunlit room; change the solution twice a week. When blossoms open, use the branches in flower arrangements. —*M. T.*

WHAT TO DO IN YOUR GARDEN IN MARCH

PLANTING

☐ CELEBRATE ARBOR DAY. First observed in 1872, Arbor Day is now celebrated on varying dates in different areas. This year, Arbor Day is officially observed on March 14 in New Mexico and April 25 in Arizona and Nevada. It's a great day to plant a tree suited to your garden's climate and conditions. Consider planting your state tree: piñon *(Pinus edulis)* in New Mexico, littleleaf palo verde *(Cercidium microphyllum)* in Arizona, and bristlecone pine *(P. aristata)* or singleleaf piñon *(P. monophylla)* in Nevada. *For more information: www.arborday.org*

☐ ORDER FLOWER SEEDS, PLANTS. Check Southwest growers' offerings. Consider brilliant yellow *Alyssum montanum* 'Mountain Gold', *Solidago* 'Wichita Mountains' (golden torch), and 'Santa Fe Garden Mix' hollyhocks in shades of red, pink, and yellow; all are available as small plants from High Country Gardens *(www.highcountrygardens.com or 800/925-9387)*. Other unthirsty choices include scarlet and gold Plains coreopsis and orange and yellow Western wallflower, available as seeds from Plants of the Southwest *(www.plantsofthesouthwest.com or 800/788-7333)*.

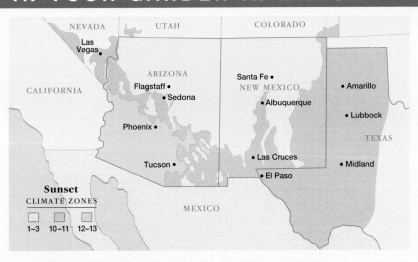

Sunset
CLIMATE ZONES
☐ 1–3 ☐ 10–11 ☐ 12–13

☐ PERENNIALS, SHRUBS. *Sunset* climate zone 10 (Albuquerque): Plant aster, chrysanthemum, coreopsis, *Dalea frutescens* 'Sierra Negra', hollyhock, and *Muhlenbergia capillaris* 'Regal Mist'. Zones 11–13: Plant brittlebush, creosote bush, desert marigold, globe mallow, lantana, salvia, and verbena.

☐ VEGETABLES. Zones 1A–3B (Flagstaff, Taos, Santa Fe): Plant garlic sets in the garden. Indoors, start seeds of celery and onions for transplanting in six weeks. Zone 10: Outdoors, sow seeds of broccoli, cabbage, carrots, cauliflower, kohlrabi, radishes, and spinach. Indoors, start seeds of eggplant, peppers, and tomatoes for transplanting in six weeks. Zones 11–13: Direct-sow bush beans, cucumbers, melons, okra, and summer squash. At month's end, set out transplants of eggplant, peppers, and tomatoes.

MAINTENANCE

☐ MULCH. Spread a 4- to 6-inch layer of mulch around plantings to insulate roots from increasing heat and to conserve soil moisture. Good mulches include aged compost, shredded bark, and wood chips.

☐ PRUNE SHRUBS. At month's end, prune frost-damaged, diseased, or crossing wood from dalea, oleander, and other shrubs. Use sharpened pruners; after each cut, clean blades with a solution of 1 part bleach to 10 parts water to prevent spread of diseases. —*K.N.*

Dining and gardening go hand in hand in this small, elegant potager, where herbs and vegetables grow near the table.

Living Well
IN THE GARDEN

Home landscapes these days are more than places to grow plants. They are sanctuaries from the outside world where we find physical and spiritual well-being. This special section is filled with ideas to help you enjoy outdoor living.

Growing supper

Raising produce is a pleasure
in this Southern California potager

By Sharon Cohoon • Photographs by Steven Gunther

If you want to get the most out of your garden with a soupçon of style, consider copying the French. That's what Linda and Steven Brombal did at their home in Newport Beach, California, and the whole family is delighted with the results. Their kitchen garden, inspired by the classic French *potager,* feeds the family and provides an outdoor room that looks *très joli*.

The Brombals chose this type of garden because they wanted to experiment with growing vegetables and herbs at their Provençal-style tract home. Since this space would also be their primary outdoor-living area, they planned out a yard that would be attractive and easy to maintain.

As in a classic potager, the Brombals' crops grow in small rectangular, square, and circular beds separated by walkways. The little plots and generous paths make weeding, watering, harvesting, and other chores accessible. And the geometric patterns add order to the garden.

Early in the season, when crops are young and a lot of bare earth is still visible, the layout and brickwork become the focal points of the garden. When the growing season is going strong and plants are lush and full, the potager's arrangement keeps the herbs' and

The side yard repeats the kitchen-garden theme. Pots filled with herbs sit on bricks between Mediterranean shrubs. Linda Brombal picks flowers with dog Sophia (at right).

vegetables' growth in check, with charming spillover onto the pathways. "Either way," Linda says, "it's pretty."

Crops for freshness and flavor

In their garden, the Brombals have had great luck with different kinds of lettuce, turning 11-year-old daughter Sydney, who didn't eat salads before, into a greens lover. Linda didn't alter her salad-dressing recipe—it's still olive oil, champagne vinegar, and freshly grated Parmesan. "But now the chives or scallions I add are right out of the garden," she says of the dressing she pours over just-picked lettuce. "And fresh greens taste absolutely amazing," she says, adding that now "Sydney

requests salads and loves to harvest the lettuce."

The Brombals have also grown artichokes, arugula, chard, and lots of herbs, including basil, chives, and lemon verbena. There are also some permanent plants in the beds—mostly aromatics like lavender and salvia. Linda has always used herbs in her cooking, but now that they're growing right outside her kitchen door, she uses them more spontaneously. "If I want to add rosemary to roast potatoes, sage to roast chicken, or arugula to the salad, or sprinkle basil on sliced tomatoes, it's right there," she says. "No need to drive to the supermarket."

Having plenty of parsley and opal

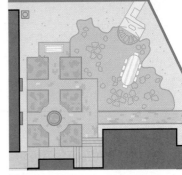

Fireplace and free-form patio, sited diagonally, embrace the geometric raised bed area.

Aging a garden, instantly

Making a new tract garden—or any yard—look like it belongs to an old French farmhouse is easy to do. Here's how Nancy and Greg Putman of Putman Construction & Landscaping *(949/552-6610)* helped the Brombals achieve their goals.

Use "aged" materials. The bricks that form the paths and define the vegetable beds in the potager, from Robinson Brick Company *(www.robinsonbrick.com or 800/477-9002),* aren't very old. They've just been tumbled until they look that way. The process not only rounds off the edges of the brick, it fades the color. The flagstones in the dining area are also tumbled.

Simulate Old World style. On the fireplace (page 58), the fine-textured stucco was deliberately overtroweled to a point past smooth, creating a mottled color—a good substitute for centuries of weathering. Provençal-style shutters embellish the garage wall (at right).

Invest in mature trees. Bringing in a California sycamore tree and several birches—all in 36-inch boxes—gave the Brombals needed privacy. (You see the birches behind the umbrellas on pages 68–69.) More important, the large trees made their garden look more established. If they'd opted for young saplings instead, the faux-aged materials and other instant-weathering tricks wouldn't look so convincing.

Small beds separated by brick paths make tending all crops easy. Low growers like Santa Barbara daisy surround pot in the center.

Grayish blue Provençal-style shutters decorate the garage wall; pansies and scented geraniums fill the window box beneath it.

basil to garnish plates and fragrant herbs like lavender and lemon verbena to create casual centerpieces is nice too, she adds. "There's always something in the garden I can use to make meals a little special."

No wonder the Brombals don't have a problem getting Sydney and 12-year-old son Morgan to settle down for family dinners. When the family moves a meal outdoors, dining together gets even easier—and cozier. "We light the fireplace and bring out candles," Linda explains. That creates an atmosphere so mellow that everyone slows down and enjoys the food and each other's company more, she says. "In the garden, even an ordinary meal is a special occasion." ◆

Five herbs for making tea grow in a raised bed designed by *Sunset's* Bud Stuckey.

Tea in the garden

It's a pleasure that bridges generations

By Sharon Cohoon and Lauren Bonar Swezey

Agatha Youngblood and her granddaughter Caroline take iced tea in their garden, which is marked with a handmade sign.

If you want a child's undivided attention, host a tea party, suggests Agatha Youngblood, a gardener in Rancho Santa Fe, California. There's something about the ceremony of brewing and sipping tea that soothes and settles everyone, she says, even the young and restless. Set aside a special place in the garden just for this activity. Add enough props to make it magical. And solicit your young guests' help in creating the scene. "That really makes the tea garden theirs," says Youngblood.

It worked for her. She turned the area near her California pepper tree into a tea garden. With the help of her granddaughter Caroline, then 7, Youngblood laid down a brick floor, brought in some French cafe furniture, and hung sun catchers (circles of colored glass) on transparent plastic fishing line from the tree's branches. This last touch is what created the magic, Youngblood says. "The way the sun bounces off the glass in the late afternoon makes you feel like you're inside a colored light," she says. "We both love it." ◆

An herbal tea plot

Many herbs make excellent teas; we grew the following in *Sunset's* test garden. Most of these plants prefer full sun and well-drained soil (in hot climates, give mint some shade). Buy plants in 3-inch pots.

Ⓐ Anise hyssop *(Agastache foeniculum).* This member of the mint family produces a light licorice flavor. It also attracts bees and hummingbirds. *Sunset* climate zones A3, 1–24.

Ⓑ Bee balm *(Monarda didyma).* This herb makes a tea with a predominantly citrusy flavor—a mingling of orange and lemon. Zones A2, A3, 1–11, 14–17.

Ⓒ Chamomile. We planted the common ornamental chamomile (*Chamaemelum nobile,* a perennial), but flowers of German chamomile (*Matricaria recutita,* an annual) make a better-tasting tea. Zones 2–24.

Ⓓ Lemon grass *(Cymbopogon citratus).* This is a tropical perennial grass with a zesty lemon flavor. Zones 12, 13, 16, 17, 23, 24, H1, H2.

Ⓔ Mint *(Mentha).* Most members of this genus make good teas. We grew peppermint *(M.* x *piperita)* and orange mint *(M.* x *p. citrata),* but spearmint and 'Chocolate Mint' are tasty too. Zones A2, A3, 1–24.

To prepare an herb tea, add boiling water to your chosen leaves. Start with 2 teaspoons fresh herb for each 6-ounce cup of water. Steep for 5 to 10 minutes. For stronger flavor, increase the amount of herb.

Mail-order source for herbs: www.mountainvalleygrowers. com or 559/338-2775.

Good food, good health

The smallest vegetable beds can pack in lots of nutrients—and great flavor—if you choose plants carefully

By Jim McCausland

Photographs by Thomas J. Story

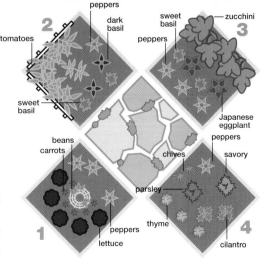

peppers
dark basil
tomatoes
sweet basil
sweet basil
beans
carrots
peppers
lettuce
thyme

sweet basil
peppers
zucchini
Japanese eggplant
peppers
chives
savory
parsley
cilantro

First we heard from Hippocrates: "Let your food be your medicine." Then our grandmothers chimed in: "Eat your vegetables; they're good for you." And finally, seed grower Renee Shepherd advises: "The more color on your plate, the healthier your meal is."

All of them are right: as you eat higher quantities of a wide variety of fruits and veggies, your risk of heart disease, cancer, and stroke declines. And when you grow what you eat, you can get incomparably sweet,

vine-ripened produce that beats anything you can buy. Fresh really *is* best.

All this good news isn't lost on plant breeders, who are developing vegetables that are higher in certain vitamins and antioxidants, such as lycopene and beta-carotene. If you include some of their offerings (many are

Raised-bed vegetables

You don't need lots of space to grow herbs and vegetables. Last spring, at *Sunset's* headquarters, test-garden coordinator Bud Stuckey planted this organic vegetable garden in four raised beds, each 4 feet square and made of 2-by-6 composite lumber called Trex. Before planting, he double-dug all beds, turning the soil to a depth of about 22 inches, then amended it with compost. Here's what we grew and liked.

QUADRANT 1: 'Blue Lake' bush beans, lettuce (dark red leaf, 'Red Grand Rapids', and dark 'Lollo Rosso'—located in the shade of the beans' obelisk to prevent bolting), 'Bolero Nantes' carrots (between the lettuce plants), and peppers ('Golden Summer', 'Ariane', and 'Purple Beauty').

QUADRANT 2: 'Celebrity' and 'Early Girl' tomatoes, 'Dark Opal' basil, 'Long Red Cayenne' peppers, 'Sun Gold' cherry tomato, and sweet basil.

QUADRANT 3: 'Ambassador' zucchini, Japanese eggplant, 'Orange Bell' peppers, and sweet basil.

QUADRANT 4: Mostly herbs. Chives, English thyme, golden lemon thyme, parsley (triple curled and Italian), nonbolting *rau ram* (Vietnamese cilantro), savory, and a few 'Inferno' peppers. 'Blue Horizon' ageratum and white sweet alyssum surround the bed.

listed on these pages) in your vegetable garden this year, you'll eat healthier.

We polled plant breeders, seed sellers, and food scientists to learn what should go into a health-promoting vegetable garden. Then we talked with nutrition-savvy vegetable gardeners and cultivated our own garden at *Sunset,* including herbs to use as fresh flavorings.

Nutritionists say that you get major health benefits from eating at least five servings of fruits and vegetables per day. That sounds like a lot until you grow your own; then those servings become some of life's delicious little pleasures.

Summer fruits and vegetables

Beans. Cooked dried beans (you can let them dry on the vine) provide protein. Fresh beans contain fiber, vitamin C, and beta-carotene. 'Purple Peacock' is a flavorful pole bean whose green leaves contrast with its purple pods, stems, and flowers; it's also very heat tolerant. 'Helda' is a tasty Romano type of bean.

Peppers. Rich in vitamin A, peppers get even better when you allow them to ripen fully and develop their colors, which can range from yellow and red through purple. Try Jewel Tone sweet bell pepper mix.

Squash and pumpkins. Grow 'Hi-Beta Gold' spaghetti squash—it has high levels of beta-carotene—and near-black 'Raven' zucchini for high antioxidant levels. Winter squashes also have abundant beta-carotene. Try the mildew-resistant 'Cornell's Bush Delicata' or Cornucopia Mix.

Tomatoes. 'Health Kick' is high in the antioxidant lycopene, while 'Vita-Gold' was bred for increased beta-carotene. So far, most tomatoes bred for increased nutrition are saladette types (about 4 ounces each); they tend to be less flavorful than standard tomato varieties. Use them for paste, or mix

Sunset garden intern Michelle Ventura brings in the harvest: peppers (purple, cream, and green), tomatoes ('Celebrity', 'Early Girl', and small, yellowish 'Sun Gold'), and zucchini. 'Inferno' pepper and zucchini, below, were both prolific producers. Lightly thin zucchini leaves to expose flowers to pollinators.

different colors of tomatoes in a salad and top with a tangy dressing. Garden Candy cherry tomato mix has seeds for gold, red, and orange cherry tomatoes, but you can easily assemble your own blend.

Watermelons. Our favorite melons for summer picnics are much more nutritious than anyone might have realized: they're loaded with antioxidants. Rainbow Sherbet mix produces a good 4- to 7-pound fruit. The mix includes seeds for watermelons with yellow, orange, and pink flesh.

Leaf and heading vegetables

Broccoli. The vegetable that presidents love to hate is extremely high in nutrients overall, with plenty of vitamins A and C, as well as the antioxidant lutein. 'Shogun' continues to produce side heads after the main head is cut. All-Season Blend is a mix whose varieties have staggered maturity dates for an extra-long season of harvest.

Cabbage. It's the only leaf vegetable that stores well long after harvest, and it's packed with good things—vitamin C, carbohydrates, and fiber. To save garden space, look for miniature varieties like 'Arrowhead II' and 'Red Express', which are the size of a large grapefruit at maturity. Among full-size cabbage, grow Savoy types.

Kale. One of the most nutritious leaf vegetables you can grow, it includes calcium, folic acid, vitamin C, and potassium. It's at its best after frost has sweetened it. Try 'Lacinato' (sometimes sold as 'Black Tuscan' or under the nickname "dinosaur kale"), 'Red Bor', or 'Winter Bor'.

Lettuce. Nutritionally, it's a lightweight, but you benefit from its fiber. Romaine has the most nutrients.

Mesclun. "Mesclun" means "mixture," so a mesclun blend can include any of a number of leaf vegetables, usually starting with lettuce. From a nutritional standpoint, mesclun's diversity recommends it, and blends that include oriental vegetables or mustard and kale usually rank very high on the nutrition scale. Keep plants well watered.

Spinach. Rich in the antioxidant lutein. 'Oriental Giant' grows on a very large plant (double the size of conventional spinach), and its smooth leaves are perfect for salads.

Swiss chard. High in calcium and lutein. 'Bright Lights' is colorful.

Root crops

Carrots. They're valued for their high levels of beta-carotene (which the body uses to make vitamin A). 'Healthmaster' is especially packed with beta-carotene, and 'Nutri-Red' has an increased amount of lycopene. Sunshine Mix is colorful.

Potatoes. This staple is high in vitamin C and potassium. Potato skins are a good source of fiber. 'Yukon Gold' is a productive favorite, while russets have slightly higher levels of vitamin C. ◆

'Bolero Nantes' carrots (from Renee's Garden seeds) will deliver a sweet crunch.

Seeds and seedlings

You can buy seedlings of many vegetables at nurseries. Or order seeds by mail; the following companies sell seeds of healthful fruit and vegetable varieties.

Johnny's Selected Seeds: *www.johnny-seeds.com or (207) 861-3901*
Natural Gardening Company: *www.naturalgardening.com or (707) 766-9303*
Nichols Garden Nursery: *www.nicholsgardennursery.com or (541) 928-9280*
Renee's Garden: *www.reneesgarden.com or (831) 335-7228*

Seeds of Change: *www.seedsofchange.com or (505) 438-8080*
Territorial Seed Company: *www.territorial-seed.com or (541) 942-9547*
West Coast Seeds: *www.westcoast-seeds.com or (604) 952-8820*

Plants separate patio (top right) from kids' play lawn. Island planting hides dog's area. Concrete edging (right) makes mowing easy.

Family garden

How to design your landscaping for kids, a dog, and a very full life

Story and photographs by Jim McCausland

In Stacie Crooks's garden, mornings are magic. As she and husband Jon breakfast on the patio, they can look through a leafy screen to see son Dylan bouncing on a trampoline. Or they can glance across flowering perennials to the main lawn, where son Trevor roughhouses with the family's Jack Russell terrier. Stacie doesn't worry that the dog might damage the lawn or that an errant soccer ball could snap shrub branches—the garden is designed for her active family.

The Crooks's garden accommodates plants, entertaining, pets, and play. Best of all, this high-performance landscape takes Stacie only about three hours per week to maintain. That's good, because she has many activities beyond family responsibilities. She loves to kayak, ski, and manage the docent program at Seattle's E. B. Dunn Historic Garden, and she runs her own garden-design business *(crooksgardens@aol.com)*. "When prospective clients come over to discuss their own gardens, this garden always wins them

over," Stacie says of her home's landscaping.

With all these demands on her time, plus kids and a dog romping through the yard, how does Stacie keep her garden beautiful enough to turn heads? By thoughtful design and smart plant choices.

Careful planning

The rear garden fans out from a patio filled with pots of perennials that echo the border plants, while a Japanese maple near the patio gives the space a sense of volume and is a great place to hang the bird feeder.

The lawn, bordered by a paved mowing strip that makes edging easy, gives the kids and dog space to run. Two extensions of the lawn are partially camouflaged by shrubs: one section contains the trampoline, while the other, concealed by a small island of perennials and shrubs, serves as the dog's comfort station. The dog was trained to do its business here and nowhere else, which makes cleanup fast and easy.

For privacy, Stacie planted a screen of Leyland cypress along the back lot line. It took six years to fill in, and the trees now block not only the view of her uphill neighbor's house but also the path of airborne weed seeds.

Shrubs, perennials, and grasses pack

How to plan your space

• **Divide the garden** into separate areas, by function. Consider a patio for quiet dining, lawn for kids to romp on, a corner for the dog.

• **Separate each space** with shrub borders, level changes, or low hedges. Dividing the garden makes the property look bigger and more functional.

• **Match plants to spaces.** Put soft-textured but tough plants around places where kids play. Ornamental grasses, sword ferns, and heathers are good choices.

• **Use a tough lawn grass** that is easy to care for and bounces back quickly from foot traffic. Less-thirsty dwarf tall fescues stay evergreen year-round in warm climates. Perennial rye is a good choice for the Pacific Northwest. Seeded lawns are generally more durable than sod for heavy traffic use because they establish deeper roots.

most of the border between screen plants and the lawn. "It's a fusion garden that looks like a medieval tapestry and shades out weeds," Stacie explains. In the undulating perimeter bed, she experiments with plant combinations. The bed also serves as a nursery from which plants can be divided and moved into other parts of the garden. The area contains a vegetable bed— the domain of 9-year-old Trevor, who is rapidly becoming a gardener in his own right.

Smart plant choices

"One of my goals," Stacie explains, "is to demonstrate that there are lots of drought-tolerant, low-maintenance plant choices for the Northwest, and I try them here before I recommend them for anybody else's garden." Many of these plantings are shrubs that she mixes freely in the border with low perennials and grasses.

Some of Stacie's favorite shrubs include viburnums for hedging, backgrounds, and fillers; small-leafed rhododendrons, which are more sun-tolerant than most; Tatarian dogwood (*Cornus alba* 'Elegantissima') for its red winter twigs and variegated summer leaves; and most of the less-than-3-foot *Euonymus* species.

Among ornamental grasses, Stacie likes 7-foot-tall maiden grass (*Miscanthus sinensis* 'Gracillimus') for its coppery plumes that mature to cream, and a 20-inch variegated sedge, *Carex morrowii*, which is a good edging plant. Of the dozens of species of perennials she grows, she has particular favorites that add lovely splashes of color. They include *Euphorbia x martinii, Salvia nemorosa* 'Ostfriesland' (or East Friesland), asters, single-flowered Japanese anemones, *Hosta* 'Francee', Corsican hellebores, and a range of true geraniums ('Ann Folkard', 'Ballerina', and 'Gravetye' top the list). ◆

Timesaving tricks

"Low maintenance" is always a relative phrase. Most perennials, for example, demand more upkeep than shrubs. In all, Stacie Crooks's garden gets a weekend of serious attention in March, about three hours of attention per week from then through fall, then nearly a week of cleanup in November. During the growing season, she tries to do all of the maintenance at once—on a Saturday morning, for example—because it's easier and more practical than trying to work in piecemeal garden time while juggling her kids' schedules and her own business.

• **Shade out weeds** by planting shrubs and perennials close together. Stacie also treats weed-prone areas with a preemergence herbicide to stop stray seeds from germinating.

• **Fertilize effectively.** Stacie's plants get a dose of organic 5-5-5 fertilizer at planting time, then again every spring. Beyond that, she applies only composted horse manure every second autumn.

• **Group plants by water needs** to make the watering easier. The lawn, which is watered only by rain, goes dormant in summer.

• **Use a mowing strip** of paving material to keep grass out of the planting beds and make edging easier.

Billowy shrubs partially hide a trampoline.

Azaleas are seasonal highlights.

Pollinator pots

Fill pots with native plants for birds, bees, and butterflies

By Sharon Cohoon
Photographs by Claire Curran

A. Golden yarrow, tall coast sunflower, orange monkey flower, penstemon.
B. White 'Canyon Snow' Pacific Coast iris, pink coral bells, and creeping snowberry.
C. Lavender *Salvia clevelandii* with white prickly poppy and pink coyote mint.

The iridescent flash of hummingbirds' wings, the fluttery beauty of butterflies, and the friendly buzz of bees can bring a garden alive. If you fill pots with carefully chosen plants, you can entice these creatures to your yard.

"Natives are the easiest, least-demanding plants I've grown," says Steven Rowland (pictured), a contractor living in Villa Park, California, whose pots are shown at right. "California natives don't need a lot of water. They rarely need to be fed. They can almost get by without you."

Native plants are magnets for wildlife; they evolved with the insects and animals. Bees especially are the plant kingdom's most important pollinators, says Mike Evans, co-owner of Tree of Life Nursery *(949/728-0685)*, which specializes in California native plants. But shrinking habitats threaten the existence of bees and many other wild creatures. Growing nectar-rich flowers to attract and feed wildlife is not just good entertainment, it's a public service. Butterflies, moths, hummingbirds, and other pollinators will come for the banquet too.

The plants listed at right are California natives, but many of them also grow well in other areas of the West. Some, like penstemon, are found throughout the West but in different forms. Mountain and desert gardeners, for instance, can substitute the hardier firecracker penstemon *(P. eatonii)*—hummingbirds love it.

When potting, select a fast-draining, light-weight soil that's not too rich in organics. Add controlled-release fertilizer to the mix at planting time and replenish it yearly. Water thoroughly when the top inch of the soil is dry. ◆

Irresistible plants

Coast sunflower *(Encelia californica)*: bees.
Common yarrow *(Achillea millefolium)*: butterflies.
Coral bells *(Heuchera)*: hummingbirds.
Coyote mint *(Monardella villosa)*: bees, butterflies.
Creeping snowberry *(Symphoricarpos mollis)*: bees.
Penstemon *(P. centranthifolius and P. spectabilis)*: bees, hummingbirds.
Prickly poppy *(Argemone corymbosa)*: bees.
Salvia *(S. clevelandii, S. 'Dara's Choice', and S. greggii)*: bees, butterflies, hummingbirds.
Sticky monkey flower *(Mimulus aurantiacus)*: hummingbirds.

This dramatic outdoor room, about 10 feet across, is the perfect setting for intimate gatherings. Tiles brighten the patio floor, and paint adds vivid color to the wall and columns.

Creating the mood

A small patio needs just a few elements to become a welcoming spot for chatting with friends over a relaxing supper.

Privacy. Tall shrubs, hedges, or vine-covered fences make a detached patio private. The columns (pictured at left) create the illusion of walls without appearing confining.

Eye candy. Outdoor art, colorful walls, interesting floor tiles, and containers create a sense of drama around the patio.

Comfort. Choose cushioned chairs and a roomy table.

Candlelight. Whether small votives or hurricane lamps, candles never fail to enhance the ambience.

Fragrance. A pot of jasmine, gardenia, or *Bouvardia longiflora* sends out delicious scents, especially on balmy nights.

Gathering friends

An artful detached patio sets the stage for intimate parties

By Steven R. Lorton • Photographs by Norm Plate

What would a garden be without an inviting patio on which to celebrate the joys of friendship? Daniel Sparler and Jeff Schouten turned a sunny spot in their Seattle garden into such a place. But unlike most patios, which are connected to the house, theirs is located down a winding path, in an area surrounded by lush shrubs, perennials, and annuals. It's a destination with all the ambience of a campfire in the woods, only guests gather around a cozy table instead of a firepit. "We wanted this part of the garden to be a place set apart," Sparler says. "We wanted to make a reference to the classics—classic design."

To make space for the hexagonal patio, Sparler and Schouten first cleared some shrubs and perennials from a planting bed, then encircled the space with a low wall and five columns of varying heights, all of reinforced concrete. The columns were poured in place at the same time as the walls between them, then coated with exterior latex paint in rosy mauve tones (the walls are purple). For added drama, vertical indentations were painted hunter green and purple. Floor tiles echo these colors.

Friends gather on the patio for alfresco dining or a glass of wine by candlelight, accompanied by talk and laughter. ◆

Potted plants (like this agave) and garden ornaments sit on platforms of scrap wood atop concrete columns. Pots and platforms are secured to the tops with long bolts.

Big ideas, tiny trees

Curator David De Groot explains
what makes bonsai beautiful

By Jim McCausland
Photographs by John Granen

You walk slowly through a hushed, white-walled gallery, studying the interplay of light and shadow falling on each piece of living sculpture. A small, perfect grove of maples catches your eye; an ancient-looking bald cypress beckons a few feet away. The trees' tiny sizes are astounding. So are their ages and histories. One, a Sierra juniper, is 1,000 years old, though its stint as a bonsai began just 30 years ago. Another, a trident maple, went into training as a bonsai as early as 1880.

Assembled by the Weyerhaeuser Company for the 1989 Washington State Centennial, the Pacific Rim Bonsai Collection in Federal Way is the Louvre of miniature trees. But whereas the Louvre has a slew of knowledgeable curators, the Pacific Rim collection has just one: David De Groot.

De Groot came to bonsai (pronounced bone-sigh, not bahnz-eye) from a career as a percussionist with the New Orleans Symphony. But even as a musician, he was interested in miniature trees. "The leap from music to bonsai is not as big as you might imagine," he says. "The principles of aesthetics [proportion, tension, resolution, contrast] are common to all the arts."

Bonsai originated in China, but it was introduced to the Western World by Japan. For this reason, we know the art by its Japanese name, which

A gallery of living art, the Pacific Rim Bonsai Collection sits in the midst of the Weyerhaeuser campus. De Groot uses a brush to remove the outer bark from a Chinese juniper (below).

means "tray planting." As De Groot explains it, "Natural dwarfs were collected mostly from the seaside and mountaintops, placed in containers, and pruned to maintain their small size.

"As time passed and wild specimens became harder to find, people started growing their own trees.

They trained them to take on the kinds of exotic shapes that they liked so much in wild trees."

The fact that people covet certain traditional shapes is no coincidence, De Groot says. "You see the triangle used a lot in bonsai. Its natural shape follows the coniferous model—the classic form of Japanese black and white pines. In Eastern thought, the three points of the unequal triangle represent heaven, man, and earth."

In other words, there's a whole lot of philosophy wrapped up in a very small tree.

How to "read" a bonsai

Pick up a free guidebook and take a self-guided tour of the Pacific Rim collection anytime, or join a guided tour any Sunday at noon. De Groot also gives frequent lectures at the garden from May through Sep-

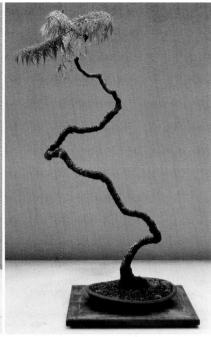

Multiple tops of 'San Jose' junipers are individually pruned into triangles; together they make a much larger triangle of foliage. The peaceful shape resolves the tension created by crossing trunks below. The abstract piece is meant to recall the trees that grow along one of Japan's ancient, windswept coastal roads.

Staghorn sumac is trained in single-trunk, zigzag "literati" style, mimicking the thin, rustic trees painted by scholars in medieval Japan.

Relatives of this Fuji beech are indigenous to the southeast foothills of Mt. Fuji. The tree's formal, upright shape reflects the mountain's serenity and simple beauty.

This 3½-foot-tall bald cypress started out as a 30-foot-tall tree. Its top was cut off, its trunk reshaped, and new growth was trained into a perfect representation of the mature tree.

Meticulously hand-pruned, this 50-year-old Japanese white pine gains visual strength from its large, gnarled trunk and a sense of movement from its asymmetrically balanced top.

tember. If he's not available when you visit, here are some of his tips for observing the highly prized collection.

• Look for balance between open and dense parts of the composition.

• Notice male- and female-specific traits. "You see the masculine in a formal trunk, strong movement, coarse texture, and deep color; you see the feminine in an informal,

curved trunk, gentle movement, smooth texture, and light color," De Groot says.

• Learn to distinguish between representational (relatively straightforward) and abstract (extremely stylized) specimens.

• Note how the color of the container often echoes or contrasts with that of the bark or leaves, depending on the artist's intent. ◆

Behold the bonsai

The Pacific Rim Bonsai Collection is open 10–4 Fri–Wed; admission is free. It's located on the Weyerhaeuser Corporate campus in Federal Way, Washington. From I-5, take exit 143 (S. 320th St.), go east ¼ mile, turn right on Weyerhaeuser Way South, and follow the signs. *For more information, visit www.weyerhaeuser.com/bonsai or call (253) 924-5206.*

A GRAPEVINE-COVERED PERGOLA frames a grassy path in this backyard "cottage garden" in Bellingham, Washington. To create a cottage-style garden of your own, see our planting and design tips on pages 98–105.

April

Darwin hybrid tulips playfully echo eggs nestled in a basket of newly sprouted lawn grass.

Grow grassy nests for Easter eggs

For a visual treat at Easter, Phyllis and Richard Null tuck grass-filled baskets into their entry garden. Nestled into the grass, colored eggs look as if the Easter bunny has just hidden them. Their bright colors harmonize beautifully with surrounding Darwin hybrid tulips, 'Hino-crimson' azaleas, and low-growing perennials like Labrador violets and 'Georgia Blue' veronica.

The Nulls pick up baskets at garage sales. Three weeks before Easter, they fill the unlined baskets with thoroughly moistened potting mix. Atop the soil, they thickly sow seeds of a lawn-grass blend of perennial rye and red fescue sold as a sun-and-shade mixture.

Then the Nulls arrange plastic eggs on the seedbed, so the grass grows up around them. They place the baskets on a plastic sheet in a room with good light and mist the seeds with a spray bottle several times a day.

When the grass appears, the plastic eggs can be replaced by more elaborate ones made of glass or stone. If the grass grows too tall and conceals the eggs, the Nulls cut it back with scissors.

When the baskets are ready, the couple positions them around the front yard, tucking them between stones and in window boxes, and even hanging them from tree branches. —*Mary-Kate Mackey*

Pipe dream in Paradise Valley

"It's very amusing to see humble material transformed into something so pretty," says Arizona homeowner Madge Kunkel. She is referring to the "pots" pictured at left, which hold bacopa, geraniums, and sweet alyssum. The elegant-looking planters are actually segments of hard-fired clay sewer pipe, known in the trade as sewer tiles, which are sold at some building supply stores.

One of the tiles camouflages an unsightly electrical junction box, slipping over it like a sleeve. In that tile, the plant is nestled inside a removable container. Another group of tiles acts as a multilevel water feature. The water trickles from the highest to lowest tile through copper tubing and into a basin, from which it is recirculated back to the top with minimum evaporation.

Steve Sternke of Magic Gardens, who designed these combination planter/water features, used 4- to 10-inch-diameter sewer tiles cut into 18- to 60-inch lengths. —*Sharon Cohoon*

Sunscreen for veggies

In Las Vegas, the native soil is poor in organic matter and so hard that people use jackhammers to break ground for planting. To overcome these challenges, Master Gardener Tina Cesaretti and her husband, Luke, designed raised beds and filled them with a mix of potting soil, sand, and compost.

The four triangular beds sit in the corners of a 23- by 23-foot area. Each bed is 15 feet long at the base with sides that are 10 feet long and 18 inches high. They're framed with untreated redwood 2-by-6s and lined with landscape fabric. The beds surround a circular planter made of interlocking pavers.

During the first year she gardened in the beds, Tina saw that many of the plants were sunburned. To shield the crops, the Cesarettis made canopies of 50 percent shadecloth (it blocks 50 percent of the sunlight) and suspended them from 8-foot-tall posts at the corners of

each bed. Shadecloth panels also shield the sides of the beds and provide wind protection in late winter and spring (for more about shadecloth, see the story on page 117). In the shaded beds, the Cesarettis grow cucumbers, eggplant, lettuce, melons, peppers, squash, and tomatoes. The beds are watered by drip irrigation. —*Julie Chai*

STEVEN GUNTHER; TOP: NORM PLATE

A pretty little willow

With its compact size and variegated foliage, the dappled willow (*Salix integra* 'Hakuro Nishiki') is one of the prettiest landscape plants to have been introduced at nurseries in recent years. The foliage emerges pink, then turns light green mottled with white. After the leaves drop, deep pink stems add winter interest.

Grown as a shrub, the plant reaches 6 feet tall with an equal spread. This willow is also sold as a grafted, 4- to 6-foot-tall standard that can be allowed to assume a gently weeping form or can be sheared into a rounded patio tree. Standards may reach 10 to 12 feet tall.

Dappled willow can be grown in *Sunset* climate zones 3–9 and 14–17 and is hardy to –20°. It does best in partial shade and needs ample water. As a shrub, it works well in beds, especially in moist areas of the garden. Standards make a lovely accent in small spaces. Set out container-grown or balled-and-burlapped plants anytime the ground is workable.

Two good mail-order sources for dappled willow are Forestfarm in Williams, OR (www.forestfarm.com or 541/846-7269) and Greer Gardens in Eugene, OR (www.greergardens.com or 541/686-8266). —Dick Rifkind

Climbing roses and clematis cover an arbor leading into the garden, where a raised bed (below left) holds zinnias and peas.

Mixing things up

European by birth and American by choice, Portland's Margaret de Haas van Dorsser combines elements of both worlds in her landscape designs (Margaret's Enchanted Gardens, *503/645-5007*). Her own garden, for example, begins with a continental plan in which four rose-covered arbors serve as portals into a 50- by 50-foot space encompassing a dozen raised beds framed with pine lumber.

But the formality ends there. The beds can barely contain a potpourri of flowers and vegetables, giving the garden a casual look. She allows self-sowing annuals like California and Shirley poppies to take over some beds. In others, she lets flowers grow around the edge but keeps the center clear for beans, peas, and other crops. —*Jim McCausland*

Focus on flowers

These hanging baskets use colorful blooms creatively

There are dozens of reasons to grow hanging baskets. They are pretty to look at, screen out sunlight, utilize vertical space, and dress up boring expanses of bare wall. But the best reason to raise plants to eye level is so you can enjoy their gorgeous detail without stooping.

Spring is the perfect time to start a hanging basket. Before you plant, keep in mind that the baskets with the greatest impact are those that pair colors well. The ones pictured here were planted by growers at Proven Winners *(www.provenwinners.com)*, but this month your local nursery will also carry a selection of ground covers, annuals, and perennials with cascading habits.

Keep your planting schemes simple—two or three colors that combine well, for instance—or go with two or three plant varieties in a single color. Start with vigorous growers in cell-packs, wire baskets 12 to 14 inches in diameter, and extra-light potting soil. Line the baskets with soaking-wet sphagnum moss. Plant the bottom level first; use shears to poke holes through the moss, then gently push the plants' rootballs through the holes from outside the basket. Add soil over rootballs, then continue planting layer by layer.

Keep plants well watered; hanging baskets dry out quickly. Feed biweekly with dilute fish emulsion for steady bloom. —*S.C.*

'Supertunia Giant Pink' petunia and 'Superbena Large Lilac Blue' verbena with chartreuse-leafed potato vine 'Marguerite'.

Lavender-pink 'Supertunia Priscilla' petunia with *Lamium maculatum* 'White Nancy'.

Other hanging-basket combos

• Coral diascia with purple verbena or petunias

• Deep purple petunias with hot pink verbena

• Hot pink verbena with white petunias

• White verbena with white-flowered bacopa

CLAIRE CURRAN (2)

Cactus on display range from towering saguaro (far left) to rotund golden barrel (left). Succulent leaves of *Agave weberi* (below) reach 3½ to 5 feet long.

Cactus reigns supreme

Visitors to one of the best collections of cactus in the country could be forgiven if they skip past the plants for a free sample of chocolate. After all, the confections are part of the famous Mars candymaking legacy. But the grounds of the Ethel M Chocolate Factory & Botanical Gardens in Henderson, Nevada, are more than just a pretty backdrop: they're a valuable resource for gardeners in the Las Vegas area and other hot, dry climates.

Created in 1981 by Forrest Mars Sr., the 3½-acre site is now home to

many mature desert-adapted plants. While cactus and succulents are the focus of the garden, the collection of more than 350 species also includes broadleaf trees and shrubs, which have a softening effect on the bristly shapes of cactus and succulents. The combinations illustrate the range of landscaping possibilities for the home gardener in the intermediate high desert (*Sunset* climate zone 11).

As shown above left, vertical saguaro cactus and fountain-shaped ocotillo reach into the dappled sun-

light cast by palo verde trees. Shorter plants like fishhook barrel cactus and *Agave bovicornuta* add texture at ground level.

Visitors also can see full-size specimens of other trees, such as mesquite, African sumac, willow pittosporum *(P. phillyreoides)*, and Anacacho orchid tree *(Bauhinia lunarioides)*.

But the stars of the garden are the many cactus and succulents, ranging from *Hesperaloe* to *Yucca brevifolia jaegeriana,* a dwarf Joshua tree.

As for the chocolate, there's an equally impressive selection of that too. About 60 kinds of confections are made at the factory on the grounds; you can view the production process through large glass windows on a self-guided tour. And it's hard to resist a free sample or two. *Garden and factory, 8:30–7 daily; free. 1 Sunset Way; www.ethelm.com or (888) 627-0990.*

—*David Becker and Liz Hartley*

Favorite natives

1. Wooly blue curls (*Trichostema lanatum*)
2. Columbine (*Aquilegia formosa*, or look for *A. caerulea* and *A. chrysantha*)
3. Firecracker penstemon (*P. eatonii*, or look for *P. palmeri*, *P. spectabilis*, *P. pseudospectabilis*, or *P. heterophyllus*)
4. Pacific Coast iris
5. Brittlebush (*Encelia farinosa*)

Going native

If you're looking for a low-maintenance, wildlife-friendly garden to fill your landscape, try the

PLANT ADVICE plants that grew up in your region. And this is the perfect month to get acquainted with native species: plants sales featuring them are popping up like wildflowers. Here are a few choice plants (good for most areas of the West) to look for while you're shopping.—*Sharon Cohoon*

Escape artist: garden designer Molly Matthews.

Tips for creating a healing garden

Many gardeners are creating peaceful places in their backyards, known as healing gardens. "My garden is a place where I can be a human being and not a human doing," says Molly Matthews,

BEST TREND owner of Molly's Touch Healing Environments in Northern California *(831/438-3992)*. To create your own healing garden: **1** Find a tranquil area of your yard, then add comfortable seating. **2** Plant fragrant, colorful, textured plants. **3** Consider adding wind chimes or a water feature. **4** Decorate with meaningful objects—personal artwork, special collections, a wagon from your childhood. —*Julie Chai*

Propagate evergreens by ground layering

To increase your supply of evergreen plants such as azalea, daphne, mahonia, and rhododendron: **1.** Bend a low-growing young, pliable branch toward the ground, scrape off a 1-inch piece of bark from its underside, and trim off leaves within 12 inches of the tip. **2.** Dust the wound with rooting hormone, press branch into an adjacent shallow hole amended with compost, and cover with 3 inches of soil. Anchor with a heavy rock or a piece of wire. **3.** Bend the stem tip up and tie it to a stake. **4.** Water well until roots form along the buried stem. Cut the new plant from the parent, then dig it up and replant. —*L. B. S.*

Vine-covered entry arch

The arch that Pam Purvis and Patrick Montgomery placed at the entrance to their enclosed backyard garden invites passersby to pause and peek inside. At the same time, the arch screens the garden from a busy city street. Situated on the strip between the street and sidewalk, the arch also visually connects the public and private areas of the garden.

Formed from old wire fencing, the arch is covered with golden hop (*Humulus lupulus* 'Aureus'), a gold-leafed form of the common hop. The arch stands about 8 feet tall with a 3½-foot-wide space for the flagstone path beneath.

This fast-growing deciduous vine thrives in full sun and tolerates cold and drought. In this Denver garden, the hop vine completely concealed its wire frame in a single summer. The foliage emerges golden yellow in spring, then darkens to green as the season progresses. It bears conelike fruits called hops, which age from pale green to amber brown and remain attractive all winter.
—*Marcia Tatroe*

Columnar junipers and wall-mounted art decorate Mickey Ackerman's rooftop garden.

Rooftop aerie in Denver

Architectural designer Mickey Ackerman resides in a historic two-story, red-brick structure within earshot of Coors Field in downtown Denver. Ackerman loves to garden, but he had no ground. "I didn't have a front yard, I didn't have a backyard, so I went up," he says. Ackerman found 1,100 square feet of rooftop space he could use for gardening, displaying art, and entertaining.

He grows everything from flowers to trees in 55 plastic containers and a dozen hanging baskets. The pots are filled with lightweight potting soil amended with well-rotted manure and wood chips, which help retain moisture. After six seasons, Ackerman's 22 trees—including dwarf varieties of apple, pear, and plum—stand tall enough to cast a bit of shade onto the cedar decking he

installed over the roof's asphalt surface. Tennis nets stretched between wood frames provide privacy, screening the view from neighboring buildings.

Around the garden, Ackerman displays small-scale cast-resin replicas of arches from ancient churches, as well as a modern mask sculpture made of metal.

Each weekend, Ackerman hosts a barbecue in the garden. Various groupings of tables, chairs, and benches accommodate anywhere from a handful to a hundred friends. The rooftop is even more dramatic at night, when spotlights shine on the fruit trees and columnar junipers sparkle with tiny white lights. And on evenings when the Colorado Rockies are playing ball across the street, Ackerman and his guests can hear fans roar when the home team scores. —*Colleen Smith*

Organic seeds

If you already garden organically, you might want to take your commitment to another level and start your crops from certified organic seeds. These seeds are harvested from plants grown without the use of synthetic chemical fertilizers or pesticides, and they have not been treated with fungicides or any other synthetic chemicals from the time of seed harvest to sale. They are certified by independent organizations, such as California Certified Organic Farmers, to meet the USDA's National Organic Program guidelines.

Oregon-based mail-order firm Territorial Seed Company *(www.territorialseed.com or 541/942-9547)* was one of the first businesses in the country to offer certified organic seeds. Botanical Interests seeds *(www.gardentrails.com),* found at many nurseries, recently joined the organic ranks.

Getting a plant to the seed-producing level organically is twice as challenging as growing organic produce, says Tom Johns, co-owner of Territorial Seed. "The plants are in the ground much longer, giving pests and diseases more opportunities," he says. Consequently, certified organic seeds are often slightly more expensive than regular seeds. "But, if you believe in sustainable agriculture, this is a great way to support it," Johns says. "Seeds start the circle."

Other good sources are Johnny's Selected Seeds (www.johnnyseeds.com or 207/861-3900) and Seeds of Change (www.seedsofchange.com or 888/762-7333). —S. C.

Organic seeds of many crops, from tomatoes, carrots, and beans to lettuce, basil, and sunflowers, are now available. Look for the word "organic" or the "organic certified" symbol on the packet.

Play yard is a winner

This colorful play area pictured above takes the children's-garden concept in bold new directions. Designed by Topher Delaney for a San Francisco family, it won an award in *Sunset's* 2003 Western Garden Design Awards program for its use of small space.

The structures—a climbing rock, basketball hoop, and sand bowl—are all scaled for kids. Multipurpose paving, made of black rubber SAF DEK with interlocking orange, red, and yellow circles, is soft enough to cushion falls, yet provides a flat surface on which to drive vehicles. Removable circles cover putting holes.

A stainless steel trellis planted with trumpet vine encloses the garden.

DESIGN: T. Delaney Inc./Seam Studio, San Francisco *(415/621-9899).*

—Lauren Bonar Swezey

RICHARD W. HARTLAGE; LEFT: E. SPENCER TOY

Closely spaced Benary's Giant Mix zinnias bloom profusely despite limited water at Denver's Alamo Placita Park.

Zinnias thrive in thirsty times

Few annuals rival zinnias for steady bloom and their ability to get by, once established, on little water. Last summer, during one of the worst droughts in Colorado history, zinnias put on a riotous color show in four beds at Alamo Placita Park in central Denver.

City horticulturist Bob Aragon chose Benary's Giant Mix (also sold as Park's Picks Mix), which produces 3- to 4-foot-tall plants with 5- to 6-inch-wide flowers in shades of crimson, pink, salmon, white, and yellow. Seeds were started in greenhouses in late May and germinated within a week. Within two weeks, the seedlings were ready for transplanting. On June 10, when outdoor temperatures were already in the 90s, 140 zinnias were planted 14 inches apart in each bed. That might seem like a late start, but zinnias thrive on heat and seedlings will languish if planted in the ground much earlier.

Initially, the plants were watered daily, but midsummer irrigation restrictions limited the beds to about 20 minutes of watering three days per week. During the heat of the day, the flowers wilted (sometimes severely), but cool nights brought relief and the blooms perked up again by morning, Aragon says.

The zinnias flourished until they were hit by powdery mildew late in the season. Aragon notes that a colleague in another city park successfully combated powdery mildew on zinnias by spraying two June applications of Soap-Shield, an organic fungicide available from Gardens Alive (*www.gardensalive.com or 812/537-8650*).

A good source for Benary's Giant Mix is White Flower Farm (www. whiteflowerfarm.com or 800/503-9624). Park's Picks Mix is sold by Park Seed (www.parkseed.com or 800/845-3369). —C.S.

WHAT TO DO IN YOUR GARDEN IN APRIL

PLANTING

☐ **ANNUAL FLOWERS.** Set out cool-season annuals like calendula, English daisy, pansy, snapdragon, stock, sweet alyssum, and viola. Start seeds of warm-season annuals like marigolds, petunias, and zinnias in a coldframe or greenhouse for transplanting next month.

☐ **COOL-SEASON VEGGIES.** Plant seedlings of broccoli, cabbage, kale, lettuce, spinach, and Swiss chard. Sow seeds of carrots, peas, and radishes; plant seed potatoes.

☐ **FLOWERING TREES, SHRUBS, VINES.** *Sunset* climate zones 1–3: You can still plant bare-root fruits, shrubs, trees, and vines, but act fast. Zones 4–7: Plant container-grown azaleas, lilacs, and rhododendrons, plus flowering vines like clematis and wisteria.

☐ **HERBS.** Set out seedlings of chives, lavender, marjoram, mint, oregano, rosemary, sage, tarragon, and thyme anytime. Sow seeds of basil and cilantro after frost danger has passed. In zones 1–3, if you want to grow rosemary, plant an extra-hardy variety like 'Arp', 'Hill Hardy', or 'Salem'.

☐ **LAWNS.** Zones 1–3: Lay sod or sow grass seed as soon as the soil warms up. Zones 4–7: Start lawns from sod or seed anytime.

☐ **PERENNIALS.** Set out basket-of-gold, bleeding heart, columbines, Corsican hellebore, evergreen candytuft, forget-me-nots, primroses, rockcress, sweet woodruff, and wallflower.

☐ **WARM-SEASON VEGETABLES.** Start seeds of corn, cucumber, eggplant, melons, peppers, and tomatoes in peat pots or flats of potting mix. To encourage germination, set the containers on a seedling heat mat (available from Charley's Greenhouse & Garden, *www. charleysgreenhouse.com or 800/ 322-4707*). Given plenty of light, seedlings will be ready for transplanting outdoors in four to six weeks. Don't plant nursery seedlings in the ground yet; it's still too early and the ground is too cold.

MAINTENANCE

☐ **CONTROL APHIDS.** As tender new growth unfolds, aphid populations explode. Blast them off foliage with a jet of hose water.

☐ **CONTROL SLUGS.** Handpick and destroy slugs whenever you see them. You can also set out beer traps. Or spread chemical baits: Methaldehyde is an effective poison but must be kept away from children, pets, and wildlife. A safer alternative is iron phosphate-based bait, but it's not as effective.

☐ **FERTILIZE.** Give plants a fast start in cool soil by applying liquid fertilizer. Or use an organic food like blood meal that has both quick- and slow-release nutrients. Feed lawns about 2 pounds of actual nitrogen per 1,000 square feet of turf.

☐ **MOW LAWNS.** Grass growth peaks this month and next. Mow often enough so that you never cut off more than a third of the blade at once (don't cut more than 1 inch off a 3-inch-tall lawn, for example). ◆

MAP: DEBRA LAMBERT

WHAT TO DO IN YOUR GARDEN IN APRIL

PLANTING

☐ **ANNUALS.** *Sunset* climate zones 7–9, 14–17: Annuals in 4-inch containers can add a splash of color nearly instantly. But if you have time to wait for seedlings to grow in, sixpacks are less expensive and the plants grow quickly. Choices often include ageratum, globe amaranth, impatiens, lobelia, marigold, petunia, phlox, portulaca, statice, sunflower, sweet alyssum, verbena, and zinnia.

☐ **BARE-ROOT PLANTS.** Zones 1–2: The most effective and economical way to start deciduous plants like cane berries, flowering shrubs, flowering vines, fruit and nut trees, grapes, rhubarb, roses, and strawberries is with bare roots. Set plants in the ground as soon as you get them home.

☐ **PERENNIALS.** Zones 7–9, 14–17: Shopping for perennials by color is simple when plants are in bloom. Try low-maintenance, sun-loving armeria, catmint, coreopsis, delphinium, dianthus, diascia, echinops, erigeron, gaillardia, gaura, heuchera, penstemon, rudbeckia, scabiosa, scaevola, sedum, verbena, and yarrow.

☐ **WATER-WISE PLANTS.** Zones 7–9, 14–17: Summers in Northern California are usually dry. So it makes sense to plant shrubs and perennials that don't need much water once established. At nurseries, look for artemisia, ceanothus, cistus, cotoneaster, fremontodendron, lavender, rosemary, salvia, and santolina.

Eureka
Redding
CALIFORNIA
NEVADA
Mendocino
Santa Rosa
Sacramento
Sunset
CLIMATE ZONES
San Francisco
San Jose
☐ Mountain (1–2)
☐ Valley (7–9)
☐ Inland (14)
☐ Coastal (15–17)
Fresno
Monterey

MAINTENANCE

☐ **AMEND SOIL.** Zones 7–9, 14–17: Before planting annuals or perennials in garden beds, dig organic matter such as compost into the soil.

☐ **CORRECT CHLOROSIS.** Zones 7–9, 14–17: If foliage on azaleas, camellias, citrus, and gardenias is yellowish with green veins, plants may be suffering from iron deficiency. Spray leaves with a foliar fertilizer containing iron and zinc or, for longer-lasting results, apply chelated iron to the soil; water well.

☐ **DIG OR HOE WEEDS.** Zones 7–9, 14–17: Dig up deeply rooted weeds like dandelions with a hand weeder or trowel. For young or shallow-rooted weeds, use a hoe to sever roots just below the soil's surface. Compost weeds if they haven't set seed; otherwise, trash them.

☐ **FEED ACID LOVERS.** Zones 7–9, 14–17: After azaleas, camellias, and rhododendrons finish blooming, feed them with a fertilizer made especially for acid-loving plants. Also pinch off spent blooms, but take care not to damage new growth.

PEST CONTROL

☐ **CONTROL MOSQUITOES.** Zones 7–9, 14–17: Stagnant water is a favorite breeding ground for mosquitoes, so be sure to drain standing water from saucers, buckets, and anywhere else that water collects. If you have a pond or fountain, add mosquito fish *(Gambusia affinis)*, available at nurseries that sell water plants. Your local mosquito- and vector-control department may also provide free mosquito fish.

☐ **DETER ANTS.** Zones 7–9, 14–17: Ants feed on the sweet honeydew secreted by aphids. They also protect aphids from predators and help safeguard their eggs. To break the ant-aphid cycle on trees and shrubs, wrap the trunk with a sticky barrier like Tanglefoot *(available at nurseries; product information and store locations at www.tanglefoot. com or 616/459-4139).* ◆

WHAT TO DO IN YOUR GARDEN IN APRIL

PLANTING

☐ ROSES. Flowers often look quite different on the plant than they do in catalogs. Visit nurseries this month to see blooming roses, if only to get ideas for the ones you'll plant bare-root next January. Also tour public gardens like the Huntington Botanical Gardens' Rose Garden *(www.huntington.org or 626/405-2100)*. If you're looking for a rose that will do well in partial shade (six hours or more of dappled sunlight or at least three hours of direct sun), consider single-petaled varieties such as 'Playboy' and 'Playgirl'. Hybrid musks, such as 'Ballerina', 'Kathleen', and 'Penelope', are also generally shade tolerant. Noisettes like 'Mme. Alfred Carrière' do well too, as do polyanthas like 'The Fairy'.

☐ SPURIA IRISES. For a strong vertical accent in a flower border, consider spuria iris as an alternative to foxglove or delphinium (see page 114). To buy spurias and see them in bloom, visit Ventura County's Greenwood Daylily + Iris Gardens *(www.greenwoodgarden.com or 562/494-8944)* in Somis. The fields are open from 9:30 to 4 every Saturday from April through June, and peak bloom is in late April. Greenwood also will sell spuria irises at the Southern California Spring Garden Show at South Coast Plaza in Costa Mesa) as well as at Brita's Old Town Gardens in Seal Beach, Burkard Nurseries in Pasadena, the Orangery in Orange, and Roger's Gardens in Corona del Mar.

☐ SUMMER PERENNIALS. To prolong color in your garden, look for plants that will bloom into summer and beyond. Good choices include blue lace flower *(Trachymene coerulea)*, chrysanthemum, daylily, gaillardia, gaura, lion's tail, penstemon, phygelius, salvia, and yarrow.

☐ VEGETABLES. Coastal gardeners *(Sunset* climate zones 21–24) can continue to plant quick-maturing, cool-season crops like chard, leaf lettuces, radishes, and spinach. Inland (zones 18–21), switch to planting warm-season crops like beans, corn, cucumbers, eggplants, melons, peppers, pumpkins, squash, and tomatoes. In the high desert (zone 11), frost is still possible; wait two to four weeks to plant.

MAINTENANCE

☐ CONTINUE FERTILIZING. Feed trees, shrubs, ground covers, perennials, turf grasses, and other permanent ornamentals that did not get a dose of fertilizer last month. Don't forget to feed houseplants; they're growing again too.

☐ THIN FRUIT. Continue thinning apples, pears, and stone fruits when they are about $\frac{1}{2}$ inch in size. Space fruit 4 to 6 inches apart, or leave one fruit per spur.

☐ TREAT IRON DEFICIENCY. Camellias, citrus, gardenias, and other plants often exhibit yellowing leaves with green veins at this time of year—an indication of iron deficiency. To remedy, feed them with a fertilizer containing chelated iron (follow package directions).

PEST CONTROL

☐ MANAGE ROSE PROBLEMS. Strip aphids from plants by hand (wear thin, disposable rubber gloves if you're squeamish). Or dislodge the pests with a strong blast of water from a hose. Sawfly larvae, which can leave rose leaves so skeletonized that they look like lace, show up around the same time. To discourage sawflies, spray foliage—including the undersides—with neem oil or pyrethrum. ◆

MAPS: DEBRA LAMBERT

WHAT TO DO IN YOUR GARDEN IN APRIL

PLANTING

☐ ANNUALS. Four to six weeks before the average date of the last frost in your area, start seeds indoors of drought-tolerant warm-season flowers such as coreopsis, globe amaranth, lion's tail *(Leonotis leonurus)*, and rudbeckia. In mountain areas, start seeds of cool-season flowers and vegetables indoors this month.

☐ LAVENDER. Sun-loving lavender thrives in poor, dry soils. English lavender *(Lavandula angustifolia)* varieties are the most resilient, hardy to *Sunset* climate zone 2. Many hybrid lavenders are hardy to zone 3. High Country Gardens in Santa Fe *(www.highcountrygardens. com or 800/925-9387)* features 11 types of lavender, including hardy pink-flowered 'Melissa' and violet-blue 'Mitcham Grey'.

☐ "OWN-ROOT" SHRUB ROSES. Roses propagated on their own roots are generally more weather-resistant and drought-tolerant than grafted roses. When planting, bury the bottom 3 to 4 inches of the canes in soil. Then spread a 4- to 6-inch layer of mulch on top, keeping the mulch several inches from the canes. Two good sources for own-root shrub roses are Heirloom Roses *(www.heirloomroses.com or 503/538-1576)* and High Country Roses *(www.highcountryroses.com or 800/552-2082).*

Sunset
CLIMATE ZONES
☐ 1–3   ☐ 10–11

☐ TREES. Consider planting one of these drought-tolerant trees for Arbor Day: American plum *(Prunus americana)*, bristlecone pine, burr oak *(Quercus macrocarpa)*, cockspur thorn *(Crataegus crus-galli)*, curl-leaf mountain mahogany *(Cercocarpus ledifolius)*, Gambell oak, common hackberry *(Celtis occidentalis)*, piñon pine, ponderosa pine (Montana's state tree), and upright junipers.

MAINTENANCE

☐ ATTRACT BENEFICIAL WILDLIFE. As frogs, toads, salamanders, and snakes emerge from hibernation, encourage them to stay in your garden and help control pests. Set shallow bowls or birdbath basins on the ground and fill them with water. Rinse and refill regularly.

☐ CLEAN OUT, MOUNT BIRDHOUSES. Remove and discard old nests, wipe each birdhouse with a solution of bleach (4 tablespoons of bleach per gallon of water), and mount it on a pole or a tree, 6 to 20 feet from the ground. A wide range of birdhouses is offered by Audubon Workshop *(http://audubonworkshop. com or 513/354-1485).*

☐ GUARD AGAINST DAMPING OFF. Seedlings started indoors in pots are especially susceptible to a fungus disease called damping off, which causes young plants to suddenly wilt and die. There is no cure, but you can prevent the disease by using sterile potting soil. Allow the soil surface to dry out slightly between waterings. Place pots in a shallow, water-filled container and let them wick moisture from the bottom up.

☐ PREPARE FLOWER BEDS. Cut off dead stalks and leaves from perennials, then top-dress the beds with 2 to 3 inches of compost and a sprinkling of fertilizer. Spread 4 to 6 inches of light, fluffy mulch between the plants, being careful not to cover the new growth. Good mulch choices include hay and pine needles. —*M. T.* ◆

WHAT TO DO IN YOUR GARDEN IN APRIL

PLANTING

☐ CITRUS. *Sunset* climate zones 11–13 (Las Vegas, Tucson, Phoenix): Set out grapefruit ('Marsh' and 'Rio Red'), 'Lisbon' lemon, mandarins ('Fremont' and 'Kinnow'), sweet oranges ('Hamlin', 'Marrs', 'Trovita', 'Valencia'), and 'Minneola' tangelo. For container plantings, try calamondin or 'Dwarf Bearss Seedless' lime.

☐ SHADE TREES. For a more comfortable microclimate in your outdoor living areas, plant shade trees suited for small spaces. Consider 'Desert Museum' palo verde, rosewood *(Dalbergia sissoo)*, shoestring acacia *(A. stenophylla)*, and Texas ebony *(Pithecellobium flexicaule)*.

☐ SUMMER COLOR. Create a cottage garden by planting colorful plants of varying heights. Zones 1A–3B (Flagstaff, Taos, Santa Fe): After frost danger has passed, set out transplants of perennial blue flax *(Linum perenne)*, gayfeather *(Liatris spicata)*, hollyhock, and Jupiter's beard. Zones 10–11 (Albuquerque, Las Vegas): Try *Lobelia laxiflora,* mallow *(Malva sylvestris),* pincushion flower *(Scabiosa caucasia),* and salvia. Zones 12–13 (Phoenix, Tucson): Sow seeds or set out transplants of hyssop *(Agastache),* salvia, verbena, yarrow *(Achillea),* and zinnia. In all zones, fill gaps with scented geraniums, nasturtium, and sweet alyssum.

☐ SUMMER VEGGIES. Zones 1A–3B: Set out transplants of broccoli, cabbage, and kale. Sow seeds of beets, carrots, salad greens, spinach, and turnips. Zone 10: Set out transplants of eggplant, peppers, and tomatoes. Sow seeds of beans, corn, cucumbers, melons, okra, pumpkins, and squash. Zones 11–13: Set out transplants of eggplant, peppers, and tomatoes. Sow seeds of black-eyed peas, lima and snap beans, carrots, corn, cucumbers, green onions, melons, okra, radishes, and squash.

MAINTENANCE

☐ GUARD AGAINST WILDFIRE. In fire-prone areas, create a defensible zone around your house by removing dead vegetation and trimming branches that hang over the roof. Clear fallen leaves and pine needles from your roof and gutters. Store firewood away from structures.

☐ MULCH. Spread a 3- to 4-inch layer of compost, bark chips, or other organic matter around plants to retain moisture.

☐ PROPAGATE CACTUS, SUCCULENTS. From stem cuttings, start new plants of cactus such as *Cereus,* cholla, pincushion, and prickly pear *(Mammillaria),* plus ice plant; start *Gasteria, Kalanchoe, Sansevieria,* and *Sedum* from leaf cuttings. With a sharp knife, remove a stem or leaf from the parent plant, then dip the cut end into a rooting hormone, make a small hole in sterile potting medium, and insert the cutting. Firm the soil around it and water gently. Place cuttings in bright, indirect light, and keep the soil moist for several weeks as roots develop.

—Kim Nelson

This eclectic blend of plants in Eugene, Oregon, includes (front to back) lavender-blue scabiosa and red *Astrantia*; rosy *Pimpinella* and *Alstroemeria*; lacy white *Eupatorium rugosom* 'Chocolate' (left) and creamy *Clematis recta* (right); and deep purple delphiniums. On the opposite page, lavender is backed by purple sage.

Carefree & colorful

Use our planting and design tips to create
a cottage garden with a Western twist

By Kathleen N. Brenzel, Sharon Cohoon, and Jim McCausland

When you hear the term "cottage garden," you might automatically picture a flowerful plot in front of a rustic country cottage in England. But you don't need a rural address to create such a garden. Cottage gardening is an attitude, not a location. All you need is a passion for plants and a willingness to mix them all up.

As Western gardeners are proving, you can achieve a cottage effect in the heart of the city as well as the suburbs. While English-style gardens draw heavily on hardy perennials, you can accomplish the same look of artful chaos with any plants appropriate to your climate. Indeed, Mediterranean plants and succulents like agaves work splendidly in coastal and desert plantings.

The owners of the gardens pictured on these pages will never be convinced that less is more. Perennials, annuals, vegetables, herbs, vines, roses, and other flowering shrubs—they find room for all of them. The result is cheerful, charming exuberance.

Plants for a cottage effect

Cottage gardens may appear wild and romantic, but it takes the right combination of colors, textures, and accessories to pull off the look. The prettiest gardens blend at least a few of the following types of plants into the collage. Choose plants appropriate for your climate and the site.

Billowers. Pillowy shrubs and perennials, like this phlox spilling over a rain barrel, add softness. Others: breath of heaven *(Coleonema),* ceanothus, lavatera, lilac.

Drapers. Twining plants, like this wisteria, climb walls or trellises and spill over fences or arbors.

Lacy accents. Wispy foliage and delicate flowers, like those of love-in-a-mist, create an airy effect.

Edgers. Ground covers soften the hard edges of paths and patios. Here, chartreuse Scotch moss fringes a pond and steppingstones. Others: blue star creeper, creeping thyme.

Spires. Plants with tall flower spikes, like gayfeather *(Liatris),* make bold contrasts to lower-growing ones. Others: delphinium, foxglove, hollyhock.

Roses. They're naturals in cottage gardens. Plant shrub roses among perennials, climbing types over arbors and against fences or walls.

Plant closely for a generous look. Soften the garden with billowers, drapers, and edgers.

Four-season appeal in Portland

How long does it take to create a show-quality cottage garden? About 18 months for the beauty shown above—and most of that was growing time. Soon after garden designer Darcy Daniels (BloomTown Garden Design; *www.bloomtowngardendesign.com or 503/331-1783*) moved into this Portland property, she ripped out a ragtag lawn, then began planting the rich tapestry pictured here in late spring. "I plant densely in a layered fashion, striving for a generous and abundant look. Over time, I will have to edit some plants out," she says.

A couple of principles guide Daniels's plant choices. Her coordinated use of color—burgundy, chartreuse, pink, purple, and blue—ties the garden together. Creating four-season interest is also critical. "In spring and summer, nearly everything looks good, but I use plants that hold their places in the off-season so I won't be looking at bare ground." Among her favorites are several kinds of *Euphorbia*, evergreen *Clematis armandii,* grasses, and New Zealand flax.

Perennials and shrubs form a multilayered tapestry of flowers and foliage in Darcy Daniels's front yard. To the left of the path, the mauve blooms of *Erysimum linifolium* 'Variegatum' and the burgundy leaves of New Zealand flax are backed by white 'Iceberg' rose, yellow-flowered *Achillea* 'Moonshine', and the violet blooms of *Allium* 'Globemaster'. To the right of the door, deep blue flowers cover *Ceanothus* 'Victoria'.

South African flavor in Southern California

Even if your favorite plants aren't traditionally used in cottage gardens, don't assume that they won't work; the trick is to use multiple varieties and plant them for an unstudied effect. That's the lesson behind Alan and Angelika Wilkinson's exotic cottage garden in Los Angeles.

When the Wilkinsons moved to Southern California, Alan realized that the climate offered the opportunity to use plants that he had grown up with in South Africa. (Both Southern California and South Africa's Western Cape Province have Mediterranean climates, characterized by long, dry summers and mild but wet winters.) Alan started a wish list of plants—including acacia, aloes, arctotis, kalanchoe, and leucadendron—and asked landscape designer Robert Cornell *(626/398-5581)* to help him fit them all in. Alan's desires matched Cornell's cottage-garden approach: "Plant-intensive, naturalistic gardens are my style," Cornell says.

African daisies with reddish orange flowers skirt the front of the Wilkinsons' garden. Just behind are *Aloe marlothii* with saffron-colored flower spikes and kalanchoe with pink bell-shaped blossoms (left). Evergreen shrubs bring up the rear; from far left to right are New Zealand tea tree (*Leptospermum scoparium* 'Ruby Glow'), *Leucadendron* 'Safari Sunset', and a treelike protea.

Finishing touches

Placing sculptural elements among plants or using them imaginatively as backdrops adds magic and romance to cottage gardens. Use them sparingly, to accentuate the plants rather than overwhelm them.

Curved paths. Allow walkways to meander among plantings, and put an interesting focal point, like a bench, at the path's end. These steps lead to a trellised rose.

Recycled materials. Integrate a flea-market find into your garden. This window-gate frames a moss-lined path leading to Darcy Daniels's rear garden.

Bird feeders. Use them as accents among drifts of flowering plants like these roses.

Sculptures. Set a piece of outdoor art or a gazing ball on a pedestal among plantings.

Rock walls. Build a stone wall to add structure and texture. This one, fringed with Scotch moss, curves past lilies and other perennials.

Birdbaths. Place one among perennials and keep it filled with water to serve thirsty birds and catch reflections of surrounding flowers.

Create focal points with sculptural plants or intriguing objects like gazing balls.

Carefree style fits anywhere

You don't need much space to achieve a carefree, cottagelike look. You can create the same bursting-with-blooms appearance by arranging potted plants on a deck or rooftop. Or plant a portion of your existing garden, perhaps an island bed, with a cottage-style mix of perennials and roses.

On a rooftop ▲
Pots filled with astilbes, delphiniums, and roses create a cottage effect on a San Francisco rooftop.
DESIGN: Sonny Garcia

In a patio bed ▲
Layered plants, from the fringe of white bacopa in front to the red 'Simplicity' rose in the center to the blue delphiniums at rear, create a colorful centerpiece for Carol Brewer's Southern California patio.

In an island bed ▶
Pink 'Ballerina' and red-and-white 'Eye Paint' roses share an island bed with blue catmint in Sharon Brasher's garden in Reno.

CLOCKWISE FROM BOTTOM LEFT: CONNIE COLEMAN; JERRY HARPUR; BOB WIGAND; MARK TURNER; NORM PLATE

In a sunny corner at *Sunset* ▾

In this springtime scene from *Sunset's* test garden in Menlo Park, California, drifts of California poppies *(Eschscholzia californica)* are backed by ornamental grass, purple Spanish lavender *(Lavandula stoechas),* and a tree mallow with rosy blooms. The poppies reseed freely.
DESIGN: Bud Stuckey

For more information

You'll find more design tips in the new book *Cottage Gardens* (Sunset Publishing Corporation, Menlo Park, CA, 2003; $15; www.sunset.com). The 128-page softcover contains ideas for regional variations of cottage-garden style, plus details about plants and structures. Look for it in home centers and bookstores. ◆

In a backyard

A grapevine-covered pergola frames a grass path in Jasmin Liepa's garden in Bellingham, Washington. The soft pink blossoms of an herbaceous peony contrast with the towering spikes of foxgloves.

Front-yard design

Three fresh ways to perk up the space outside your front door

Creating an inviting front yard can be a challenge, especially on a small lot that is exposed to the sidewalk and street traffic. But as the gateway to your house, this space deserves some careful consideration.

Rather then simply carpeting the soil with lawn and edging it with foundation plants, Westerners increasingly are rethinking their front yards in interesting ways. They make every square foot count by expanding outdoor living space; replacing lawns with low-maintenance, water-wise plants; or adding gracefully curved beds. Some gardeners with shady backyards are using sunny front yards for vegetable beds and fruit trees.

The following pages show three innovative approaches that people have taken to their street-facing spaces. —*Julie Chai*

This rich tapestry of plants includes nandina and Japanese maples as well as, at right, bronze coral bells, lime green *Lysimachia*, and blue star creeper.

Reclaim it for outdoor living

What can you do with a front yard on a busy street corner? Plenty, as garden designer Doug Stapleton found out when he began developing his small front lot in a Seattle neighborhood.

Before the redesign, the space amounted to little more than lawn and foundation plantings, and it was wide-open to the street. Stapleton wanted to create places to sit outdoors. He also wanted a sense of enclosure without feeling fenced in, distant from the hubbub of the street yet open enough for him to greet passing neighbors while he gardened.

Stapleton began by stripping the yard of sod. Next he enclosed it with an open-grid cedar-and-copper fence atop a dry rock wall. He set two small, irregularly shaped patios at opposite ends of the yard; Pennsylvania blue-stone pavers lie on a bed of 2 inches of gravel and 2 inches of sand with crushed rock between the stones.

Stapleton decided to rely mostly on leaf texture and color for interest, rather than flowers. He planted small-scale trees, perennials, shrubs, and ground covers to form the garden's backdrop.

Keep it simple

Because front gardens such as Doug Stapleton's are in full view of the neighborhood, they need regular maintenance to keep up their appearances. But the work doesn't have to be complicated or time-consuming. Stapleton suggests these ways to simplify.

Make daily rounds in early morning or late afternoon to check out your plantings (keep clippers handy). Snip off any spent foliage and flowers. Pull weeds as soon as they appear. Prune errant branches. Make these little routines part of savoring your garden; that way, they never build up into huge chores.

Allow plants to naturalize. Many plants will spread and multiply if they are happy. They'll fill in plantings for you.

Do two annual cleanups. In early spring and again in late autumn, clean up garden debris. In fall, dig and divide any clumping perennials that need it; cut back others to keep growth compact.

Mulch. In late winter or early spring, top-dress garden beds with 2 to 4 inches of organic material such as compost. This feeds the plants, conserves water, protects roots in cold as well as scorching weather, and reduces weed germination.

Be generous. Share plants with friends and neighbors. Invite people in to look around and talk. That's half the fun, and you'll learn a lot too.

A raised container and a curving path add form to the garden.

Low plants include blue star creeper, thyme, and pink-flowered *Lewisia.*

Along the fence and rock wall, he combined low, flowering ground covers to create the effect of an alpine rock garden. Then he tucked in bulbs to pop up in spring. As the seasons change, a horticultural symphony progresses throughout the garden.

To come up with the plant combinations pictured here and on pages 106 and 107, Stapleton roams nurseries by section, from sun lovers to shade lovers, mixing and matching plants for foliage color, form, and texture. He's willing to experiment. What works stays put. What doesn't gets moved to a new spot.

And when Stapleton relaxes on his patio with a newspaper and a cool drink, he can really enjoy his front yard.

DESIGN: Doug Stapleton, Garden Design, Seattle *(206/706-9170)*

—*Steven R. Lorton*

MAGGIE MacLAREN (2)

Plan it for low maintenance

When Don Terwilliger and Brian Capon travel, they seldom worry about their beautiful Mediterranean garden—they simply set the automatic irrigation timer, then go.

Terwilliger and Capon live in Del Mar, California, a beach community where the sun shines year-round and water is a limited resource. Their classic Mediterranean home is U-shaped, opening toward the street, with rooms leading into a courtyard that serves as an outdoor-living room.

The public space outside the courtyard is a waist-high garden bed (the home sits several feet above street level to escape potential flooding). To design the plantings, Capon drew on his own background as a professor emeritus of botany at California State University in Los Angeles; he's also a self-taught artist and the author of *Botany for Gardeners: An Introduction and Guide* (Timber Press, Portland, 1990; $30; 800/327-5680). He used Mediterranean and dry-climate plants such as lavender, salvia, santolina, and other plants that conserve moisture. "English

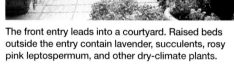

The front entry leads into a courtyard. Raised beds outside the entry contain lavender, succulents, rosy pink leptospermum, and other dry-climate plants.

gardens are lovely," Capon says, "but out of place in Southern California."

The garden requires little care. Weeding is minimal, because spaces between plants stay dry enough that weeds seldom sprout. Capon deadheads plants once a month, pruning out stray branches and keeping plants compact. He fertilizes once a year, at the beginning of the rainy season.

Even the courtyard pots—planted with bougainvillea, crotons, impatiens, pansies, pentas, and more—require little attention beyond regular irrigation with a watering can. —*Nan Sterman*

Easy-care tips

• **Plant in zones.** Fill the front yard—the public zone—with plants that need little supplemental water or care. Then spend your water and gardening time in your property's more private spaces—such as a courtyard or patio.

• **Choose tough, unthirsty plants.** See what grows easily in your region and climate with minimum fuss—native ferns, perhaps, or tough shrubs or cactus. Then fill the front yard with them.

• **Establish points of interest.** Brian Capon focused on leaf color and texture. Eye-catching succulents such as *Aeonium, Euphorbia tirucalli* 'Sticks on Fire', and *Kalanchoe* add punch to the foreground. Spiky bronze New Zealand flax *(Phormium)* grows in the background. Generous coral pink bougainvillea arches over the plantings.

• **Install a drip-irrigation system.** Run by an automatic timer, it'll do the watering for you.

...ds for seasonal interest

...emporary approach to planting beds ...long house foundations created an entirely new look for Bob and Suzette Ferguson's front yard in Oakland, California. Before the redesign, huge rhododendrons were jammed against the house and obscured lovely arched windows while darkening the home's interior. In their place, garden designers Shari and Richard Sullivan created a rich tapestry of plants that complements the house's style.

The Sullivans removed some of the lawn and expanded the planting bed out from the house, giving it a gentle curve and finishing it with a sinuous rock wall. To fill the bed, the Sullivans chose mostly shrubs and small trees that provide interesting color, texture, and form throughout the year.

Tall shrubs, including camellias, hydrangeas, and variegated weigela, were carefully positioned so they wouldn't completely block the windows. In front of the large shrubs are winter-blooming daphne and hellebores, ferns, 'Pia' dwarf hy-

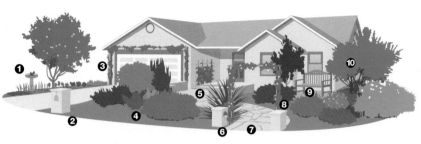

drangeas, and a red laceleaf Japanese maple. 'Akebono' pink flowering cherries add spring color to the corners of the property.

For added summer color, Shari tucks tall ageratum, 'Bluebird' nemesia, calibrachoa, dahlias, and impatiens between the shrubs.

Fall brings its own magic when the orange and red dogwood, maple, and viburnum foliage set the garden aglow. With plants that provide year-round color, the Fergusons' garden now spans all seasons.

DESIGN: Shari and Richard Sullivan, Enchanting Planting, Orinda, CA *(925/258-5500) —Lauren Bonar Swezey*

Other front-yard accents

1. Plant vegetables. Mix them into borders of perennials, or create separate beds in a sunny area.

2. Dress up the mailbox. Consider enclosing it in a stone or wood column with a built-in light above.

3. Trellis the garage. Build a sturdy trellis over the garage and plant a climbing rose or wisteria at its base.

4. Build a berm. A mound of soil covered with plants can help provide privacy from the street.

5. Build an entry patio. Define it with low seat walls.

6. Add lighting. Flank the pathway with low night-lights.

7. Curve the entry path to enhance the journey to the front yard and create an unfolding view. For added interest, use flagstones and put plants such as creeping thyme between them.

8. Trellis the garden's entry. A trellis covered with a fragrant climbing rose is welcoming.

9. Create a secret garden. In an area hidden by berms, trees, or hedges, place a few chairs or a lovely bench on a small paved patio.

10. Plant in layers. A well-mannered tree, several shrubs below it, and ground covers enhance privacy.

In spring, 'Mariesii' viburnum blooms behind a red laceleaf Japanese maple.

A perennial morning glory twines along a cable mounted to the cottage wall.

How to use plants

- *I. indica* blooms in one year from seed, but you can also start with young plants. It's a perennial (to 30 feet tall) in *Sunset* climate zones 8, 9, and 12–24, annual elsewhere (in frost-prone areas, it dies to the ground in winter). Needs sturdy support; use it to cover a bank, fence, trellis, or unsightly structure (like a chain-link fence).

- *I. tricolor* is an annual (to about 15 feet tall) and grows in all zones. Use it for quick color on arbors or trellises, or plant it in large containers; provide tall stakes or wire cylinders for it to climb. Plants reseed profusely; hoe out unwanted sprouts as soon as they appear.

- For cut flowers, pick stems with buds in various stages of development; place them in a deep vase. The buds will open on consecutive days.

Vines that say good morning

How to use these colorful easy growers

By Debra Lee Baldwin
Photographs by Claire Curran

There's something magical about morning glories, which do indeed bloom gloriously in the morning, then swirl closed as the day fades.

For growers Sheryl and Marshall Lozier, that's just what makes these vining annuals and perennials so irresistible. As you see in the photo above, perennial blue dawn flower *(Ipomoea indica)* scrambles up the side of their cottage. Elsewhere, another five-year-old plant weaves through a white-flowered potato vine *(Solanum jasminoides)* to cover a stucco arch.

"It's not for every garden," Sheryl says of the blue dawn flower. "It'll come in your doors and windows if you let it." To keep the vines in check, the Loziers prune them to 3 feet tall each January.

If you don't have room for this rambunctious rambler, consider its annual counterpart, *I. tricolor.* Sheryl trains them along the wire fencing of a maze. "They're a must-grow," she says. "Structures that support them don't have to be as strong as for perennial types."

The Loziers' Summers Past Farms *(www. summerspastfarms.com or 619/390-1523),* a 5-acre herb farm and nursery near San Diego, is one good place to see and buy morning glories.

No matter which variety you choose, spring is the perfect time to plant. Nurseries stock perennial morning glories in pots and sell seeds of annuals. Plant in well-drained soil after all danger of frost has passed. ◆

I. tricolor

'Tie Dye' morning glory *(I. tricolor)*

Clockwise from right: *Petasites japonicus giganteus,* 'Atrosanguineum' ornamental rhubarb, and *Hosta sieboldiana* 'Elegans'.

Going for the bold

Large-leafed plants add drama to garden beds

By Lauren Bonar Swezey

A beautiful planting is like a play. The small-leafed plants—bit players—create a textural backdrop that complements large-leafed ones—the stars—whose commanding presences make them standouts. Place a 6-foot-tall 'Black Magic' elephant's ear in a bed or border, for instance, and you have a striking focal point.

Plants with flamboyant foliage come in a variety of shapes and sizes. A prehistoric-looking gunnera with hairy green leaves that spread to 8 feet wide is a true giant among bold-leafed plants. But only a grand space can support such a behemoth. In more diminutive gardens that benefit from slightly smaller plants, try 'Eola Sapphire' hosta (4 feet wide) or one of the other large-leafed hosta hybrids to add drama without dominating surrounding plants.

Also consider hardiness when choosing big plants. Although some of the ones listed on the facing page are tropical in origin, most are widely adaptable. In cold-winter climates, you can grow tender plants in containers, then move them into protected areas for winter. Or plant them in the ground during the warm season, then dig them out and store them indoors through the cold season. Wait to set out tender plants until after last frost.

Give these plants room to spread. Use shade-loving annuals and perennials beneath large leaves to hide bare soil.

Huge gunnera leaves dominate a border. Top right: Yellow-flowered *Ligularia*. Right: 'Cleopatra' and 'Tropicanna' cannas.

Big leaves for large spaces

Banana *(Ensete, Musa).* Large, lush leaves range from 3 to 4 feet long for smaller types of *Musa* to 10 to 20 feet long for *Ensete* and tall *Musa* varieties. *E. ventricosum* 'Maurelii' (*Sunset* climate zones 13, 15–24, H1, H2) has dark red leafstalks and red-tinged leaves. Leaves of *M. acuminata* 'Zebrina' (zones 8, 9, 14–24, H1, H2) are green with maroon stripes. Japanese banana *(M. basjoo),* which grows to 15 feet tall, is the hardiest banana (zones 2 and 3 with protection; 4–9, 14–24, H1, H2). Full sun or partial shade. Regular to ample water.

Canna. The most dramatic cannas, including striped 'Minerva', 'Pretoria', and 'Tropicanna', grow to 4 to 6 feet tall. The shorter varieties (1½ to 3 feet tall) generally have green leaves and are suitable for smaller borders. Plant in full sun (except for 'Tropicanna'; leaves fade in full sun, so plant in partial shade) and well-composted soil. Regular water. Zones 6–9, 12–24, H1, H2; dig and store rhizomes in colder climates.

Cardoon *(Cynara cardunculus).* Silvery-leafed plant closely related to artichoke, but much larger (5 feet tall and 4 feet wide). Purple artichoke-type flowers can be cut and dried. Full sun. Regular water. Zones 4–9, 12–24.

Elephant's ear *(Colocasia).* Fast-growing plants to 6 feet tall with leathery, heart-shaped leaves up to 3 feet long. Ornamental varieties include 'Black Magic' (deep purple leaves), 'Illustris' (black leaves with greenish veins), 'Nancy's Revenge' (deep green leaves with white midveins). In colder climates, dig and store bulbs for winter. Tops die down at 30°. Plant in filtered shade and well-composted soil. Ample water; good beside ponds. Plants can overwinter in the ground in zones 12, 16–24 (mulch thickly in zones 14 and 15), H1, H2.

Gunnera *(G. tinctoria).* Lobed, toothed 4- to 8-foot-wide leaves develop on 4- to 6-foot-tall stalks. In mild-winter climates, leaves re-main for more than a year; in colder climates, they die back each year. Plant in partial shade in rich, well-composted soil; feed three times a year beginning when new leaves appear. Needs ample water. To keep foliage moist in dry climates, use overhead sprinkling. Zones 4–6, 14–17, 20–24.

Ornamental rhubarb *(Rheum palmatum).* Large plant 6 to 8 feet tall and 6 feet wide with 2- to 4-foot-wide, deeply lobed leaves. White flowers to 8 feet tall. 'Atrosanguineum' has reddish- to coppery-colored leaves and red flowers. Plant in full sun or light shade and well-composted soil. Ample water. Zones 2B–7, 14–17.

Petasites *(P. japonicus giganteus).* Creeping rhizomes produce 4-foot-diameter round leaves on 5-foot stalks. Fragrant white daisies appear before the leaves in spring. Plant in confined areas near ponds or in other moist locations (rhizomes can become invasive). 'Variegatus' has slightly smaller leaves with white markings. Partial to full shade; full sun in cool climates. Ample water. Zones 2B–9, 14–17.

Modest growers for smaller pots

Hosta. There are hundreds of hosta varieties to choose from, but the grandest forms have 1- to 1½-foot-wide leaves: 'Elegans' (metallic blue-green), 'Eola Sapphire' (dark green aging to blue), 'Frances Williams' (blue-green leaves edged with yellow), 'Sum and Substance' (chartreuse leaves). Plant in partial or full shade and well-composted soil. Regular water. Zones 1–10, 14–21.

Ligularia. Large clumps to 3 feet wide with heart-shaped or deeply lobed, 12- to 20-inch-wide leaves. Flower stalks, topped with yellow or orange daisy flowers, can reach 6 feet tall. *L. dentata* 'Desdemona' has purple leafstalks, veins, and leaf undersides; upper leaf surfaces are green. Plant in partial shade in well-composted soil (plants also thrive in large containers as shown above). Ample water. Zones 1–9, 14–17 (*L. dentata* 'Othello' and *L. stenocephala* grow in A2, A3). ◆

Spuria irises have a long vase life.

'Ada Perry'

'Dena's Delight'

Growing tips

• Choose a planting site in full sun and amend the soil with plenty of compost or other organic matter. If soil is acidic, also add lime.

• Get rhizomes into the ground immediately; they can't tolerate drying out. Plant 1 inch deep in heavy soil, 2 inches deep in sandy soil. Space rhizomes at least 2 feet apart. Keep them well watered from planting through bloom period.

• You'll get more blooms if you feed spuria consistently. One strategy: apply a balanced, controlled-release fertilizer in early spring and again in early autumn.

• Once spuria have finished blooming, you have two options: continue watering, but less frequently, in order to enjoy foliage longer; or stop watering completely and let the plants go dormant. Gardeners in hot-summer areas like Arizona generally follow the latter practice.

• When foliage declines, cut back to 8 to 9 inches. Resume watering when new foliage emerges.

• Spuria irises don't like to be disturbed and should only be divided every 5 to 10 years. Expect them to go dormant briefly after planting or transplanting. Bloom might be sparse and foliage shorter the first year, too.

Ideal iris

Spuria's abundant blooms add weeks of color in most Western climates

By Sharon Cohoon
Photographs by Norm Plate

If you like Dutch iris, you're going to love spuria iris. Though its flowers resemble those of Dutch iris, they're bigger—up to 5 inches across. Not only does spuria produce larger flowers than Dutch types, it produces more of them: three to four buds per stalk is typical; seven is possible. And spuria's stalks are taller (3 to 5 feet) and stronger than their Dutch cousins, so they're better able to resist wind and rain. This all adds up to quite a show that lasts for several weeks.

Spuria blooms in late spring, just as tall bearded iris start tapering off. It lasts longer in the vase than Dutch iris and comes in a wider variety of colors. You'll find a full range of blues and purples, yellows, and snowy whites, plus exotic browns, red-browns, even off-blacks.

The leaves, which reach up to 5 feet tall, are impressive too. With their swordlike shape and neutral green hue, they're a great background in the perennial garden, even when the irises are out of bloom. If you have the space, plant them separately in large groups for a glorious spring display.

You could certainly call spuria robust. This plant withstands almost any climate: It grows in *Sunset* climate zones 2–24; when mulched it can tolerate temperatures to –20°. And though spuria prefers well-drained, slightly alkaline soil, it adapts easily to most soils.

Visit, or order by mail

Despite all of its virtues, spuria can be hard to find. Few nurseries carry this iris, so your best bet is one of these growers.
Aitken's Salmon Creek Garden, Vancouver, WA. Iris fields open for viewing during bloom season, April 1–July 1. *www.flowerfantasy.net or (360) 573-4472.*
Greenwood Iris + Daylily, Somis, CA. Fields open Saturdays, April–June, plus the last Friday and Sunday of April. *www.greenwoodgarden.com or (562) 494-8944.*
Iris Gallery, Fort Bragg, CA. Open May 10–June 16. *www.allthingsiris.com or (800) 757-4747.*
Shepard Iris Garden, Phoenix. Open in April. *(602) 841-1231.* ◆

Plant a tomato tepee

Train four seedlings up poles to save space and reap fruits aplenty

By Sharon Cohoon and Lauren Bonar Swezey

You don't need a big yard to grow tomatoes successfully. In *Sunset's* test garden last summer, we grew four different tomato varieties on a single compact tepee and harvested great crops. We grew 'Marvel Stripe' and 'Mortgage Lifter', both of which bear fruits weighing a pound or more, and 'Dona' and 'Black Krim', which produce smaller fruits in prodigious quantity. These are all indeterminate types, meaning that the plants continue to grow and bear tomatoes over a long season.

What's the secret of this method? No sprawling allowed! From the time the tomatoes go into the ground, they're trained up the tepee's bamboo poles. As the vines grow, they're tied to the poles, and side shoots are pinched off to preserve a single main stem. This foliar thinning helps ensure good air circulation and channels the plant's energy into fruit production.

TIME: About 1 hour to assemble.
COST: About $40.

MATERIALS

- 1 roll sturdy **twine**
- 4 **bamboo poles,** each 8 feet long
- 2 cubic feet of **compost**
- 4 **tomato seedlings** of indeterminate types, from 4-inch pots
- 25-foot **soaker hose**
- 4 to 6 **metal drip-tubing stakes**

DIRECTIONS

1. Use twine to lash the poles together near the top. Raise them to form a tepee, spacing the bases about 2 feet apart. To anchor the tepee, push the base of each pole 6 to 8 inches into the ground.

2. Amend the soil beside the base of each pole by digging in a 2- to 3-inch layer of compost or other organic amendment.

3. Dig a deep hole in the amended soil (see "Tips for Planting" and bottom right photo), and plant one tomato seedling in each hole, slightly tilting the plant toward the pole. Remove the lowest set or two of leaves from the main stem and bury the stem up to the next set of leaves. Roots will emerge from the buried portion of the stem.

4. Encircle the tepee with a soaker hose, staking it down next to the plants.

5. As plants grow, tie vines to poles with twine or plastic tape. Pinch off large side shoots that emerge from the main stem. ◆

Tips for planting

Before planting a tomato seedling, clip off the lowest set or two of leaves (top). Dig a hole deep enough to bury the stem up to the next set of leaves.

Abundant gardening

Planting and design tips from an organic grower

By Julie Chai

More than a decade ago, Craig Murray began growing hard-to-find tomatoes and peppers in Los Altos Hills, California. His organic methods yielded so much beautiful produce that he planted other vegetables, herbs, and flowers to sell at a roadside stand.

Many crops now grow in Murray's 1-acre plot, from zinnias, rudbeckias, and dahlias to tomatoes—'First Lady', 'Big Beef', and heirloom 'Caspian Pink' are among Murray's favorites—and peppers, such as 'Gypsy' and 'Vidi'.

Murray, a landscape designer, contractor, and horticultural consultant *(650/941-1301)*, says his garden enables him to connect with the community as well as the earth. "This is a gathering place," he explains; customers come to chat and exchange recipes.

For his summer garden, Murray sows seeds in a greenhouse in late winter, then sets seedlings in the ground when they reach planting height, about 10 inches tall. He uses no chemical fertilizers or pesticides and says they're not needed in a healthy garden that's visited by beneficial insects, which eat insect pests. "If you provide sun, water, enriched soil, and the best [seed] varieties you can find, you'll get results," he adds. ◆

Coppery 'Cherokee Sunset' rudbeckia, pink celosia (*C. spicata* 'Flamingo Feather'), and a blue-and-white bicolor salvia thrive in narrow raised beds.

Steps to success

You can duplicate Murray's method by following these steps before planting:

Start plants from seed so you can grow unusual varieties that are not available as seedlings in nurseries. Murray annually orders new and unusual varieties as well as tried-and-true types. "There's a lot of joy in germinating seeds and watching them grow to maturity," he says.

Prepare the soil. Dig in several inches of compost and a balanced organic fertilizer. Or use Murray's method: in midfall, plant cover crops of barley, clover, legumes, oats, and vetch, then till them into the soil in spring.

Create narrow rows (30 to 36 in. wide) for easy harvest. Mound the soil in these beds to 8 inches high for good drainage.

Lay drip tape or soaker hoses lengthwise, close to where you'll set out seedlings. Irrigate for several hours to moisten the soil.

Cover rows and drip tape with plastic mulch and bury the edges with soil to keep it in place. (For sources and more information about plastic mulch, see "Landscape Fabrics," on the facing page.)

Now that the rows are ready for planting:

Use a tighter-than-usual spacing method for seedlings so that plants will support each other and protect foliage from sunburn. Cut 4-inch Xs in the plastic; through the openings, plant seedlings atop the mounds.

Support plants with a simple stake-and-string method: place a post at each corner of the bed and run plastic twine horizontally from post to post at every 8 to 10 inches of height.

Landscape fabrics

Dress your garden for success

By Jim McCausland

From the ground up, synthetic fabrics make gardening easier by performing a variety of problem-solving functions. The chart below outlines the main choices available to home gardeners. Be aware that suppliers often sell nearly identical products under different names.

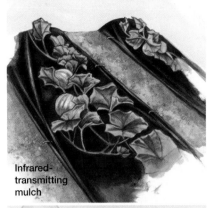

Infrared-transmitting mulch

MATERIAL	COST(per 100 sq. ft.)	FUNCTION, BENEFITS, NOTES
Mulches Made for different purposes, including weed control, warming soil, conserving moisture, and repelling insects. Hold down the edges with soil, staples, or stakes.		
Black sheet plastic	$5–$7	Absorbs heat to warm soil. This impermeable mulch works best when drip tubing is run beneath the plastic.
Infrared-transmitting (IRT) mulch (brown or green plastic)	$6	Allows infrared light to penetrate plastic, warming soil. Boosts yields of cucumbers, melons, peppers, squash.
Rapid Red plastic film (also sold as Selective Reflecting Mulch or SRM-Red)	$7	Reflects infrared light up to plant. Boosts yields of tomatoes and strawberries.
Silver mulch (high-density plastic)	$7	Protects crops by repelling insect pests such as aphids, flea beetles, thrips, and white flies.
Weed control fabric (black synthetic fiber)	$10–$27	Insert permanent plants through slits cut in fabric. Lasts 10 years or longer if covered with bark or gravel.
Floating row covers Made of synthetic fibers, these covers "float" over rows to protect crops against many insect pests and light frost.		
Extra-light fabric (summer-weight) fabric	$6–$8	Insect barrier only. Light enough to leave on in the heat; 85% light transmission.
Standard floating row cover	$6–$9	Insect barrier, frost protection to 28°–30°; 75%–85% light transmission. Remove when temperatures top 80° or plants will overheat.
Frost blanket	$13–$17	Enhanced frost protection down to 24°–26°; 50% light transmission. Must remove during day when temperatures rise above 32°.
Shadecloth Reduces the intensity of sunlight. Density rating is based on the percentage of sunlight blocked.		
52%–70% density knit poly "yarn" (sold in rolls)	$25–$40	Stretch fabric over crops to protect from sunburn, especially in desert areas.
30%–66% density knitted panels	$40–$70	Usually sold with finished edges and grommets, they're designed to hang from hooks over greenhouses, patios.

Rapid Red plastic film

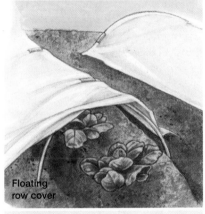

Floating row cover

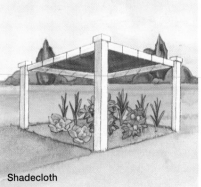

Shadecloth

SOURCES: Most nurseries and garden centers offer at least a few basic garden fabrics. For more options, try one of these mail-order suppliers: **Gardener's Supply Company** (www.gardeners.com or 800/427-3363), **Gardens Alive** (www.gardensalive.com or 812/537-8650), or **Territorial Seed Company** (www.territorialseed.com or 541/942-9547). For shadecloth and mulch choices, contact **Charley's Greenhouse** (www.charleysgreenhouse.com or 800/322-4707). ◆

LINDA HOLT AYRISS (4)

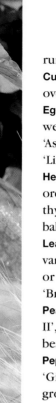

'Farmers' Long' eggplant dangles 10-inch fruits.

Crops that thrive in pots

You don't need much space if you plant the right veggies and herbs

By Jim McCausland

Growing in just a few big pots set in a sunny corner of a deck or patio, a compact container garden can reward you with a steady stream of vegetables from spring through fall.

From carrots to zucchini, a surprisingly wide variety can be grown successfully in containers. (Large, space-consuming plants like corn, melons, and pumpkins are still best grown in the ground.)

The basics

Large containers (18 inches or more in diameter) made of thick-walled terra-cotta or plastic work best for vegetables because they allow ample room for root growth, retain moisture well, and provide insulation against day and night temperature extremes.

Fill containers with good potting soil amended with a complete organic or controlled-release fertilizer. Apply fish emulsion or liquid fertilizer (such as 20-20-20 formula) every two weeks for the entire season.

Install supports like stakes, trellises, and tomato cages at planting time. Place pots in a spot where they'll get at least six hours of sun per day. Water whenever the top inch of soil dries out.

For more tips, see *The Bountiful Container*, by Rose Marie Nichols McGee and Maggie Stuckey (Workman Publishing, New York, 2002; $17; www.workman.com or 800/722-7202).

The menu

Beans. Bush-type 'Blue Lake' green bean is a popular choice. Try scarlet runner bean on a trellis or tripod.

Cucumbers. Let lemon cukes trail over the rim or grow up a trellis.

Eggplants. Japanese types work well; we've had excellent success with 'Asian Bride', 'Farmers' Long', and 'Little Fingers'.

Herbs. Plant seedlings of basil, chives, oregano, parsley, rosemary, sage, and thyme. Keep spreaders like lemon balm and mint in their own containers.

Leaf crops. Choose looseleaf lettuce varieties like 'Oak Leaf' or 'Red Sails', or any mesclun. It's hard to beat 'Bright Lights' Swiss chard.

Peas. Bush-type 'Oregon Sugar Pod II', which reaches only 2½ to 3 feet, bears sweet, crisp pods.

Peppers. For large, sweet peppers, try 'Giant Marconi'; for hot peppers, grow 'Habanero', 'Super Cayenne', and 'Thai Dragon'.

Root crops. Plant 'Chantenay #1' or 'Sweetness II' carrots, any kind of radish, and almost any potato (red ones like 'Buffalo' and 'Red La Soda' are especially good).

Tomatoes. Among slicing types, choose determinate varieties like 'Bush Celebrity', 'Pik Red', and 'Solar Set'; for cherry tomatoes, go with 'Sun Gold', 'Sweet Million', and 'Yellow Pear'.

Zucchini. Try one of the bush types such as 'Eight Ball', 'Raven', 'Ronde de Nice', or 'Spacemiser'. ◆

'Thai Dragon' peppers turn red when ripe.

THOMAS J. STORY (2)

Get a glimpse of paradise

At Open Days, sneak a peak at glorious private gardens

By Sharon Cohoon
Photographs by Steven Gunther

The best private gardens, like this one in L.A., open for tours this month.

You don't need to know a *Brachyscome* from a *Boltonia* (fyi: both are daisies) to enjoy a garden tour. Sure, visiting private gardens is a great way to learn about plants—and about design, hardscape materials, and every other aspect of the landscapers' art too.

But let's be honest. Touring is also a great way to snoop without guilt. Having a peek at someone else's masterwork is like slipping on another life for a while. Would I like living in this neighborhood, city, state? Could I embrace this climate, lifestyle, income bracket? In other words, garden touring is "Let's Pretend" for grown-ups.

There is no better way to engage in such flights of fancy than by taking in the Garden Conservancy's Open Days Program. A New York–based nonprofit organization, the conservancy identifies outstanding properties throughout the country and then organizes a calendar of viewing days so the rest of us can see them for a charge of $5 per visit. Of the nearly 400 gardens in this year's program, 136 are in the West. Tour dates for the West range from late March to July; visit the conservancy's website, listed below, for the full schedule.

While the gardens that are open to the public vary from year to year, they are, almost invariably, stunning. The formal Italian garden with boxwood hedges and billowing roses shown here is one of the highlights of the Open Days Program on April 27 in Los Angeles. A terraced garden with a panoramic view of the San Francisco skyline and a tropical oasis in Portland are featured this year.

To take advantage of the program, you need to invest in the Open Days Directory, which lists the gardens and the dates they're open. Site descriptions and detailed driving instructions are also included.

There is a national version, which covers the entire program, and this year, there is also a West Coast edition covering only Washington, Oregon, and California. Complete directory: $16 plus $4.50 for shipping and handling; Western version: $5 plus $1.95. With either, you can obtain a certificate good for admission to one garden. To order: *www. gardenconservancy.org or (888) 842-2442.* ◆

The Garden Conservancy

Great private gardens are fragile creations, ones that often don't survive their owners' deaths or the sale of property. The Garden Conservancy is a nonprofit organization founded in 1989, dedicated to preserving exceptional private gardens for the public. Although the conservancy is based in New York, it has Western roots. Ruth Bancroft's famous succulent garden in Walnut Creek, California, was the achievement that prompted the formation of the conservancy and also was its first preservation project. For a glimpse of the Bancroft grounds (which you can visit) and other conservancy projects, see the organization's website, listed at right.

HIDDEN BEHIND A STONE WALL, this expansive garden in Ketchum Idaho, coaxes abundance out of a short summer. Learn the gardener's clever growing tricks on pages 134–137.

NORM PLATE

May

Reflections from home

"**M**y best ideas spring from emotion and intuition," says Del Mar, California, gardener Lynne Blackman. Her "moon mirror" is a good example.

Blackman's close friends Jim and Nancy Matison live in Guatemala. Though the three rarely have a chance to visit, they are alive in each other's minds and hearts. Once, when the moon was full, Blackman stood in her garden—at the edge of a bluff over-looking the sea—and sent a wish to the moon on her friends' behalf. "When I told them about it later, Nancy and Jim loved the idea," says Blackman. "After that, whenever there was a full moon, we knew we were looking at it and thinking of each other."

The spot where Blackman did her gazing is where she later hatched the notion to send her reflection to the moon. Installing a pool was her first idea, but using a mirror instead seemed both more practical and more mysterious.

The mirror—round, naturally, to echo the shape of the moon—rests on a bed of builder's sand and is framed by a ring of blue fescue. Now, when the moon is full, Blackman writes her messages on the mirror—sometimes with her finger, sometimes with an erasable marker—trusting they will be reflected and relayed to Guatemala.

This section of the garden generates plenty of daytime magic too. Dark red bougainvillea and blue bearded iris provide color, rose-scented geraniums add perfume, and two frothy gray licorice plants frame the view. In the afternoon, it's her cat Zorro's favorite place to lounge. —*Sharon Cohoon*

STEVEN GUNTHER

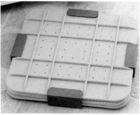

Orchid vine thrives in desert heat

Two species of heat-loving orchid vine (*Mascagnia*) thrive in the intermediate and low-desert areas around Tucson and Phoenix (*Sunset* climate zones 12 and 13). Both kinds bear five-petaled flowers and seedpods reminiscent of butterflies atop branches. Either can be grown over an arbor, or on a trellis to create a privacy screen or to provide shade.

Yellow orchid vine (*M. macroptera,* pictured above) is a vigorous, fast-growing plant native to Baja California and Sonora, Mexico. It blooms from late spring through summer. This twining vine will climb 15 to 30 feet if provided with support. Hardy to about 22°, it is damaged by hard frost but recovers quickly when temperatures warm up in the spring.

Lavender orchid vine (*M. lilacina),* native to the Chihuahuan Desert of Mexico, has slightly smaller lilac-colored blossoms and seedpods. This vine grows more slowly to 15 to 20 feet. Tiny hairlike structures on its leaves can cause mild skin irritation for some people, requiring gloves and long sleeves for tending. Hardy to about 15°, the vine remains evergreen in the warmest winter microclimates.

Nurseries sell these plants in 1- or 5-gallon containers. Plant them in full sun and well-drained soil near support structures. Water every few days until plants are established, then only twice monthly.

—Kim Nelson

UNTHIRSTY WESTERNERS
Blanket flower

One of the easiest native Western wildflowers to domesticate, blanket flower (*Gaillardia aristata*) also happens to be one of the few perennials that bloom all summer long. Hardy in most *Sunset* climate zones, blanket flower isn't fussy about soil or water (it does need good drainage). The plant bears red-and-yellow daisies 2 to 4 inches across over clumps about 2 feet tall and wide.

To start plants in your garden, scatter seeds in a sunny spot any time of the year and keep the soil moist until they germinate. Or sow the seeds in early spring or late fall and let nature do the work for you. To keep flowers coming all summer, remove faded blossoms frequently or shear the whole clump back by half several times a season. Always leave a few flowers on the plant to go to seed. Though not long-lived, blanket flower self-sows readily.

A good source for seeds is Plants of the Southwest *(800/788-7333 or www. plantsofthesouthwest.com).* Note: Many nurseries carry the hybrid *G.* x *grandiflora* rather than the wild form of the plant.

—Marcia Tatroe

Press blooms instantly in the microwave

Instead of waiting weeks for flowers to dry in a traditional press, you can preserve richly colored blossoms in minutes by pressing them in your microwave.

We experimented with the Microfleur Microwave Flower Press and found that it worked best with thin, fairly flat petals like those of bougainvillea, pansies, and violas. The microwave-pressed blossoms held their color well and had essentially the same texture as those pressed by conventional methods.

Microfleur press is available in two sizes: 5 inches square and 9 inches square. Each comes with absorbent pads and fabric liners that draw moisture from the flowers and expel it through vents in the press. You'll have to adjust the drying time and power level to accommodate the strength of your microwave and the density of the flowers being pressed.

The Microfleur is available from Gardener's Supply (www. gardeners.com or 800/427-3363) for about $35 (small) or $50 (large) plus shipping.

—Julie Chai

The perfect delphinium for smaller gardens

Towering as high as 6 to 9 feet, standard English delphiniums can look out of scale in some gardens. Now, however, you can enjoy the same elegant flowers on a shorter plant. New Heights Mix reaches only 3½ to 4 feet. Discovered and hybridized in Holland, these plants come in a range of colors, including iridescent purple, turquoise, sky blue, yellow, cream, white, pink, and mauve. Bloom season extends from late May to early July, with an occasional round of fall flowers. Because of their shorter stature, they pair well with many other annuals and perennials, like the white-flowered nicotiana and deep maroon Oriental poppy shown here in Stephanie Niedermeyer's garden in Eugene, Oregon.

Cultivate New Heights Mix as you would taller delphiniums. Niedermeyer stakes her plants with branches pruned from her apple trees.

Look for New Heights Mix in 4-inch pots at local nurseries. If they don't carry them, ask the staff to order from Log House Plants (wholesale only) in Cottage Grove, Oregon. *Visit www. loghouseplants.com for a list of retail nurseries that carry New Heights Mix.*

—Mary-Kate Mackey

Ground cover forms minimountains

Visitors to the Bloedel Reserve on Bainbridge Island, Washington, admire *Euonymus radicans* 'Kewensis', an evergreen ground cover that forms mounds resembling miniature mountain ranges. People often ask the garden staff how they prune the plant to achieve that effect, but 'Kewensis' grows that way naturally.

Native to China, 'Kewensis' has delicate leaves ¼ to ⅝ inch in diameter. It grows well in sun and tolerates substantial shade. For the planting pictured above, gardeners set out 4-inch pots of 'Kewensis' at 8-inch intervals. At first, the plants hugged the ground, but after five or six years they began developing their own topography. This plot is never fed and is watered only during the driest parts of summer.

When 'Kewensis' touches a wall or another plant, it can start climbing. Bloedel's gardeners only trim the ground cover to keep it out of the dwarf white pine (*Pinus strobus* 'Nana') shown in the photo.

'Kewensis' is hardy to at least 0°. It is sold by some nurseries, and it's available by mail from Forestfarm in Williams, OR *(541/846-7269 or www.forestfarm.com). —Jim McCausland*

Happy birthday, Master Gardeners

Born 30 years ago, the Washington State University Master Gardener Program was the model for a movement that has since spread to 36 states and four Canadian provinces. After taking an eight-week course to earn certification as Master Gardeners,

volunteers must complete 60 hours of free instruction in subjects ranging from plant identification to composting. Then, they donate about 60 hours their first year and 25 hours each year thereafter at gardening clinics and other public venues. For information about the program in Washington, go to *http://mastergardener.wsu.edu;* in other states, call the Cooperative Extension office in your county.

The seven cheerful men and women pictured at left are among the more than 90 volunteers who maintain the 1½-acre Skagit County Master Gardener Discovery Garden located at the WSU Mount Vernon Research Unit. This idea-packed garden is divided into 12 segments, including a test plot for vegetables and small fruit trees.

Dawn–dusk daily; free. 16650 State 536 in Mount Vernon. —Steven R. Lorton

Peony fields in the Willamette Valley

The Pacific Northwest ranks among the best places on earth for growing peonies. Their large, multipetaled flowers can be red, pink, white, coral, or bicolored; new hybrids that are crosses of herbaceous peonies and tree peonies come in purple and yellow ranges. You can see thousands of them in full bloom at either of two peony growers located in the Willamette Valley of Oregon. Each welcomes visitors during peak bloom season, and each

sells both potted plants and cut flowers. You can also place orders for delivery at fall planting time.

Just outside Canby, **Pacific Peonies & Perennials** (shown above) carries more than 300 varieties of herbaceous peonies and about 100 kinds of tree peonies. Be sure to see the best-selling 'Coral Charm' and the spectacular hybrid yellow 'Bartzella'. The farm also sells freeze-dried peony arrangements, plus a wide range of perennials.

Apr 24–Jun 14, 10–5 daily. 11466 S. Mulino Rd.; www.pacificpeonies.com or (503) 263-6353.

In Salem, **Adelman Peony Gardens** offers around 150 varieties of herbaceous peonies. The 6-acre farm's grassy lanes are awash with the fragrance of the blooms, many of which are the size of dinner plates. *Peak bloom is May 15–Jun 7. Open May 1–Jun 15, 9–7 daily. 5690 Brooklake Rd. N.E.; www.peonyparadise. com or (503) 393-6185. —J.M.*

Purple fountain grass waves over pink petunias.

Flowers thrive on gray water

Last summer, in the midst of Colorado's worst drought in recorded history, when many area gardens turned brown, the flower beds on the golf course at Valley Country Club in Aurora remained verdant—without violating any local water-use restrictions. The flower beds were irrigated with "tertiary treated effluent"—or gray water, as it's commonly known—from a nearby treatment plant.

Designed by the club's horticulturist/arborist Patrick Myers, the beds feature heat-tolerant annuals that are also tough enough to withstand the voracious voles that make their homes in them. In the bed behind the first tee (pictured above), white trumpets of tall *Nicotiana sylvestris* dangle over raspberry dahlias and purple fountain grass (*Pennisetum setaceum* 'Rubrum'). Below the grass are Tidal Wave Hot Pink petunias, dusty miller, and 'Blackie' and 'Terrace Lime' sweet potato vines.

Gray water is wastewater from bathing, washing dishes, and laundry that can be safely reused for landscape irrigation. Regulations governing gray water vary from state to state; check with your water provider. For a good overview, go to *http://cahe.nmsu.edupubs/_m/m-106.html*

—*M. T.*

This gazania tolerates drought

Each year, the Plant Select program introduces a few new plants that perform exceptionally well in the West's intermountain areas and the high plains. Among this year's winners is *Gazania krebsiana* 'Tanager', an unthirsty perennial that bears dazzling orange daisies from spring through fall. The 2-inch-wide flowers are borne on spreading plants that reach 4 inches tall by 10 inches across.

A short-lived perennial, 'Tanager' can be grown as a summer annual in all zones, but it is hardy enough to overwinter in *Sunset* climate zone 3A (Grand Junction, Colorado, and Salt Lake City). It tolerates full sun or partial shade. 'Tanager' is rated as a Xeriscape plant, and according to horticulturist Mike Bone of Denver Botanic Gardens, it actually lives longer if it is grown *without* irrigation.

Look for 'Tanager' in pots at local nurseries. Go to *www.plantselect.org* to review the six other Plant Select winners for 2003. —*M. T.*

Orchids in Oakland

For the serious collector or anyone looking for a Mother's Day gift, the annual sale at **Orchids Fiori D'Amore** may be just the place to find a blooming treasure.

Nina and Paolo Di Candia began growing orchids at their home more than 25 years ago, fell in love with the flowers' longevity, and turned their passion into a business. The Di Candias specialize in unusual varieties (one of their favorites is rusty orange Mighty Remus

'Enos' cymbidium). Of course, uncommon beauty is pricey: the rarest orchids cost up to $500 each, but there are plenty of varieties in the $10–$60 range.

Store is open by appointment only except during the annual sale; call for 2004 dates; free. 4526 Fair Ave.; (510) 530-4884. Di Candia orchids are also available at several Bay Area farmers' markets, including those in Pleasanton (*W. Angela and Main Streets*) and in Oakland (*Jack London Square*). —Lauren Bonar Swezey

BACK TO BASICS

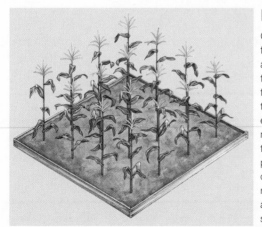

Plant corn in blocks

Corn plants carry both male and female flowers. The male flowers are on the tassels at the top of the plant; the female flowers form the silk that hangs out of the developing ears. In order for ears to produce a full set of kernels, wind must distribute pollen to all of them. To ensure good pollination, plant corn in blocks of no fewer than 16 plants (four rows of four plants). Plant seeds at least 12 inches apart in rows spaced 3 feet apart. —L.B.S.

Lavender fields forever

Visits to Provence inspired Ellen Sullivan and her husband, Paul Bernhardy, to grow lavender as a cash crop. Sullivan praises "the herb's lovely flowers and exquisite fragrance," adding that "it's one of the hardiest plants to grow, loves sunny southern slopes, needs very little care, and really dislikes rich soil."

A dream came true for the couple in 1998 when they purchased a 9-acre farm in the hills of Valley Center, in San Diego County. The couple broke ground and began propagating and planting in 1999. They now grow 28 varieties—up to 6,000 plants—on three acres. "We hand-cut all our bundles in spring and early summer when the plants are in full bloom," Sullivan says. The farm, now officially known as the **Lavender Fields,** offers group tours, classes, and more.

Open to the public on weekends in May and June; free. Second annual Lavender Harvest Festival in June. For directions and hours: www.thelavenderfields.com or (888) 407-1489. —Debra Lee Baldwin

Less is more on this desert island

Part of the beauty of the desert lies in its sparseness, notes Edward Abbey in his book *Desert Solitaire*. In the desert, he writes, the flora is "scattered abroad in spareness and simplicity, with a generous gift of space for each herb and bush and tree, each stem of grass, so that the living organism stands out bold and brave and vivid against the lifeless sand and barren rock."

That sentiment is appreciated by Tucson landscape architect Margaret Joplin. When she moved to a 1950s-era neighborhood, she inherited a front yard dominated by a driveway that curved around an island inhabited only by a mesquite tree, a date palm, and a single prickly pear cactus surrounded by pea gravel. Yet Joplin didn't rush to fill the space. She first identified the parts of the area that were most visible from indoors, then slowly began establishing small areas of vegetation within the large space. Her first planting was the grouping (shown at left above) of aloes, golden barrel cactus, and *Trichocereus* under the mesquite tree. "This is the view I see from my dining room," she says. Another group is developing around the prickly pear; if you look closely, you'll see baby cactus, started as cuttings below the mother plant.

Joplin also added a few woody perennials like yellow lantana. But she wants to keep it spare, with plenty of gold decomposed granite between plants and, more importantly, plenty of room to stroll. "Usually all we can do is walk *by* plants," she says. "But here I can walk all *around* mine, surveying them from every angle. That's what I love most about this space." —S.C.

WHAT TO DO IN YOUR GARDEN IN MAY

PLANTING

☐ **ANNUAL FLOWERS.** As soon as danger of frost has passed and soil warms, you can sow or plant any annual. If you begin with nursery seedlings, harden them off first by putting them under a tree or on a sheltered patio for a few days before planting. In sunny spots, grow cosmos, geraniums, marigolds, petunias, and zinnias. In light shade, use begonias, coleus, impatiens, and violas.

☐ **FUCHSIAS.** Plant them in patio pots, hanging baskets, or in lightly shaded garden beds. Pinch back the growing tips every couple of weeks to make plants bushy and dense; feed and water regularly through summer for maximum bloom.

☐ **HERBS.** Sow seeds of basil and cilantro. Harvest the cilantro as soon as it leafs out, since it goes to seed with lightning speed. Oregano and thyme like soil on the dry side, mint likes it damp, and chives and parsley get by with normal watering.

☐ **PERENNIALS.** Shop for astilbe, bleeding heart, campanula, columbine, ferns, lady's-mantle, lupine, poppies, and sweet woodruff. You can also plant summer and fall bloomers like aster, black-eyed Susan, chrysanthemum, coreopsis, and Shasta daisy.

☐ **SUMMER BULBS.** Set out dahlia tubers and gladiolus corms in a sunny location with well-drained soil. Callas and cannas (usually sold as potted plants this month) also like full sun, and they can take damp soil. Plant tuberous begonias in shade. Start montbretia from container stock.

☐ **VEGETABLES.** As soon as danger of frost has passed, sow beans and corn and set out seedlings of eggplant, peppers, and tomatoes. Start cucumbers, melons, and squash from seed if you have a long, warm growing season; otherwise set out transplants.

MAINTENANCE

☐ **CONTROL APHIDS.** They colonize tender new growth. Knock them off with a jet of water from the hose whenever you see them. In extreme cases, use insecticidal soap.

☐ **CONTROL SLUGS.** Handpick them on nights after you've watered, or put out a pet-safe bait like iron phosphate. If you use a methaldehyde-based bait, put it where pets and birds can't get to it, since it can poison them.

☐ **FEED LAWNS.** Apply 1 pound of actual nitrogen per 1,000 square feet of turf early this month.

☐ **FERTILIZE PLANTS.** Dig slow-release or controlled-release organic fertilizer into the backfill of everything you plant this month. To feed existing plants, apply liquid fertilizer or a complete granular fertilizer over the root zones every month during active growth.

☐ **MAINTAIN SPRING BULBS.** When bloom fades on plants like daffodils, grape hyacinths, and tulips, fertilize lightly and keep watering until leaves start to die back. This helps the plant prepare for bloom next spring.

☐ **PRUNE SPRING-BLOOMING VINES, SHRUBS.** Immediately after bloom, prune azaleas, camellias, forsythias, lilacs, and rhododendrons for shape. This gives them time to produce buds this summer for next spring's bloom. ◆

WHAT TO DO IN YOUR GARDEN IN MAY

PLANNING

☐ **BULBS ON SALE.** To get the best prices, order your fall bulbs during preseason catalog bulb sales, starting now and lasting until mid-August. Look for Brent and Becky's Bulbs *(www.brentandbeckysbulbs.com or 877/661-2852)* and Park's Bulbs from Park Seed *(www.parkbulbs.com or 800/845-3369).*

☐ **GIFT FOR MOM.** A beautiful blooming plant can bring any mother joy long after Mother's Day has passed. Some choices include azalea, calla, hydrangea, miniature rose, moth orchid, Oriental lily, tulip, and 'Wonder Bells Blue' double campanula.

PLANTING

☐ **FLOWERS FOR CUTTING.** Long-blooming perennials provide a good source of cut flowers. Try alstroemeria, coreopsis, gaillardia, gloriosa daisy, lavender, *Limonium perezii,* Mexican sunflower, purple coneflower, scabiosa, Shasta daisy, and yarrow *(Achillea).*

☐ **JAPANESE MAPLES.** Specialty maple nurseries carry many common and unusual varieties. The following three Northern California nurseries are good sources: Marca Dickie Nursery, Boyes Hot Springs *(800/990-0364, open by appointment only);* Mountain Maples, Laytonville *(www.mountainmaples.com or 888/707-6522, open by appointment only; mail-order catalog free, ships Sep–May);* Wildwood Farm Nursery and Sculpture Garden, Kenwood *(888/833-4181).*

Sunset CLIMATE ZONES

- ☐ Mountain (1–2)
- ☐ Valley (7–9)
- ☐ Inland (14)
- ☐ Coastal (15–17)

☐ **PLANT FOR PERMANENCE.** Now is a good time to plant almost any perennial, shrub, tree, or vine (in *Sunset* climate zones 1 and 2, wait until after the last frost to set out tender plants). When shopping at the nursery, look for plants that have good leaf color (green leaves should be a deep green, not pale and yellowish) and attractive form. Check container bottoms to make sure roots aren't growing out of them (which may mean plants are rootbound). Plants should also be well watered.

☐ **VEGETABLES.** It's not too late to set out plants of cucumber, eggplant, peppers, tomatoes, and squash. For pumpkins by Halloween, sow seeds now. Try 'Cinderella's Carriage' from Renee's Garden *(seeds available at nurseries or online from www.reneesgarden.com)* or 2- to 3-inch-wide 'Jack Be Little' and ivory white 'Baby Boo' from Ornamental Edibles *(www.ornamentaledibles.com or 408/929-7333).*

☐ **WATERMELON.** Summer's favorite melon is healthier than you may think. USDA researchers found that it contains on average about 40 percent more lycopene (an antioxidant associated with reduced risk of certain cancers) than raw tomatoes. It's also fat free and contains vitamins A, B_6, C, and thiamin. The best indicator of a nutritious watermelon is red, ripe flesh. Seedless watermelons tend to contain more lycopene than seeded varieties. Though not specifically tested for lycopene content, two seedless varieties to try from Park Seed *(www.parkseed.com or 800/845-3369)* are 'Everglade' and 'Sweetheart'.

MAINTENANCE

☐ **AERATE LAWNS.** If your lawn gets a lot of use and has compacted soil, aerate it to help improve air and water movement to the roots. You can rent an aerator from an equipment supply store (look in the yellow pages under "Rental Service Stores & Yards"). Rake up the cores and topdress with mulch. If you haven't fertilized recently, apply a lawn fertilizer and water in well. ◆

WHAT TO DO IN YOUR GARDEN IN MAY

PLANTING

☐ **CULINARY HERBS.** Plant basil, chives, lemon grass, lovage, mint, oregano, parsley, rosemary, sage, sorrel, tarragon, thyme, and other edible herbs. A good source for unusual basils and other out-of-the-ordinary herbs is Herban Garden in Fallbrook *(800/407-5268)*.

☐ **SUBTROPICALS.** This is the best time to plant avocados, bananas, cherimoyas, citrus, mangos, and other tropical and subtropical fruits, if they are appropriate for your area. Subtropical ornamentals like bougainvillea, mandevilla, palms, and thunbergia can be planted now too.

☐ **SUMMER PERENNIALS.** Nurseries are well stocked with spring perennials now, but to prolong color in your garden, look for plants that will bloom into summer and beyond. Good unthirsty summer bloomers include aster, gaillardia, gaura, helianthus, lion's tail, penstemon, salvia, verbena, yarrow, and zauschneria.

☐ **VEGETABLES.** Set out heat lovers like cucumber, eggplant, melons, okra, peppers, tomatoes, and summer and winter squash. If you like growing pumpkins for Halloween, try 'Cinderella's Carriage' (also sold as 'Rouge d'Étampes'). Dark red-orange with deep, rounded lobes, it looks just like it sounds. Seeds from Renee's Garden are available at well-stocked nurseries or online from *www. reneesgarden.com*. In the low desert (zone 13), plant Jerusalem artichoke, okra, peppers, and sweet potatoes.

MAINTENANCE

☐ **CHECK IRRIGATION SYSTEMS.** Look for leaks, broken sprinkler heads, and clogged emitters, then fix any problems to avoid water waste.

☐ **FERTILIZE.** All plants will benefit from a feeding now. If you want to go organic, try this garden tea: Mix 1 tablespoon fish emulsion and ½ teaspoon seaweed or kelp in 1 gallon of water. Irrigate root zones and spray onto foliage every few weeks during the growing season. The recipe comes from the University of California Cooperative Extension Common Ground Garden Program in Los Angeles County.

☐ **RENEW MULCH.** Apply a fresh layer of mulch around trees, shrubs, and established perennials in order to keep roots cool, preserve soil moisture, and discourage weeds. While homemade compost is ideal, you can also use shredded bark or wood chips.

PEST & DISEASE CONTROL

☐ **CONTROL ANTS ON CITRUS.** First get rid of aphids (the ants are traveling up the tree trunks to feed on the honeydew secreted by the aphids); wash foliage with a forceful spray of water to knock them off. Apply Tanglefoot around the tree's trunk, following label instructions, to stop the ants from carrying the aphids back up the tree.

☐ **MANAGE ROSE PROBLEMS.** Aphids usually appear this month. To control them, strip them from plants by hand (wear thin disposable rubber gloves if you're squeamish), or dislodge them with a strong blast of water from a hose. Sawfly larvae, which can leave rose leaves so skeletonized they look like lace, show up around the same time. To discourage sawflies, spray foliage with neem oil or pyrethrum, including the undersides. Powdery mildew is the third rose problem that appears this month, especially along the coast. Control by spraying foliage with the following formula: 1 tablespoon baking soda plus 1 tablespoon summer oil to 1 gallon of water. ◆

WHAT TO DO IN YOUR GARDEN IN MAY

PLANTING

☐ **SUMMER COLOR. At lower elevations:** Plant drought- and heat-tolerant annuals such as amaranth, blackfoot daisy, *Centaurea rothrockii, Cosmos sulphureus,* creeping zinnia (*Sanvitalia procumbens*), desert marigold (*Baileya multiradiata*), *Gaillardia pulchella,* gazania (see item on page 123), globe amaranth (*Gomphrena*), *Ipomopsis aggregata* and *I. rubra,* lantana, *Nolana paradoxa,* portulaca, *Salvia coccinea* and *S. farinacea,* scaevola, *Silene armeria,* strawflower (*Helichrysum*), sunflower, tidytips (*Layia platyglossa*), *Verbena bonariensis,* and vinca (periwinkle). Wildseed Farms (*www.wildseedfarms.com* or *800/848-0078*) carries some of the more unusual annuals. **At higher elevations:** Start annuals indoors after May 1 for transplanting after June 1. Candidates include begonia, clarkia, cosmos, Iceland poppy, lobelia, nasturtium, painted tongue, pansy, petunia, schizanthus, snapdragon, and sweet William.

☐ **VEGETABLES.** In drought-impacted areas where permitted, consider planting less-thirsty alternative crops such as amaranth, New Zealand spinach, orach, Russian kale, and tepary beans.

☐ **WATER-WISE CONTAINER PLANTING.** Plant drought-tolerant annuals such as those listed at left. To boost the water-holding capacity of potting mix, add a soil polymer such as Hydrosorb (available from Territorial Seed Company, *www.territorialseed.com* or *541/942-9547*). Cover the soil surface with several inches of mulch.

Sunset
CLIMATE ZONES

☐ 1–3   ☐ 10–11

MAINTENANCE

☐ **CHANNEL RUNOFF FROM ROOF.** Install drain-spout extensions to direct runoff water from the roof to established trees or to low-lying areas of the garden. These devices are available from Gardener's Supply (*www.gardeners.com* or *800/427-3363*).

☐ **DIVIDE SPRING BULBS.** After the leaves turn brown, dig up crowded clumps of daffodils, tulips, and other spring bulbs and gently pull the bulbs apart. Before replanting, dig 2 inches of compost and a handful of complete fertilizer into the soil. The dormant bulbs need very little summer water.

☐ **GUARD AGAINST WILDFIRE.** In fire-prone areas, create a defensible zone around your house by removing dead vegetation and trimming back branches that overhang the roof. Clear dead leaves and pine needles from your roof and rain gutters. Store firewood away from structures.

☐ **KEEP HOUSEPLANTS INSIDE.** Normally, indoor plants appreciate spending the summer outside. But in drought-impacted communities, keep them inside this summer. They'll need less frequent watering, perhaps only once a week, than the daily drink they'd require outdoors. You can still take houseplants outside periodically for a short vacation; place them on a porch or patio sheltered from direct sun and strong wind.

☐ **LOW-TECH DRIP FOR TRANSPLANTS.** Recycle a 1-gallon plastic milk jug to create a constant water source for small transplants. Poke a hole in one corner of the jug with a pin, fill it with water, and place it where it will drip slowly onto the rootball of the plant.

☐ **WATER TREES, SHRUBS DEEPLY.** To help preserve valuable established trees and shrubs, water them deeply at least once a month from May through September. For more irrigation tips, see "10 Drought-Fighting Tactics" on page 150.

—M. T.

WHAT TO DO IN YOUR GARDEN IN MAY

PLANTING

☐ **HERBS.** Sow seeds or set out transplants of unthirsty herbs such as bee balm, lavender, marjoram, oregano, rosemary, sage, and thyme. Other herbs to plant now include epazote, lemon basil, and lemon grass.

☐ **LIVING FENCE.** Zones 10–13: For a drought-tolerant privacy screen, consider planting a border of ocotillo *(Fouquieria splendens).* Many nurseries sell 5-foot-wide panels of ocotillo branches that are wired together and ready to plant between support posts.

☐ **PALMS.** Zones 10–13: Among the species with low to moderate water requirements are Guadalupe palm *(Brahea edulis),* pindo palm *(Butia capitata),* Mexican blue palm *(Brahea armata),* and windmill palm *(Trachycarpus fortunei),* which is cold-hardy to 10°.

☐ **SALVIA BED.** The sage family is hard to beat for colorful flowers and aromatic foliage. Why not devote an entire bed to water-thrifty *Salvia* species and varieties? Plant them in groups with the tallest ones at the rear and the shorter ones up front. Rear: Cleveland sage *(S. clevelandii),* Mexican bush sage *(S. leucantha),* or purple sage *(S. leucophylla).* Middle: autumn sage *(S. greggii),* germander sage *(S. chamaedryoides),* or scarlet sage *(S. coccinea).* Front: golden sage *(S. officinalis* 'Aurea', also known as 'Icterina'), *S. officinalis* 'Purpuras-

Sunset
CLIMATE ZONES
☐ 1–3 ☐ 10–11 ☐ 12–13

cens', or *S. officinalis* 'Tricolor'. Shop for these plants at local nurseries or order most from Mountain Valley Growers *(www.mountainvalleygrowers. com or 559/338-2775).*

☐ **SUMMER COLOR.** Sow seeds or set out transplants of these water-wise color makers. Zones 1A–3B (Flagstaff, Santa Fe, Taos): Ageratum, blanket flower (see item on page 123), coreopsis, and gaillardia, after danger of frost has passed. Zones 10–13 (Albuquerque, Las Vegas, Phoenix, Tucson): Blanket flower, cosmos, flax (blue *Linum perenne* and scarlet *L. grandiflorum* 'Rubrum'), Mexican hat *(Ratibida columnifera),* portulaca, and purple coneflower. Seeds are available from Roswell Seed Company *(505/622-7701).*

☐ **VEGETABLES.** All zones: Sow seeds or set out transplants of cucumbers (Armenian or lemon types), melons (try 'Cassava', 'Sugarbaby', 'Winter Queen'), peppers ('Anaheim M', 'De Arbol', 'Española Improved'), squash ('Delicata' or dark green zuc-

chini), and tomatillos. Seeds of all these are available from Plants of the Southwest *(www.plantsofthesouthwest. com or 800/788-7333).*

MAINTENANCE

☐ **CHECK GRAPEVINES.** Watch for inch-long, yellow-and-black larvae of grapeleaf skeletonizers; handpick any you find.

☐ **FEED CITRUS, ROSES.** After a deep watering, feed citrus trees with high-nitrogen fertilizer; give roses a balanced fertilizer (6-6-6, for example).

☐ **WATER WISELY.** Whenever you irrigate, make every drop of water count. See "10 Drought-Fighting Tactics" on page 150. —*K. N.*

Secrets behind a garden wall

Clever growing tricks from an Idaho gardener

By Suzanne Touchette Kelso • Photographs by Norm Plate

On the west side of Alex and Gina Macdonald's contemporary log home in Ketchum, Idaho, a dry-stacked stone wall surrounds the garden. The artfully arranged stones form a picturesque and utilitarian barrier, which allows the Macdonalds to grow a bountiful array of flowers and vegetables that would otherwise be devoured by passing deer and elk. The wall also creates a warmer microclimate, extending the too-short growing season here at an elevation of 6,500 feet.

The inspiration for the walled garden came during a trip the Macdonalds took to Provence. In France, they saw ancient stone walls surrounding virtually every garden.

Back home in Ketchum, Gina—a veteran gardener, farmer, and rancher—worked with Webb Landscape to design walls that would be sturdy enough to keep out elk and withstand a heavy snow load in winter. Using buff-colored Utah sandstone, they built 7-foot-tall walls that taper from 4 feet wide at the base to 2 feet wide at the top.

Besides barring unwanted wildlife from the expansive garden, the walls block the cold wind, and the stone retains solar heat that radiates into the garden. The longest walls, which face west and south,

From shrub roses like 'What A Peach' (left) to strawberries (bottom), the garden blends ornamentals and edibles. The metal trellis holds pots of geraniums and honeysuckle.

receive maximum solar exposure. Consequently, the garden stays about 10° warmer than the ambient air temperature. Gina figures that the wall extends Ketchum's average 75-day growing season by at least 21 days.

To squeeze even more abundance out of the short summer, Gina employs other devices. Early in the season or whenever temperatures dip, she shields vegetables with row covers or plastic sheeting suspended over frames made of metal or PVC pipe. She grows warmth-loving artichokes, basil, and tomatoes in a 120-square-foot plastic greenhouse.

In addition to edibles, Gina grows 30 kinds of perennials. Near the house, which bounds one side of the garden, she grows towering delphiniums and hollyhocks for their strong vertical interest. Nearby, peonies yield soft pink blossoms that she harvests for indoor arrangements. Gina likes carnations and sweet Williams for their spicy fragrance and season-long color. Indestructible bearded irises are scattered throughout the garden. She keeps lavenders and lemon trees in pots, which she moves indoors for

Pots of roses and lavender surround the patio. Creeping thyme fills the cracks between flagstones.

Gina's favorite plants

FLOWERS
Bearded iris 'Sugar Blues'
Bee balm 'Scorpio'
Columbine McKana Giants
Delphinium Magic Fountains Mix
Dianthus 'Zing Rose'
Foxglove 'Apricot'
Gaillardia x *grandiflora* 'Portola Giants'
Hollyhock 'Chater's Double'
Lavender 'Provence'
Peony 'Raspberry Sundae'
Purple coneflower 'Magnus'
Rudbeckia hirta Rustic Colors Mix
Scabiosa atropurpurea Imperial Giants Mix
Shasta daisy 'Christine Hagemann'
Sweet William 'Magic Cherry'

VEGETABLES
Asparagus 'Jersey Giant'
Broccoli 'Bonanza'
Carrot 'Royal Chantenay'
Green bean 'Vernandon'
Lettuce Napa Valley Lettuce Mix
Pea 'Super Sugar Snap'
Potatoes 'All Blue', 'Kerr's Pink', 'Peruvian Purple', 'Yukon Gold'
Spinach 'Bloomsdale Longstanding'
Strawberry 'Tristar'
Tomatoes 'Brandywine', 'Early Girl', 'Super Sweet 100'

SOURCES
Flowers: Many of the plants on Gina's list are sold by White Flower Farm *(www. whiteflowerfarm.com or 800/ 503-9624)* and Wayside Gardens *(www.waysidegardens. com or 800/845-1124),* which also sells Canadian Explorer series roses.

Vegetables: Seeds for many of the varieties mentioned are available from W. Atlee Burpee & Co. *(www.burpee.com or 800/888-1447)* and Shepherd's Garden Seeds *(www. shepherdseeds.com or 800/503-9624),* which also offers an assortment of seed potatoes.

Row covers: These are available from Charley's Greenhouse *(www. charleysgreenhouse.com or 800/322-4707)* and Gardener's Supply Company *(www.gardeners.com or 800/863-1700).*

Outside the wall, a willow trellis topped with fabric softener sheets keeps deer and elk from eating irises. Petunias in window boxes add color.

winter. She plants tender climbing vines such as wisteria and sweet peas so they can cling to the warm stone walls. As for roses, Gina favors cold-hardy, repeat-blooming varieties from the Canadian Explorer series, including 'William Baffin', 'Martin Frobisher', and 'Jens Munk'.

Each spring, Gina broadcasts granular fertilizer over the flower beds. Starting in June, she scatters dry fishmeal over the entire garden once a month. In early and midsummer, she spreads a 1- to 2-inch layer of compost around vegetable plants. In autumn she cuts back perennials and wraps roses with insulated shrub cloth. Then she covers the entire garden with a mulch of fine bark mixed with well-rotted steer manure, applying 1 to 2 inches over vegetable beds and 3 to 5 inches over perennials. The manure breaks down over winter and is ready to provide gentle nourishment to crops and flowers when the growing season begins.

WALL DESIGN: Webb Landscape, Ketchum, ID *(www.webbland.com or 208/726-4927)*

Gina's secrets for success

Jump-start veggies. Plastic sheeting over PVC frames gives extra warmth to lettuce (front) and broccoli (rear) in chilly weather.

Some like it hot. Tender crops like tomatoes and basil thrive in the warmer air and soil inside the greenhouse.

No bare ground. Closely spaced plants keep out weeds. Here, irises and gladiolus are underplanted with Johnny-jump-ups and marigolds.

More garden tips

• **Go organic.** Amend soil yearly with compost and manure.

• **Let nature work.** Plant self-sowing flowers like columbine and cosmos that scatter their own seed.

• **Befriend birds.** Set out feeders and water-filled containers to invite birds to dine on insect pests.

• **Deadhead.** Remove faded flowers to stimulate repeat bloom. ◆

In Woodlake, good techniques result in great harvests. Climbing crops wind up trellises like the one pictured above; the trellis was made by tying sturdy string in horizontal rows between end posts, then vertically lacing the rows together. At right: 'Floristan' sunflower and 'Zebra' eggplant.

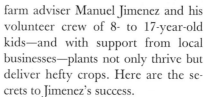

Summer school

How to raise the tastiest vegetables where temperatures soar

By Lance Walheim • Photographs by Norm Plate

Growing vegetables in hot summer climates isn't easy, especially where weeds flourish and bugs are voracious. But at Bravo Lake Botanical Gardens, a 13-acre community garden in the Woodlake area of California's Central Valley, plots filled with flowers and vegetables are beautiful and productive. Thanks to careful planning, planting, and tending by garden founder and University of California Cooperative Extension farm adviser Manuel Jimenez and his volunteer crew of 8- to 17-year-old kids—and with support from local businesses—plants not only thrive but deliver hefty crops. Here are the secrets to Jimenez's success.

• **Choose the right variety.** Of the thousands of vegetables grown in the garden, the ones listed on the facing page are Jimenez's warm-weather favorites.

• **Control weeds.** A couple of weeks before planting, sprinkle empty beds with water to germinate weed seeds, then lightly rake out any sprouts that emerge.

• **Amend the soil.** Before planting, mix in a balanced (16-16-16) fertilizer.

• **Build raised beds.** Form the soil into 4-inch-high by 20-inch-wide raised beds; leave 12 inches between rows.

• **Mulch with black plastic.** Just before planting, lay drip lines or soaker hoses, then cover beds with black plastic mulch. Cut Xs through the plastic near *(Continued on page 140)*

Jimenez removes a row cover from maturing squash plants to allow pollination. Late-summer harvest includes 'Sunnyside' cabbage, top left, and 'Calsweet' watermelon and 'Golden Crown' melon, left.

Hot-weather varieties

Letters adjacent to vegetable names refer to sources listed below.

BUSH BEANS. 'Xera' **(J)** is compact and consistently produces small, fine-flavored beans.

CUCUMBERS. 'Tasty Green Hybrid' **(B)** produces beautiful, flavorful fruits.

EGGPLANTS. 'Machiaw' **(J)**, 'Neon' **(J)**, and 'Zebra' **(J)** are gorgeous, productive, and tasty.

MELONS. 'Savor' **(J)**, a French Charentais melon, and 'Golden Crown' **(W)** have exceptional flavor. 'Calsweet' **(L)** watermelon is a reliable producer.

PEPPERS. Medium-hot 'Cherry Bomb' **(T)** and sweet 'Biscayne' **(T)** are tasty and ornamental.

TOMATOES. For sweet flavor, choose 'Sun Gold' **(J, T)** and 'Super Sweet 100' **(B)** cherry tomatoes; 'Ace 55' **(T)** and 'Quick Pick' **(T)** full-size red varieties; 'Carolina Gold' **(S)** and 'Lemon Boy' **(T)** yellow and orange tomatoes; and heirlooms 'Evergreen' **(T)** and 'Brandywine' **(T).**

Seed sources:
(B) W. Atlee Burpee & Co.
www.burpee.com or (800) 888-1447.

(J) Johnny's Selected Seeds
www.johnnyseeds.com
or (207) 437-4301.
(L) Lockhart Seeds
(209) 466-4401.
(S) Stokes Seeds
www.stokeseeds.com or (800) 396-9238.
(T) Tomato Growers Supply Company
www.tomatogrowers.com
or (888) 478-7333.
(W) West Coast Seeds
www.westcoastseeds.com or (604) 952-8820.

Community spirit lives

"People feel as good as their surroundings," says garden founder Jimenez (far right). "Planting beautiful gardens makes everyone feel better." That's why Jimenez started planting flowers and vegetables around Woodlake 11 years ago. Bravo Lake Botanical Gardens is one of the newest.

During some years, 1,000 varieties of flowers and vegetables grow in up to five locations around town. The kids— volunteers from Jimenez's neighborhood and through word of mouth—raise transplants in green-houses, care for the gardens, and sell vegetables to help pay for equipment and supplies. "The gardens are about more than making Woodlake look better," Jimenez says. "The kids get tremendous satisfaction and pride in growing plants and producing food."

each nozzle, then plant through the holes. Set smaller vegetable crops, such as bush beans, on both sides of a single drip line.

· **Group plants by water needs.** Plant melons, cucumbers, and other frequent water-users along one drip line or soaker hose; irrigate regularly. Put tomatoes, which need deep, infrequent irrigation once fruit starts to ripen, on a separate line.

· **Trellis plants.** Build trellises of 1- by 1-inch wood posts—evenly spaced down the row and connected with string—for vining vegetables such as cucumbers and pole beans. Trellises can also be used to support upright plants like tomatoes and eggplants.

· **Use row covers.** To keep insects away from plants, cover insect-free seedlings with floating row covers. Secure each cover by burying its edges in soil. Once plants are mature, remove the cover to allow pollination and fruit set.

· **Fertilize.** Six to eight weeks after planting, pull weeds, then apply another dose of fertilizer to give vegetables a boost so they can compete with—and beat—weeds.

· **Root out pests.** Regularly inspect older leaves for signs of whitefly eggs or pupae. If you find damage, cut off, bag, and discard infested leaves. Immediately pull out and throw away any bean plants infested with spider mites. ◆

Make more hydrangeas

How to create new plants by taking cuttings

By Jim McCausland
Photographs by Robin Cushman

'Blauer Prinz' hydrangea produces blue to purplish blooms when growing in acid soils and pink flowers in neutral to alkaline soils.

Nearly every month of the year, Fred and Kit Fulton successfully multiply garden hydrangea *(H. macrophylla)* varieties at Alsea River Gardens *(541/563-5599)*, the hydrangea cut-flower operation they own in Waldport, Oregon. "We're pruning and thinning constantly," explains Fred, which means they always have cutting material for new plants.

The Fultons began the business by taking cuttings from healthy-looking hydrangeas around town. They selected plants with thick, sturdy leaves and large, clean (unspotted) blooms.

Though the Fultons occasionally make new plants by pushing hydrangea sticks into garden soil, they get better results when they are a bit more scientific about it and start cuttings in small pots using rooting hormone.

Here we show their simple step-by-step process. Spring through early summer—while new growth is at the softwood stage—is one of the best times to make new plants. Start with a variety you really like, since all of its offspring will be identical. Cuttings take about a month to root. New plants occasionally produce a few flowers the first summer after rooting. By the third summer, they should be blooming heavily.

Hydrangea step-by-step

TIME: 30 minutes

MATERIALS
- **4-inch pots** or other containers
- Potting soil
- Sharp pruning shears
- Rooting hormone
- Pencil

DIRECTIONS

1. Fill pots with soil. Take cuttings early in the morning. Choose nonflowering, vigorous shoots. Make tip cuttings 6 to 8 inches long, snipping each one just above a set of leaves. Remove all but the top two sets of leaves on each cutting.

2. Cut the remaining leaves in half, crosswise. Trim the stems off to within $\frac{1}{2}$ inch of the lowest leaf node. Dip the cut ends in rooting hormone.

3. Poke a 2-inch-deep hole in the center of the soil with a pencil. Set the stem in the hole and cover with soil. Water thoroughly after planting and then again whenever the top $\frac{1}{2}$ inch of soil is almost dry. Set the pots in a shady location that is protected from wind. When new growth appears, move into filtered light.

In four weeks, check for root formation: if stems resist when gently tugged, roots are developing. When cuttings are well rooted, transplant into larger containers or directly into garden beds. ◆

Spring-summer. Fanlike leaves of Japanese aralia anchor this grouping of burgundy coleus, bronze *Ipomoea* 'Sweet Dreams Bronze', pink Hiemalis (Rieger) begonias, and chartreuse *Lamium* 'Aureum' growing in a 21- by 30-inch ceramic glazed pot.

Fall-winter. The warm-season arrangement lasts until late fall, when it's replaced with pale yellow *Primula obconica,* white cyclamen, *Liriope spicata* 'Silver Dragon', and bacopa (for mild climates only). Fall-planted freesias pop up in late winter.

Containers for all seasons

Start with an evergreen shrub, then add seasonal flowers

By Lauren Bonar Swezey • Photographs by Thomas J. Story

Container plantings that look good all year long are floral designer Jean Manocchio's specialty. Manocchio creates many such plantings every year for her clients at Belli Fiori in Redwood City, California, so she has developed strategies for simple but spectacular living bouquets that need sprucing up just twice a year.

She starts by anchoring the arrangement with a single plant that can live year to year and look attractive in every season—a weeping blue Atlas cedar, Japanese aralia, or sago palm, for instance.

To accommodate the rootball (such plants are typically sold in 1- to 5-gallon pots), Manocchio sets it in a container partially filled with potting soil. She then builds a composition around it using annuals, bulbs, ground covers, or perennials.

Some arrangements feature foliage plants with interesting textures and forms; adding a few bulbs or annuals for a spot of color every spring and fall is usually all that's needed. For added drama, Manocchio sometimes also packs in colorful, long-blooming plants, then replaces them at the season's end.

Choose an anchor

Select your anchor plant first. Choose one that's suitable for the pot's style, location, and exposure.

- Citrus
- Feather reed grass
- Japanese aralia (*Fatsia japonica*)
- Lily-of-the-valley shrub (*Pieris japonica*)
- New Zealand flax (*Phormium tenax*)
- Princess flower (*Tibouchina urvilleana*)
- Sago palm (*Cycas revoluta*)
- Silver spear (*Astelia nervosa chathamica*)
- Weeping blue Atlas cedar (*Cedrus atlantica* 'Glauca Pendula')

Spring-summer. Sago palm anchors this composition in a 22- by 24-inch glazed urn. Below it are 'Orange Profusion' zinnias, yellow *Pachystachys lutea,* and trailing variegated vinca.

Steps to an all-year show

To create your own long-lasting living bouquet, follow Manocchio's guidelines:

Determine the site. Locate the pot where it will be most visible—by the front door, on a patio, or in view of a window.

Select a container. It should be in scale with its surroundings (a large pot can overwhelm a small entryway), and in a style and color that go with your house's architecture. Be sure to choose one that will look attractive with the existing plants that grow nearby. Make sure it has drain holes.

Design the planting. Colors that match the flowers and foliage already growing in your garden have a unifying effect; contrasting or complementary colors create a visual diversion. If the container will be viewed from indoors, you may prefer to take color cues from your home's interior. Also consider style. Do you want a casual planting or a sculptural one? Bold or lacy? Vertical or horizontal? Tall or short? Choose plants accordingly; group them on a cart at the nursery to see how they'll look together.

Fall-winter. Cool-season bloomers replace summer flowers. They include English primrose and violas. *Ficus pumila* replaced the vinca, which tends to get shaggy in winter.

Container care

Potting mix. Use a high-quality mix (price is a good indicator); blend in a controlled-release fertilizer according to package directions. Where water supplies are limited, consider adding soil polymers (such as Broadleaf P4) to the mix. These tiny granules absorb water that would otherwise drain away. They release moisture to the roots longer than potting mix alone, allowing more time between waterings. (Follow package directions carefully; many polymers can turn the soil too soggy for most plants.)

Watering. Be diligent about irrigation, especially for plants that need lots of water to thrive. Manocchio uses a drip system that is connected to an automatic controller, but hand-watering also works.

Feeding. For an extra boost during the growing season, give plants a shot of water-soluble fertilizer, diluted according to directions.

Refreshing the planting. When flowers and foliage start to fade on filler plants such as annuals and bulbs, replace the plants, adding fresh potting mix and controlled-release fertilizer before replanting. ◆

Choose fillers

Make sure they grow shorter than the anchor plant, share its cultural requirements, and harmonize with its colors and textures. New Zealand flax with pink-toned leaves, for example, blends well with pink flowers. Add trailers such as bacopa and vinca to soften the pot's edge.

Spring fillers: In addition to the many annuals, long-blooming perennials, and bulbs (particularly tuberous begonias and dahlias) sold in bloom at nurseries, many houseplants make lovely additions to container plantings once the weather has warmed.

Fall fillers: In mild climates, many plants suitable for containers are sold in bloom in fall, including chrysanthemums and violas. In colder climates, use hardy foliage plants with interesting color and texture, such as ornamental cabbage and kale, and underplant them with spring-blooming bulbs.

Tree-friendly remodeling

A guide to protecting valuable trees from construction damage

By Kathleen N. Brenzel and Julie Chai • Illustrations by Arthur Mount

During a remodel, bad things can and often do happen to trees. Among the mishaps we've observed recently in neighborhoods around the West: A lovely, large Japanese maple, dug up during the heat of summer, left for a month atop the soil with its rootball exposed, then planted just a few feet from a new foundation. Young oaks, also dug up during summer, replanted next to a sidewalk; they died by fall. The tops of tall liquidambars lopped off to make way for an expanded roof line. Magnolia branches, broken by trucks, left hanging from stubs. And root zones cut in half to dig basements or trenches for computer cables.

Such damage is no surprise: When a 1950s ranch house is razed and replaced with a mini-mansion that fills much of a suburban lot, or a house is expanded outward, trees are often in the way. Designing a house addition to nudge or hug a large tree is not the answer; this solution does not allow for the tree's future growth, or for its movement during strong winds.

The time to protect mature trees on your property—if you decide to save them—is during the planning stage, *before* construction starts. Otherwise, you could end up paying many thou-

TROUBLE SPOTS

The canopy

Broken branches. Large branch stubs, left by breakage or careless pruning, seldom heal over. **Topping.** Pruning back the topmost, terminal branches to make way for roof overhangs cuts back a tree's food-making potential.

The trunk

Injuries. Heavy equipment and machinery can gouge the trunk, exposing the tree to disease and insect pests.

The roots

Most roots are within the top 24 inches of soil, and they can extend far beyond the drip line. They're susceptible to damage from the causes shown below.

drip line

PROTECTIVE MEASURES

The canopy

• If low branches need removal to make way for heavy equipment, hire an arborist to do it.
• Instead of topping, cut selected branches back to lower laterals.

The trunk, branches

• If you need to work close to the trunk, prop hay bales against it to protect the bark.
• Use rope to tie thinner, flexible branches up and out of the way of trucks and machinery.

The roots

• Put a fence around the tree as far outside the drip line as possible.
• Lay plastic tarps over the ground out to the drip line to keep out soil contaminants.

LEADING CAUSES OF ROOT DAMAGE

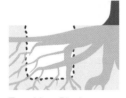    

Trenching. Digging trenches for utilities too close to the trunk can seriously injure or sever tree roots.

Solid paving. Nonporous paving under the canopy can prevent water and air from reaching roots.

Grade change. As little as a couple of inches of fill dirt, if it does not have good drainage, can smother roots.

Soil contamination. Spilling wet concrete, paint, and solvents within the root zone can poison the tree.

Compaction. Heavy equipment or materials such as pallets of pavers can squash a tree's shallow surface roots.

sands of dollars to replace trees that are injured or killed.

There are a number of steps you can take before and during a remodel to protect your trees. Following them will pay off in the long run; indeed, trees are your landscape's most valuable assets—adding beauty and cooling shade around your house.

Crucial tree questions: save, relocate, or remove?

Before finalizing house expansion plans that may involve areas near established trees, consult an arborist certified by the International Society of Arboriculture (ISA). The arborist can evaluate the tree's health, age, present and future size, and any hazards it may pose. If the tree is healthy and in a strategic location such as a front yard, saving it may be worth the effort. If the tree is in the way of proposed construction, ask whether it should be removed, or, if it's young and healthy, if it can be moved. Also ask the arborist how far any solid paving should be from the tree's trunk to avoid suffocating the roots.

For a large, established tree such as an oak or redwood that will remain in its present location, avoid building within its root zone. "If you stay outside the canopy, we can almost assure the tree's survival," says arborist Jim Clark of HortScience in Pleasanton, California. As a guideline, allow at least 1 foot of space between the trunk and the structure for every inch of trunk diameter measured at 54 inches above soil level.

To further protect roots, learn where any new underground lines will go, and if possible, reroute them away from trees. If it's not possible for contractors to work outside the root zone, up to one-third of a healthy tree's roots can be removed without severely harming the tree.

If you decide to remove a big tree, make sure you are allowed to. Without prior approval, some communities prohibit the removal of trees whose trunk caliper (diameter) is more than a certain number of inches.

Before breaking ground

It's a good idea to have the arborist consult with your contractor to find out exactly where the construction will take place and how to coordinate the building process with the tree's preservation. That way, the arborist can perform any pruning needed to allow clearance for moving heavy equipment onto the site.

Hang signs or otherwise prominently mark the trees to be saved so there's less chance of them being seriously injured by trucks or heavy equipment.

If a tree is to be relocated, make sure the new site has well-drained soil, proper light exposure (whether sun or shade), and enough room to accommodate future growth of roots, canopy, and trunk. Ideally, the tree should be moved when it's dormant, before buds break, then planted so that the rootball sits 1 to 2 inches above its previous grade level.

Water the transplanted tree deeply, making sure that moisture penetrates the original rootball, not just the soil around it. Allow a hose to trickle slowly and move it periodically over several hours. Or lay a soaker hose on the soil around the tree between its trunk and the drip line.

Any trees to be removed should be cut down and their stumps ground up (not pulled out) to avoid injuring roots of nearby trees.

During the remodel

"Half of the tree is below ground, so it's really important to [protect] the root system," says Robert Tate, executive director of ISA's Western Chapter. When roots are compacted by heavy equipment or severed by trenching, chances are you won't see the damage immediately. But injured roots are often unable to take up water, air, or nutrients, resulting in the decline and eventual death of the tree, even years later. Disease organisms or pest infestations that enter unhealed wounds can also, in time, kill the tree.

To ensure that the tree comes through the remodel with its health intact, protect its roots, trunk, and canopy as indicated to the right of the illustration on the facing page. If heavy equipment must be moved over the root zone, cover the area from the trunk out to the drip line with a 12-inch-thick layer of wood chips, then top the mulch with interlocking sheet-metal plates or plywood sheets to minimize soil compaction.

Make sure your contractor knows your wishes regarding your trees and will convey them to workers; the best way to do that is to spell them out in the remodeling contract. ◆

The value of trees

It's hard to put a price on beauty, but property values of homes whose landscapes include mature trees are 5 to 20 percent higher than those without them.

Located where they'll shade windows from hot afternoon sun, mature trees can lower cooling costs by 10 to 40 percent. One such tree can cool a house as well as five average room air conditioners running 12 hours a day. Trees planted to block winter wind can reduce heating bills by 10 to 50 percent.

For more information

• Colorado State University Cooperative Extension. *See "Protecting Trees During Construction" at www.ext.colostate.edu/ pubs/garden/07420.html*

• HortScience, a horticultural consulting firm in Pleasanton, California. *(925) 484-0211*

• The International Society of Arboriculture. *www. isa-arbor.com or (217) 355-9411*

• PlantAmnesty, a Seattle-based group, promotes respect for trees and encourages proper pruning practices. *www. plantamnesty.org or (206) 783-9813*

'Fairy Wings' lavender, shown here in ceramic pots, produces an abundant show of delicate lilac-colored flowers.

Compact lavenders

Enjoy their fragrant, easy grace in pots or as border edgings

By Lauren Bonar Swezey
Photographs by Thomas J. Story

What's not to love about lavender? Flowers of many varieties have a fragrance so heady that they're used to make potpourri, soap, and perfume; some are also used in cooking. Most lavenders dry beautifully for bouquets and attract bees and butterflies. There's a species for just about every region, from the coast to inland valleys, mountains, and deserts.

Dwarf lavenders, which stay under 2 feet tall (see list at right), are compact alternatives to the varieties that can grow to 4 feet or taller. They're particularly suitable for small beds, border edgings, even containers. Best of all, they're simply smaller lavenders with all of the same great qualities as their parents.

When you shop, keep in mind that 'Hidcote' and 'Munstead', two well-known compact varieties, are often grown commercially from seed rather than cuttings; that means their growth habit and flower color will vary. Always buy these varieties in bloom (or from a nursery that sells only cutting-grown plants) so you know what color you're getting.

12 small lavenders

Of the many dwarf lavenders we grew in *Sunset's* test garden, the ones mentioned here are some of our favorites. Heights listed include foliage and flowers; when not in bloom, plants range from 8 to 14 inches tall.

Many lavenders are sold under more than one name, which we note in parentheses.

English

Lavandula angustifolia. Most dwarf types are varieties of English lavender, all with wonderfully fragrant flowers. Foliage is gray-green unless noted. All grow in *Sunset* climate zones 2–24 from the *Western Garden Book*.

'Compacta'. Light purple flowers. Very compact growth to 1½ feet tall.

'Hidcote' (sometimes sold as 'Hidcote Blue'). One of the darkest purple flowers of any lavender; short stems. Grows 1½ to 2 feet tall. Look for cutting-grown plants.

'Irene Doyle' ('Two Seasons Lavender'). Light purple flowers. Medium green to gray-green foliage. Grows 1½ to 2 feet tall.

'Loddon Blue'. Dark violet-purple blooms. Grows 1½ to 2 feet tall.

'Martha Roderick'. Light purple flowers. Gray foliage. Grows 1½ to 2 feet tall.

'Nana Alba' ('Dwarf White', 'Baby White'). White flowers. Very compact growth to just 1 foot tall.

'Rosea' ('Jean Davis'). White to pink buds, pale lilac-pink flowers. Light green foliage. Grows 1½ to 2 feet tall.

'Sarah'. Purple flowers. Medium green to gray-green foliage. Grows to 1½ feet tall.

'Silver Frost'. Deep lavender-blue flowers. Silvery white foliage. Grows to 15 inches tall. A hybrid of woolly lavender and English lavender.

Spanish

L. stoechas. Blocky flower heads produce showy top bracts that look like rabbit ears or wings. Spanish lavenders bloom from spring into summer and will usually repeat bloom if flowers are sheared off after they fade. Flowers have a piney lavender scent. Foliage is gray-green. Zones 4–24.

'Dwarf'. Rosy purple flowers. Grows to 1½ feet tall.

'Fairy Wings'. Particularly long lilac-pink bracts. Grows to 1½ feet tall.

'Ron Lutsko's Dwarf'. Medium purple flowers on short bloom stalks. Very compact growth from 1 to 1½ feet tall.

Lavenders by mail

If you can't find the varieties you want at your local nursery, try these mail-order sources.
Dutch Mill Herb Farm, *6640 N.W. Marsh Rd., Forest Grove, OR 97116; (503) 357-0924.*
Goodwin Creek Gardens, *Box 83, Williams, OR 97544; www.goodwincreekgardens.com or (800) 846-7359.* ◆

Purple 'Compacta' with pale pink 'Rosea'.

Lavender basics

PLANTING. Choose a spot in full sun with well-drained soil, or plant in raised beds or containers. Keep soil off the crowns (base) of the plant. In hot climates that experience humidity in summer (most notably the Southwest during the monsoon season), plant in an area that gets good air circulation and avoid crowding.

WATERING. Young plants need regular watering to keep the soil moist. Once plants are established, slowly cut back on frequency so the top 2 inches of soil go fairly dry between waterings.

FERTILIZING. A light application of organic fertilizer in spring should be sufficient (plants are not heavy feeders).

PRUNING. To keep plants bushy, cut off spent flowers and about one-third of the foliage after bloom.

Purple flower spikes of *Salvia* 'Mainacht' stand 2 to 2½ feet tall in rear and front gardens (below).

High impact

Colorful low-water plants thrive in these rock gardens

By Marcia Tatroe • Photographs by Paul Bousquet

From the Cascades and the Sierra to the Rockies, the West is richly supplied with mountains. It's only natural, then, that rock gardens should fit so well into our landscapes. Designer Alison Peck takes rock-gardening style to new heights at this home on a mesa overlooking Boulder, Colorado. But Peck's design isn't merely stylish, it's sensible, making use of low-water plants.

Peck replaced a thirsty bluegrass lawn with a water-wise landscape that complements views across the Continental Divide.

At the front of the house, a sculptural rock garden evokes the craggy mountain peaks of the Divide. Peck used locally quarried andesite, a brittle stone that fractures into sharp, angular shapes and has a sparkly surface. Colorful plants are nestled in pockets among the stones. In early summer, the flower spikes of blue *Salvia* x *sylvestris* 'Mainacht' and rosy *Veronica spicata* 'Red Fox' stand tall against the rocks, while the soft pink blossoms of *Dianthus nardiformis* and hot pink daisies of ice plant hunker down against the stone.

In the rear, another rock garden frames a red sandstone patio. Since plants here are exposed to the full force of sun and wind, Peck used perennials she calls the "toughest of the tough"—magenta wine cups, *S*. 'Mainacht', and white evening primrose.

The new plantings require very little maintenance and are watered by drip irrigation. The rest of the property is planted with native grasses, including blue grama and buffalo grass. For her water-conscious design, Peck received a Xeriscape merit award from the Excellence in Landscape competition sponsored by the Associated Landscape Contractors of Colorado. ◆

Peck's plant palette

Dianthus nardiformis. From the *Sunset Western Garden Book,* climate zones A2, A3, 1–24.

Ice plant *(Delosperma cooperi).* Zones 2–24.

Salvia x *sylvestris* 'Mainacht'. Zones 2–10, 14–24.

Veronica spicata 'Red Fox'. Zones A2, A3, 1–9, 14–21.

White evening primrose *(Oenothera caespitosa).* Zones 1–3, 7–14, 18–21.

Wine cups *(Callirhoe involucrata).* Zones 1–3, 7–14, 18–24.

Tips from the Dunn Gardens to yours

Curators Charles Price and Glenn Withey explain how to make your garden look like a great estate

By Steven R. Lorton

This year, Seattle celebrates the centennial of its commission of Frederick Law Olmsted and his stepbrother, John Charles Olmsted, who together designed more than 37 parks and gardens in the Emerald City. Though not the first or the most noted of the Olmsteds' designs, the E. B. Dunn Historic Gardens is, from a gardening standpoint, perhaps the most interesting. That's because its curators, Charles Price and Glenn Withey, are not only among the most noted gardeners and plantsmen in the country—they're best known for their contribution to the famous mixed border at the Bellevue Botanical Garden—but also excellent teachers for the rest of us.

"When it comes to developing ideas, be an intellectual omnivore and a shameless pirate," says Price. "Read books and periodicals, visit other people's gardens, walk around neighborhoods. Most important, immerse yourself in nature."

To celebrate the continuing legacy of the Olmsteds, we went to the Dunn Gardens to talk to Price and Withey. We asked them what lessons this venerable 88-year-old garden holds for the average homeowner.

Celebrate the Olmsted legacy

When John Charles Olmsted visited Seattle in May 1903, he spoke enthusiastically about what he called "the natural advantages for parks." In that same year, the Olmsted brothers were commissioned by the then-small, young, and remote Seattle to produce a complete landscape design for the city. These days, Seattle is known as the Emerald City, and the Olmsteds get the credit for that. Hilary Bramwell of the Seattle Parks Foundation says, "The Olmsteds set the standard for park and green-space development and preservation that we still actively pursue today."

From May 1 through 4, the city will host the National Association of Olmsted Parks Conference. Throughout the year, join in Olmsted-related activities, from volunteer work parties to docent-led walks through various Olmsted parks (10–12 on the third Saturday of every month). *For centennial information, visit www.seattle. gov/friendsofolmstedparks or call (206) 332-9915. For walking tour information, call (206) 332-9900 or visit www.seattleparksfoundation.org*

Visiting the garden

Dunn Gardens is in Seattle's Broadview District. To visit, sign up for a guided tour (2 P.M. Thu, 10 A.M. and 2 P.M. Fri, and 10 A.M. Sat; $10). *Tour reservations, directions, and information on what's in bloom: www. dunngardens.org or (206) 362-0933.*

Shade ▲

The garden's tall trees allow only pockets of sun. Price and Withey have found that many plants can be shade tolerant. "Be as aggressive in your search for shade lovers as you are for plants that take full sun," Price says.

Plant a tree ▲

"If you are lucky enough to have an old [tree] in a garden you acquire, take good care of it," Price says. "Spend the money to have it properly pruned, increasing the health of the tree and bringing more light into the garden. If your garden does not have great trees, plant small ones. You'll enjoy watching them grow, and you'll be giving the wonderful gift of a great old tree to your grandchildren."

Mass bulbs to make a statement ▲

"Buy lots of bulbs of the same variety and plant them in grand sweeps," Withey advises. "A mass of bulbs is a great swath of color. Dotted here and there, they lose their impact."

◄ Flowers are nice, foliage is essential

"Form, color, and texture are as vivid and varied in foliage as they are in flowers," says Withey. "Flowers come and go. Foliage lasts longer."

Cluster containers ▲

"We like the informal look of clustered containers," says Price. "It gives us the freedom to showcase certain plants, rearrange the groupings for various effects, and completely change the look when we want. It's movable gardening." ◆

10 drought-fighting tactics

How to make every drop of water count during dry times

By Dick Bushnell and Jim McCausland

As the severe drought persists across much of the Intermountain West, gardeners here are facing another dry growing season. Last year, some communities in Arizona, Colorado, and New Mexico asked residents to voluntarily reduce water use, while others issued mandatory restrictions on outdoor watering.

Now, as summer approaches, many reservoirs are still less than half full. To conserve scarce supplies, water managers will probably have to implement restrictions again. In severely impacted communities, one of two scenarios is likely to prevail. In the less drastic scenario, lawn watering would be restricted to two days a week, if water supplies allow. In the worst case, lawn watering would be banned and only trees and shrubs could be watered. In any case, there are water-saving practices you can adopt to maintain your existing plants.

1 Assess your priorities. Survey your landscape: What areas or individual plants do you want most to save? There's no point in wasting water by trying to keep alive scraggly or diseased plants. No matter what else you have to sacrifice, give top priority to irrigating established trees and shrubs; they're virtually irreplaceable. Consider perennials a second priority.

2 Identify root zones. The roots of various plants grow to different depths; the trick is to apply just enough water to moisten the roots without going beyond. Most tree roots are located in the top 2 feet of soil. The drip line of a tree or shrub runs around the perimeter of the canopy and virtually outlines the root zone on the ground below. Once you identify the root zone, focus your resources on that area.

3 Check soil moisture. To determine how dry or moist the soil is below the surface, dig down at least 12 inches with a trowel or spade and take a handful of soil and squeeze it; still-moist soil will hold together in a tight ball. An even better way to investigate is to invest in a sampling tube to "read" your soil. When you push the metal tube into the ground and twist it back out, it extracts a 12-inch or longer core showing in cross section how wet or dry the soil actually is. For example, if your soil sample is powder dry on top and barely damp below, it's time to water. Tube samplers ($23 and up, plus shipping) are available from Forestry Suppliers *(www.forestry-suppliers.com or 800/647-5368)*.

4 Build watering basins. Mound soil berms around young trees and shrubs such as roses to concentrate water on the root zones. Form the main berm just outside the tree's drip line; make a second berm 4 to 6 inches from the trunk to keep water off it.

Don't use your thumb to direct water from a bare hose end. Install a soft spray head or watering wand with an on-off valve. Don't spray water on foliage; apply it directly to the soil or mulch around plants' root zones.

5 Irrigate slowly and deeply. Slow soaking limits runoff and encourages plants to develop deep root systems that are better able to tolerate drought.

To minimize evaporation, irrigate in the early morning or evening, when the air is cool and calm.

6 Modify lawn care. If local restrictions allow lawn irrigation, there are some things you can do to reduce the amount of water you apply.

Mow grass higher—2 to 3 inches for bluegrass, 2½ to 3 inches for tall fescue—to help shade the roots below. Don't overfertilize; too much nitrogen only encourages thirsty new growth. Some gardeners cut back to 1 inch of water every two weeks; under this regime, lawns turn straw-colored and semidormant but bounce back after the weather cools in fall.

7 Apply mulch. To conserve soil moisture, spread a 2- to 4-inch layer of organic mulch such as shredded bark, straw, or weed-free hay over the root zones of permanent plants. Mulch trees all the way out to the drip line, but keep the mulch 6 inches from the trunk to prevent rot. Mulch also blocks weeds, which steal water and nutrients needed by desirable plants

9 Deep-root irrigators. These hose-end devices have forked or needlelike shafts that inject water into the ground. You insert the shaft 6 to 12 inches or deeper into the soil around trees and shrubs. After watering in one spot along the drip line, you move the irrigator to another spot until you complete one round trip. For a tree with a 12-inch-diameter trunk, which needs 60 minutes of water (flowing at 2 gallons per minute), you would insert the irrigator at six points around the drip line, letting it run 10 minutes at each point. The needle-type Root Irrigator ($25, plus shipping) is sold by Gardener's Supply (see tactic 8).

10 Be water-wise with containers. Use glazed terra-cotta or plastic ones, which hold water better. For extra insulation, nest smaller pots inside larger ones, or bury pots in the ground up to the rims. ◆

8 Use soaker hoses. These porous hoses ooze water along their length. Run them among flowers and shrubs or along hedges or rows of vegetables. Coil them under the drip lines of large trees; you'll need 50 or 100 feet. For a small tree or shrub, consider using a Soaker Ring ($13, plus shipping), a hose-end device that forms a closed circle around the trunk; it's available from Gardener's Supply *(www.gardeners.com or 800/427-3363)*.

REMINISCENT OF A MISSION COURTYARD, this water-wise entry garden features California classics in bold serape colors. For details, see page 160.

June

Wild mock orange

7 great natives

Bearberry *(Arctostaphylos uva-ursi).* This 4- to 6-inch-high ground cover with glossy evergreen leaves bears white or pinkish flowers in spring, followed by red berries. *Sunset* climate zones 1–3.

Golden currant *(Ribes aureum).* A 3- to 6-foot-tall shrub, it bears yellow flowers in spring; edible currants appear in summer. Zones 1–3, 10, 11.

Redtwig dogwood *(Cornus stolonifera).* Pink spring flowers cover this 7- to 9-foot-tall shrub, followed by white fruit. Bright red leaves in autumn drop to reveal red twigs. Zones 1–3.

Saskatoon serviceberry *(Amelanchier alnifolia).* Small white blossoms blanket this 20-foot-tall shrub in early spring, followed by fruit similar to blueberries. Foliage turns red in fall. Zones 1–3.

Silver buffaloberry *(Shepherdia argentea).* After tasting the reddish-orange fruit of this 6- to 12-foot-tall shrub, Lewis compared its flavor to cranberry. Zones 1–3, 10.

Snowberry *(Symphoricarpos albus).* This 2- to 6-foot-tall shrub was described by Lewis as "a kind of honeysuckle which bears a white bury [*sic*]." Zones 1–3, 10, 11.

Wild mock orange *(Philadelphus lewisii).* Named for Lewis, this 6- to 9-foot-tall shrub bears fragrant, satiny summer blossoms. Zones 1–3, 10.

Lewis & Clark heritage plants

During their famous overland expedition, Lewis and Clark collected more than 200 specimens of plants, many of them new to botanists. Some of these natives, especially the seven described at right, are worth growing in today's intermountain gardens. Look for them in nurseries that offer native plants, or ask garden-center staff to order from Lawyer Nursery (wholesale only) in Plains, Montana. These plants are deciduous unless noted. —*Suzanne Touchette Kelso*

Silver buffaloberry

Redtwig dogwood

Lupines cloak an Idaho hillside

The hillside below Gene and Judy Whitmyre's home in Ketchum, Idaho, used to be barren. So the Whitmyres hired a landscaping firm to hydroseed the slope: seeds of grasses and wildflowers that also included Russell hybrid lupines were mixed with water and sprayed over the ground. The landscaper advised them that the grasses would eventually crowd out the wildflowers. But on the Whitmyres' slope, even more flowers appeared in the third year. The next summer, after the lupines finished blooming, Judy gathered their dry seedpods and tossed them on grassy patches. Each year since, she has continued to scatter seeds. Now, six years after the initial planting, the whole slope turns deep purple and blue in June, as thousands of lupines burst into bloom.

Hybrid lupines are hardy in *Sunset* climate zones 1–3. Russell hybrids come in shades of blue, purple, red, pink, yellow, and white. New Generation hybrids are sturdier than other lupines and usually last seven or eight years. —*S. T. K.*

UNTHIRSTY WESTERNERS

Firecracker penstemon

When *Penstemon eatonii* is in bloom, hummingbirds will fly out of their way to sip nectar from its scarlet blossoms. Native throughout much of the Southwest, this short-lived perennial reseeds readily in rocky, well-drained soil. The evergreen foliage is waxy to the touch. In spring, 1-inch-long flowers are borne on 2- to 3-foot-tall spikes.

Firecracker penstemon is hardy in all *Sunset* intermountain climate zones. Seeds are available from Plants of the Southwest (*www.plantsofthesouthwest. com* or 800/788-7333), and plants from High Country Gardens (*www. highcountrygardens.com* or 800/925-9387).

—*Marcia Tatroe*

Compact, colorful, carefree entry

With the help of landscape designer Jocelyn Chilvers, Belinda and Bill Nygren of Denver transformed their small front yard into a relaxing outdoor living area that complements the Mediterranean architecture of their Spanish colonial bungalow. During warm weather, the Nygrens eat most of their meals on a patio behind a low wall near the entry. A more private seating area is screened from the street by aspen trees and boulders.

The patio is fringed by a colorful mix of flowering perennials and shrubs that needs little water and only an hour's care each week. Blooming here in May are chartreuse lady's-mantle, scarlet roses, coral bells (*Heuchera micrantha* 'Palace Purple'), crimson Jupiter's beard, purple *Salvia* 'Superba', and magenta cranesbill. A mulch of bark chips helps conserve soil moisture around the plants. Light fixtures illuminate the garden at night. —*M.T.*

Stellar fruit

Supermarket star fruit is just expensive parsley, says Alex Silber, owner of **Papaya Tree Nursery** in Granada Hills. Its five-pointed golden yellow slices look pretty garnishing a plate, but they're nearly tasteless. Silber says it's because commercial growers don't choose the best varieties and often pick the fruit green.

A homegrown, fully ripe 'Arkin', 'Florita', 'Golden Star', or 'Kary', on the other hand, provides a delightful flavor, he says. The fruit is juicy and sweet-tart like an orange, and smells like flowers. Star fruit, also called carambola *(Averrhoa carambola),* is a surprisingly easy crop to grow in frost-free areas of Southern California. Once established, trees can survive temperatures as low as 28° for a brief period. The tree likes good drainage, full sun (though it can tolerate less), and regular irrigation (soil should be moist but not wet). It's not a heavy feeder, but it is susceptible to chlorosis in alkaline soils, so it needs chelated iron regularly. Star fruit also appreciates protection from wind.

In Southern California, mature trees generally reach 8 to 15 feet tall; they're densely clothed in small green leaves and bear fruits heavily twice a year. The winter star fruit crop is especially appreciated, says Fullerton gardener Patricia Sawyer, who has grown 'Arkin' for nearly 10 years. "It's like having a decorated Christmas tree in the yard," she adds.

Papaya Tree Nursery: open by appointment, (818) 363-3680. Pacific Tree Farms in Chula Vista: mail order available, (619) 422-2400. Laguna Hills Nursery: (949) 830-5653. —Sharon Cohoon

UNTHIRSTY WESTERNERS

Harison's yellow rose

Few roses are as adaptable or indestructible as *Rosa* x *harisonii.* Commonly known as Harison's yellow rose, this old hybrid persists—without fertilizer or irrigation—in pioneer settlements around the West. In late May and early June, it produces a profusion of clear yellow 2-inch-wide double blossoms with a scent often described as sweet. Reaching 6 feet tall and 4 feet wide, this shrub rose is hardy in all *Sunset* climate zones. Once established, it is drought-tolerant.

Plants are available from High Country Roses (www. highcountryroses.com or 800/552-2082).

—*M.T.*

Tubular flowers give way to curved fruit pods (below).

Devil's claw, a summer surprise

For centuries, a low-growing herbaceous shrub called devil's claw *(Proboscidea)* has been cultivated by the native peoples of the Southwest as a source of food and as fiber for basket-making. With its showy flowers and edible pods, this fast-growing, heat-tolerant annual makes an unusual addition to a summer garden.

Reaching 2 to 3 feet tall and wide, the plant produces 2-inch creamy white to pinkish purple flowers followed by green fruit pods that resemble those of okra in appearance and flavor. If you want to eat the pods, harvest when they are small (no more than 2 inches long) and tender;

they become bitter and pithy as they mature. Cook them as you would okra, either sautéing in butter or stewing in gumbo. When left to ripen on the plant, the pods dry and split open to form two curved "claws." Basketmakers strip the black fibers from the claws to weave into baskets.

Seeds of wild and domesticated devil's claw are sold by Native Seeds/SEARCH *(www. nativeseeds.org or 520/622-5561).* Seeds germinate in the heat and humidity that accompany the Southwest's monsoon season. As summer thundershowers commence, sow them $\frac{1}{2}$ inch deep in amended soil.

—*Cathy Cromell*

TOP: STEVEN GUNTHER; FAR LEFT: CHARLES MANN; COURTESY NATIVE SEEDS (2)

Plumes of astilbe paint the shade

Cora and Ray Paulson have lived and gardened on the same property near Bremerton, Washington, for 60 years. Consequently, they've become experts at matching plants and habitats. For example, the drifts of astilbe pictured above thrive in compost-rich soil in a partly shaded area—just what this perennial needs.

Altogether, Cora has about a dozen kinds of astilbe. Many were gifts from friends, but she bought a few choice varieties. "I don't know their names," she says, "but I do know how to grow them. Over the years, I've divided them again and again, digging compost into the soil every time I replant. That's all they need to give me a show from late May into July."

Cora divides the astilbes in fall, when they become dormant. She replants the divisions fairly closely so the emerging spring leaves shade out weeds. For companion plants, Cora uses ferns, hostas, Japanese irises, and primroses.

If you'd like to start your own astilbe collection, shop nurseries now for blooming plants in the colors you like. —*Jim McCausland*

A redwood bridge crosses the creek bed to link with a flagstone path and patio.

CHARLES MANN

Herbs thrive around a dry creek

June is peak bloom time in Santa Fe, and Ed and Nancy Lane's walled garden is no exception. Aromatic herbs are the mainstay of their garden. Lavender—the showiest plant in the central island where most of the herbs are concentrated—loves this hot, sunny, southern exposure. Yellow-and-orange gaillardia thrives here too, as does yarrow in mixed pastel colors.

Around the island, several varieties of creeping thyme *(Thymus serpyllum)* form carpets that substitute for a lawn.

"Thyme is pretty tough. You can't play football on it," Ed explains, "but walking across it occasionally doesn't seem to do it any harm."

The Lanes also like the herbs' ability to attract bees, hummingbirds, and especially butterflies. "Clouds of painted ladies feast on the flowering thyme some years," says Ed. "I know you're supposed to cut the flowers off to keep thyme from getting woody. But I can't bear to do it. I'd rather enjoy the painted ladies."

Lamb's ears, which hugs a dry creek bed, is so happy basking in the sun that the Lanes have to divide it every year to keep the fuzzy-leafed perennial under control.

The creek bed runs through the property and helps collect the sparse rainfall. "Fortunately, these are xeric plants [those with low water needs], because there's been precious little rain lately," notes Nancy. And even without water, the creek bed adds interest to the garden. —*Sharon Cohoon*

Rose lovers' tips for prize blooms

He loves to cultivate roses; she loves to use them in prize-winning flower arrangements. So between them, Ed and Joan Conn worked out a system for growing large, perfect roses in their Corvallis, Oregon, garden. Here's how they do it.

Selection. Joan's favorite roses for color are 'Barbra Streisand' (lavender), 'First Kiss' (pink), 'Full Sail' (white), 'Gold Medal' (gold; shown), 'Olympiad' (red), and 'Timeless' (rose pink). For fragrance, she likes the tea scent of 'Voodoo' (orange) and the citrus essence of 'Sombreuil' (white).

Planting. In each hole, the Conns combine their garden's heavy native soil with an equal amount of planter's mix. Most roses go in full sun.

Mulching. An 8- to 12-inch layer of mint-hay compost in the fall keeps down weeds and holds in moisture. The mulch breaks down over winter so that only a couple of inches remain by spring.

Watering. Roses are deep-watered by a drip-irrigation system twice a month (more often during very hot weather).

Feeding. Granular 15-15-15 fertilizer is applied three times between March and September. Ed alternates those feedings with three foliar spray applications of 20-20-20 liquid fertilizer, mixing in 1 tablespoon of epsom salts (magnesium sulfate), which promotes the growth of new canes.

Pinching. To produce bigger flowers, the Conns pinch out all but one bud in each cluster.

Pest control. To control disease, Ed sprays plants with a fungicide every month during the growing season. When he sees insects start to gather on plants, he hoses down the foliage in the morning or midafternoon. —*J. M.*

'Gold Medal'

A few seeds, a lot of lupines

How far does a packet of lupine seeds go? Jo and Vern Ford of Yakima, Washington, found out when they planted the garden pictured above.

The Fords grow fruit professionally, but they do their flower gardening on an exposed hilltop that's too rocky for apple trees. The site gets plenty of sunshine, and the dark basalt boulders make a perfect visual foil for perennial flowers.

In early spring of a few years ago, Vern started seeds of Russell hybrid lupines in his greenhouse. He moved the seedlings into the garden in late spring, interplanting them with tall bearded irises. Together, they make a spectacular late-spring show that comes back year after year. In late May, he also sows patches of zinnias, raking the seeds into the soil and watering. After the irises and lupines finish blooming, the zinnias take over.

The Fords fertilize once in spring and once in fall with a complete fertilizer (16-16-16 formula).

Start your own lupine garden by setting out nursery plants now, or wait until early next spring to sow seeds.

—*J. M.*

BACK TO BASICS

Tips for tree pruning

To correct or slow growth on fruit trees, shade trees, and spring-flowering trees—particularly young ones—prune in early summer (midsummer in cold climates). **1. Correct the structure:** Cut off broken and diseased branches, as well as ones that are hanging too low or growing in an unwanted position. Remove vigorous, upright branches that may compete with the central leader. Make each cut just outside a branch bark ridge at the point of attachment; do not leave a stub. **2. Thin the canopy:** If growth is too dense, prune back some branches to vigorous side shoots (red marks on illustration). —*L. B. S.*

CLAIRE CURRAN

Serape colors in a water-wise garden

For anyone who took a childhood field trip to California missions, flowers in the colors of a Mexican serape—such as red bougainvillea, yellow euryops, and purple statice—probably remain a vivid memory.

When Matthew Midgett bought and restored a mid-20th-century adobe, he chose those very plants to brighten its entry. But the plants do more than evoke Midgett's memories of a boyhood visit to Mission San Fernando. They work because they're more suited to California's predominantly Mediterranean climate and terrain than many of the pastel-flowered plants used in traditional gardens. They get by on minimal water and care, and their bright colors complement mission-style architecture.

The curved wall pictured above is an attractive backdrop. The scarlet bougainvillea, yellow *Euryops pectinatus,* pink ivy geraniums, purple sea lavender (*Limonium perezii),* and succulents such as aeonium, echeveria, and jade plant surround a dramatic-looking agave. Behind the wall, a pink-flowered *Nerium oleander* makes a splash of bright color against the grassy green fronds of a ponytail palm. These dazzling colors are repeated throughout the garden. In the backyard, bird of paradise plants flank a fountain that's reminiscent of those found in mission courtyards.

Californians see these plants so frequently that they view them as common, Midgett says. But when they're planted together, they can form a beautiful tapestry. —*D.L.B.*

Billowy mounds blooms include scented geraniums (left) and orange nasturtiums (right).

Path of discovery

"Wide enough to be comfortable, narrow enough to be romantic"—that's how Francesca Filanc describes the garden path outside the Rancho Santa Fe house she shares with her husband, Peter.

Just 4 feet across and covered with mulch, the path connects the house with a horse corral at the bottom of a gentle slope. But what makes it so magical are the billowing mounds of yellow, orange, and purple blossoms that overlap and soften its edges.

To get that softly romantic look, Francesca lined the path with stones, then planted French lavender and scented geraniums on both sides. She seeded drifts of wildflowers (including California poppies, clarkia, linaria, and scarlet flax), as well as coreopsis, hollyhocks, and trailing nasturtiums. To fill in bare areas, she added succulents, bulbs, lemon trees, and apple trees "so I can pick apples on my way to the horses."

The nasturtiums reseed prolifically and grow year-round in this nearly frost-free climate (*Sunset* climate zone 23).

—*Debra Lee Baldwin*

Masses of grasses

Ornamental grasses capture sunlight and sway in the slightest breeze, adding visual and kinetic interest to the garden. When they develop flower spikelets and seed heads, grasses catch even more light, transforming them into nearly magical plants.

To see this energy in action, visit the all-grass border at the Grace Kallam Perennial Garden in the Los Angeles County Arboretum and Botanic Garden. Pictured at left, a tall fountain of *Miscanthus sinensis* is partnered in the garden with softer deer grass (*Muhlenbergia rigens*) and stiffer-textured blue oat grass (*Helictotrichon sempervirens*). Cross a bridge to the opposite side of the stream, and you'll find sedges, reeds, and other grasslike plants interplanted with delicate spring bulbs.

To reach the Kallam garden, take the farthest western path in the arboretum to just north of the falls. 9–4:30. 301 N. Baldwin Ave., Arcadia; www.lacountybotanicgarden.org or (626) 821-3222.—S.C.

Outdoor rooms in Sonoma

Artist John Holmes turned the garden of the Sonoma County mountaintop retreat he shares with his wife, Kathleen, into a series of outdoor rooms. There's a fruit orchard, a secret garden surrounded by large shrubs, a shade garden, and a lush ornamental vegetable garden—all divided by a wisteria arbor. "The arbor is like an entrance hall," explains Kathleen. "All of the garden rooms lead off of it."

The vegetable garden, pictured above, pairs flowers and edibles; gloriosa daisies, hollyhocks, roses, and sunflowers mingle with squash, tomatoes, and other crops. Purple snap beans scramble over a trellis. Chairs offer a place to relax between garden chores.

Although the Holmeses live in deer country, none of their plants has been munched by marauders, thanks to an 8-foot fence. To foil gophers, the couple planted *Euphorbia biglandulosa*. They make their own compost, which they use to enrich the volcanic soil. A drip system, put together with help from M2 Landscape *(415/816-3403),* keeps plants watered.—*L.B.S.*

Made for shade

Of all the plants that garden designers Freeland and Sabrina Tanner grow in their Napa garden, oakleaf hydrangea (*H. quercifolia* 'Snowflake') is a standout.

This 4- to 6-foot-tall selection looks good year-round. In midspring, 6-inch-long lime green and white flowers appear. As the season progresses, each floret produces a new one until, by the end of summer, the blooms extend to 12 inches or more.

In fall, foliage turns shades of purple and red. The plant's peeling bark is also attractive in winter.

Plant 'Snowflake' in partial shade or in an area that receives only morning sun. Water regularly.

If you can't find them at your local nursery, plants can be ordered from Hydrangeas Plus (www.hydrangeasplus.com or 866/433-7896). —L. B. S.

WHAT TO DO IN YOUR GARDEN IN JUNE

PLANTING

☐ **ANNUALS.** Sow seeds of cosmos, marigold, portulaca, sunflower, sweet alyssum, and zinnia early in the month, or plant seedlings of these, plus coleus, geranium, impatiens, Madagascar periwinkle, pansy, and petunia.

☐ **BULBS.** Early in the month, plant canna, dahlia, gladiolus, montbretia, tigridia, and tuberous begonia for late-summer color.

☐ **HERBS, VEGETABLES.** You can plant every kind of herb this month. And there's still time to plant bush beans as well as leaf and root crops.

☐ **JAPANESE AND SIBERIAN IRISES.** Both of these late-spring bloomers are hardy in *Sunset* climate zones 1–7 and 17. Japanese irises are voluptuous beauties that love water (you even can grow them with their feet in a shallow pond). Siberian irises also need consistent moisture but don't like waterlogged soil. Both kinds come in blue, purple, maroon, yellow, and white, some with yellow throats. Buy plants in bloom in nurseries, or visit a specialty grower like Walsterway Iris Gardens *(360/668-4429)* in Snohomish, WA.

☐ **LAWNS.** Zones 4–7, 17: You can lay sod almost anytime during the growing season. Zones A1–A3, 1–3: If you have sufficient water where you live, sow seed or lay sod now so turf grass will have time to become established over summer.

☐ **PERENNIALS.** Set out seedlings of these flowering perennials: aster, blanket flower, chrysanthemum, columbine, coreopsis, delphinium, erigeron, feverfew, foxglove, gilia, heuchera, hosta, Oriental poppy, penstemon, perennial sweet pea, potentilla, purple coneflower, and salvia. Fill gaps with these foliage plants: artemisia, dusty miller, and golden or purple sage.

☐ **PERMANENT PLANTS.** Plant containerized trees, vines, ground covers, and shrubs; many varieties of roses (especially landscape types) are now sold in bloom.

MAINTENANCE

☐ **CONTROL SLUGS.** Remove and kill them at night after you water (or after a rain).

☐ **DIVIDE PERENNIALS.** Immediately after flowering, dig up your spring-blooming perennials and divide them. Some plants, such as Oriental poppies, can be separated root by root; others, like irises, have to be cut apart with a shovel or knife.

☐ **FERTILIZE.** Feed spring-flowering plants right after bloom.

☐ **PRUNE SPRING-BLOOMING TREES AND SHRUBS.** Thin and shape them now, before they set next spring's flower buds (which happens later in summer).

☐ **THIN APPLES.** To keep apple trees from producing too much small fruit, wait until after June drop, when trees spontaneously abort unpollinated fruit, then go through and break off excess fruit. Thin triple clusters to doubles, double clusters to singles.

☐ **WEED.** Hoe tiny weeds early on a hot day when the soil is dry; they'll be dead by dark. ◆

WHAT TO DO IN YOUR GARDEN IN JUNE

SHOPPING

☐ **GIFTS FOR DAD.** One of these gifts is sure to please any gardening dad on Father's Day: A dwarf citrus tree such as 'Clementine' tangerine, 'Oroblanco' grapefruit/pummelo hybrid, or, for cooler climates, 'Improved Meyer' lemon; Wonder Gloves waterproof gloves, available at some nurseries or from Garden Works *(425/455-0568);* or a stainless steel and ash-handled spade, edging knife, or other Heirloom Tool from Smith & Hawken *(www.smithandhawken.com or 800/776-3336).*

PLANTING

☐ **CILANTRO.** To make sure you have plenty of cilantro for cooking all summer, sow successive crops of seeds every six to eight weeks. A variety that's slow to go to seed is 'Slow-bolt' from Renee's Garden, sold on nursery seed racks and online *(www. reneesgarden.com).*

☐ **HERBS.** For flavoring salads, sandwiches, soups, and grilled meats, plant basil, chives, oregano, rosemary, tarragon, and thyme. For seeds of harder-to-find plants like French sorrel, visit an herb specialty nursery, such as Sycamore Farms in Paso Robles *(800/576-5288).*

☐ **LOW-MAINTENANCE SHRUBS.** *Sunset* climate zones 7–9, 14–17: For attractive color and form with minimal water, try blue hibiscus, cape mallow, ceanothus, coast rosemary *(Westringia fruticosa),* euphorbia, Jerusalem sage, lavender, New Zealand flax hybrids (two new hybrids are 'Apricot Queen' and 'Rainbow Warrior'), plumbago, rockrose, rosemary, Russian sage, and tree mallow.

Sunset
CLIMATE ZONES
☐ Mountain (1–2)
☐ Valley (7–9)
☐ Inland (14)
☐ Coastal (15–17)

☐ **SUMMER PERENNIALS.** To prolong color in your garden, look for plants that will bloom through summer and beyond. Good choices include daylilies, gaillardia, *Gaura lindheimeri,* gloriosa daisy, lion's tail, *(Leonotis leonurus),* penstemon, phygelius, salvia, and yarrow.

☐ **VEGETABLES.** June is prime planting time for warm-season vegetables. Sow seeds of beans (bush and pole types) and corn (try one of the supersweet or sugar-enhanced varieties, which stay sweeter longer after harvest). Set out transplants of cucumbers, eggplant, melons, okra, peppers, pumpkins, squash, and tomatoes.

MAINTENANCE

☐ **CHECK SPRINKLERS.** Inspect your sprinkler system for broken, malfunctioning, or misaligned heads. Turn the system on and inspect each head, then replace broken ones. If a head nozzle bubbles or squirts irregularly, it may be clogged; check

slits for dirt or small pebbles. If you can't unclog it, replace it. To readjust a misaligned head, turn it until it sprays in the right direction.

☐ **SHEAR SPRING-BLOOMING PERENNIALS.** To keep basket-of-gold, candytuft, common aubrieta, moss pink, rockcress, and other low-growing, spring-blooming perennials full and compact, remove spent blooms and 1 or 2 inches of growth. Use sharp grass shears, hedge shears, or Classic English Trimming Shears from Kinsman Company *(www. kinsmangarden.com or 800/733-4146).*

☐ **TRANSPLANT WATER PLANTS.** If your water plants need transplanting, make sure to use a mineral-based soil, not one with a base of peat moss or compost. The latter types can cloud the water and clog filters and pumps. One type to look for is Schultz Aquatic Plant Soil (available in 10- and 25-pound bags). If you can't find it at your local nursery or home improvement center, you can order it from Star Nursery Online Store *(www.yardsupply.com).* ◆

WHAT TO DO IN YOUR GARDEN IN JUNE

PLANTING

☐ **DAYLILIES.** They're among the easiest blooming perennials you can find. But look for these rust-resistant varieties—'Butterscotch Ruffles', 'Frankly Scarlet', 'Lavender Dew', and 'Plum Perfect'.

☐ **HERBS.** For flavoring salads, sandwiches, soups, and grilled meats this summer, plant basil, chives, mint, oregano, rosemary, tarragon, thyme, and many other herbs. For harder-to-find plants like anise hyssop *(Agastache foeniculum)*, lovage, rau ram (Vietnamese coriander), or French sorrel, visit a specialty herb nursery, such as Sycamore Farms in Paso Robles *(800/576-5288)* or Herban Garden in Fallbrook *(800/407-5268)*. Or order herbs from Mountain Valley Growers *(www.mountainvalleygrowers.com or 559/338-2775)*.

☐ **SUBTROPICALS.** It's not too late to plant avocado, citrus, cherimoya, mango, and other subtropical fruit trees. You can also plant ornamental flowering trees like bauhinia, crape myrtle, plumeria, and tabebuia; ornamental shrubs like gardenia, hibiscus, and princess flower; and bougainvillea, passion vine, thunbergia, and trumpet vines.

☐ **VEGETABLES.** Set out seedlings of cucumbers, eggplants, melons, peppers, squash, and tomatoes. Sow seeds of beans, corn, cucumbers, okra, pumpkins, and summer and winter squash. In the high desert (*Sunset* climate zone 11), sow seeds of corn, cucumbers, melons, okra, and squash.

Sunset
CLIMATE ZONES
1–3 7–9 11 13 14–24

MAINTENANCE

☐ **HARVEST VEGETABLES.** Pick all beans, cucumbers, okra, and squash as they ripen. Otherwise, fruit left on the vine and allowed to grow too large will lose flavor and drain the plant's energy, resulting in a smaller remaining harvest.

☐ **PROTECT FRUIT.** To keep birds from stealing your ripening fruit, enclose trees with broad-mesh netting several weeks before fruit matures. Or hang flash tape—Mylar tape that is silver on one side, red on the other—on the branches to keep birds at bay.

☐ **PRUNE CORAL TREES.** If your coral tree is growing too rapidly, now is the time to cut it back. Shorten long shoots by a third to a half, and remove any branches that cross. If possible, reduce the amount of water the tree receives to slow its growth.

☐ **TURN COMPOST.** To speed up decomposition, use a spading fork to move material from bottom to top and from sides to center of the compost pile; moisten the compost during the process.

PEST & DISEASE CONTROL

☐ **CONTROL POWDERY MILDEW.** When morning fog brings "June gloom," moisture causes powdery mildew to thrive on roses and vegetable crops like cucumbers, melons, and squash. Combat this fungus disease by washing spores off foliage with a hose. Do this in the morning to let foliage dry by evening.

☐ **PREVENT BLOSSOM-END ROT.** The dark brown or black sunken areas that develop on the bottom of tomatoes are caused by inadequate calcium uptake, fostered by uneven watering. Irrigate plants thoroughly and regularly to prevent the disease, and apply mulch to retain moisture. Also avoid high-nitrogen fertilizers, which tend to block calcium uptake. If you've been doing all this and your tomatoes still get blossom-end rot, try spraying foliage with seaweed extract to supply calcium directly to the leaves. ◆

MAP: DEBRA LAMBERT

WHAT TO DO IN YOUR GARDEN IN JUNE

PLANTING

☐ **LANDSCAPE PLANTS.** Where water-use policies allow, plant trees, shrubs, and perennials. Choose species and varieties with low water needs and buy the largest pot available, because larger rootballs require less-frequent watering. After planting, use soil to build a watering basin around each plant just outside its drip line or rootball. Spread 2 to 4 inches of mulch over the root zone, keeping it a few inches from the bases of plants. For the first few weeks, shade new transplants with evergreen boughs or extra-light (summer-weight) floating row covers, which are available from Gardener's Supply Co. *(www.gardeners. com or 800/427-3363)* and Territorial Seed Co. *(www.territorialseed.com or 541/942-9547)*.

☐ **SUMMER FLOWERS.** When the weather warms up, sow seeds of cosmos, four o'clock *(Mirabilis jalapa)*, morning glory, portulaca, sunflower, and zinnia directly in the ground. For instant color, set out nursery seedlings of drought-tolerant African daisy *(Osteospermum)*, gazania, globe amaranth, Madagascar periwinkle, petunia, *Salvia coccinea* and *S. greggii*, scaevola, and *Zinnia angustifolia*.

☐ **X-RATED PLANTS.** A free brochure and website from Garden Centers of Colorado *(www.xratedgardening.com or 303/850-7589)* rate annuals, perennials, shrubs, and trees according to their water needs. Designations range from a single X for plants like

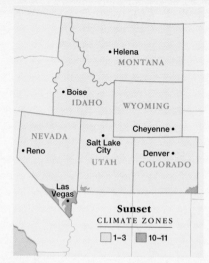

Sunset
CLIMATE ZONES

☐ 1–3   ▨ 10–11

bacopa that tolerate slightly dry conditions to XXX for plants like portulaca that thrive in very dry conditions.

MAINTENANCE

☐ **APPLY ANTITRANSPIRANT.** To help reduce moisture loss during drought, spray the foliage of valuable evergreens, perennials, and shrubs with an antitranspirant. Try Wilt-Pruf, a clear, pine oil–based product, which is available from home- and garden-supply centers.

☐ **LET DORMANT LAWNS REST.** If lawn watering is banned in your community this summer, continue mowing until the grass stops growing. While the turf is dormant, don't use fertilizers or pesticides and don't aerate or dethatch the lawn. Stay off the grass—foot traffic can further damage drought-stressed turf.

☐ **PROVIDE WATER FOR BIRDS, WILDLIFE.** When natural water sources dry up, birds and other wildlife rely on the fresh water you provide. Refill birdbaths regularly, and put basins on the ground for frogs, snakes, and toads.

☐ **SET OUT BEE SHELTERS.** Attract pollinating bees to your garden by putting up bee houses. For instructions on building your own boxes, go to the Xerces Society website *(www. xerces.org)*. Territorial Seed Co. *(www.territorialseed.com or 541/942-9547)* sells a number of nesting boxes and canisters ($17 and up) designed for bumblebees and mason bees.

☐ **USE FLOW METERS.** If your local water provider recommends giving trees and shrubs a certain amount of water based on the plants' size, don't waste water by guessing. Instead, attach a flow meter to the hose to accurately measure water output in gallons. This device is available from H$_2$O Watch *(www.h2owatch.net or 866/426-9282)*.

☐ **WATER WITH SOAKER HOSES.** Use them to water trees, shrubs, and flower beds. Those made from recycled tires can be pinned down and left in place year-round. They last longer if covered with mulch to protect them from sunlight. —*M. T.*

WHAT TO DO IN YOUR GARDEN IN JUNE

PLANTING

☐ ANNUAL FLOWERS. *Sunset* climate zones 1A–3B (Flagstaff, Prescott, Santa Fe, Taos): Try 'Touch of Red' calendula, 'Mr. Majestic' marigold, and 'Candy Cane' zinnia, all from Territorial Seed Co. *(www. territorialseed.com or 541/942-9547).* Zones 10–11 (Albuquerque, Las Vegas): Consider 'Pink Candle' celosia, Tea Time series four o'clock, Summer Showers series geranium, 'Wild Thing' impatiens, Kaleidoscope Mix larkspur, and Burpeeana Giants Mix zinnia, all from Burpee *(www. burpee.com or 800/888-1447).* Zones 12–13 (Phoenix, Tucson): Try 'Dancing Petticoats' cosmos, 'Black Watchman' hollyhock, 'Starfire' signet marigold, 'Marble Arch' salvia, 'The Joker' sunflower, and 'Scarlet Flame' zinnia, all from Renee's Garden *(www.reneesgarden.com or 888/880-7228).*

☐ HERBS. All zones: In an 18-inch container filled with potting soil, plant six to eight 4-inch pots of various basils such as sweet basil, purple-leafed 'Purple Ruffles' or 'Swiss Sunset', or dwarf bush 'Finissimo Verde a Palla' (from Territorial Seed Co.; see above). Harvest leaves regularly to promote denser foliage; use the leaves fresh in pastas and salads. Zones 1A–3B: Sow seeds of cilantro, dill, and parsley directly in the ground. In zones 10–13, set out transplants of marjoram, oregano, rosemary, and thyme.

☐ LANDSCAPE PLANTS. As drought conditions persist in the Southwest, choose species and varieties that need little or no supplemental irrigation once established. Accent plants: *Agave geminiflora* and *A. schidigera* 'Durango Delight', *Hesperaloe parviflora* 'Yellow', and tree bear grass *(Nolina matapensis).* Evergreen shrubs: 'Irene' rosemary and *Tecoma* 'Orange Jubilee' and 'Sunrise'. Ground cover: *Acacia redolens* 'Desert Carpet'. Ornamental grasses: *Muhlenbergia capillaris* 'Regal Mist' and *M. lindheimeri* 'Autumn Glow'.

☐ SHADE TREES. Good candidates include Arizona mesquite *(Prosopis velutina),* 'Desert Museum' palo verde, rosewood *(Dalbergia sissoo),* shoestring acacia *(A. stenophylla),* and Texas ebony *(Pithecellobium flexicaule).*

☐ VEGETABLES. Zones 1A–3B: Sow seeds of broccoli, brussels sprouts, cabbages, carrots, chard, radishes, and turnips. Zones 10–13: Sow seeds of Armenian cucumbers, black-eyed peas, corn, early-maturing green beans, melon, and summer and winter squash. Set out sweet potato transplants.

MAINTENANCE

☐ MULCH. Apply a 4- to 6-inch layer of mulch around annuals, landscape plants, and vegetables. This insulating layer cools the root zone and keeps moisture in the soil.

☐ PROTECT CROPS. To protect fruits and vegetables from birds and insects, drape trees and plants with bird netting or shadecloth. To prevent sunscald, cover the entire vegetable patch with 50-percent shadecloth; this also reduces temperatures, increasing blossom set and fruit production of tomatoes and peppers. —*Kim Nelson*

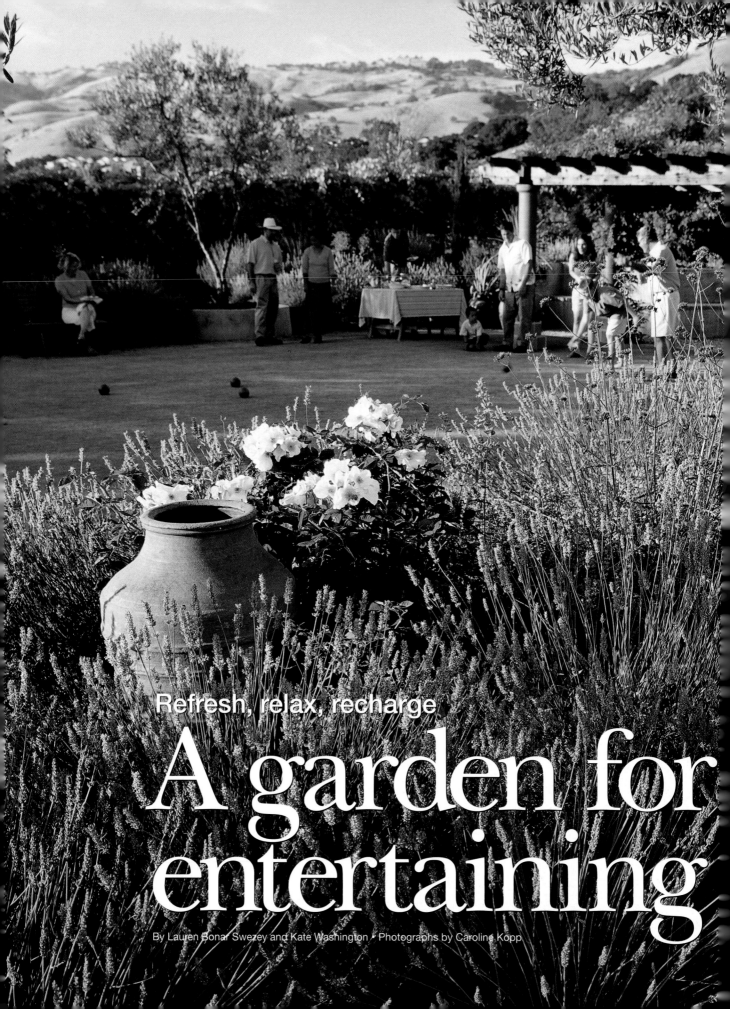

Refresh, relax, recharge

A garden for entertaining

By Lauren Bonar Swezey and Kate Washington · Photographs by Caroline Kopp

Drifts of lavender frame the bocce court. Guests enjoy Campari-Orange Sodas over a game.

Some gardens, like some hosts, really know how to throw a party. With the right mix of recreation areas, conversation nooks, and inviting plantings, a great party garden invites guests to play, relax, and dine—and it's no worse for wear after they depart. Offer an easy, flavorful buffet and friends and family will enjoy lingering outdoors for hours.

The casual, welcoming backyard of Joyce and Warren Hackbarth in Northern California is just such a garden. Its bocce court, water features, vine-covered arbors, and aromatic, low-maintenance plants are the main attractions

Scene setters

Bocce court. The level playing field, 80 feet long by 30 feet wide, is planted with hybrid Bermuda grass that is kept short (about 1 inch) to create a smooth, fine-textured surface. On either end, wisteria-covered arbors provide shade during game time.

Water. A rivulet trickles along a channel just above the bocce court into a nearby bowl, providing soothing, refreshing sounds.

Roomy patios. Two terraces serve the Hackbarths' entertaining needs: one, off the back of the house, has a barbecue and an overhead arbor; another, on an upper level, invites dining and taking in great views.

Swimming pool. Just off the lower terrace, it's a summer gathering spot for kids and adults.

A tiny plunge. Edged with rock to resemble a miniature mountain lake, this unheated pool is just big enough for cooling soaks on hot summer days.

Mini gardens. Scattered throughout the landscape are spots where guests can linger in small groups, including a secret escape with a foliage-surrounded bench for two.

during the couple's spontaneous summer gatherings. David LeRoy, who designed the landscape with David Warren, describes it as "an Italian garden that went wild."

Beyond the manicured bocce court, a mown green path leads visitors up a hill through a meadow of lavender, salvia, yarrow, and other Mediterranean-climate plants. In late spring and summer, the lavender's heady fragrance fills the air along the way. Farther up the path, partygoers encounter groves of fruit trees and olive trees, a chamomile and thyme lawn, a secret garden with a bench for relaxing or intimate conversation, and a natural-looking swimming hole. The path ends at a large entertainment patio with stunning views of the golden south San Jose hills.

Several arbors and a garden swing all constructed from ceramic flue tiles and wood decorate the property. Trees scattered throughout the landscape provide escape from the hot summer sun.

DESIGN: David LeRoy, Santa Cruz, CA *(831/ 462-1828)* and David Warren, Oakland, CA *(510/531-7144)*

Elements of a party garden

• **Large, open areas** for groups to gather. Tile, flagstone, lawn, and decomposed granite are all suitable party surfaces.

• **Intimate spaces** for cozy gatherings of two or more. A swing, secluded patio, small dining area, and firepit ringed with benches are inviting places to chat.

• **Seating.** Place groupings of outdoor furniture throughout the garden; supplement them with seat walls.

• **Sport courts.** Provide space for group activities such as badminton, bocce, or volleyball. If you have room, consider a pool or spa, natural crowd pleasers.

• **Cooking facilities.** Tuck a freestanding or built-in barbecue on a patio within reach of the kitchen. If you don't have an outdoor refrigerator, fill large buckets or ceramic bowls with ice to keep drinks cold. Or, for portability, substitute a clean wheelbarrow (line it with black plastic before adding ice). Use colorful, unbreakable glasses and dishes.

• **Lighting.** For nighttime parties, supplement light fixtures with portable lighting. Hang up strings of low-wattage party lights. Cluster candles in key locations—place lanterns atop patio tables or seat walls; put floating types in a pond.

At left, a buffet tablecloth echoes hues of lavender flowers. The swimming hole, surrounded by boulders and ornamental grasses, has the look of a mountain lake. It was constructed like a hot tub but has no heating element. Willow trees grow on the hill's crest. Above, water trickles between rows of blooming catmint into two terra-cotta bowls.

All-star gerberas

How to grow summer's show-off daisies

By Kathleen N. Brenzel • Photographs by Thomas J. Story

If ever there were a flower tailor-made for bold color, it's the gerbera. This happy-faced daisy, loved by flower arrangers, artists, and photographers, unfurls shapely petals, all neatly arranged around a tufted or velvety center. It comes in a rainbow of glowing colors: sunny yellow, sassy orange, vivid red, flaming coral, hot pink, and deep fuchsia. If subtle colors suit your taste, you'll also find the blooms in creamy white and a range of soft, sherbet shades like pale lemon and seashell pink.

As cut flowers, gerberas are practically unsurpassed. Their sturdy stems, topped with 4- to 5-inch-wide blooms, rise from rosettes of dark green, wavy-edged leaves. Flowers are

Large flowers, vibrant colors, and sturdy stems make gerberas standouts in the garden and in bouquets. Most hybrids have blooms with two or more rows of petals.

mostly fluffy doubles, with brown or yellow centers. "Buying a single plant is cheaper than buying a bouquet, because a plant can bloom for years," says Luen Miller, a grower with Monterey Bay Nursery in California. The trick is to give it optimum conditions (see "Care Tips," below right).

Modern hybrids of *Gerbera jamesonii* come from parents native to South Africa's Transvaal region; many strains are now sold. Those grown predominantly as cutting flowers are propagated by tissue culture to ensure consistency in flower color, stem length (up to 24 inches), and general appeal. For bedding plants, dwarf types (about 7 inches tall) are usually grown from seed, so they vary in petal count, color, and stem length.

In the West, gerberas are perennial in *Sunset Western Garden Book* climate zones 8, 9, 12–24, H1, and H2, where they bloom most heavily in

Raise the bed for top results

One way to give gerberas the excellent drainage they need is to plant them in mounds of garden soil. Here's how: (**1**) Amend soil with compost or leaf mold and a bit of horticultural sand. (**2**) Mound soil into foot-tall beds, then lay drip tubing or soaker hoses down the center. (**3**) Cover bed with black plastic sheeting. (**4**) Cut Xs in the plastic far enough apart to allow good air circulation between plants (8 to 10 inches for dwarf types, 2 feet for larger ones), then plant gerberas through them. To avoid crown rot, set the plants so their crowns rise about an inch above surrounding soil. Cover the plastic with a thin layer of fir bark or similar mulch, taking care not to mound it around plant crowns.

Care tips

EXPOSURE. Near the coast, give plants full sun; inland, partial shade.

SOIL. It should be loose, rich, and fast-draining. In pots, use a packaged potting mix.

WATERING. Irrigate deeply, then let soil go nearly dry before watering again. Avoid wetting the leaves and watering at night, which can cause powdery mildew or crown rot.

FEEDING. Fertilize monthly during spring and summer with a dilute liquid plant food according to label instructions.

Three 'Sunburst Red' gerberas fill this redwood patio box; *Helichrysum petiolare* 'Limelight' fringes the edges.

Cutting gerberas for the vase

Just two or three elegant blooms, displayed in a simple vase like the one pictured, can brighten a whole room.

To prepare cut flowers for bouquets: Using sharp shears, cut the stem under warm water to the desired length; make the cut at a sharp angle, as shown above. Remove the stem from the water and cut a 1/2-inch slit up one side of the stem, as shown here, before arranging it in a water-filled vase. Replace the vase water every day or two.

If flower heads start to droop after a few days, recut stems under warm water.

late spring and summer. Although flowers can appear anytime—even in winter—plant growth slows when temperatures drop below 65°. Irrigate plants as needed to supplement rainfall. In other zones, grow gerberas as annuals. In the hottest desert areas (zones 12 and 13), plant them in fall for winter and spring color. In intermountain areas, you may find potted plants at florists; grow them indoors in a cool, sunny room.

Shop for blooming plants at nurseries in 6-inch pots and 1-gallon cans. To enjoy peak bloom, cluster pots on a patio or group several plants in a patio box like the one pictured on the facing page. Then, after bloom is through, move them to a more permanent home in separate containers or raised beds.

For cutting flowers, plant at least a dozen tall-stemmed kinds in garden beds. Group dwarf plants at the front of a bed or border, or tuck them in window boxes. Pick off old or tangled leaves regularly; bait or handpick snails and slugs. If mildew appears, snip off affected leaves. ◆

ARTHUR MOUNT

Against the house wall are a shower and an equipment-storage closet, as well as an outdoor sink (bottom right). The gate elevates a potted plant.

Side-yard solutions

Ways to make use of this overlooked space

By Sharon Cohoon • Photographs by Steven Gunther

Pity the poor side yard. It's one of the most visible and frequented parts of the landscape. Yet we often treat it like a dog run at a kennel—all paving, no plants. Narrow as these spaces may be, it's possible to turn them into real gardens, or to use them for extra living space. Two side yards, pictured on these pages, offer proof.

Utility with charm

Robyn and Dana Hogan and their teenage son Chad have messy hobbies— scuba diving, boogie boarding, and spearfishing. That means wetsuits need to be rinsed off and gear stored away. And very big fish—halibut and sea-bass—need cleaning. Such tasks are better done outdoors whenever possible, so the Hogans decided to install stations to handle these chores in the side yard of their home in Monarch Beach, California. Since this narrow corridor is visible from indoors, Robyn also wanted it to look pretty when it isn't in use. Capistrano Beach landscape architect Theresa

Clark managed to fit in an outdoor closet for scuba and fishing gear, a shower to use before and after water sports, and a sink for cleaning fish. (Robyn found the antique limestone sink in France.) "I also use the sink as a prep station when I'm working with cut flowers," says Robyn. "All the mess stays outside." There's a dog door to the space just big enough for the Hogans' pair of tiny papillons, Roxy and Lucy.

A trellis covered with a white-flowered potato vine *(Solanum jasminoides)*

Silvery green *Lamium* and deep green ajuga fill spaces between pavers in this narrow garden.

Small-space strategies

• **Create an espalier.** Training a plant to grow flat against a wall or fence is a great way to soften a narrow space. A wide variety of flowering shrubs and fruit trees lend themselves to this treatment. For sunny spots, consider citrus, 'Climbing Cécile Brunner' rose, *Cotoneaster lacteus,* crabapple, edible fig, mirror plant (*Coprosma repens),* and pyracantha. Camellia, goldenchain tree (*Laburnum watereri),* Texas mountain laurel (*Sophora secundiflora),* and vine maple (*Acer circinatum)* are good in part shade. For support, tie the plant's branches to a lath trellis or to a system of wires attached to the wall.

• **Attach planters to walls.** Flat-backed terra-cotta or stone containers can dress up walls outside windows. Or place flower boxes atop block walls and fill them with plants that have cascading habits, such as bacopa; this trick can also block out views from neighboring windows, providing more privacy.

• **Grow vines overhead.** For added privacy, install an elevated, horizontal trellis and train vines across it, creating a green roof over your side yard.

• **Hang art.** Use the wall between your house and your neighbor's as an art gallery. Mount a stone bas-relief, a copper sun god, or a wrought-iron gate or other piece of found art.

creates a picturesque focal point that draws attention away from the neighbor's house. Garden bench, urns, and antique door trim are final proof that no space is too small to be lovely.

Plant a pocket garden

When Herb and Karen Niles moved into their new house in Huntington Beach, California, they wanted to rework the narrow passageway that connects their front yard to a back patio. Despite the fact that the space measures just 6 feet wide and is in shade much of the day, the best option seemed to be a pretty garden viewed from inside the house. "We didn't want our only view to be of our neighbor's gray wall," Karen says.

To create pleasant views, Huntington Beach garden designers Sandy Atherton and Sherry Lewis planted tall, narrow, fast-growing shrubs—including camellias and *Podocarpus gracilior*—in front of the neighbor's wall (at right above). For a dash of color in a sunnier spot near the front, they added clematis vines. They left wide strips between large (2- by 2½-foot) slabs of Arizona flagstone for planting, and filled the spaces with giant ajuga and *Lamium maculatum* 'White Nancy'. Autumn ferns, begonias, and *Loropetalum chinense* 'Razzleberri' spill out into the pathway from beds beside the path.

"Because the garden is so shady, we relied on the texture and color of foliage instead of blooms," says Lewis. "And as a result, the garden looks great year-round." ◆

Lemon Grass–Coconut Sorbet

PREP AND COOK TIME: About 1 hour

NOTES: If you do not have an ice-cream maker, pour lemon grass mixture (after step 3) into a 9- by 13-inch dish and freeze just until firm, 2 to 4 hours. Scrape with a large fork to form a slushy ice; serve at once.

MAKES: About 1 quart; 4 to 6 servings

10	stalks fresh lemon grass (about 12 oz.), rinsed
1½	cups sugar
¼	teaspoon salt
¼	cup lemon juice
1	cup coconut milk (stir before measuring)

1. Peel toughest outer layers from lemon grass; discard. Cut into ½-inch lengths. In a 2- to 3-quart pan over high heat, combine lemon grass, sugar, salt, and 2½ cups water. Stir until liquid comes to a boil. Reduce heat; simmer, stirring occasionally, until light golden, about 20 minutes.

2. Pour through a fine strainer into a bowl, pressing on solids; discard solids. Nest bowl in a larger bowl of ice water and stir syrup until cool, about 5 minutes. Stir in lemon juice.

3. Whisk in coconut milk. If mixture is lumpy, pour through a fine strainer.

4. Pour into an ice-cream maker (at least 1 qt.) and freeze. Scoop into bowls or, for a firmer consistency, freeze airtight up to 3 days.

Per serving: 293 cal., 25% (74 cal.) from fat; 1.2 g protein; 8.2 g fat (7.1 g sat.); 58 g carbo (0 g fiber); 104 mg sodium; 0 mg chol.

Lemon zest

Plant a fast-growing herb with an aromatic zing

By Sharon Cohoon and Kate Washington
Photograph by Thomas J. Story

In the garden, lemon grass forms handsome clumps that reach 3 to 4 feet tall and nearly as wide, with lime green leaves rising from swollen bases. When harvested, the bulbous stems look like scallions, but pale yellow and more fibrous. When you cut them, the stems release essential oils, which immediately perfume the air with the mouthwatering aroma of freshly cut lemon combined with the clean bite of ginger.

Thai and Vietnamese cooks use lemon grass in marinades, stir-fries, curries, and soups. But this fragrant herb isn't limited to Asian cuisine. Make a sugar-syrup infusion to spice up lemonade or to use as the start of a dessert such as Lemon Grass–Coconut Sorbet (left).

Fresh lemon grass can be hard to find at the supermarket. But you can buy a small potted plant now, and you'll grow a large clump of your own by summer's end.

What lemon grass needs

EXPOSURE: Full sun.

SOIL: Rich, with good drainage.

WATER: Ample during growing season; less in winter, when it goes dormant.

FEED: Monthly with half-strength fish emulsion during the growing season.

CLIMATE NOTES: *Cymbopogon citratus* is a perennial in *Sunset* climate zones 12, 13, 16, 17, 23, 24, H1, and H2. Elsewhere, grow it as an annual or treat it like a geranium or other tender perennial by bringing the entire plant or a potted cutting indoors for the winter.

HARVEST: When stems are about ½ inch thick. Push an outside stem to the side, then twist and pull it off. Discard leaves and woody outer layers; save the white inner core.

PLANT SOURCES: Nichols Garden Nursery *(www.nicholsgardennursery.com or 800/422-3985)*. ◆

How to make a serene space

Create privacy.
Enclose the area with a fence, arbors, trellises, tall shrubs, or robust vines.

Use easy-care plants.
Choose ones that don't need lots of water or fussing over once established. Avoid plants that drop copious amounts of litter—maintenance shouldn't be a burden.

Add sensory elements.
Include a small fountain or water bowl. Fill pots with fragrant plants such as gardenia.

Include seating.
Add a bench, chair, or swing.

Illuminate.
Use low-voltage lights or portable lanterns. Float candles in water containers.

Make it your own.
Fill the space with favorite furnishings and garden art. Shop flea markets and junk stores for pieces that speak to you.

A water bowl is underplanted with diascias, hen and chicks, and *Salvia* x *superba*. Below, potted plants embellish a driveway.

A tranquil place
Create your own outdoor escape

By Lauren Bonar Swezey • Photographs by Norm Plate

One of the best places to find respite from the outside world is your garden. There, surrounded by greenery, fragrant flowers, and objects you love, you can relax and reconnect with nature.

For Cindy Jo Rose, who created these two sanctuaries at her home in Capitola, California, there is another benefit too. Her house is so small, she says, that her comfortably furnished outdoor nooks add to her living space.

For one tranquil corner, Rose screened part of the driveway with easy-care plants and bamboo trellises. Then she added a rattan chair and table, a water bowl, and garden art.

In the backyard, Rose, collaborating with designer Lynn Robinson *(831/426-5452),* used a fountain as the focal point of her "stone circle," which is paved with gravel, marbles, and beach rock. Paper umbrellas and a bench add to the magic. "The garden is my haven," says Rose. ◆

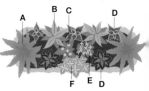

What to plant
This rich, mostly foliage composition contains **(A)** Medusa ferns *(Nephrolepis obliterata)*; **(B)** purple-leafed Persian shield; **(C)** 'Triple Yellow' *Datura metel;* **(D)** coleus; **(E)** fragrant, white-flowered bouvardia; **(F)** lamium.

Paradise in a pot

Common nursery plants can turn your patio into the tropics

By Sharon Cohoon • Photograph by Thomas J. Story • Container design by Bud Stuckey

Imagine Bali, the Indonesian island that enjoys perfect weather nearly year-round. Picture its lush green palms and ferns, its bright flowers. Breathe in the spicy-sweet scents of jasmine, tuberose, and frangipani.

The materials to create a Balinese corner in your garden are as close as your neighborhood nursery. Start in the houseplant section, and select a few plants to re-create that tropical mood with foliage. Add flowers too, especially if they have a rich tropical fragrance like *Bouvardia longiflora* or datura. But keep in mind that a pot containing primarily foliage will be easier to maintain.

The following plants thrive through summer and well into fall (when frost is immi-nent, bring the containers indoors). House-plants: arrowhead vine *(Syngonium);* bloodleaf *(Iresine);* bromeliads, especially billbergia, neo-regelia, and vriesea; calathea (peacock plant, zebra plant); cordyline; ctenanthe; and maranta (arrowroot, prayer plant, rabbit's foot). Foliage annuals: dwarf cannas; New Guinea impatiens; plectranthus; purple-leafed basil; shiso *(Perilla frutescens);* and variegated nasturtium. For fragrance, plant nicotiana or tuberose.

Consider adding exotic garden art to your pocket paradise. Mike and Robin Abrams of Los Altos, California, placed Balinese and Javanese statues by their tropical containers (one is shown above). ◆

More tropicals

HOUSEPLANTS:
• Aluminum plant *(Pilea cadierei)*
• Bromeliads
• Corn plant *(Dracaena fragrans)*
• Dieffenbachia
• Inch plant *(Callisia elegans)*
• Purple passion vine *(Gynura aurantiaca)*

FOLIAGE ANNUALS:
• Amaranth
• *Euphorbia marginata* 'Summer Icicle'
• Polka-dot plant *(Hypo-estes phyllostachya)*
• Zonal geraniums

Summer cleanup made easier

A shopper's guide to electric trimmers

By Jim McCausland

Just as detail work can make a car shine, edging and trimming make a garden look really sharp. Power trimmers can help you accomplish these tasks quickly and efficiently.

Gasoline-operated versions of these tools are available, but our focus is on electric models; as a group, they are lighter, cheaper, quieter, and cleaner to operate. And the best ones have more than enough power for small to medium jobs.

Electric models are classified by their power source.

Plug-in units. Running on the standard 120-volt current, these are usually more powerful and less expensive than battery-operated models. Extension cords are sold separately (expect to pay about $10 for a 100-foot cord).

Battery-operated models. Energized by rechargeable batteries, these tools offer cordless mobility and generally quieter operation—but they have less power than plug-ins and they're apt to run out of juice on longer or harder jobs. The batteries typically power a unit for 20 to 40 minutes on a single charge. Recharging takes from 3 to 24 hours, depending on the type of battery used. To extend operating time, you can also buy an extra battery ($30–$60).

Troy-Bilt's string trimmer ($75) has the preferred shaft-mounted motor.

String trimmers reach where mowers can't

They're great for edging lawns and trimming around sprinkler heads, sidewalks, and fences. They can reach under shrubs, too.

- If you want a plug-in unit, get one that has two lines of synthetic monofilament string with a cutting area 15 to 16 inches in diameter.

- Battery-powered units are usually limited to a single string with a smaller cutting area, usually 7 to 12 inches in diameter.

- Most string is .065 to .08 inch in diameter; the thicker the string, the longer it should last. When you run out of string, reload the spool with fresh line (about $7 for 140 feet).

- Trimmers whose motors are mounted at the top of the shaft usually have superior balance and longer life than those whose motors are mounted on the cutting head. (Head-mounted motors won't last as long because they operate in the dust kicked up by the whirling strings.)

- Heavy-duty motors (rated at 5 amps or more) perform better and last longer.

PRICE: $30–$100

CAUTION: When using a string trimmer, wear eye protection. Avoid nicking the trunks of trees and shrubs; these cuts can injure or kill the plant by girdling the bark. Commercial-grade line can damage asphalt driveways.

Hedge trimmers clip plants cleanly

Although they're made to cut back bushes, hedge trimmers can also be used for touch-up pruning on perennials, grasses, and ground covers.

- Dual-action trimmers with two moving blades cut more cleanly, quickly, and with less vibration than single-action models.

- Blade lengths vary: 16 inches is standard for small hedges, 18 inches for medium hedges, 20 inches or more for larger hedges. A longer blade makes it easier to trim the sides of the hedge in one even plane.

- Most hedge trimmers are labeled according to the size of the largest branch they can cut: $^3/_8$ inch is a good minimum; some units cut $^5/_8$ inch or larger. But actual cutting power depends on how stringy and hard the wood is—juniper, for example, can be very tough.

- Battery units are useful for touch-up pruning on fine-textured shrubs like boxwood, but they lack sufficient power for extended jobs.

PRICE: $30–$100

CAUTION: Be extremely careful when operating hedge trimmers: they can and will cut any object in front of the handguard. ◆

Hedge trimmer by Black & Decker ($70), with 22-inch blades, cuts an even plane.

CAREFUL PLANNING HELPS ASSURE that the abutilon, lavender, Santa Barbara daisy, and other flowering perennials in this garden will bloom along with the roses—right on time for a special event. You'll find tips on planting for a party on page 192.

SAXON HOLT

July

From driveway to sun garden

The leafy Oak Bay neighborhood of Victoria on Vancouver Island, British Columbia, is not the place you'd expect to find a colorful Mediterranean garden. Valerie Murray bought her home here 13 years ago because she was smitten with the huge Garry oaks on the property. Then she started attending meetings of the local hardy plant society and soon became equally smitten with the sun-loving Mediterranean plants she saw.

But the only sunny part of her property was a long asphalt driveway that passed by the back door. When her family started using that door as the main entrance, Murray dressed it up with some favorite containers. That first winter, she discovered that the overhanging eaves sheltered the more tender plants. So one hot summer day, when the asphalt was softened by the sun, Murray took a pick and started chipping away. Surmising that the resulting holes might make fine niches for sunken containers, she amended the underlying soil with compost and planted a *Euphorbia characias* and a tree lupine. Surrounded by warm asphalt, the plants thrived.

Then Murray rented a jackhammer and, with the help of her teenage son, she began to remove larger sections of the blacktop and fill them with plants. Now her driveway garden has at least 20 sunken containers and just as many above ground. They're filled with a variety of tender perennials and succulents such as aeoniums, echeverias, fancy-leafed geraniums, New Zealand flax, rockrose, and salvias. She likes to display flowers set against a background of green and silvery gray foliage. —*Fiona Gilsenan*

Stumped?
Go natural

Taking his cue from nature, Les Bugajski deftly planted a delphinium in an old juniper stump. "Nature would never have left that stump empty. Eventually, something would have seeded and grown in there. I just did it faster," says Bugajski, an artist and garden designer based in Vancouver, Washington.

In this woodland tableau, the stump is backed by a weeping form of Atlas cedar *(Cedrus atlantica)* on the left and a gold-tinged American arborvitae *(Thuja occidentalis* 'Rheingold') on the right. In the foreground are azalea, blue fescue, and heather.

Other tall-stemmed flowers that could work in a similar situation are cardinal flower *(Lobelia cardinalis)*, common foxglove *(Digitalis purpurea)*, and Joe Pye weed *(Eupatorium purpureum)*. —*Steven R. Lorton*

Costa Rican butterfly vine

Bow tie–shaped flowers cover Costa Rican butterfly vine *(Dalechampia dioscoreifolia)* in summer. Sold during the warm season in 4-inch containers, this tender vine can overwinter outdoors only in the mildest part of coastal Oregon (*Sunset* climate zone 17). Everywhere else in the Northwest, it makes the most sense to immediately transplant the vine into a 16-inch container, train the plant up a freestanding 4-foot trellis, and keep it in a warm, mostly sunny location. In fall, cut back the vine to about 1 foot and bring it into a frost-free porch or greenhouse for the winter.

Look for Costa Rican butterfly vine at nurseries and garden centers. If you can't find the vine locally, ask the nursery staff to order it from Log House Plants (wholesale only) in Cottage Grove, Oregon. Visit www.loghouseplants. com for a list of retailers.
—*Jim McCausland*

Kitchen garden in the round

When Tom and Jean Coghill invite friends to dine outdoors under the midnight sun at their home near Fairbanks in North Pole, Alaska, the food couldn't be any fresher. Surrounded by a circular kitchen garden, the Coghills and their guests are within arm's reach of arugula, kale, lettuce, spinach, Swiss chard, and an assortment of herbs. Salad ingredients are picked, washed at a nearby sink, and served within minutes at a festive table in the center of a 30-foot-diameter circle of lawn.

"We just created an outdoor room and used vegetables to decorate it," Jean says. Alternating bands of red- and green-leaf lettuce and heads of purple and white flowering cabbage highlight the 4-foot-wide bed. The garden is accented by a rustic willow birdhouse and a 1940s-era cast-iron stove nestled among nasturtiums, sunflowers, and herbs.

In this part of interior Alaska (*Sunset* climate zone A1), there are only 108 frost-free days in the growing season. Jean gets a jump-start by sowing vegetable and flower seeds in her garage in March. By June 1, the seedlings are ready to go into the bed, which has been thoroughly amended with compost. To keep the garden productive all summer, Jean applies liquid fertilizer monthly throughout the growing season and plugs in new seeds when she pulls out ripe crops.

The garden also entices wildlife. "This is a great moose salad bar," Jean explains, adding that she doesn't hesitate to yell and wave her arms to ward off the four-legged visitors. —*Nancy Tarnai*

Dinner is served in the center of a 30-foot-wide circle of lawn ringed by vegetables and flowers.

Grow your own scrubber

If you like to scrub with a sponge, why not grow one of your own? The gourds of *Luffa aegyptiaca* (sometimes sold as *L. cylindrica*) form on vines that are undeterred by the desert's intense summer heat, quickly scrambling 20 feet or more. The cleaned gourds make loofahs, great scrubbers for everything from rough elbows to kitchen sinks.

Pick a site that gets full sun and amend the soil with compost or organic matter. Provide a fence, trellis, or other sturdy support for the tendrils to climb. Such supports allow the 1- to 2-foot-long gourds to hang vertically in the air, where they aren't likely to rot (as they might on moist ground).

The gourds take about 120 days to reach maturity. Let them turn brown and dry on the vine (bottom right). Cut off one end, shake the seeds out, and save them for planting next year. Soak the gourds in water for a few hours to soften the outer shell, then peel or scrape it off to reveal the spongy fibers inside. Rinse the loofah thoroughly and hang it in the sun to dry. Once dry, it has a natural tan color. If you prefer a lighter, brighter sponge, soak the loofah overnight in a solution of 1 part household bleach to 10 parts water, then rinse and dry.

Luffa seeds are sold by Nichols Garden Nursery, www.nicholsgardennursery.com or (800) 422-3985.
—*Cathy Cromell*

UNTHIRSTY WESTERNERS

Sulfur flower

A member of the wild buckwheat family, *Eriogonum umbellatum* is one of those rare perennials that look good in or out of bloom. In summer, 3-inch-wide clusters of sunny yellow flowers are borne on sturdy 1- to 2-foot-tall stems over low mats of olive green leaves. Bees and butterflies are attracted to the blooms.

Hardy in all *Sunset* climate zones, sulfur flower tolerates heat and a wide range of soil conditions; it prefers full sun and needs only one deep soaking each month.

A robust selection called 'Shasta Sulfur' is offered by High Country Gardens, www.highcountrygardens. com or (800) 925-9387.
—*Marcia Tatroe*

Raising veggies in water-wise waffle beds

In the arid Southwest, Native Americans have traditionally planted small sunken gardens to collect sparse rainfall, creating an efficient water-harvesting method. When many of these square basins were dug in close rows, they formed a pattern resembling the grids of a waffle iron. Modern-day desert gardeners who have adopted this ancient practice call the sunken gardens waffle beds.

Master Gardener Linda Trujillo of Chandler, Arizona, grows a variety of crops in the waffle beds she forms in her backyard. In spring and summer, she raises beans, black-eyed peas, chilies, corn, melons, okra, and squash.

First, cultivate soil so it's loose and easy to work. Then push a plastic nursery flat into the soil, sliding it back and forth to shape uniform squares with level bottoms. The number of indentations will vary depending on the amount of space you have. As a guide, form waffles 15 to 18 inches square and 3 to 4 inches deep. Allow 4 to 6 inches of space between the squares.

In anticipation of monsoon rains, you can sow seeds of corn, melons, and squash directly in the squares.
—*C. C.*

Mojave style in Las Vegas

When architect Steven Carpenter designed his home in Las Vegas, he utilized earthy colors to complement the natural hues of the surrounding Mojave Desert. For the sunny, south-facing front yard, Carpenter wanted a simple and sensible landscape. He enlisted Brian Patterson, landscape architect for the WLB Group *(702/458-2551),* to create plantings that would tolerate the harsh conditions.

Patterson painted a desert scene by arranging plants in groups as they appear in nature: low-growing *Acacia redolens* 'Desert Carpet', deer grass (*Muhlenbergia rigens*), desert spoon *(Dasylirion wheeleri),* and purple prickly pear *(Opuntia violacea santa-rita).* He dotted the yard with boulders, which are softened by the deer grass and trailing *Lantana* 'New Gold'. Single specimens of other unthirsty plants were chosen for their sculptural form and seasonal color, including barrel cactus, blue palo verde *(Cercidium floridum),* and spiky ocotillo *(Fouquieria splendens).* Inside the arched entry, an inviting courtyard is planted with red bird of paradise *(Caesalpinia pulcherrima), Ficus pumila,* and *Pittosporum tobira* 'Variegata', with more ocotillo on the right.

The yard is watered by a drip-irrigation system. A 2-inch layer of palomino coral granite over the soil helps conserve moisture. —*Gail Mueller*

Betsy Miller's picks

Aquilegia 'Betsy's Bonnet'. Doug Miller bred this pinkish lavender columbine and named it for his wife. Blooms May through July; 18 to 20 inches tall.

Dianthus deltoides 'Brilliancy'. Fuchsia-blue blossoms emerge in sprays June through July; only 6 inches tall.

Erigeron speciosus 'Azure Fairy'. Soft lavender-blue flowers tolerate mid- to late-summer heat and drought; 18 inches tall.

Gaillardia x *grandiflora* 'Burgundy'. Wine red flowers come in late summer; 20 to 24 inches tall.

Heliopsis helianthoides 'Summer Sun'. Profuse semidouble yellow blooms appear July to frost; 30 to 36 inches tall.

Knautia macedonica Melton Pastels. Flowers resembling pincushions, in shades of blue, mauve, pink, or crimson, appear July through September; 20 to 30 inches tall.

Maltese cross (*Lychnis chalcedonica*). Neon orange-red flower clusters appear June through August; 3 to 4 feet tall.

Betsy and Doug Miller check a bed of pink *Centaurea dealbata* and lavender-blue *Campanula persicifolia*. Below: *Gaillardia* x *grandiflora* 'Burgundy' (right) and *Erigeron speciosus* 'Azure Fairy'.

Acres of hardy perennials

Seven years ago, Betsy and Doug Miller and Betsy's mother, Margaret Larsen, jumped into the wholesale nursery trade by growing 16,000 tomato seedlings in their basement. Soon, however, they decided to shift their focus from annuals to perennials. Today, as the owners of Montana Perennial Farms, the Millers and Larsen cultivate more than 450 kinds of cold-hardy perennials on 20 acres in Belgrade, Montana, just north of Bozeman. While the three sell most of their plants to nurseries and garden centers, they also sell directly to the public, welcoming visitors to their farm and gardens from May 15 through September 30. They also offer weekend workshops on designing, planting, and maintaining a perennial garden. Seven of Betsy's favorite bloomers are described above, at left.

Montana Perennial Farms, 2545 Spain Bridge Rd.; (406) 388-0425. Call for directions.

—*Kim Thielman-Ibes*

Edelweiss grows high in the Rockies

Jane R. and Klaus Hendrix of Breckenridge, Colorado, don't find that gardening at an altitude of 10,000 feet is a challenge. The couple's Mountain View Experimental Gardens (at their home) inspire other high-elevation gardeners. Despite frigid winters and short summers, they grow more than 600 species of flowering plants on a suburban-size lot.

One of their favorites is the beloved Swiss alpine wildflower, edelweiss (*Leontopodium alpinum*). Its starlike flowers appear all summer through October. This perennial is hardy in *Sunset* climate zones 1–9. The 6- to 12-inch-tall plant prefers full sun and well-drained alkaline soil, and it likes a gravel mulch spread over its crown. In the planting pictured above, edelweiss is backed by scarlet *Lychnis x arkwrightii* 'Vesuvius'.

Edelweiss plants are available from Siskiyou Rare Plant Nursery, www. siskiyourareplantnursery. com or (541) 772-6846.
—*M.T.*

Clematis columns accent a fence

In this Denver garden, clematis form striking vertical accents on a wood fence. James Love, a gardener with Frances Shure Designs, planted the deciduous vines along the base of the fence at 3- to 6-foot intervals, depending on the size of the variety. He then trained the vines up plastic-coated wire mesh, tying the stems with twine to hold them in position. Among the hybrids blooming here in early summer are 'Ernest Markham' (right) and 'Niobe' (center).

There's an old saying about growing clema-

tis: flowers in the sun, feet in the shade. In this garden, the east-facing fence allows the clematis to bask in gentle sun all morning, then snooze in the shade most of the afternoon. To help keep them cool, the clematis roots are overplanted with New Guinea impatiens, petunias, and *Houttuynia cordata* 'Variegata' with ivylike leaves. Love generally doesn't fertilize the clematis, but the soil is amended every other year with a high-quality compost.

—*Colleen Smith*

Drought-proof color in Colorado Springs

When Eric and Rita Von Sacken landscaped their home in Colorado Springs, they wanted to take a water-thrifty approach. Eric, an advocate of xeriscaping, served as superintendent of water systems for Colorado Springs Utilities before retiring recently. And last summer, as the drought bore down with a vengeance on the Intermountain states, the Von Sackens' garden not only survived, it was vibrant with color all summer.

The Von Sackens' rock garden is well suited to the 6,800-foot foothills

environment. In the view at left, drifts of fragrant 'Hidcote' English lavender flow down the hill. Seeds of this fragrant plant took root in the cracks between the boulders. In July, the 1½- to 2-foot-tall lavender spikes contrast with bright yellow gloriosa daisies (*Rudbeckia hirta*) and white Shasta daisies that have naturalized above the wall. Low-growing partridge feather (*Tanacetum densum amanii*), with silver foliage and tiny yellow flowers, spills over the boulders in the foreground. —*M. T.*

Avocado for small yards

A new Guatemalan-type avocado tree, named 'Holiday', is ideal for the backyard grower. Among its many virtues, 'Holiday' grows to only 10 to 12 feet tall—small for an avocado tree. Nonetheless, it produces generously, and the avocados it bears are large, weighing 15 to 30 ounces each.

None of this would matter, of course, if the fruit weren't tasty. But 'Holiday' avocados have a rich, mellow flavor. They ripen at a welcome time, August through December, when other varieties have finished bearing.

Because of its oversize avocados, 'Holiday'—one of thou-sands of seedlings developed in the breeding program at UC Riverside—seemed to have no commercial potential. But Julie Frink, curator of the avocado variety collection at the University of California South Coast Research and Extension Center in Irvine, recognized the seedling's backyard potential and became its relentless champion. "She's the guiding force that got it to market," says Bob Bergh, emeritus specialist at UC Riverside. "She rescued it from oblivion."

'Holiday' will be available this summer at nurseries throughout Southern California. —Sharon Cohoon

Bali chair grows tropicals

Giving an old chair a second life as an amusing planter is not a new idea. But the tropical planting pictured here, at Mystic Gardens in San Juan Capistrano, gives this concept a fresh spin.

Its designers, Carlos and Carmen Hernandez, removed the seat from a used chair and replaced it with a sling of black nursery shadecloth, stapling the cloth in place. They lined the sling with moss, filled it with potting soil, then planted a lush bird's nest fern and *Spathiphyllum*. For brilliant color, the couple chose several varieties of coleus, a flowering bromeliad, and pink impatiens. Variegated ivy and periwinkle trail over the chair's edges.

Not feeling crafty? Drop by Mystic Gardens *(27401 Ortega Hwy.; 949/ 488-0074)* for inspiration.
—*S. C.*

A garden fit for a hacienda

Garden designer and artist Dinah Grisdale believes that a garden should fit the style of the house it surrounds. It's no wonder, then, that the landscaping around her hacienda-style house in San Diego's Mission Hills neighborhood looks like a bit of Spain or old Mexico.

The house, designed by legendary architect Cliff May during the 1930s, is a sprawling low-profile structure that nudges the outward curve of a corner lot. It has a secluded inner courtyard filled with potted plants and artifacts that Grisdale and husband Michael collect on their travels, and a narrow strip of yard facing the street.

Drawing upon her love for the desert, Grisdale planted the streetside landscape, pictured at right, to suit not only the house but also San Diego's arid climate. Outside the front door, a huge variegated *Agave americana* and a pair of stately *Opuntia* cactus stand sentry. Nearby are blue-green agaves, low-water perennials, and a large angel's trumpet *(Brugmansia)* that dangles fragrant blooms in spring.

Left of the front door are irregularly shaped planting beds edged with dry-stacked Arizona flagstone. Grisdale placed rocks in the beds for a backdrop, then used plants as architectural elements and color echoes. The raised-bed plantings, which include aeonium, Jerusalem sage *(Phlomis fruticosa),* and sedum, repeat the same shades of sunny yellow as the angel's trumpet blooms and the variegated aloe.

A sea of rounded river gravel sur-

rounds the planting beds; Grisdale thinks of the gravel as a beautiful grass substitute—one that requires no mowing or watering.

By echoing the house's hacienda style, Grisdale has created a stunning garden that requires little water or maintenance. Cliff May would be proud. —*Nan Sterman*

Planting for a party

If you're planning to host a backyard garden tour, wedding, or dinner party this summer, you might want to take a few tips from Sebastopol-based landscape designer Maile Arnold, who regularly prepares home landscapes for special events (see photo at right and on page 182). For each occasion, Arnold's goal is always the same: flower power.

Rather than planting for a succession of blooms through all seasons, she follows a timetable so that every one of the plants will be blooming together when the big day arrives. She plants annuals— or sets out containers of them—to fill bare spots between shrubs, perennials, and trees, choosing ones whose flower colors complement existing plants. See the detailed "Countdown to bloom time" at right. —*Lauren Bonar Swezey*

Dog tunnel

Landscape designer Pamela Simonds of Pleasant Hill wanted her Border collie–terrier mix, Rudy, to enjoy the entire backyard, not just a dog run. Yet she couldn't allow him to destroy plants. Her solution, a tunnel through a planting mound, was inspired by Rudy's agility training; he had learned how to run through tunnels along an obstacle course.

Simonds fashioned the 7-foot-long tunnel from an 18-inch-diameter black ADS (advanced drainage system) pipe. To allow for drainage, she sunk the front end about 5 inches into the soil, raised the rear end about 3 inches, and lined the bottom with 3 to 6 inches of decomposed granite. A mound of soil covers the pipe; dry-stacked (without mortar) broken concrete holds it in place.

—*L. B. S.*

Countdown to bloom time

Eight weeks out: Fill bare spots between shrubs and trees with annuals. To save money, use small plants from sixpacks.

Six weeks out: Prune flowers from all plants that can rebloom—annuals, perennials, roses, and shrubs.Clip off open flowers as well as buds. Do not cut back foliage. Keep in mind that plants take longer to rebloom when the weather is cool and wet.

Start fertilizing all plants once a week. Finely spray leaves with a half-strength water-soluble fertilizer, one that's low in nitrogen and high in phosphorous and potassium. Maile Arnold uses Miracle-Gro Water Soluble All Purpose Plant Food, but other kinds, such as Omega 1-5-5 *(available from Peaceful Valley Farm Supply, www.groworganic.com or 888/784-1722),* also work well. When the weather is hot, feed early in the morning or in the evening; do not foliar feed when temperatures rise above 85°.

Water plants regularly; annuals may need irrigation daily during hot or windy weather.

Two weeks out: For an instant effect, plant annuals from 4-inch pots and 1-gallon cans, perennials from 1-gallon cans. Discontinue fertilizing all plants until after the event, but continue regular watering.

BACK TO BASICS

Irrigate trees

Now that summer's dry days are upon us, trees—particularly those planted within the past five years—need water. Deep irrigate them when the top 2 to 3 inches of soil are almost dry. Build a berm of soil around the tree's drip line. Turn on the hose to a slow trickle, and allow it to run into the basin for about 30 minutes. Check moisture penetration by digging down with a trowel; water longer if necessary. To irrigate more mature trees, use a deep root irrigator. On the ground beneath the canopy, encircle the trunk with several soaker hoses spaced about 3 feet apart. —*L. B. S.*

WHAT TO DO IN YOUR GARDEN IN JULY

PLANTING

☐ **ANNUAL COLOR.** For flowers or foliage color from now until frost, try bedding or wax begonias, coleus, impatiens, marigolds, million bells, petunias, and zinnias.

☐ **CROPS FOR FALL HARVEST.** Sow seeds of these crops directly in the ground: beets, broccoli, bush beans, carrots, chard, Chinese cabbage, kohlrabi, lettuce, peas, radishes, scallions, spinach, and turnips. A good Northwest source is Ed Hume Seed (*www.humeseeds.com*).

☐ **LAWN.** *Sunset* climate zones A2–A3: Sow grass seed or lay sod. Use Kentucky blue grass in sunny areas, red fescue in shade. Water the lawn regularly until fall dormancy.

☐ **PERENNIALS.** Shop nurseries for asters, black-eyed Susan, canna, chrysanthemums, coreopsis, and purple coneflowers. Plant immediately.

MAINTENANCE

☐ **CARE FOR FUCHSIAS.** Deadhead faded blooms to keep new flowers coming. Feed container plants with a complete liquid fertilizer every two weeks; plants in the ground need only monthly feeding.

☐ **CONTROL SLUGS.** Use one or more of these methods: handpick them at night, set out beer traps, or spread a chemical bait. There are two kinds of bait: relatively safe but less-effective iron phosphate–based products, and those containing metaldehyde, which must be kept away from children and pets.

☐ **DIVIDE BEARDED IRISES.** As foliage tips start to die, stop watering bearded irises. When most foliage is withered, dig up the rhizomes and use a knife to cut them into pieces 3 to 4 inches long (they should be firm and white inside). Trim leaf fans back to 6 inches. Let the rhizomes dry in the shade for a few days, then replant 1 foot apart.

☐ **DIVIDE ORIENTAL POPPIES.** After tops die down, dig up clumps, separate the intertwined roots, and replant divisions (one parent can easily yield a dozen new ones).

☐ **FEED MUMS.** To stimulate fall bloom, use a high-phosphorus liquid fertilizer every three weeks until buds start to show color. Once the first blooms open, feed weekly.

☐ **FERTILIZE STRAWBERRY BEDS.** After you harvest June-bearing strawberries, apply 2 pounds of 10-10-10 fertilizer per 100 square feet.

☐ **MAINTAIN GROUNDCOVERS.** Shear them back with a lawn mower, string trimmer, or brush cutter. Then scatter a complete granular fertilizer (10-8-6, for example) over the bed and water it in well.

☐ **SPREAD MULCH AROUND SHRUBS.** Put a 2- to 4-inch layer of organic mulch such as leaf mold or shredded bark over the root zones of shrubs, especially azaleas, camellias, and rhododendrons.

☐ **WATER WISELY.** Irrigate early in the morning to minimize evaporation.

☐ **WEED.** Hoe young weeds on a warm, dry morning, and the sun will bake their exposed roots by evening. Pull mature weeds right after watering, when their taproots can be easily removed from damp soil. ◆

WHAT TO DO IN YOUR GARDEN IN JULY

PLANTING

☐ **GOPHER RESISTANT PLANTS.** If gophers are troublesome in your garden, try growing some of the following plants. Ruth Valiquette, who has grown all of them in her Manteca yard for years, finds these plants to be free of gopher damage. **Trees:** apricot, avocado, eucalyptus, 'Marshall' seedless green ash, Japanese maple ('Senkaki' and 'Koshimino'), lemon, fruitless mulberry, plum, pomegranate. **Shrubs:** banana shrub (*Michelia figo),* bottlebrush, breath of heaven, butterfly bush, *Caesalpinia, Ceanothus, Escallonia, Euonymus japonicus,* fuchsia, *Grevillea,* heavenly bamboo, hydrangea, India hawthorn, lavender, rose, rosemary, strawberry tree, toyon. **Perennials, herbs:** borage, catnip, coral bells, ferns, fibrous begonia, lantana, *Nierembergia,* penstemon, periwinkle, Shasta daisy.

☐ **PATRIOTIC POTS.** To fill a pot or two with flowers in patriotic colors for a Fourth of July gathering, choose from these plants. **Red:** annual phlox, celosia, dahlia, geranium, nicotiana (flowering tobacco), petunia, scarlet sage *(Salvia splendens),* or tropical sage *(S. coccinea).* **White:** annual phlox, dahlia, dwarf cosmos, geranium, heliotrope, nemesia, nicotiana, petunia, sweet alyssum. **Blue:** gentian sage *(S. patens),* lobelia, mealycup sage *(S. farinacea),* nemesia, petunia, or verbena. All of these plants require full sun.

Sunset
CLIMATE ZONES

☐ Mountain (1–2)
☐ Valley (7–9)
☐ Inland (14)
☐ Coastal (15–17)

MAINTENANCE

☐ **CARE FOR FRUIT TREES.** To prevent limb breakage on apple, peach, pear, and plum trees, use wooden supports to brace limbs that are sagging with fruit. Also, clean up and discard fallen fruits (worms, diseases, and other pests may be living in them).

☐ **DIVIDE IRISES.** Dig up old clumps with a spading fork, then cut the rhizomes apart with a sharp knife; be sure that each division includes at least one leaf. Replant the younger, vigorous sections of rhizomes.

☐ **FERTILIZE CYMBIDIUMS.** Every time you irrigate, also apply a liquid fertilizer (such as 20-20-20) that's been diluted to half the recommended strength.

☐ **PROTECT AGAINST FIRE.** In fireprone areas such as Lake Tahoe, Marin County, and the Oakland hills, now's the time to protect your house and garden from wildfires that can ignite when days are hot and dry and vegetation on adjacent wildlands is drought stressed. Mow weeds and thin out shrubs for at least 30 feet around your house (or to within the property line, whichever is closer). Prune off tree limbs that hang over the roof. Remove fuel ladders—bushy shrubs that touch low-hanging tree branches. Clear your roof of debris such as fallen leaves.

☐ **REST YOUR ROSES.** *Sunset* climate zones 7–9, 14: Heat-stressed roses will provide a much more spectacular bloom in the fall if you allow them to rest now. Instead of deadheading, let rose hips form. Stop fertilizing the plants. Irrigate often enough to keep them healthy. To encourage a flush of fall bloom, trim off the hips in late summer, then apply fertilizer.

PEST CONTROL

☐ **CONTROL BUDWORMS.** Zones 7–9, 14–17: If your geraniums, nicotiana, penstemons, and petunias appear healthy but have no flowers, suspect budworms. Look for holes in buds and black droppings on the leaves. Spray affected plants every 7 to 10 days with *Bacillus thuringiensis* (Bt), available at most nurseries or by mail from Harmony Farm Supply & Nursery in Sebastopol *(www. harmonyfarm.com or 707/823-9125).* ◆

WHAT TO DO IN YOUR GARDEN IN JULY

PLANTING

□ **ANNUALS.** It's not too late to plant annuals in pots or garden beds, if you stick to heat lovers like celosia, marigold, portulaca, vinca, and zinnias.

□ **BIENNIALS.** For bloom next spring, sow seeds of Canterbury bell, foxglove, hollyhock, Sweet William, and verbascum now. In the fall, transplant seedlings to the garden when plants are about 4 inches tall.

□ **CITRUS.** If your garden is small but you want to grow citrus, try an Ultra-Dwarf Citrus tree, which grows just 6 feet tall—ideal for containers. Plants (grapefruit, lemon, lime, mandarin, orange, tangelo) are available at Armstrong Garden Centers *(www.armstronggarden.com or 800/557-2687).*

□ **ORNAMENTALS.** Bring the tropics to your garden by planting palms, philodendrons, tree ferns, and other heat-loving evergreens. Now is also the time to plant flowering shrubs such as angel's trumpet *(Brugmansia),* bougainvillea, hibiscus, night jessamine *(Cestrum nocturnum),* passionflower, thunbergia, and trumpet vines. Fill containers with bromeliads and croton.

□ **PERENNIALS.** Plants that put on a good show in summer and well into fall include asters, coreopsis, gaura, lion's tail, marguerite daisies, and rudbeckia.

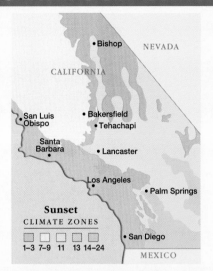

□ **SUBTROPICAL FRUITS.** Avocado, cherimoya, guava, mango, and other exotic fruit trees are plentiful in nurseries now.

□ **SUMMER VEGETABLES.** Coastal *(Sunset* climate zones 22–24) and inland (zones 18–21) gardeners can continue to plant summer vegetables. Set out cucumber, eggplant, pepper, squash, and tomato plants. Sow snap beans and corn. For varieties beyond the usual nursery choices, try mail-order companies that specialize in vegetables. Two good ones are Territorial Seed Company *(www.territorialseed.com or 541/942-9547)* and Seeds of Change *(www.seedsofchange.com or 888/762-7333).*

MAINTENANCE

□ **ADJUST MOWING HEIGHT.** To keep their roots shaded and to conserve soil moisture, allow tall fescues to grow 2 to 3 inches tall during hot weather. Warm-season grasses like Bermuda and St. Augustine, on the other hand, should be kept below 1 inch tall to lessen thatch buildup.

□ **FEED SELECTIVELY.** Feed annual flowers and vegetables, container plants, cymbidium orchids, roses, tropicals, and warm-season lawns. If you didn't fertilize citrus and avocado last month, do that now.

□ **SPEED MELON HARVEST.** To keep ripening melons off damp soil that could rot them, place melons on upside-down aluminum pie pans. The pans also will speed up ripening.

□ **WATER CAREFULLY.** Give shade trees a slow, deep soak once a month. Water established shrubs and perennials deeply too. Shallow-rooted citrus and avocados need more frequent irrigation. Water once a week inland, every other week along the coast. Container plants need more frequent watering; small pots may need a daily soaking.

PEST CONTROL

□ **WATCH FOR TOMATO HORNWORMS.** Handpick them from tomato plants. The green worms will be easier to spot if you sprinkle the tomato foliage lightly with water first. The worms will shake off the water, a motion that makes them more visible. ◆

WHAT TO DO IN YOUR GARDEN IN JULY

PLANTING

☐ **REPLACE COOL-SEASON ANNU-ALS.** Iceland poppies, lobelia, pansies, and stock can't stand intense summer heat. When they start looking ragged, pull them out and replant beds and containers with heat-loving annuals such as gazania, globe amaranth *(Gomphrena),* Madagascar periwinkle, petunia, portulaca, sunflower, and zinnia.

☐ **SET OUT IRISES.** Bearded irises tolerate long periods without irrigation, especially when they are dormant in mid- to late-summer. A good mail-order source for bearded types and many other irises (as well as daylilies) is Willow Bend Farm in Eckert, Colorado *(www.willowbendirisfarm.com or 970/835-3389).*

MAINTENANCE

☐ **DIVIDE BEARDED IRISES.** The best time to divide overcrowded clumps of bearded irises is six weeks after they finish blooming. Lift and dig up the rhizomes with a spade, then use a sharp knife to cut them into pieces about 3 to 4 inches long. Trim back leaf fans to 6 inches. Let the rhizomes dry in the shade for a few days, then replant 1 foot apart. Before replanting, amend the soil by digging in compost or well-rotted manure and a handful of balanced fertilizer.

☐ **DIVIDE ORIENTAL POPPIES.** After tops die down, dig up clumps, separate the intertwined roots, and replant divisions (one parent can easily yield a dozen new ones).

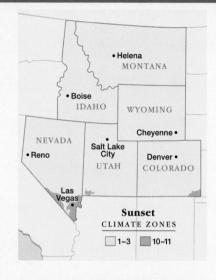

Sunset
CLIMATE ZONES

☐ 1–3   ☐ 10–11

☐ **DON'T NEGLECT HOUSEPLANTS.** Before you go on vacation, place your houseplants in the bathtub or a shower enclosure in a cool bathroom. Water until the soil is saturated, then cover the plants loosely with a sheet of clear plastic to hold in moisture. Leave the light on; the plants should be okay for up to two weeks.

☐ **FERTILIZE STRAWBERRY BEDS.** After you harvest June-bearing strawberries, apply 2 pounds of 10-10-10 fertilizer per 100 square feet.

☐ **GET DROUGHT HELP ONLINE.** These websites offer many useful tips for coping with drought: *http://drought. colostate.edu,* sponsored by Colorado State University; *www.greenco.org,* sponsored by the Green Industries of Colorado; and *www.xeriscape.org,* sponsored by Xeriscape Colorado.

☐ **PROTECT APPLE TREES.** Larvae of apple maggot flies and coddling moths damage fruit by boring into it. Hang yellow sticky traps and sticky red spheres in trees to trap apple maggot flies before they lay eggs. To prevent damage from coddling moth caterpillars, release parasitic *Trichogramma* wasps, available from Gardens Alive *(www.gardensalive.com or 513/354-1482).*

☐ **SPRAY PESTS WITH SUMMER OIL.** To control outbreaks of aphids, leafhoppers, leaf miners, mealybugs, mites, sawfly larvae, and whitefly, spray affected plants with lightweight summer oil such as Ultra-Fine (available at garden centers), which effectively suffocates these pests. Thoroughly spray product on the tops and undersides of leaves.

☐ **WATER WISELY.** Most plants die if overwatered, so irrigate only when needed and check soil moisture first. To reduce evaporation, water when temperatures are cool and the air is still, usually in the early morning or evening. Apply enough water to moisten the soil in the root zone, generally 6 to 12 inches deep. Soaker hoses are an efficient way to deliver water along rows of vegetables or flowers. —*M. T.* ◆

WHAT TO DO IN YOUR GARDEN IN JULY

PLANTING

☐ **GOURDS.** For centuries, gourds have been cultivated for use as canteens, ladles, and musical instruments. Sow groups of three seeds 3 feet apart; when seedlings reach 2 inches tall, thin to the single strongest plant in each group. Harvest fruit after the first frost and allow them to cure in a warm, dry place. Some varieties to try include 'Bird's Nest' from Seeds of Change *(www.seedsofchange.com or 888/762-7333),* 'Buffalo Gourd' from Plants of the Southwest *(www. plantsofthesouthwest.com or 800/788-7333),* and 'O'odham Dipper' or 'Tarahumara Canteen' from Native Seeds/SEARCH *(www.nativeseeds.org or 520/622-5561).*

☐ **LANDSCAPE PLANTS.** *Sunset* climate zones 10–13: Set out drought-tolerant trees and shrubs, including acacia, desert ironwood *(Olneya tesota),* feather bush *(Lysiloma thornberi),* jujube *(Ziziphus jujuba),* Mexican-buckeye *(Ungnadia speciosa),* palms, and Texas ebony *(Pithecellobium flexicaule).* Add accent or specimen plants such as agave, aloe, euphorbia, ocotillo, and yucca.

☐ **SUMMER COLOR.** Set out heat-tolerant plants such as agastache, amaranth, celosia, cosmos, creeping zinnia *(Sanvitalia procumbens),* four o'clock, gaillardia, gazania, globe amaranth *(Gomphrena),* hollyhock, kochia, lisianthus *(Eustoma grandiflorum),* Madagascar periwinkle, marigold, portulaca, and zinnia.

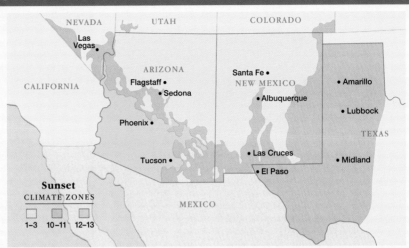

Sunset
CLIMATE ZONES

☐ 1–3 ☐ 10–11 ☐ 12–13

☐ **WARM-SEASON VEGGIES.** Zones 1A–3B (Flagstaff, Taos, Santa Fe): Sow bush beans, collards, cucumbers, eggplants, melons, okra, snap beans. Zones 10, 11 (Albuquerque, Las Vegas): Sow corn, cucumbers, melons, pumpkins, and squash. Zones 12, 13 (Tucson, Phoenix): Sow black-eyed peas, corn, melons, okra, pumpkins, and squash. The sources listed above left in "Gourds" offer seeds of crops suited for the Southwest.

MAINTENANCE

☐ **COLLECT RAINWATER.** In anticipation of summer monsoons, mound soil into berms around trees and shrubs to form catch basins for rainwater. Install downspout extensions *(available from Gardener's Supply, www. gardeners.com or 800/427-3363)* to direct runoff from roof into basins or low-lying areas of the garden.

☐ **CONTROL INSECT PESTS.** If you see green aphids on new growth or white cottony cochineal scale infesting prickly pear pads, blast them off plants with a strong jet of water.

☐ **CONTROL OLEANDER GALL.** This bacterial disease causes blackened and deformed flowers and wartlike galls on oleanders. To prevent its spread, prune out all infected wood. After each cut, clean the blades with a solution of 1 part bleach to 10 parts water.

☐ **XERISCAPING AID ONLINE.** These websites can help you plan and maintain a water-thrifty landscape. Check out "Plants and Water" at *http://ag.arizona.edu/gardening/plantwater.html.* Read about "Landscape Water Conservation" at *www.cahe.nmsu.edu/pubs/_h/h-707.html.* Visit *www.cabq.gov/hot/xeriscape.html* to see six "Free Xeriscape Designs." —*Kim Nelson*

BEFORE

Cinderella makeover

How a barren backyard in Oregon became a dreamy space

By Mary-Kate Mackey • Photographs by Janet Loughrey

Not too long ago, this backyard in Beaverton, Oregon, looked so bleak that the homeowners admit they used to leave the curtains down all the time "because it was so gross out there." Then one day, Oprah Winfrey announced that she was searching for a "nightmare yard" to transform as a topic on her show. So the homeowners submitted a video of the barren 86- by 35-foot backyard, showing a dead fir surrounded by straggly grass (above). Then they crossed their fingers.

Their wish came true. The yard was chosen for an instant garden makeover. To accomplish a swift transformation, the *Oprah Winfrey Show's* producers enlisted the help of Los Angeles landscape designer Nicholas Walker of Jardin du Jour and Portland-based Craig Prunty of All Oregon Landscaping.

"I'd done a makeover before in three days," Walker explains, "but Oprah's people said, 'You have to do it in

Colorful foliage plants now sweep across the once-bleak corner shown at left. Red-leafed Japanese barberries play off green-and-white hostas and deep red 'Bloodgood' Japanese maple (far right). Behind, a golden deodar cedar and rich green incense cedars create a privacy screen.

12 steps, from paper to party time

1. Draw up a basic design with separate divisions for dining or just relaxing.

2. Order paving materials, plants, and furnishings.

3. Remove any dead or unwanted plants. Strip sod from old lawns.

4. Form berms around fences to create a raised planting area with greater visual interest. Use the flat area near the house for lawn and beds.

5. Enrich the soil. The remodel team amended the existing heavy clay soil with sandy loam, lime, and mushroom compost.

6. Place stonework, including boulders. The team laid basalt slabs as steps leading up to a bench.

7. Install electrical or irrigation lines.

8. Put down paths.

9. Lay out all trees and shrubs atop the soil to find the best arrangement, then plant them.

10. Move in furnishings and structures such as playhouses or storage sheds.

11. Install sod lawn.

12. Spread mulch over the beds. The remodel team here used dark hemlock bark mulch. Relax and enjoy the garden.

Awash in dwarf periwinkle, stone slabs step up to a seating area at the base of an oak tree. Behind the concrete bench are pink 'Rosamundi' rhododendrons and white-flowered dogwood.

two.' We made it happen because we all worked together as a team."

In those two whirlwind days, a 20-person team regraded the hillside, forming wide berms for borders around the perimeter; planted trees and flowering shrubs; added finishing touches like a garden bench; and installed a lawn of perennial rye grass sod. They even installed a cheerful 4- by 4-foot playhouse in one corner for the couple's daughter.

By choosing plants the owners could maintain easily, the design team ensured that this wonder garden wouldn't disappear once the television crew departed. The designers relied mainly on trees and shrubs with striking foliage color and texture, plus a few seasonal bloomers like rhododendrons. Plants needing more maintenance, like annuals, perennials, and roses, were used only as accents.

Two years later, the yard looks more lush than the day it was planted. Instead of shunning it as they once did, the homeowners say they now plan events around the garden.

The landscape is filled with ideas, like the multilayered plantings on the berms, a dry creek bed that runs from the fence and spills into the lawn, and a boulder that forms a gently bubbling fountain near the patio.

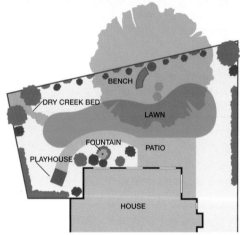

Unless you have a fairy godmother (or Oprah) with a magic wand, expect that a major garden remodel like this would take a contractor three to four weeks from planning to installation, according to Prunty.

DESIGN TEAM: Nicholas Walker, Jardin du Jour, Los Angeles *(310/557-2700);* Mario Navarro, All Oregon Landscaping, Portland *(503/646-6426)*

INSTALLATION: Craig Prunty, All Oregon Landscaping (see above)

PLAYHOUSE: Barbara Butler, Barbara Butler Artist-Builder, San Francisco *(415/864-6840)*

ILLUSTRATION: ARTHUR MOUNT

Left: Smooth river rocks form a dry creek bed fringed by tawny leather leaf sedges, white-edged 'Patriot' hostas, and barberries.
Middle left: 'Crimson Pygmy' barberry contrasts with 'Goldflame' spiraea.
Middle right: Water bubbling out of a boulder is pumped up from a collecting basin at the base through a pipe hidden in the rock.

Plant palette

TREES AND SHRUBS

Deciduous

Azalea 'White Lights'. *Sunset Western Garden Book* climate zones A2, A3, 1–7.

Japanese barberry (*Berberis thunbergii* 'Aurea', 'Crimson Pygmy', 'Rose Glow'). Zones A3, 2B–24.

Japanese maple (*Acer palmatum* 'Bloodgood'). Zones A3, 2–10, 12, 14–24.

Japanese snowdrop tree (*Styrax japonicus*). Zones 4–9, 14–21.

Kousa dogwood (*Cornus kousa*). Zones 2–9, 14–17.

Norway maple (*Acer platanoides* 'Crimson Sentry'). Zones A2, A3, 1–9, 14–17.

Spiraea japonica 'Goldflame'. Zones A2, A3, 2–10, 14–21.

Weeping beech (*Fagus sylvatica* 'Pendula'). Zones A3, 2B–9, 14–21.

Weigela 'Briant Rubidor', *W. florida* 'Java Red'. Zones 1–11, 14–21.

Evergreen

Azalea 'Girard's Fuchsia', 'Glacier'. Zones 4–9, 14–24.

Golden deodar cedar (*Cedrus deodora* 'Aurea'). Zones 3B–10, 14–24.

Heavenly bamboo (*Nandina domestica* 'Gulf Stream'). Zones 3 (with protection), 4–24.

Hinoki false cypress (*Chamaecyparis obtusa*). Zones A3, 2B–6, 15–17.

Incense cedar (*Calocedrus decurrens*). Zones 2–12, 14–24.

Rhododendron 'Cunningham's White' (hardy to –15°), 'Purple Gem' (hardy to –25°), 'Rosamundi' (hardy to –5°). Zones 4–6, 15–17.

Thuja occidentalis 'Emerald Green'. Zones A2, A3, 1–9, 15–17.

VINE

Clematis montana. Zones 3B–9, 14–17, 21–23.

PERENNIALS

Dwarf periwinkle (*Vinca minor* 'Bowles' Variety'). Zones 1–24.

Hosta 'Patriot'. Zones 1–10, 14–21.

Leather leaf sedge (*Carex buchananii*). Zones 2B–9, 14–24.

Western sword fern (*Polystichum munitum*). Zones A3, 2–9, 14–24. ◆

This 16-square-foot playhouse is furnished with a child-size table and chairs, perfect for playing games or hosting tea parties.

Signature palms

How to use them in your garden

By Sharon Cohoon • Photographs by Steven Gunther

Forget the Hollywood sign. The real symbol of Southern California—and the low desert—is a crown of palm fronds against a light blue sky. Palms line our streets, punctuate our skylines, edge our pools, and create jungle canopies over our gardens.

We love them because they are inherently exotic looking, and also because they are eminently practical. Palms have compact root systems, and many species are easy to transplant even when mature, enabling us to create instant landscaping. Palms can be squeezed into narrow parkways or planted close to homes, since their roots won't break up sidewalks, curbs, or foundations.

Because palms produce minimal litter, they are useful beside pools, where their tropical silhouettes are reflected in still water. As if that weren't enough, they're generally low-maintenance and pest free.

Following is a list of popular garden-scale palms. All are single trunked and take full sun unless noted.

Pygmy date palms edge a driveway in Rancho Palos Verdes, CA. Above left: Mexican blue palms pair with blue-gray senecio in a poolside planter designed by Pamela Palmer, Artecho Architecture and Landscape Architecture (310/399-4794).

Palm care

Don't expect much growth the first year; the palm will be busy creating a new root system.

• **Planting.** Before transplanting a large palm, dig a hole the same depth as the tree's rootball but several feet wider. If soil is heavy clay or highly alkaline, dig a small amount of compost into the backfill; otherwise, use unamended native soil.

• **Watering.** Keep newly planted palms well irrigated, especially in sandy soil. Once established (one to two years), many palms will tolerate drought, but all grow faster with regular watering.

• **Fertilizing.** Feed established palms regularly in spring and summer. Use a fertilizer specially formulated for palms, containing micronutrients like magnesium and manganese.

• **Pruning.** Some palms, such as *Archontophoenix,* naturally shed old leaves, leaving a smooth trunk. Most, however, do not, requiring leaves to be cut off (although even these leaves can be dislodged by high winds). *Washingtonia* palms develop "skirts" of old fronds; a popular option is to remove them but keep leaf bases intact to form an attractive lattice pattern. Although removing healthy green fronds is a common practice, especially in the Southwest, it is both unnecessary and ill-advised. It stresses the palms, making them more susceptible to disease and insects.

Mediterranean fan palms complement a blue-green *Agave attenuata* in Sue and John Major's Rancho Santa Fe, CA, garden.

Small (10 to 35 feet tall)

Use them singly as accents or in clusters. Good near pools or in patios, and in large garden beds with succulents or Mediterranean plants.

Chinese fountain palm *(Livistona chinensis)*. Widespreading crown. Bright green, fan-shaped leaves with drooping tips. Best with regular watering. Grows very slowly to 25–30 ft. Hardy to 22°. *Sunset Western Garden Book* climate zones 13–17, 19–24, H1, H2.

Foxtail palm *(Wodyetia bifurcata)*. Narrow trunk, luxurious plumelike leaves, and gray-green crownshaft (a smooth pillar of leaf bases at the top of the trunk). Beautiful solo specimen or small street tree. Needs good drainage. Grows slowly to 25 ft. Hardy to 30°. Zones 21–24.

Mediterranean fan palm *(Chamaerops humilis)*. Produces multiple trunks, which are covered with a dense mat of old leaf bases. Foliage varies from dark green to silvery gray. Grows slowly to 20 ft. Hardy to 0°. Zones 4–24, H1, H2.

Mexican blue palm *(Brahea armata)*. Striking silvery blue, fan-shaped leaves. Grows slowly to 35 ft. Hardy to 18°. Zones 10, 12–17, 19–24, H1.

Pindo palm *(Butia capitata)*. Stout trunked, with arching, gray-green, feather-shaped leaves. Grows slowly to 10–20 ft. Hardy to 15°. Zones 8, 9, 12–24, H1, H2.

Pygmy date palm *(Phoenix roebelenii)*. Fine-textured, feather-shaped leaves. Somewhat resembles a tree fern. Often planted in multiples. Best with regular watering; appreciates light shade away from coast. Grows slowly to 10 ft. Hardy to 26°. Zones 13, 23, 24, H2.

Shaving brush palm *(Rhopalostylis sapida)*. Feather-shaped leaves stand upright from crownshaft, making it a good accent plant. Best with regular watering. Grows slowly to 30 ft. Hardy to 27°. Zones 17, 23, 24, H1, H2.

Triangle palm *(Dypsis decaryi)*. Leaf bases form a triangular trunk. Long (to 15 feet) feather-shaped leaves are gray-green to blue-green. Sun or light shade; drought tolerant. Grows slowly to 20 ft. Hardy to 28°. Zones 20–24, H2.

Windmill palm *(Trachycarpus fortunei)*. Dark green, fan-shaped leaves atop stiff-looking trunk covered with brown, hairy fiber. Moderate to fast growth to 35 ft. Hardy to 10° or lower. Zones 4–24.

Mature queen palms shade pygmy date palms. Top right: A king palm dangles a flower cluster above a bench. Bottom right: Mexican fan palms.

Medium (40 to 60 feet)

Use these palms in lawns or as street trees.

Australian fan palm *(Livistona australis)*. Dark green, 3- to 5-ft.-wide leaves. Best with regular watering. Grows slowly to 50 ft. Hardy to 20°. Zones 13–17, 19–24, H1, H2.

King palm *(Archontophoenix cunninghamiana)*. Slender trunk with a green crownshaft. Has 8- to 10-ft.-long leaves and showy lilac-colored flowers. Looks best when protected from wind. Older specimens difficult to transplant. Grows quickly to 50–60 ft. Hardy to 28°. Zones 21–24.

Paradise palm *(Howea forsteriana)*. Also known as kentia palm. Slender trunk and 6- to 12-foot-long, dark green leaves. Light shade; best near the coast. Grows slowly to 30–40 ft. Hardy to 26°. Zones 17, 21–24, H1, H2.

Queen palm *(Syagrus romanzoffianum)*. Tall, straight trunk. Plumelike leaves are 10–15 ft. long. Grows quickly to 50 ft. Hardy to 25° or lower. Zones 12, 13, 15–17, 19–24, H1, H2.

Giant (above 60 feet, except as noted)

Use these palms on large properties.

Bismark palm *(Bismarckia nobilis)*. Very large, full crown with fan-shaped leaves, which are gray-blue, stiff textured. Its broad canopy needs room to spread. Moderately fast grower to 30–60 ft. Hardy to 28°. Zones 13, 21–24.

Canary Island date palm *(Phoenix canariensis)*. Trunk is massive (to 3 ft. across) with a 40-ft.-wide crown at maturity. Leaves are dark green, feather shaped. Drought tolerant. Slow to establish a trunk, then grows moderately to 60 ft. Hardy to 20°. Zones 9, 12–24, H1, H2.

Date palm *(Phoenix dactylifera)*. Wide crown of stiff, gray-green, feather-shaped leaves atop a slender trunk. Multistemmed when young. Drought tolerant. Moderately fast grower to 80 ft. Hardy to 15°. Zones 9, 12–24, H1, H2.

Mexican fan palm *(Washingtonia robusta)*. Tall, slender trunk with compact crown, dark green leaves. Drought tolerant. Grows quickly to 100 ft. Hardy to 20°. Zones 8, 9, 10 (warmer parts), 11–24, H1, H2. California fan palm *(W. filifera)* has a thicker trunk, grows to only 60 ft., and is slightly hardier. ◆

Buying and learning

SPECIALTY NURSERIES

Jungle Music. *Encinitas, CA; www.junglemusic. net or (619) 291-4605.*
Pacific Palms Nursery. *Phoenix; www. pacificpalms.com or (602) 867-2602.*
Plant World Nursery. *Las Vegas; www. plantworldnursery.com or (702) 878-9485.*
Rancho Soledad Nurseries. *Rancho Santa Fe, CA; www. ranchosoledad.com or (858) 756-3717.*
Worldwide Palms. *Palm Desert, CA; (760) 346-9251.*

CLUBS

International Palm Society. *www.palms.org*
Palm and Cycad Association of Arizona. *Contact president Mark Kiah at (602) 721-2835, or visit Pacific Palms Nursery website (see above).*
The Palm Society of Southern California. *www.palms.org/socal or (949) 361-3652.*

LITERATURE

An Encyclopedia of Cultivated Palms, by Robert Lee Riffle and Paul Craft (Timber Press, Portland, 2003; $50; 800/327-5680).

Bright coral walls make a vivid backdrop for this courtyard pool's blue tiles and echo the hues of the potted geraniums.

A splash of color

Paint can wake up a quiet garden corner

By Lauren Bonar Swezey

Color is a powerful design tool, most often introduced into a garden with flowers or accessories such as tiles and fabrics. But paint—applied to walls, paving, arbors, or even pots—can achieve remarkable results of its own.

Used carefully, colored walls and structures create different effects. Some colors seem to expand the garden; others make it smaller. Warm oranges and reds can make an outdoor space vibrate; cool blues, grays, or greens create a sense of calm.

San Francisco landscape designer Topher Delaney often uses paint to dress up her landscapes and to act as a foil for plants. To ensure that hues are compatible, Delaney chooses her paint first, then selects the plants.

Landscape architect Chad Robert of Phoenix uses strong colors to add accents to a sparse design. "The desert blooms subtly," he says. "Color from paint offers another opportunity to create interest."

So experiment. As Robert says, "If you don't like the color, you can always paint over it."

Using powerful hues

Selecting paint can be as simple as picking a color that appeals to you. But before you get carried away with lipstick red, keep in mind that a strong hue will look very intense when applied to a large area. Here are some other things you should know.

· Cool colors (blues, greens) make an object recede, as shown at right. Below, warm colors (reds, oranges, yellows) bring it to the foreground.

· A simple shift in a color's shade (its lightness or darkness) can determine whether a particular combination works. Celadon green and light violet are gorgeous together, says Delaney. But pair that same green with dark violet, and the combination is less appealing.

· To avoid making mistakes at the outset, check the color wheel below before you buy paint. If you want to use more than one color, choose two complements (those opposite each other on the color wheel, such as yellow and violet or blue and orange), or use three noncontiguous colors (orange, violet, and green, or yellow, red, and blue). Shades of the same color make a more subtle accent. ◆

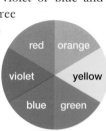

Colorful tasks

Make a focal point.
Painting a gate or a pair of chairs in a vivid hue and setting them at the end of a lawn will draw your eye to them. A highly colored wall can draw attention away from an unattractive view. A bright picket fence stands out and makes a garden corner feel more enclosed than a brown fence.

Create a foil for plants.
Use colored walls to make plants more visible, or use plants as a backdrop for colored walls. Magnolia flowers backed by a wall of soft blue-gray or olive green will stand out. On the other hand, a tall, dark green cypress hedge behind a bright orange wall will make the wall pop (as shown at right).

DESIGN
Page 206: Exteriors by Chad Robert, Phoenix *(www.exteriors-cr.com or 602/252-6775).*

This page, top: George Little and David Lewis, Bainbridge Island, WA *(www.littleandlewis.com or 206/842-8327)*

This page, bottom: Topher Delaney, San Francisco *(415/621-9899)*

A large clay pot reflects the purple and blue of the wall behind it.

Indian sari colors inspired these dazzling walls in Fremont, CA.

THOMAS J. STORY; JERRY HARPUR (TOP)

Soft lighting and water—which trickles along the wall's top and into the pond—set the mood.

Exotic nights

This garden sets the stage for parties with lighting and artful details

By Lauren Bonar Swezey
Photographs by Norm Plate

At dusk, Richard Holden and Sandra Moll switch on the lights in their San Jose backyard, instantly transforming the tranquil garden into paradise. Chinese lanterns stuffed with sparkling white lights dangle from arbors. A large dining patio radiates a warm glow from the back of the garden. And a dramatic fiery orange light bathes an ancient-looking wall relief.

But the lights are only part of what gives this landscape—inspired by designer and contractor Cevan Forristt's global travels—its dazzle and mystery. Each area of the garden is filled with interesting details that invite lingering looks.

To accommodate the 50 to 100 people who

Potted bougainvillea and a broken-pottery edge dress the table. Soaking tubs double as coolers.

Details you can adapt

Chill drinks in unexpected containers. Holden and Moll use the 39-inch-long soaking tubs pictured below left. When the party's over, the vessels revert to soaking tubs (supplied by hot- and cold-water spigots nearby). You could also use smaller glazed ceramic bowls from the nursery as coolers.

Hang portable lighting fixtures. White lights are instant magic, strung overhead or threaded into baskets. Holden and Moll also put floating candles in their pond, lanterns on seat walls, and tiki torches among tropical foliage.

Fill a pond with water lilies. Choose from tropical kinds, whose large blooms (5 or more inches wide) typically stand well above the water, or hardy kinds, which usually lie at the water's surface. A mail-order source is Lilypons Water Gardens (*www.lilypons. com* or *800/999-5459*).

Embellish plain surfaces with insets of broken pottery. Save ceramic pieces to dress up birdbaths or other stone surfaces; for greatest effect, use pottery bits sparingly and in limited colors. Here, they make striking accents around the edges of Holden and Moll's 16-foot-long concrete table and the nearby pillars.

Grow bougainvillea in a pot. Its brilliant blooms act as an all-summer flower arrangement. Best varieties for pots include 'Brilliant Variegated' (brick red bracts); 'Crimson Jewel' (crimson bracts); 'Hawaii' (also sold as 'Raspberry Ice'; red bracts, variegated foliage); and 'Singapore White' (white bracts).

attend Holden and Moll's frequent fundraising events, the garden is divided into "rooms." Guests can circulate freely from the spacious patio, with its raised pond and portable firepit, to the lattice-sheltered buffet table and through the keyhole opening back to the pond. "Every element has a double or triple function," says Forristt. The concrete table seats 12, for example, but without chairs it makes a perfect buffet table.

DESIGN: *Cevan Forristt, San Jose (408/297-8538)* ◆

Black and yellow bamboo poles are lashed into a grid that pairs elegantly with Mexican feather grass.

Zen fence

It's easily built with bamboo

By Lauren Bonar Swezey

Using bamboo poles, you can erect a 12-foot-long fence like this one, built by Bob Davenport and Joe House of Lotus Valley Nursery *(530/622-2321)* in California's Sierra foothills.

Harvest culms (stems) from your garden (cut ones that are at least three years old), or buy poles from a nursery or other source. You can substitute other kinds of bamboo. Adjust dimensions if necessary: the top pole needs to be $1^{1}/_{2}$ to 2 feet longer than the fence.

Materials

Black bamboo (*Phyllostachys nigra*) poles: one at 14 feet, two at 4 feet • Gravel • Two 90-lb. bags concrete • Two four-foot-long 4x4 redwood fence posts • Eight 3-inch nails • Yellow groove bamboo (*P. aureosulcata*) poles: three at 12 feet, two at 4 feet • $1/2$-inch copper pipe: one at 4 feet • 18-gauge copper wire • Two lightweight concrete finials (optional)

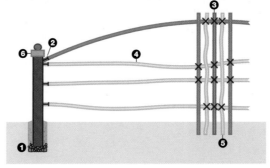

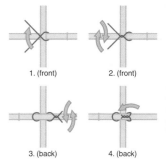

HOW TO LASH

1. (front) 2. (front)

3. (back) 4. (back)

Directions

❶ Dig two holes 1 foot deep, 10 inches wide, and 12 feet apart (measured from the outside of each post). Put a 2-inch layer of gravel in each hole. Mix concrete with water according to package directions. Set a post in each hole, then fill around them with concrete, angling the surface so water drains away from the posts. Allow concrete to set until thoroughly dry (at least a day).

❷ Pound a nail about halfway into the inside face of each post 2 inches below the top, at a slight angle as shown. Cut 7 inches off one end of the 14-foot-long top pole, then slip the cut end over the nail. Gently flex the pole and slip the other end over the nail in the opposite post. If the curve is too extreme, cut more off the pole.

❸ Place the copper pipe halfway between the posts vertically, and pound it about 5 inches into the ground. Lash it to the bamboo top piece with wire as shown (above right); twist ends closed with needlenose pliers.

❹ Measure the exact distance between posts; then, to install the three 12-foot crosspieces, cut each to fit (you'll need to trim about 7 inches). Pound three nails into the inside face of each post at 1-foot intervals, starting $1^{1}/_{2}$ inches below arch. Slip the end of one pole over a nail; then, gently flexing the pole, slip the other end over the nail in the opposite post. Using wire, lash it to the copper pipe. Repeat for the other two crosspieces.

❺ Pound two 4-foot-long yellow bamboo poles on either side of the copper pipe as shown. With wire, lash each one to the arch and to the bottom crosspiece. Install the 4-foot black bamboo poles; lash them to the top two cross poles.

❻ Add finials (optional). ◆

Pairing mulch with plants

For best effects, choose mulches in colors that echo those of the succulents—cool colors for serenity, hot ones for drama.

Agave americana medio-picta

Echeveria

Aloe aristata hybrid

Sedum

Tumbled blue-green glass surrounds *Pachyveria* and variegated aeonium (center).

Echeveria on ice

Glass mulch adds a cool touch to potted succulents

By Sharon Cohoon
Photographs by Steven Gunther

Succulent plants such as agaves, aloes, and echeverias are often associated with heat-loving landscapes. But put glass mulch—instead of gravel—over the soil under their fleshy leaves, and suddenly these plants take on a cool, fresh look. "It's like placing jewels on a velvet cloth," says Los Angeles garden designer Judy M. Horton, whose potted plants are shown here. "The contrast really makes the plants stand out."

Pieces of frosty tumbled glass also emphasize succulents' other-worldly qualities. "Succulents remind me more of sea creatures than plants," Horton says.

There are two things to keep in mind. Although glass mulch looks cool, it can get hot, especially in small pots exposed to full summer sun. In the desert or other hot inland locations, move containers to a lightly shaded area to avoid burning plants. Also, glass pebbles look best when they are litter-free. To make them easier to clean, lay landscaping fabric over the soil surface before adding pebbles. That way you can brush the pebbles into a colander to wash them as needed.

Sources

Horton's glass mulches come from the **Glass Garden,** Los Angeles *(www.landscape2go.com or 213/368-9220).* They are made from recycled glass, so the availability of certain colors might be limited or variable. Cost is $65 plus shipping for a 50-pound bag.

For a smaller amount, check with well-stocked pet- or aquarium-supply stores, which often sell flattened glass marbles in a variety of sparkling colors for about $6 a pound. ◆

THIS TROPICAL-LOOKING WATER GARDEN in Vancouver, Washington, was inspired by the sensual scenery of Hawaii. For details, see page 219.

August

Flowers make good neighbors

Two adjacent gardens form a tapestry of color that flows across property lines here in Breckenridge, Colorado. In the foreground, Pat Steiner's colorful garden of hardy annuals and perennials was started almost entirely from seed. In this area, the native soil is rich, a rare commodity in mountain gardens. In the fall, when snow was forecast, Steiner simply roughed up the surface with a rake, then broadcast a Rocky Mountain wildflower mix over the ground.

She repeated this process the next spring, just as the snow was melting. All the seeds germinated, resulting in a riot of wildflowers. Since then, Steiner has saved seeds from her favorite flowers for fall sowing to ensure a repeat performance every summer. Blooming here in August are white Shasta daisies, sweet William in shades of pink and magenta, and yellow wallflowers.

The front yard of neighbor Carol Erickson is just to the right of the path. Her property was covered by rocks, so before she could do any planting, several truckloads of soil had to be hauled in.

To achieve instant gratification, Erickson set out mostly 1-gallon-size perennials. Just one year later, her garden—a profusion of delphiniums, foxgloves, Iceland and Oriental poppies, and Shasta daisies—was featured on the Summit County Garden Club's annual tour.

As they work side by side in their gardens, Steiner and Erickson enjoy each other's company, passing along advice, stories, and plants. Both women mulch around plants with wood chips, which also cover the path that runs between their gardens. —*Marcia Tatroe*

Heads up with a horizontal trellis

In garden beds, plastic 6-inch by 6-inch mesh netting is practically indispensable. Install it horizontally over cutting-flower seedlings to support varieties that tend to flop over. 'Blue Boy' bachelor's button, carnations, delphiniums, dianthus, lilies, scabiosa, and tall calendulas can grow up through it.

Try the following method to support the netting. Width varies; seed grower Renee Shepherd and her staff used 4-foot-wide netting to cover the bed in her Felton, California, test garden. Cut the netting the length of the bed plus 8 inches, then wrap and staple each end around a sturdy, 4½-foot-long wooden stake, leaving 3 inches of uncovered stake at each end. On four additional 4- to 6-foot-long stakes, halfway sink nails every 6 inches into one side of each (depending on the ultimate height of the flowers), starting 2 feet from the stakes' bottoms. Angle the nails upward.

Pound the four stakes 12 inches into soil at each corner of the bed so the heads of the nails face away from the longest edges of the bed. Stretch the netting across the bed, and rest the netting stakes on the nails at the appropriate height for the plants. If the bed is longer than 10 feet, add vertical stakes along the long edges to support the netting.

Plastic mesh is available by mail from Peaceful Valley Farm Supply (www.groworganic.com or 888/784-1722). —Lauren Bonar Swezey

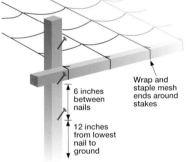

6 inches between nails

12 inches from lowest nail to ground

Wrap and staple mesh ends around stakes

An adjustable system of stakes and netting keeps flowers from flopping.

Succulents made for artisan pots

"Desert succulents are so inherently architectural, they seem custom-made for distinctive pots," says Jane Evans, co-owner of Plants for the Southwest in Tucson. The photo below precisely illustrates her point. *Agave ocahui* is ensconced in a container handcrafted by Tucson artist Jan Bell, who fired the clay with a copper carbonate stain. This agave will live contentedly in its pot for several years, says Evans, and will maintain its neatly symmetrical shape better here than if planted in the ground.

Look for artisan pots at specialty nurseries like Plants for the Southwest (520/628-8773) or at craft fairs. —*Sharon Cohoon*

When is it time to pick?

All summer you've watered and tended your vegetables, and now they're ready to harvest. Or are they? Here's how to tell.

Eggplants. Harvest fruits when they're immature and shiny. Dull-skinned mature eggplant has hard seeds and flesh that separates into channels; its flavor isn't as good.

Peppers. You can pick any pepper when the pod is firm and fully developed. But for best flavor, pick hot peppers—jalapeños, serranos—after the pods show color. (Jalapeños turn red; serranos can go red, orange, brown, or yellow.) Sweet peppers are most flavorful when mature; that's usually signaled, but not always, by color change. Bell peppers can mature green as well as red, orange, yellow, or maroon; pimientos ripen red; wax types go from yellow to orange or red.

Tomatoes. Pick after fruit colors fully. In fall, when night temperatures drop below 55°, pick any tomatoes with some color and ripen them indoors on a windowsill (dark green fruit never ripens). —*Jim McCausland*

A harvest basket holds eggplants, peppers, and tomatoes (yellow 'Sunny Goliath' and red 'Big Beef' picked late in the season).

COURTESY FULCRUM PUBLISHING;

UNTHIRSTY WESTERNERS

Wine cups

Too much water and fertilizer can be the undoing of many native wildflowers—but not wine cups (*Callirhoe involucrata*), also known as poppy mallow. The more you pamper this perennial, the bigger it gets. In unirrigated beds, it typically grows 1 foot across, but given fertile soil and twice-weekly water, it can spread to 10 feet. The 2-inch-wide magenta blossoms first appear in late spring, then continue nonstop until the first hard frost. The flowers are borne above dark green leaves.

Wine cups are hardy in all *Sunset* intermountain climate zones. They self-sow readily. In winter, the stems die back to the ground. Use this plant alone as a 6-inch-high groundcover, or allow the stems to weave through upright companions such as Rocky Mountain penstemon.

Check garden centers, or order by mail from High Country Gardens (www. highcountrygardens.com or 800/925-9387). —M. T.

Dripless in Denver

The hanging containers that delight summer visitors to the Denver Pavilions overflow with flowers and foliage, yet they never spill so much as a drop of water. Designed by Western Proscapes, a Denver-based landscape design and maintenance firm, 130 containers are planted with dramatic combinations of bedding plants. The water-thrifty pots are made of nonporous plastic, which holds water much longer than clay, and they have no drainage holes. Such containers would be ideal for apartment dwellers who can't use conventional hanging pots that might drip onto neighbors' balconies below.

Before planting, the containers, which are 20 inches in diameter and 24 inches deep, are filled to just below the halfway level with perlite, then topped off with a peat moss–based mix with 5 percent sand. Plantings vary depending on whether the container is to be hung in sun or shade (see "Plant Picks," right).

The pots are held in place by wrought-iron collars bolted to railings. Western Proscapes irrigates at two- to three-day intervals to prevent water from

pooling up in the bottom. Plants are fed with liquid fertilizer every 10 days.

Made by Riverside Plastics, the pots come in various shapes and colors. You can order Riverside containers with or without drainage holes through Simple Gardens (800/351-2438). —Colleen Smith

Plant picks

For sun: Ivy geranium, million bells (*Calibrachoa*), petunias, 'Ruby Crystals' ruby grass, salvia, sweet potato vine, verbena, vinca.

For shade: Caladium, coleus, impatiens, lobelia, purple fountain grass.

NATIVE PLANTS
for High-Elevation
Western Gardens

Janice Busco
and Nancy R. Morin

PUBLISHED IN PARTNERSHIP
WITH THE ARBORETUM AT FLAGSTAFF

BOOKSHELF
Native plants for high places

During periods of drought, gardeners quickly appreciate the merits of native plants. After all, natives survive in the wild solely on natural precipitation. But after reading *Native Plants for High-Elevation Western Gardens*, by Janice Busco and Nancy R. Morin (Fulcrum Publishing, Golden, CO, 2003; $30; www.fulcrum-books.com or 800/992-2908), you'll appreciate why natives make a valuable addition to the home landscape anytime.

The authors, both horticulturists at the Arboretum at Flagstaff in Arizona, begin with a discussion of planting and maintaining the native garden. The next section is devoted to descriptions of more than 150 species native to higher elevations of the Rocky Mountain region and the Southwest, including grasses, perennials, shrubs, and succulents. Each plant is introduced by a color photograph. —*Julie Chai*

Bougainvillea for a slope

Bougainvillea is a choice plant for inclines where soil drains fast and water is minimal. The trick is to choose a variety with a spreading habit and prune it carefully, says La Quinta landscape architect Ray Martin.

For the Palm Desert garden pictured here, Martin chose 'La Jolla' to cover the upper slope and dwarf 'Oo-La-La' to cover the more densely planted lower slope. Both kinds spread a delicate tracery of bloom among bold, sculptural agaves, cactus, and desert spoon. And they create bright spots of color among sand-colored boulders, along with brittlebush *(Encelia farinosa)*, purple and yellow lantana, and flowering trees— *Acacia smallii* and palo brea *(Cercidium praecox)*.

'Oo-La-La' gets a lot of competition from other plants in this garden and for that reason hasn't spread much, Martin says. "It just pops up here and there like a bright surprise." 'La Jolla' needs more maintenance. Any shoot that grows straight up is cut off immediately so the plant doesn't get shrubby.

DESIGN: Ray Martin, Ray Martin Design & Associates, La Quinta, CA *(760/771-2071) —S. C.*

Mosaic memories

Garden writer Pat Welsh is bringing back the old Southern California tradition of embellishing walls with Mexican river rock and whimsical objects. Her planter, pictured here, is decorated with old tools, craft projects from her children (the three tile plaques), and gifts from gardening friends (the toy watering can and the angel).

Welsh decorated her wall with help from builder Dean Johnson. She arranged objects on heavy paper in the exact dimensions of the wall, then outlined each one with a permanent black marker. Then, using the paper as a template, Welsh and Johnson transferred the design to the wall and glued each object in place with thin-set cement. To finish, they filled in the remaining space with grout and rock. —*S. C.*

Bookshelf

CONTAINER GARDENING. *Contain Yourself: 101 Fresh Ideas for Fantastic Container Gardens,* by Kerstin P. Ouellet (Ball Publishing, Chicago, 2003; $25; www.ipgbook.com or 800/888-4741), includes photographs, a useful list of colorful plant choices, and planting plans.

SUCCULENTS. These sculptural plants are enjoying renewed popularity. You'll see why when you view the striking photographs in *Succulents for the Contemporary Garden,* by Yvonne Cave (Timber Press, Portland, 2003; $30; www.timberpress. com or 800/327-5680).

HERBS. *Celebration of Herbs: Recipes from the Huntington Herb Garden,* edited by Shirley Kerins and Peggy Park Bernal (Huntington Library Press, 2003; $30; www.huntington.org or 626/405-2131), is an amazing value for the price. The book is packed with information, including how to grow, harvest, and dry herbs; where to buy them; and how to cook with them. More than 200 recipes are provided, such as goat cheese and basil ravioli, Thai beef and mint salad, and lemon thyme poached peaches. Hungry yet?

This *Doritaenopsis* seedling has 20 to 25 flower spikes and blooms that last two months or more.

Orchid news

You probably know moth orchids, but *Doritaenopsis?* Maybe not. These moth-orchid hybrids—part *Doritis* and part *Phalaenopsis*—don't yet have a common name, but they're so easy to grow that they're bound to become popular.

Besides the exquisite beauty of their long-lasting flowers, *Doritaenopsis* have much to recommend them. Smaller than their thoroughbred moth-orchid cousins, they fit more comfortably on a windowsill; they flower in spring and summer, after most moth orchids have finished.

The best *Doritaenopsis* choices are plants with multiple flowering spikes and at least four leaves. Named varieties (tags sometimes label the plants with the abbreviation "Dtps.") cost a bit more than seedlings, but they bloom longer, produce more spikes, and come in more colors.

Grow *Doritaenopsis* in an east- or north-facing window, water only when the potting mix dries out, and fertilize with half-strength liquid fertilizer (such as 10-10-10) every second week during active growth and flowering.

You can buy Doritaenopsis from specialty nurseries or on the Web from Norman's Orchids in Southern California (www.orchids.com or 888/467-2443). —J.M.

A soothing plug-in fountain

The sight and sound of water pulsing from a fountain adds a refreshing element to any garden. Installing this type of water feature used to be a complex undertaking that required plumbing skills. Not anymore. With Beckett's Ceramic Watering Vase ($99–$129), you do little more than add water and plug the fountain into an outlet.

The 19-inch-tall container comes with its own plastic reservoir and submersible pump. You can dig a small hole in the ground to hold the square reservoir, or simply place the vase on a deck or patio and conceal the reservoir with decorative rocks. Before plugging it in, verify that the outlet is equipped with a ground-fault circuit interrupter.

Visit www.888beckett.com or call (888) 232-5388 to find a dealer near you.

Easy steps

1. Dig a hole just deep enough to hold the reservoir.

2. Connect the pump to the vase's uptake tube. Fill the reservoir with water and close the lid.

3. Conceal the lid beneath a layer of river rocks. Plug in the pump. —*Peter O. Whiteley*

BACK TO BASICS

Pesticide safety

Poison centers received 96,000 reports last year about accidental exposure to pesticides. To avoid such mishaps, follow these tips for proper use and storage of all garden chemicals.

• **Choose products with low toxicity to humans and pets;** buy only the amount you can use in a season.

• **Store them in their original containers,** locked up in a cool, dry place.

• **Follow label instructions precisely.** Do not spray chemi-cals where children play or on windy days.

• **Dispose of empty containers** and leftover products at your city's toxic-waste center.

• **For pesticide details,** visit *www.1-800-222-1222.info* or call the poison hotline at *(800) 222-1222.* —*L.B.S.*

Scatter iron phosphate snail and slug bait around plants. It's nontoxic to pets and humans.

Inspired by Hawaii

Tad and Jodie Suckling are great admirers of Hawaii. They love the lush look of the plants there, the way sunlight streams through the dense foliage, and the splashy sound of waterfalls. Inspired by such sensual scenery, they decided to turn part of their flat backyard in Vancouver, Washington, into a tropical-looking water garden.

Tad installed the entire project himself. First, he used a backhoe to dig out the pond and streambed. Then he shaped the excavated earth (supplemented with additional soil) into an elevated mound for the twin waterfalls.

Volcanic basalt was used to form the rock ledges of the falls and to edge the main pond and the stream, which channels water to a nearby koi pond. The top pond has waterproof rubber liners; the stream is lined with Gunite (a mixture of cement and sand). A pair of $^3/_4$-horsepower pumps, hidden in housing surrounded by nandina and ivy, recirculates the water.

Above the falls, a grove of evergreen English laurel reinforces the illusion that the water is plunging down a forested hillside. In the pond itself, water-loving yellow flag iris (*I. pseudacorus*) forms a fountain of foliage 5 feet tall. Ferns, cardoon (front left), assorted flowering perennials, even Japanese maples grow in soil-filled pockets around the rocks. Low-voltage lights in metal housings illuminate several pathways that connect the patio to two ponds, a perennial bed, and a cave behind the falls. —*J.M.*

NORM PLATE

Summer snow, in a pot

Snow bush (*Breynia nivosa* 'Roseopicta') loves warm, humid climates. In its native Melanesia, it can reach 6 feet tall or more; in Southern California, it typically tops out at just 3 to 4 feet tall. So why is the one in the pot pictured above, at Sherman Library & Gardens in Corona del Mar, approaching tropical height?

Extra heat, for one thing. The plant in the picture sits next to a west-facing wall that reflects a lot of the sun's warmth. Being in a container rather than the ground helps the plant too, says John Bishop, manager of horticulture at Sherman. The pot keeps the soil warm. "We

have the same shrubs in the ground, and they don't get nearly as big," he says.

Bright, diffused light is another reason snow bush does so well here. The roof overhang is covered with corrugated clear plastic panels made of Lexan that are whitewashed with a shading compound. The panels cut the sun's rays by 50 percent—ideal, according to Bishop.

This snow bush also gets plenty of water, twice a week most of the year, and is fed once a month with an acid fertilizer (Liquinox 10-10-5 Grow). Pruning each February stimulates fresh, rosy pink growth. —*S.C.*

Grow a snow bush

ZONES: *Sunset* climate zones 22–24 and H2, or indoors

POT: 36-inch-diameter plastic pot (doesn't dry out as fast as terra-cotta)

SOIL: Rich packaged mix that includes worm castings

SHADING: Lexan panels and shading compound available from Conley's, a commercial greenhouse manufacturer in Montclair *(800/377-8441 or www.conleys.com)*

Horticultural haven in Victoria, B.C.

Be it daphne or dahlias, something is blooming every month at the Horticulture Centre of the Pacific in Victoria, British Columbia. In August, for instance, fuchsias spill from hanging baskets, and beds of Asiatic hybrid lilies, dahlias, and roses provide bursts of color. The mild climate on Vancouver Island is one reason for the floriferous nature of the place, but in larger part credit goes to the hard work of hundreds of volunteers and 20 students who study landscape horticulture here.

Located on a south-facing slope above a small lake, the 103-acre site encompasses 21 display and demonstration gardens featuring plants from heather to mixed perennials. One Saturday each month, the center offers inexpensive workshops on subjects ranging from organic vegetables to Japanese gardens. Special events in 2003 included the eighth annual Artists in a Country Garden show on August 10 and the fall plant sale on September 13.

The center is open 8–8 daily year-round; $7.50 (Canadian) admission. 505 Quayle Rd.; www.hcp.bc.ca or (250) 479-6162. —Rachel Goldsworthy

Plant-swapping party

Last summer, after a tour of local gardens, a group of friends met at Debbie Teachout-Teashon's home in Kingston, Washington, to swap plants and enjoy a potluck supper.

The two dozen gardeners who attend this twice-yearly event start by emailing each other lists of the plants they have to trade plus those they seek. The potluck is also organized online, with the host providing the main course (pizza perhaps) and the others posting the foods they plan to contribute. The group holds its summer plant exchange on the same weekend as the Bainbridge Island garden tour. For the fall plant exchange near Portland, the organizer sets up a private tour of local gardens and public nurseries.

Go to www.rainyside.com/features/plantswap.html for tips on organizing your own exchange.
—J. M.

UNTHIRSTY WESTERNERS

Rabbitbrush

One of the most prevalent native shrubs in the foothills and high deserts of the Rocky Mountains, *Chrysothamnus nauseosus* is commonly known as rabbitbrush in the northern part of its range and as chamisa in the southern part. When plants are covered with yellow blooms in late summer and autumn, they give the landscape a golden cast. The 3-inch-wide flower clusters are followed by seed heads that ripen to wheat color.

Hardy in all *Sunset* intermountain climate zones, rabbitbrush thrives in full sun and well-drained soil. Ranging from 18 inches to 6 feet in height with a slightly larger spread, this plant needs little or no water once established. To give it a more compact shape, cut the branches back in spring to within a few inches of the ground.

Rabbitbrush is sold in 1- and 5-gallon containers by most nurseries. A good mail-order source is Plants of the Southwest (www.plantsofthesouthwest.com or 800/788-7333).

—M.T.

Stonehenge in the Southwest

Ancient obelisks on a South Pacific island? Olmec monoliths in the Mexican jungle? No, just an ingenious solution to a storm-damage problem in Paradise Valley, Arizona.

When a large palo verde tree in Madge Kunkel's backyard was severely injured in a summer storm, she had to have the tree removed. That left an unsightly 200-square-foot gap in the landscape.

She sought guidance from designer Steve Sternke; he suggested that, instead of replanting, they treat the space as a sculpture garden, using natural stones rather than manmade art. Before arranging the pieces of Hass granite, Sternke dug foundation holes deep enough to bury about a third of their length, leaving up to 7 feet aboveground. After the stones were hauled into place by a heavy-duty hand truck, "we still had a lot of tweaking to do so the most attractive planes were exposed," he says.

Coarse decomposed granite covers the ground around the stones, and clumps of white-flowered bush morning glory (*Convolvulus cneorum*) add soft contrast.

DESIGN: Steve Sternke, Magic Gardens, Phoenix *(602/279-1207)* —S. C.

A jewel-like new plant

Once in a while, a new plant comes along that's so special, so irresistible, it's worth showing off. Pincushion *(Nertera granadensis),* a diminutive New Zealand native, is one of them. In late summer, it covers itself with beadlike, brilliant orange berries the size of pinheads; they hold on for more than three months.

We discovered the plants at a Bay Area nursery, then planted them in a blue strawberry jar. More rich color comes from a deep green dwarf philodendron, whose glossy leaves are a foil to the pincushions' fine texture. A single pincushion in a tiny pot (each plant is just 3 inches across) makes a charming gift.

Pincushion is best treated as an annual (you can discard it when berries fade); although it will continue to live as a mounding green houseplant, it's unlikely to rebloom. In frost-free climates, try growing it outdoors in a rock garden.

Look for pincushion in nurseries, garden centers, and grocery stores. Plants cost about $7.50 each. —L.B.S.

What pincushion needs

Light: Bright, indirect light indoors, or part sun to shade outdoors (during mild weather).

Water: Keep it moist but not soggy; do not allow it to dry out.

Fertilizer: Once a month, apply a water-soluble fertilizer diluted to half the recommended strength.

Temperature: Hardy to 30°–40°.

WHAT TO DO IN YOUR GARDEN IN AUGUST

PLANTING

☐ **BULBS.** As soon as they appear in nurseries, buy and plant autumn crocus. They flower in late summer or early autumn, then disappear until spring when leaves emerge and die back. This is also a good time to order unusual spring-blooming bulbs such as miniature daffodils and species tulips. You can plant them anytime between Labor Day and the end of fall.

☐ **COOL-SEASON CROPS.** *Sunset* climate zones 4–7: Sow lettuce, radishes, and spinach now for fall harvest. Or plant beets, broccoli, cabbage, collards, kale, kohlrabi, and leeks for harvest through winter and spring.

☐ **FALL COLOR.** Nurseries still have potted asters, dahlias (mostly miniatures), and mums for sale, along with flowering cabbage and kale. Plant now for a fall show.

☐ **GARLIC.** Two of the best soft-necked varieties are 'Siberian Red' and 'Spanish Roja'. You can order them now for planting anytime before the ground freezes. A good source is Spirit of the Pacific Northwest *(541/929-4532)*. Price is $6–$10 per pound.

Sunset
CLIMATE ZONES
☐ 1–3 ☐ 4–7

☐ **LAWNS.** Zones A2–A3: Sow new lawns or repair old ones before mid-August. Zones 1–3: Sow seed now through mid-September, or lay sod anytime. Zones 4–7, 17: Wait until the weather cools off in September to sow lawn seed or to lay sod. You *can* do either successfully now, but only if your time and water supply allow daily irrigation through the heat of summer.

MAINTENANCE

☐ **COMPOST.** As you remove spent summer flowers and vegetables, combine them with green grass clippings, weeds, nonmeat kitchen waste, and manure or old compost. Wet the pile thoroughly and turn it weekly with a pitchfork. You'll have compost to dig into empty garden beds within a couple of months.

☐ **HARVEST HERBS.** Pick herbs in the morning, just after dew has dried. To preserve them for later use, lay leaves on a clean window screen in a cool, shady spot and air-dry until crisp. Store dried leaves in airtight jars.

☐ **PRUNE CANE BERRIES.** After canes bear fruit, they start to look withered. On June-bearing plants, cut these to the ground. On ever-bearing plants, cut back the top half of canes that have fruited (the lower half can still bear fruit).

☐ **RECOGNIZE BENEFICIAL INSECTS.** Your garden has more good bugs than bad ones, even though it's often hard to tell them apart. A new pocket-size photo guide can help you identify—and preserve—beneficial insects: *The Good Bugs Guide,* produced by the Local Hazardous Waste Management Program in King County, Washington. King County residents can get a free copy by calling *(206) 263-3050;* others can order a copy ($3.95) from the Seattle Audubon Society Nature Shop *(www.seattleaudubon. org or 206/523-4483).*

☐ **WATER.** Soak moisture-loving plants like rhododendrons every week to 10 days—more often in extra-hot weather or in fast-draining soil. Also, hose down plants to rinse dust off leaves and rehydrate thirsty foliage. ◆

WHAT TO DO IN YOUR GARDEN IN AUGUST

SHOPPING

☐ **ORDER SPRING BLOOMERS.** *Sunset* climate zones 7–9, 14–17: Now's the time to browse catalogs and order spring-flowering bulbs and perennials. Zones 1, 2: Make sure to specify that plants should be sent in time for September planting (in coldest, highest-elevation areas, wait until spring to plant).

PLANTING

☐ **BABY LETTUCE.** Zones 7–9, 14–17: Miniature romaine and butterhead lettuce are just the right size for a single salad. Heads grow quickly, so you can sow seeds successively a couple of weeks apart. 'Little Gem' romaine grows 5 to 6 inches tall. 'Tom Thumb', an English heirloom butterhead lettuce with a tight, solid head, grows 4 to 6 inches tall. Both are available from Territorial Seed Company *(www.territorialseed.com or 541/942-9547).*

☐ **SHRUBS.** Zones 7–9, 14–17: For a show of flowers that lasts from summer well into fall, try one of the following long-blooming shrubs or shrubby perennials: blue hibiscus, Brazilian plume flower, butterfly bush, cape fuchsia, lavatera, oleander, plumbago, princess flower, and a variety of salvias (hardiness varies; check to make sure the plant is adapted to your climate).

Sunset
CLIMATE ZONES

☐ Mountain (1–2)
☐ Valley (7–9)
☐ Inland (14)
☐ Coastal (15–17)

☐ **SWEET PEAS.** Zones 7–9, 14–17: For earliest bloom in spring, sow the Elegance series, which is bred to bloom significantly earlier than other sweet peas. New Elegance mixes in a variety of colors (sometimes called Early Elegance or Winter Elegance) will be available this fall. Also try knee-high Explorer Mix (crimson, light pink, navy blue, purple, rose, scarlet, and white flowers). Protect new growth from slugs and snails and provide trellis support for Winter Elegance. Look for packets on nursery racks from Renee's Garden or order directly *(www.reneesgarden.com or 888/880-7228).*

MAINTENANCE

☐ **IRRIGATE LARGE ORNAMENTALS.** Large, deep-rooted shrubs and trees may need a deep soaking now, even if they're watered regularly by sprinklers or drip irrigation. (Those irrigation systems don't usually run long enough for water to penetrate the soil deeply.) Use a soaker hose, deep-root irrigator, or hose turned on slowly in a basin to moisten the soil under the drip line 12 to 18 inches deep (or deeper for really large trees and shrubs).

☐ **PREPARE PLANTING BEDS.** To get garden beds ready for fall planting, cultivate the soil at least 12 inches deep, then dig in a 2- to 3-inch layer of organic matter or compost.

☐ **TEND ROSES.** Zones 7–9, 14–17: For a second flush of bloom in fall, give roses plenty of water during the warm August days and feed them with a complete fertilizer. Also, apply iron chelate if leaves look chlorotic (yellow with green veins). Make certain the soil is moist before applying, and water thoroughly afterward. Snip off old blooms and rose hips; lightly shape plants if necessary.

☐ **TRIM SHRUBS AND VINES.** After a summer of growth, some plants may need a light trimming to stay shapely. Snip off long, wayward shoots and thin out interior growth, if necessary, but wait until the dormant season to do major pruning.

☐ **WATER CITRUS.** Irrigate newly planted citrus twice a week (more frequently during hot spells), established citrus every other week or so. In clay soils, wait for top 4 to 6 inches of soil to dry between waterings. ◆

WHAT TO DO IN YOUR GARDEN IN AUGUST

PLANTING

□ **RUDBECKIAS.** Black-eyed Susans are excellent performers in Southern California; they bloom well into fall. In addition to annual kinds like 'Goldilocks', 'Indian Summer', and 'Toto', seek out perennial types. Melinda Sakioka of What Matters Most Garden Boutique in Stanton *(714/995-4868)* recommends *R. fulgida* 'Goldsturm' and the magnificent, 7-foot-tall *R. nitida* 'Herbstsonne'.

□ **SHRUBS.** Subtropical shrubs like cape honeysuckle, hibiscus, plumbago, and princess flower add color to late-summer gardens year after year. Shop soon; they are readily available in nurseries now. Many salvias also bloom late into the season.

□ **TOMATOES.** For a late crop, 'Celebrity', 'Champion', and 'Early Girl' are the varieties usually mentioned. But 'Moscow', 'Oregon Spring', 'Rutgers', and 'Siberia' are better choices, says Steve Goto of Goto Nursery *(818/767-2337)*, a tomato specialist. They'll set fruit at temperatures as low as 40° (most tomatoes need temperatures to reach 55°). If you prefer heirloom types, try 'Siletz' or 'Stupice'.

□ **WINTER VEGETABLES.** Planting vegetables this month may seem counter-intuitive, but late summer is the ideal time to start cool-weather crops from seed. In *Sunset* climate zones 11 and 18–24, try broccoli, brussels sprouts, cauliflower, chard,

Sunset
CLIMATE ZONES
1–3 7–9 11 13 14–24

collards, and kale. Start seeds in flats, out of direct sun; gradually move them into brighter light after sprouts appear, then transplant into the garden after 6–8 weeks. Want something more adventurous? Try horned mustard greens, Korean radish, molokhia (Egyptian spinach), or flowering pak choi. Kitazawa Seed Co. *(www.kitazawaseed.com or 510/595-1188),* an Asian vegetable seed specialist, carries these and more. Its new catalog has recipes too.

MAINTENANCE

□ **DETHATCH LAWNS.** Because grass grows back very quickly in late summer, now is the best time to dethatch bermuda, St. Augustine, zoysia, and other warm-season lawns. Heavy buildup of thatch (the spongy, fibrous mat of undecomposed plant material beneath grass blades) can keep air and water from reaching grass roots. By breaking it up, you reinvigorate the lawn and keep it green longer. Rent a dethatching machine, called a verticutter, from an equipment rental company; ask to

have blades set for your type of grass. Water your lawn before you pick up the machine; soil should be moist but not soggy.

□ **DIVIDE BEARDED IRIS.** Dig up old, overgrown clumps of bearded iris and divide rhizomes with a sharp knife. Discard woody centers. Trim leaves of remaining rhizomes to 6 inches. Replant divisions 1 to 2 feet apart; set with tops barely beneath soil surface.

□ **PRUNE.** Lightly trim plants that have grown rangy or leggy so they'll have time to put out new growth before winter. Watch for new basal growth on perennials. Cut back spent flower stalks to just above this growth to encourage rebloom. Prune roses lightly to stimulate fall bloom.

□ **WATER CAREFULLY.** Keeping plants well irrigated is a gardener's most important task this month. Container plants are particularly vulnerable and may need daily soaking. Water shallow-rooted citrus and avocado more frequently too: inland, once a week should suffice; along the coast, every other week. Established perennials, shade trees, and shrubs will appreciate a deep soak. ◆

WHAT TO DO IN YOUR GARDEN IN AUGUST

PLANNING AND PLANTING

☐ **ORDER SPRING BULBS.** Place orders immediately for spring-flowering bulbs to plant this fall. Bulbs that tolerate summer drought include *Allium christophii* and *A. karataviense; Calochortus; Crocus chrysanthus* and *C. sieberi;* cyclamen; foxtail lily *(Eremurus); Geranium tuberosum;* glory-of-the-snow *(Chionodoxa);* grape hyacinth; Greek windflower *(Anemone blanda); Iris reticulata; Nectaroscordum siculum;* striped squill *(Puschkinia scilloides libanotica);* and tulips. A good mail-order source for many of these is Brent and Becky's Bulbs *(www.brentandbeckysbulbs.com or 877/661-2852).*

☐ **PLANT CROPS FOR FALL HARVEST.** At all but the highest elevations, sow seeds of vegetables for fall harvest, including radishes and salad greens (arugula, loose-leaf lettuce, spinach, Swiss chard). Mulch loosely with 3 to 4 inches of straw or hay and keep the soil moist until seeds germinate. Dimension Trade Company *(www.newdimensionseed.com or 503/577-9382)* offers Asian vegetables for fall planting. Seeds of Change *(www.seedsofchange.com or 888/762-7333)* offers many kinds of lettuce and radishes.

MAINTENANCE

☐ **CARE FOR ROSES.** Continue irrigating deeply once or twice a week until midmonth, then gradually cut back on water and stop

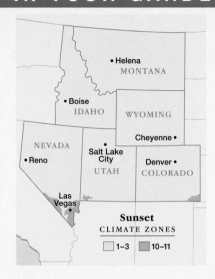

Sunset
CLIMATE ZONES

☐ 1–3 ☐ 10–11

fertilizing to prepare roses for winter dormancy. Treat black spot, mildew, or rust with fungicidal soap spray or sulfur.

☐ **FEED HUMMINGBIRDS.** Set out feeders now to entice hummingbirds to visit for a few weeks before they begin their fall migration. Place the feeder in an open area and tie red ribbons onto nearby branches or trellises to attract the birds.

☐ **HARVEST FLOWERS FOR DRYING.** Cut blooms and air-dry them for everlasting bouquets. Try amaranth, baby's breath, globe thistle, hydrangea, lavender, sea holly, sea lavender, statice, strawflower, and yarrow. Harvest blossoms before they fully open, strip leaves off stems, bind the bunches with rubber bands, and hang them upside down in a cool, dark place with low humidity, such as a closet or garage.

☐ **HARVEST POTATOES.** You can dig tubers as soon as they reach 1½–2 inches; to check progress, carefully remove soil from the plant's base. Allow the potatoes to dry for a few hours in a warm spot out of direct sunlight, then store them at 38°–45° in a dark place with at least 75 percent humidity.

☐ **TRAP YELLOW JACKETS.** These yellow-and-black wasps can be serious nuisances as their numbers increase in late summer. Several kinds of traps, using attractant or food bait, are sold at garden and home supply centers. At *Sunset's* headquarters, gardeners have had good results with Rescue! Yellow-jacket Trap by Sterling International *(www.rescue.com or 800/666-6766).*

☐ **WATCH FOR THIRSTY TREES.** Drought-stressed trees may exhibit scorched foliage or prematurely drop their leaves. To save these trees, water with a deep-root irrigator or a soaker hose placed under the drip line.

☐ **ZAP WEEDS WITH VINEGAR.** USDA Agricultural Research Service studies show that household vinegar is an effective biodegradable herbicide that kills many weeds, including Canada thistle, during their first two weeks of life. Spray young weeds with undiluted white vinegar (5 percent acetic acid) when the air is still, taking care not to spray desirable plants.

—*M. T.*

WHAT TO DO IN YOUR GARDEN IN AUGUST

PLANTING

☐ **BUTTERFLY PLANTS.** To attract butterflies to your garden, add shrubs and trees whose summer flowers supply nectar or whose foliage provide larval food. Now through October, plant Baja fairy duster *(Calliandra californica),* butterfly bush *(Buddleja davidii),* chaste tree *(Vitex agnus-castus), Dalea* species, desert hackberry *(Celtis pallida),* lantana, red bird of paradise *(Caesalpinia pulcherrima),* and *Senna* (formerly *Cassia*) species.

☐ **HERBS, VEGETABLES.** *Sunset* climate zones 1A–3B (Flagstaff, Taos, Santa Fe): Sow seeds of arugula, bush beans, carrots, mesclun, peas, radishes, spinach, and turnips. Set out transplants of broccoli, brussels sprouts, cabbage, and cauliflower. Zones 10, 11 (Albuquerque, Las Vegas): Sow beans, corn, cucumber, and squash. Set out transplants of basil, lemon balm, and pineapple sage. Zones 12, 13 (Tucson, Phoenix): Sow bush beans, carrots, collards, corn, pumpkin, scarlet runner beans, summer squash, and turnips. Set out transplants of basil, chives, and lemon verbena.

☐ **LOW-WATER LANDSCAPE PLANTS.** Select native or desert-adapted species that require little irrigation. Choose accent plants such as muhly grass (*Muhlenbergia* 'Autumn Glow' or 'Regal Mist') and ocotillo *(Fouquieria splendens);* groundcovers such as ger

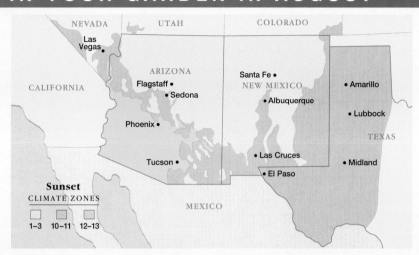

mander *(Teucrium × lucidrys)* or ice plant *(Delosperma cooperi);* and trees like acacia, desert willow, and mesquite.

MAINTENANCE

☐ **CARE FOR ROSES.** Zones 1A–3B: Reduce irrigation and eliminate fertilizer to discourage tender new growth that might be damaged by early frost. Zones 10–13: Apply a balanced fertilizer to stimulate fall bloom.

☐ **CONTROL INSECT PESTS.** Translucent patches on corn leaves are usually caused by corn borer larvae. Similar damage on grape leaves is caused by the grapeleaf skeletonizer. Both pests can be controlled by spraying plants with Bt *(Bacillus thuringiensis).*

☐ **FERTILIZE.** Feed annual flowers and vegetables with a fertilizer high in phosphorus (15-30-15, for example). Feed citrus trees with a high-nitrogen fertilizer (12-3-3).

☐ **REJUVENATE TOMATOES.** Cut indeterminate (vining-type) tomato plants back to 10 to 15 inches, fertilize, and water deeply to encourage a fall crop.

☐ **SPREAD COMPOST.** Spread a 6- to 8-inch layer of organic compost around annual flowers and vegetables to maintain soil moisture and keep roots cool. After you pull spent plants, dig the remaining compost into the soil before fall planting.

☐ **ZAP WEEDS WITH VINEGAR.** USDA Agricultural Research Service studies show that household vinegar is an effective biodegradable herbicide that kills many weeds, including Canada thistle, during their first two weeks of life. Spray young weeds with undiluted white vinegar (5 percent acetic acid) when the air is still, taking care not to spray desirable plants.

—Kim Nelson

Flying colors

Fabric panels hang from an arbor to create this magical outdoor dining room

By Sharon Cohoon • Photographs by Norm Plate

Colorful fabrics give this gazebo drama—especially when lit from within. Saris form the walls; canvas panels cover the top. The light feature is of steel tubing with fiberglass cones over 20-watt bulbs. **Far left:** Gena and Jeff Zischke with daughter Sierra. **Left:** Rosemary spills from a pot atop a sculptural pedestal.

Entering the Zischke family's courtyard in Scottsdale, Arizona, is like stepping to the other side of the world. A country bordering the Mediterranean, perhaps. The paving—chunks of broken concrete with bands of black river rock set in the mortar between them—feels Spanish. The ocher yellow and cinnabar red walls, on the other hand, suggest Morocco, while the citrus and grapevines in containers evoke Italy.

But the steel gazebo in the courtyard's center comes from the rich imagination of owner Jeff Zischke, an artist and designer. He built the frame, then hung canvas panels over the top and colorful saris around the sides to fashion a tentlike roof and "walls"; the fabric gives the space drama and a sense of enclosure. Then he and his wife, Gena, brought in artwork, colorful furnishings, and container plantings.

Jeff has spent many summers in the Mediterranean region—mostly in Provence, France, but also in Italy, Corsica, and

Make your own magic

The shade structure. The Zischkes' five-sided gazebo is about 100 square feet—within a nearly 900-square-foot courtyard—but you could substitute a smaller arbor purchased from a nursery. To provide shade, Jeff placed potted grapevines at each corner; when fully grown, they'll cover the gazebo. Until then, canvas panels block out the sun. Provençal tablecloths also would work well, as would any other colorful, lightweight fabric.

The furnishings. Colorful chairs fitted with striped cushions help brighten the courtyard's perimeter.

Lighting for every mood. "Nothing creates ambience more successfully than beautiful lighting," says Jeff, who designs lighting for restaurants. His chandelier casts a warm glow in the gazebo; sconces illuminate the courtyard's perimeter walls. Candles enhance the magic.

Pots for plants and style. Using containers of plants to soften a hardscape is a classic Mediterranean accent. In addition to grapes, Jeff and Gena grow potted citrus, geraniums, and herbs.

Monaco. These places didn't just appeal to him visually; the lifestyle—the leisurely pace, alfresco dining, and willingness to mix antiques with contemporary furnishings—captivated him too. "We wanted a garden that felt like those places but that wasn't a literal copy of any of them," says Jeff.

"We host a lot of parties in this courtyard, especially in the summer, and everybody loves it out here," says Gena. There's one problem, she adds. "Sometimes people just don't want to leave."

Although Jeff created almost everything in the courtyard, including the light fixtures, you can adapt his ideas using a purchased gazebo and colorful lightweight fabrics.

DESIGN: Zischke Studios *(480/483-9225)* ◆

A cinnabar red wall is a rich backdrop for Jeff Zischke's sculptural painted metal light fixture.

Peppers and cabbage brighten the planting bed and echo the hues of the courtyard's walls. At left, a blue bench and colorful cushion provide bold contrast, while black river rock adds detail between broken concrete pavers.

As savory as its name

This easy-to-grow herb complements summer veggies

By Sharon Cohoon and Kate Washington • Photograph by Thomas J. Story

Summer savory *(Satureja hortensis)* is not as well known as its Mediterranean cousins, sage and thyme, but once you taste it with fresh green beans, you'll wonder how you ever did without it. The aromatic leaves of this fast-growing annual have a mild peppery flavor. The taste is a little sharper than thyme, but not as hot as sage, with a pleasant earthiness all its own. Traditionally used to season snap, shelling, and dried beans, savory is also good with peas, lentils, and other legumes. We like it with root vegetables, especially potatoes, as well as summer squash. Savory also complements roast chicken; blend it with butter to rub under the skin before roasting.

Many nurseries carry this plant, but it's not too late to sow a crop. Savory seeds germinate very quickly, and you can begin harvesting leaves when plants are 6 inches high. The Romans considered savory to be an aphrodisiac, so maybe it wouldn't hurt to grow a little extra.

What summer savory needs

EXPOSURE: Full sun.

SOIL: Light, well drained, organically rich.

WATER: Regular.

GROWING TIPS: Sow directly in the ground (or large containers), barely covering seeds with soil. Thin the strongest seedlings to 12 inches apart. Pinch mature plants often to discourage flowering. If plants get floppy, mound soil slightly around their bases.

SEED SOURCES: Territorial Seed Company *(www.territorialseed.com or 541/942-9547);* Seed Savers Exchange *(www.seedsavers.org or 563/382-5990).* ◆

Warm Potato and Green Bean Salad with Summer Savory

PREP AND COOK TIME: About 30 minutes

MAKES: 4 servings

8	ounces green beans, rinsed and ends snapped off
1½	pounds Yukon Gold potatoes, peeled and sliced ¼ inch thick
2	tablespoons minced shallots
2	tablespoons white wine vinegar
¼	cup olive oil
2	tablespoons summer savory leaves, chopped
	Salt and fresh-ground pepper

1. In a 4- to 5-quart pan over high heat, bring 2 quarts water to a boil. Add green beans and cook until bright green and tender-crisp, 1 to 2 minutes. Drain well and rinse with cold water until cool (or plunge in ice water); drain again.

2. In same pan, bring 2 quarts water to a boil over high heat. Add potato slices and cook until tender when pierced, 10 to 12 minutes; drain well and transfer to a large bowl.

3. Meanwhile, in a 1-cup glass measure, combine shallots and vinegar. In a 1- to 1½-quart pan over medium heat, combine olive oil and summer savory. Stir occasionally until savory is limp and slightly darker and oil is fragrant, 10 to 12 minutes. If oil sizzles, reduce heat slightly.

4. Pour half the oil mixture into vinegar mixture and stir to combine; season with salt and pepper to taste. Pour over warm potatoes and mix gently to coat. Top potatoes with green beans and drizzle remaining oil mixture over beans. Serve warm or at room temperature.

Per serving: 262 cal., 48% (126 cal.) from fat; 4.2 g protein; 14 g fat (1.9 g sat.); 33 g carbo (3.4 g fiber); 13 mg sodium; 0 mg chol.

Playful paving

Bits of tile add fresh color and movement to paths and patios

By Lauren Bonar Swezey and Julie Chai

Renovating a patio or a path provides the perfect opportunity to bring a touch of whimsy to the garden. With the ground as your canvas, you can use patterns and colors that echo the hues of your flowers and furnishings. Or think bigger: imagine seeing the Milky Way overhead and replicating it underfoot. All you need are tiles (or tile pieces) in colors that complement their surroundings, and a little imagination.

Stardust sanctuary

When landscape designer Kathy Kane redesigned her backyard, she incorporated a secluded space for contemplation. Her 10-foot by 10-foot "blue room" features a celestial-patterned mosaic that Kane created herself in two days for less than $100. "I've always liked paving that has a lot of interest," she says. "This design reminds me of stardust."

To make her mosaic, Kane used ceramic tiles (sold as remnants for $10 per box), which she broke into fragments. Before installing them, she put down a 2-inch-thick layer of base rock, settling it with a compactor from an equipment rental yard. She used spray paint

to outline her pattern on the base rock (pictured above). Then she placed plastic netting over the pattern and laid tile fragments on the netting, securing each piece with Liquid Nails adhesive. After allowing the adhesive to dry overnight, she filled in the space between tile pieces with decomposed granite.

DESIGN: Kane Design and Associates, Menlo Park, CA (650/326-4850)

Mosaic tips

Start small. Try applying tile pieces to a stepping-stone first. Once you're comfortable with the process, move on to larger projects.

Draw a plan. If the design is complex, draw it on a smaller scale on grid paper.

Use a smooth surface. The best base for laying tiles is a level concrete pad that's free of lumps, depressions, and large cracks.

Outline the design. Use chalk to draw out the pattern on a paved surface. Once you're satisfied with the design, go over it with a marking pen.

Choose nonskid tiles. Avoid smooth tiles; choose textured ones instead.

Be safe. Before breaking a tile with a hammer, put on safety glasses and rubber gloves, and cover the tile with a cloth.

Follow the fallen leaves

Not long after purchasing their home in Marin County, California, landscape designer Michelle Derviss and partner Liam O'Flaherty began planning an artful walkway inspired by the sculptural building style of Spanish architect Antonio Gaudí. "The mosaic walkway gave us the opportunity to express our creativity," says Derviss. Its fallen-leaf pattern was inspired by the surrounding landscape of black oaks; the background reflects Derviss's love of intense colors. "Blue is a great backdrop for bright planting schemes," she explains.

In summer, Derviss fills beds along the path with succulents and herbs, including yellow variegated oregano. In fall, she swaps in yellow and orange calendula and plants daffodils for spring bloom.

You don't need special skills to work with tile, Derviss says. But a project of this size is time consuming. It took five weekends of kneeling on the ground (and a few back massages) to finish. The effort was worth it, she says. "It inspires a lot of smiles!"

DESIGN: Michelle Derviss, Landscapes Designed, Novato, CA *(415/892-3121)* ◆

THROUGHOUT THE WEST, fall is prime time to plant or revamp your garden. This month's feature articles (pages 250–281) provide inspiration and plenty of practical advice geared especially for your region. See pages 258–261 for details on the Laguna Beach entry garden shown here.

September

Casual, colorful city garden

A carpet of lawn isn't the only way to landscape a front yard. Virginia and Murray Davis don't have any typical turf in front of their house in Piedmont, California. Instead, their angular, sloping lot is filled with easy-care plants that provide colorful flowers from spring through fall.

Landscape architect Bob Cleaver developed the garden's layout, then Shari Bashin-Sullivan and Richard Sullivan of Enchanting Planting created an inviting purple, green, and white planting scheme that plays perfectly off the new decomposed granite and stone entry. Tall, lacy azara trees frame the front door

and soften a long expanse of wall. Below them, *Erysimum* 'Bowles Mauve', purple *Verbena* Tapien hybrid, and white 'Iceberg' and 'Flower Carpet' roses pump out flowers over a long season. Downslope, a patch of creeping red fescue grows naturally, requiring mowing just once or twice a year to renew growth.

"The trees, shrubs, and large boulders give volume to the slope," Bashin-Sullivan explains. "The result is a very relaxed, casual-looking garden."

DESIGN: Cleaver Design Associates *(925/934-6044);* Enchanting Planting *(925/258-5500).*

—*Lauren Bonar Swezey*

If your front yard slopes ...

• Use large boulders and stones to form a retaining wall.

• Take advantage of the upper and lower levels to create paths or patios.

• For best effect, choose medium-size shrubs (3 to 4 feet tall) and cascading groundcovers (such as 'Flower Carpet' roses).

NORM PLATE

Russian tomato thrives here

When Nik Peplenov emigrated from southern Russia to Oregon, he brought seeds of his favorite heirloom tomato. To his delight, it grew as well in the Willamette Valley as it had near the Don River. Eventually, the tomato found its way into a trial planting conducted by Gary Ibsen, founder of the Carmel TomatoFest in California. In Ibsen's tests, it was among the earliest-bearing tomatoes (about 70 days after sowing) and continued producing well into November.

With Peplenov's permission, Ibsen named it 'Sunset's Red Horizon' in recognition of *Sunset's* sponsorship of the 2003 TomatoFest. Indeterminate in habit, the plant keeps growing as long as the weather allows, bearing 4- to 5½-inch-diameter fruits weighing 2 to 3 pounds each.

Order seeds of 'Sunset's Red Horizon' to start indoors in late winter or early spring from the TomatoFest (www. tomatofest.com).

—Jim McCausland

The conservatory blooms again

On September 20, the historic Victorian glass house in San Francisco's Golden Gate Park finally reopened to the public after an eight-year, $25 million restoration. The occasion was celebrated at an extravaganza featuring live performances, horticultural demonstrations, and kids' activities.

Inside the 12,000-square-foot conservatory, visitors can view 1,500 species of rare and unusual tropical plants from more than 50 countries; the plants are displayed in six different climate chambers. Of particular interest is the Plant Explorers Exhibit (in the Lowland Tropics dome), which tells the stories and displays the gear of plant explorers past and present.

The 19th-century structure, severely damaged during winter storms in 1995, was restored thanks to the efforts of the Friends of Recreation & Parks, the National Trust for Historic Preservation, Save America's Treasures, and private citizens.

10:30–6:30; outside activities are free, entrance to the conservatory is $5. John F. Kennedy Dr.; www. conservatoryofflowers.org or (415) 666-7071.—L. B. S.

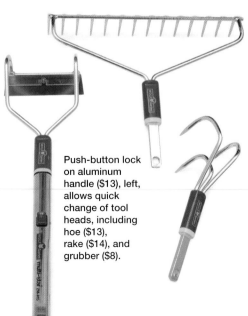

Push-button lock on aluminum handle ($13), left, allows quick change of tool heads, including hoe ($13), rake ($14), and grubber ($8).

Tools with detachable heads

If you'd like to upgrade your collection of garden tools but don't have much storage space, check out the sleek new line of Interlocken tools made in Germany by Wolf-Garten. This mix-and-match system gives you the option of using a single aluminum or wood handle with your choice of 28 detachable heads that perform a variety of tasks. For example, we tried an aluminum handle paired with three heads: a grubber, a hoe, and a rake—a package that retails for about $48. The line also includes edgers and weeders. Made of strong, chromium-galvanized steel, the heads attach to the handle with a snap-and-lock device. The tools are ergonomically designed to reduce back strain.

The handles range in price from $10 for a standard aluminum or wood shaft to $33 for an extra-long telescoping aluminum shaft. The heads run from $8 for a scuffle hoe to $42 for a lawn-edge trimmer.

Look for Interlocken tools at Lowe's and other garden centers. Or order online at *www.omygarden.com* —*Julie Chai*

Late-season fireworks

The dog days of summer don't faze Howard Justice. He knows how to stage flowers so that they look like the grand finale of a fireworks show. At the entry to his century-old farmhouse in Randle, Washington, Wave petunias in shades of lavender and cherry spill out of hanging baskets and clamber up wire frames. A mass of million bells (*Calibrachoa*) forms a low, rose-colored globe on the right side of the porch. These hues echo the red-flowered garden hydrangea growing beneath the weeping blue atlas cedar (*Cedrus atlantica* 'Glauca Pendula') that covers the shake walls. On either side of the walk, pink chrysanthemums in 10-gallon pots add floral pyrotechnics to the scene. —*J. M.*

Camass: A true Northwest beauty

Every spring in Vic Sabin's garden in Eugene, Oregon, camass *(Camassia)*, a Northwest native bulb, puts on a stunning show. The starlike blossoms start opening in April and May and go on blooming for two to four weeks. Flower colors range from dark purplish blue to light blue to white, with pink appearing occasionally, as pictured in Sabin's garden. While seldom grown in home gardens, this perennial deserves a place. Fall is prime planting time.

You're most likely to encounter these species:

· *Camassia cusickii* bears light blue to steel blue blossoms on 3-foot-tall stems.
· *C. leichtlinii* 'Blue Danube' has deep blue-violet blossoms on 4-foot-tall stems; *C. l.* 'Alba' has white flowers.

· *C. quamash* carries deep purple-blue flowers on 1- to 2-foot-tall stems; *C. q.* 'Blue Melody' bears creamy white-and-green foliage.

In the wild, camass grows in moist meadows; it needs ample water during growth and bloom. It takes full sun or partial shade. Plant bulbs 4 inches deep and 6 to 8 inches apart. Camass goes dormant in summer; to hide the leaves, which turn yellow and die down to the ground, plant camass among later-developing perennials like asters or summer bulbs such as lilies.

Look for camass bulbs at nurseries, or check out these mail-order suppliers: Brent and Becky's Bulbs (www.brentandbeckysbulbs.com or 877/661-2852) and McClure & Zimmerman (www.mzbulb.com or 800/883-6998).
—*Mary-Kate Mackey*

Weaving a leafy tapestry

By carefully composing conifers that have contrasting foliage colors and forms, Ralph Hastings and his late partner, Holly Turner, created a magnificent evergreen screen behind a garden bench.

Started 15 years ago, the planting is composed of dwarf conifers and other varieties that normally don't grow very large. Over time, the plants grew together and stretched up toward the light, just as trees do in a forest. The excellent growing conditions at Hastings's Froggwell Garden on Whidbey Island, Washington, prompted even the dwarf specimens to grow much taller than you'd expect.

The screen is flanked by a pair of Oriental arborvitae. The other plants are identified in the diagram and list at right.

If you'd like to create a similar screen, fall is an ideal time to plant conifers from containers. After planting, soak the rootballs and water as needed to keep them damp until fall rains take over. When new growth begins next spring, feed the plants with a controlled-release fertilizer.

— *J.M.*

1. *Thuja orientalis (Platycladus orientalis)*
2. *Chamaecyparis obtusa* 'Nana Lutea'
3. *Juniperus squamata* 'Blue Star'
4. *Tsuga canadensis* 'Gentsch White'
5. *C. obtusa* 'Nana Gracilis'
6. *Cryptomeria japonica* 'Elegans'
7. *Chamaecyparis lawsoniana* 'Fletchers White'
8. *Picea pungens* 'Montgomery'
9. *Chamaecyparis pisifera* 'Golden Mops'

NORM PLATE

Fresh Southwest spirit in Phoenix

When Robert Armijo and Howard Whipple decided to remodel their front yard, their challenge was to give it an updated look that would complement the Spanish colonial revival architecture of the house but still harmonize with the more traditional look of their historic neighborhood in Phoenix. "I wanted to convey the Southwest spirit, without one style overshadowing the other, as well as conserve water," Armijo explains.

To gain space for planting beds, Armijo reduced the area of an existing Bermuda grass lawn by almost half. He used a garden hose to outline possible shapes for the beds, eventually choosing a design with gently curving lines that echo the arches of the porch. Although Armijo didn't have much gardening experience, he was fortunate to live across the street from Tera Vessels, owner of Tera's Garden (602/253-4744), a local nursery. "She has so much enthusiasm for plants and really knows what will thrive in different conditions," he says. With Vessels's help, he picked out a palette of colorful but water-thrifty plants. Clumps of yellow angelita daisy (*Tetraneuris acaulis*), pink *Penstemon parryi*, *Agave angustifolia* 'Marginata' with its white-striped leaves, and *A. americana* with its bold blue leaves fill the beds flanking the walk. On the left side, a sweet acacia (*A. farnesiana*), blooming here in March, casts shade over the porch. Flowering perennials such as white evening primrose are interspersed with accent plants like *Agave murpheyi*.

Poured-concrete edging about 8 inches deep prevents the remaining grass from spreading into the beds. A mulch of Madison Gold decomposed granite was spread over the beds. Armijo continues to add or move plants as needed. "I like to watch the garden's structure and form change as it matures," he says. —*Cathy Cromell*

Winter aconite,
Eranthis hyemalis

Early-bird bulbs

Tough enough to endure the cold and occasional snow, winter-blooming bulbs deliver color when you want it most. In fall, plant these bulbs about 3 inches deep and 3 inches apart in well-drained soil.

Glory-of-the-snow *(Chionodoxa luciliae)* displays its blue, white, or pink flowers in late winter atop 6-inch stems.

Snowdrops *(Galanthus* species) sport nodding white flowers on 6- to 8-inch stems in February. Common snowdrop *(G. nivalis)* has 1-inch-long flowers. Giant snowdrop *(G. elwesii)* has 1½-inch-long flowers.

Winter aconite *(Eranthis hyemalis)* bears 1½-inch-wide buttery yellow flowers.

Find a good selection of early bulbs from mail-order sources such as Brent and Becky's Bulbs (www. brentandbeckysbulbs.com or 804/693-3966), McLure & Zimmerman (www. mzbulb.com or 877/661-2852), and Old House Gardens Heirloom Bulbs (www.oldhousegardens. com or 734/995-1486).

—J.M.

Grassy mosaic in Taos

As an alternative to a traditional lawn, Rene Mettler planted a living mosaic among the flagstones in the courtyard fronting his 200-year-old adobe home in Taos, New Mexico.

Mettler leveled the area, spread 3 inches of sand on top of the existing soil, then set the flagstones securely in the sand in a random pattern, leaving bare seams of at least 2 inches between the stones.

He filled the seams with topsoil, sowed grass seed in them, and watered daily until the seed germinated. Once the grass was well established, he cut back to weekly watering. To keep the grass looking tidy, Mettler runs a lawnmower over it once a month.

To try something similar, use a drought-tolerant grass such as blue grama *(Bouteloua gracilis* 'Hachita'), which does well in either sandy or clay soil. You can sow this fast-germinating seed in early fall (until six weeks before the first heavy frost) or wait until spring. As an alternative to seed, grass plugs can be planted in the cracks at 4-inch intervals. Blue grama turns straw-colored in its dormant winter state.

Another plant that grows well between paving stones is creeping thyme; try 'Ohme Garden Carpet' or 'Reiter'.

'Hachita' blue grama (seeds and plugs) and thyme (in 2½-inch pots) are available from High Country Gardens in Santa Fe *(www.highcountrygardens.com or 800/925-9387).*

—Susan P. Blevins

BACK TO BASICS

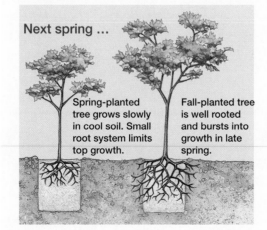

Next spring ...

Spring-planted tree grows slowly in cool soil. Small root system limits top growth.

Fall-planted tree is well rooted and bursts into growth in late spring.

The benefits of fall planting

Shrubs, trees, and groundcovers get a head start on growth when planted in fall. Set them out early enough so roots begin to grow while the soil is warm (late August to October in colder climates, September through October in mild climates, and October through November in warm climates). As the weather turns cool and fall rains come, roots will become well established by spring.

—L.B.S.

Cool-toned plants bask in the sun

Although it gets full sun, this bed looks as refreshing as a chilled fruit salad. The bracing combination of flowers and foliage was designed by Loddie Dolinski and Ebi Kondo for Denver Botanic Gardens. Altogether, they used about eight different plants, a combination of annuals and tender perennials. At left rear, plumes of purple fountain grass (*Pennisetum setaceum* 'Rubrum') wave over the toothy green-and-maroon leaves of *Perilla frutescens* and mauve-flowered 'Spumante' osteospermum. Just below them are 'Alto Blue' ageratum, deep purple 'Marine' heliotrope, and bicolored 'Merlin Blue Morn' petunia, one of the 2003 All-America Selections. And filling out the front, the burgundy leaves of perilla play off the frosty foliage of licorice plant (*Helichrysum petiolare*).

Perilla, an aromatic annual herb also known as beefsteak plant and shiso, has edible leaves that taste something like mint, something like cinnamon. In Japan, shiso is used to flavor sushi, tofu, and tempura.

—*Colleen Smith*

JAMES BOONE

A delicious potager in Denver

The garden of Judy and Ken Robins is a feast for the eyes and the palate. Known as a potager (from the French word *potage,* or soup), this style of garden mingles edible and ornamental plants. For example, in the bed at left, nasturtiums with peppery yellow and orange flowers are backed by zucchini squash and hefty heads of cabbage. The Robinses also grow arugula, broccoli, carrots, cucumbers, lettuce, onions, peppers, and turnips. Behind these crops rise tall flowering perennials such as pink and red bee balm and Joe Pye weed (*Eupatorium purpureum* 'Gateway'), with showy mauve plumes. In the center of the garden, surrounded by a 2-inch-deep layer of pea gravel, island beds planted with yellow snapdragons and summer phlox are accented by trellises entwined with sweet peas (front) and purple hyacinth bean (rear). Around the beds, black steel edging keeps the gravel in place.

Designed by Laurie Jekel, owner of the Last Detail *(303/733-5280),* a Denver-based landscaping firm, the garden owes much of its bountiful look to the soil itself. Jekel enriched it with her specialty compost of sterilized cow manure mixed with wood chips and fortified with granular iron. Jekel's staff cultivates the soil once a week. —*C.S.*

Succulents for slopes

Cascaders

Sedums such as donkey tail *(S. morganianum)* produce fat, overlapping, downward-pointing leaves. For color, you can't beat pork and beans *(S. rubrotinctum);* the more sun you give it, the redder it gets.

Clumpers

Aeoniums form lush clusters of rosettes that range from dime- to dinner plate–size, depending on the variety. Striking varieties include *A. decorum* 'Sunburst', with green, pink, and cream stripes; and *A. arboreum* 'Zwartkop', which is nearly black.

Showstoppers

One large agave or aloe packs a lot of punch, but many kinds have vicious spines. For a great backdrop plant, use smooth-edged, solid-green *Agave attenuata,* which grows 5 to 6 feet across and produces pups.

Succulent sitting area

A wreath inspired this bank planting, which curves behind my semicircular sitting area in Escondido. I'd made a wreath using various kinds of succulents, and I admired the beauty of their fleshy leaves, sculptural shapes, and colors like silver green, jade green, and bronze. So why not plant a big half-wreath to sit in? In Southern California, most succulents do fine in partial shade, and many of them cascade beautifully. The best place to view their rosettes and whorls is at eye level, in a spot designed for lingering.

In early fall, I gathered my garden's ignored aeoniums, kalanchoes, and sedums and massed them above the sitting area's wood retaining walls (where the soil is fast draining and enriched with leaf mold and a potting mix formulated for cactus and succulents). Plants that stay small went in front, larger ones in back.

Next I prowled specialty nurseries for succulents with unusual shapes and colors, such as purple-black *Aeonium arboreum* 'Zwartkop', frilly-edged echeverias, and *Aloe striata,* which resembles a fleshy gray-blue star.

In addition to their evergreen foliage, many of these succulents offer a seasonal bonus: flowers of yellow, red, cream, or coral that last a month or more. —*Debra Lee Baldwin*

WHAT TO DO IN YOUR GARDEN IN SEPTEMBER

PLANTING

☐ **COOL-SEASON ORNAMENTALS.** Set out seedlings of flowering cabbage and kale, pansies, and violas.

☐ **COOL-SEASON VEGETABLES.** *Sunset* climate zones 4–7, 17: Early in the month, set out seedlings of arugula, kale, leaf lettuce, mustard greens, radishes, and spinach for fall harvest and cabbage and purple-sprouting broccoli for late-winter or spring harvest. You can still get a crop this year from a September sowing of Asian vegetables such as baby bok choy, mizuna, tah choy, 'Crimson Lady Finger' radish, or 'Silver Bell' sweet turnip. An excellent seed source for these is Dimension Trade Company in Scappoose, Oregon *(503/577-9382 or www.newdimensionseed.com).*

☐ **COVER CROPS.** You can substantially improve the soil in garden beds by sowing them with crimson clover or vetch. They minimize erosion from wind and rain all winter. In spring, about a month before planting, till them under and the added organic matter will greatly improve the soil's texture and organic content.

☐ **LANDSCAPE PLANTS.** Fall-planted groundcovers, perennials, shrubs, trees, and vines have winter to establish roots, so they'll be ready to take off next spring. (For landscaping ideas, see the story on page 250.)

☐ **LAWNS.** Zones 1–3: Start or repair a lawn from seed any time through mid-September, or lay sod through mid-October. Zones 4–7, 17: Sow grass seed or lay sod any time this month. Keep the sod or seedbed moist until grass is up.

☐ **SPRING-FLOWERING BULBS.** For long-term performance, choose among camass (see page 238), crocus, daffodils, fritillary, grape hyacinths, *Scilla,* species tulips, and star of Bethlehem *(Ornithogalum arabicum).* Hyacinths and standard tulips remain viable for two or three years.

MAINTENANCE

☐ **CARE FOR ROSES.** After the fall flush of bloom, don't deadhead the spent blossoms. Instead, let them form hips to help the plant wind down for winter.

☐ **DIG AND DIVIDE PERENNIALS.** Divide and replant spring- and summer-flowering perennials now, including Shasta daisies, Siberian irises, peonies, and Oriental poppies. Divide fall bloomers immediately after flowering or wait until spring.

☐ **MAKE COMPOST.** Put grass clippings, dead leaves, weeds, and vegetable waste onto a compost pile. Keep the pile damp and turn it weekly with a pitchfork.

☐ **MULCH.** Zones 1–3: Apply a 3-inch layer of organic mulch over the roots of permanent plants to reduce soil erosion and freeze damage this winter.

☐ **ZAP WEEDS WITH VINEGAR.** U.S. Department of Agriculture studies show that household vinegar is an effective biodegradable herbicide that kills many weeds, including Canada thistle, during the first two weeks of life. Spray young weeds with undiluted white vinegar (5 percent acetic acid) when the air is still, taking care not to spray desirable plants. ◆

WHAT TO DO IN YOUR GARDEN IN SEPTEMBER

PLANTING

☐ BULBS. *Sunset* climate zones 7–9, 14–17: Try these less common charmers in your garden. All will give a colorful display in spring: baboon flower *(Babiana),* African corn lily *(Ixia),* dwarf *Narcissus, Freesia,* grape hyacinth *(Muscari),* harlequin flower *(Sparaxis), Homeria collina,* naked lady *(Amaryllis belladonna),* ranunculus, *Tritonia* and species tulips (such as *Tulipa clusiana, T. saxatilis),* and windflower *(Anemone coronaria).*

☐ LAWN. Zones 1–9, 14–17: Toward the end of the month, sow seed or lay sod over soil that's been rotary tilled and amended with organic matter. Zones 1–2: Plant new lawns early in the month (at highest elevations, such as the Lake Tahoe area, wait to plant seed until October; it will germinate in spring when the snow melts).

☐ PERENNIALS. Zones 7–9, 14–17: Plant perennials now so roots get established through late fall and winter. Choices include campanula, candytuft, catmint, coreopsis, delphinium, dianthus, diascia, foxglove, gaillardia, geum, Japanese anemone, penstemon, phlox, pincushion flower, salvia, *Scaevola,* and yarrow. Nurseries should have a good selection in sixpacks, 4-inch pots, and gallon cans. In zones 7–9, wait to plant until the middle or end of the month, when the weather cools a bit.

Sunset
CLIMATE ZONES
☐ Mountain (1–2)
☐ Valley (7–9)
☐ Inland (14)
☐ Coastal (15–17)

☐ VEGETABLES. Zones 7–9, 14–17: Early autumn is a great time to introduce kids to vegetable gardening. Select a small, sunny border or, if you lack garden space, plant in containers. Plant carrots; try small, round 'Thumbelina' from Territorial Seed Company *(www.territorial-seed. com or 541/942-9547).* Mix seed with $1/8$ cup of clean sand so it's easier to distribute. Also plant onion sets, snap peas (kids love to eat them fresh off the vine), and radishes (red, purple, and white 'Easter Egg II', also from Territorial, are fun to harvest, even if kids don't want to eat them).

MAINTENANCE

☐ CARE FOR ROSES. Zones 7–9, 14–17: To encourage a good flush of flowers in fall, give plants a shot of fertilizer now. (Try organic rose food, sold at nurseries and home centers.) Make sure the soil is moist before applying it; water well afterward. Also remove faded blooms and rose hips to encourage bud formation. If powdery mildew is starting to show up on

leaves, or if spider mites are present, spray foliage with a nontoxic fungicide made from sulfur (such as Safer Garden Fungicide).

☐ PICK UP FALLEN FRUIT AND LEAVES. Inspect fallen fruit. If it's diseased or infested with insects, bag it and discard in the trash. Also, clean up fallen leaves from beneath fruit trees; they may be harboring diseases. It's best not to compost fruit and leaves unless you know your pile gets hot enough to kill the pests.

☐ REMOVE MULCHES. Zone 1–2: As temperatures start to drop in fall, keep organic mulches away from warm-season crops so the sun can heat the soil.

☐ REPLANT FLOWERPOTS. Zones 7–9, 14–17: By September, summer flowers in pots may look bedraggled. To carry the container plantings through the last remaining warm days, replant them with late-summer annuals such as cosmos, marigolds, salvias, or zinnias. Or wait until the end of the month to plant cool-season annuals such as calendula, Iceland and Shirley poppies, ornamental cabbage and kale, pansies, primrose, snapdragon, stock, sweet peas, and violas. Before planting, add new planting mix and an organic or timed-release fertilizer. ◆

WHAT TO DO IN YOUR GARDEN IN SEPTEMBER

PLANTING

☐ AUTUMN FOLIAGE. Even if you don't have room for a liquidambar or ginkgo tree, you can still enjoy those wonderful amber-to-burgundy leaves that announce it is fall. Many smaller trees provide similar color—like crape myrtle, persimmon, or pomegranate. Also try shrubs like Japanese barberry *(Berberis thunbergii)*, heavenly bamboo *(Nandina)*, oakleaf hydrangea, and smoke tree *(Cotinus)*. Or plant a grapevine like *Vitis californica* 'Roger's Red', a California native that has brilliant red leaves in fall.

☐ SPRING BULBS. Nurseries are well stocked with spring bulbs. For best selection, shop early. Choices include anenome, daffodil, Dutch iris, *Leucojum,* and South African bulbs like babiana, freesia, and sparaxis. Also consider spring star flower *(Ipheion uniflorum),* a well-behaved Argentine native that blooms for several months and looks great at the edges of beds. In the high desert *(Sunset* climate zone 11), plant all bulbs now. In other zones, wait until October, except for South African bulbs, which can be planted immediately.

☐ SWEET PEAS. For best performance, plant all varieties of sweet peas this month and next. To get flowers by the winter holidays, sow 'Winter Elegance' by mid-September. 'Early Mammoth' and the dwarf variety 'Explorer' also

Sunset
CLIMATE ZONES
1–3 7–9 11 13 14–24

bloom early. Plant sweet peas in full sun and rich, fertile soil, ideally amended with aged manure. Provide a trellis or other support before planting. Keep soil moist until all seeds sprout. If you're gone during the day, it's useful to start seeds in small pots in filtered sun first, then transplant them into the garden later.

☐ WINTER VEGETABLES. From mid-September until Thanksgiving, coastal (zones 22–24) and inland (zones 18–21) gardeners can set out winter crops. Sow seeds or plant seedlings of beets, broccoli, cabbage, carrots, cauliflower, celery, chard, collards, kale, lettuce, green and short-day onions, parsley, parsnips, peas, white potatoes, radishes, spinach, and turnips. In the high desert (zone 11), plant lettuce, radishes and spinach.

MAINTENANCE

☐ FEED ROSES. For prolific fall bloom, feed roses now. Try this homemade fertilizer, courtesy of *The Rose Garden*, an organic rose-care newsletter *(www.therosegarden.mouchet. us or 661/269-1525):* For each shrub, apply 3 cups alfalfa meal, 1 cup fish meal, $1/4$ cup kelp, 1 tablespoon bonemeal, and 2 teaspoons powdered chelated iron. Scratch it into the soil and water well.

☐ PROTECT PROPERTY FROM BRUSH FIRES. In fire-prone areas, before the onset of Santa Ana winds, cut and remove all dead branches and leaves from trees and shrubs, especially those that grow near the house. Clear leaves from gutters and remove woody vegetation that is growing against structures.

☐ TREAT HYDRANGEAS. To keep blue hydrangeas blue, treat soil around plants now with aluminum sulfate. (Southern California garden writer Pat Welsh uses 1 tablespoon per foot of plant height or $1/4$ teaspoon per potted plant.) Mix it with water and apply as a soil drench. Reapply later in fall and again in spring.

PEST CONTROL

☐ PROTECT CABBAGE CROPS. To keep cabbage white butterflies from laying eggs on your broccoli, cabbage, and mustard greens, cover seedlings with floating row covers as soon as you plant. Or spray young caterpillar larvae with *Bacillus thuringiensis.* ◆

MAP: DEBRA LAMBERT

WHAT TO DO IN YOUR GARDEN IN SEPTEMBER

PLANTING

☐ AUTUMN FLOWERS. Set out fall-blooming perennials, including aster, chrysanthemum, goldenrod *(Solidago),* Japanese anemone, *Rudbeckia, Sedum* 'Autumn Joy', and wine cups.

☐ LANDSCAPE PLANTS. For a list of unthirsty grasses, groundcovers, perennials, shrubs, and trees, see page 270. Planted now, as temperatures are cooling down, they'll need less-frequent watering to get established.

☐ SHOWY FALL FOLIAGE. For colorful autumn leaves, consider these plants. *Shrubs:* Dwarf amur maple, barberry, chokeberry *(Aronia* species), cotoneaster, redtwig dogwood, *Rosa glauca,* serviceberry, *Spiraea,* sumac, viburnum, and winged euonymus. *Trees:* Alder, ash, chokecherry, crabapple, eastern redbud, goldenrain tree, hawthorn, honey locust, linden, and maple.

☐ SPRING BULBS. Crocuses, daffodils, tulips, and other spring bulbs are widely available this month. For a fresh look, consider these unusual hardy bulbs. *For sun:* Camass, foxtail lily, *Geranium tuberosum,* Greek windflower *(Anemone blanda),* spring star flower *(Ipheion uniflorum),* Juno iris *(I. bucharica),* and spider lily *(Lycoris squamigera). For shade:* Checkered lily *(Fritillaria meleagris),* English bluebell *(Hyacinthoides non-scripta),* Spanish bluebell *(Hyacinthoides hispanica),* and *Lilium henryi.* A good source for these and other bulbs is McClure & Zimmerman *(www.mzbulb.com or 800/ 883-6998).*

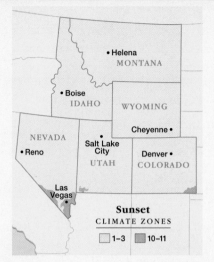

Sunset
CLIMATE ZONES

☐ 1–3   ☐ 10–11

☐ VEGETABLES. Sow seeds of lettuce and other salad greens, radishes, and spinach for late fall harvest. Use a floating row cover to shield seedlings from early frosts. Spinach can be left in the ground over winter; protect plants with a thick blanket of hay or straw.

MAINTENANCE

☐ BRING TENDER PERENNIALS INDOORS. Take cuttings from coleus and geraniums to overwinter indoors. Root the cuttings in moist vermiculite or sterile potting soil. Bedding or wax begonia, caladium, heliotrope, impatiens, Madagascar periwinkle, New Zealand flax, and *Plectranthus* can be moved indoors and grown as houseplants over the winter. As soon as you bring the plants inside, cut them back by one-third, place them in pots in a sunny window or under lights, and fertilize.

☐ HARVEST CROPS. *Apples:* When they appear ripe, cut one in half: Brown seeds indicate the fruit is ready for harvest. Pick from the sunniest side of the tree first; those in shade take longer to ripen. Light frost will not damage apples left on the tree. *Vegetables:* Pick all beans, eggplants, peppers, summer squash, and tomatoes before first frost. Green tomatoes will continue to ripen indoors if stored in a dark, cool place. When frost threatens, pull out the whole tomato plant and hang it in the garage, or store picked green tomatoes in cardboard flats, taking care that they do not touch. Beets, carrots, parsnips, and turnips can be left in the ground for winter harvest if you cover them with 6 to 12 inches of hay or straw.

☐ LIFT AND STORE SUMMER BULBS. After frost kills their foliage, dig up bulbs of calla, canna, dahlia, gladiolus, tuberous begonia, and other tender bulbs. To get a head start next spring, replant the dug-up bulbs in containers filled with fresh potting soil and store them in a cool, dry place. Keep the potting medium slightly moist all winter. Next spring, the potted bulbs will be ready to force under lights or in a sunny window. —*M. T.*

WHAT TO DO IN YOUR GARDEN IN SEPTEMBER

PLANNING

☐ NATIVE PLANT INFO ONLINE. Check out the website of your state's native plant society for regionally specific information: Arizona *(www.aznps. org)*; Nevada *(www.heritage.nv.gov/ index.htm)*; New Mexico *(http://npsnm. unm.edu)*; Texas *(www.npsot.org)*.

PLANTING

☐ COOL-SEASON FLOWERS. *Sunset* climate zones 1A–3B (Flagstaff, Taos, Santa Fe): Sow seeds of calendula, cornflower, larkspur, and poppies for spring bloom. Set out transplants of chrysanthemum, Iceland poppy, and nemesia. Zones 10–13 (Albuquerque, Las Vegas, Tucson, Phoenix): Sow seeds of snapdragon. Set out transplants of calendula, feverfew, larkspur, pansy, petunia, pincushion flower, primrose, stock, sweet alyssum, and viola.

☐ COOL-SEASON VEGETABLES. Prepare beds for fall planting by removing weeds and mixing in a 6-inch layer of compost or well-aged manure, plus a balanced fertilizer (a 10-10-10 formula, for example). Zones 1A–3B: Sow seeds of bok choy, carrots, chard, kale, radishes, salad greens, and spinach; plant garlic cloves. Zones 10–13: Sow seeds of beets, bok choy, carrots, chard, kale, kohlrabi, leeks, peas, salad greens, and turnips. Set out transplants of broccoli, brussels sprouts, cabbages, cauliflower, and green onions.

☐ GROUNDCOVERS. Zones 10–13: These tolerate drought and recover quickly from frost damage: evening primrose (*Oenothera* species), dwarf germander (*Teucrium* x *lucidrys* 'Prostratum'), trailing indigo bush (*Dalea greggii*), *Lantana montevidensis*, and verbena.

☐ IRISES. Bearded irises are most suitable for the desert Southwest. Select tall, standard, ruffled, or fringed varieties. In a sunny site with good drainage, plant iris rhizomes so that the tops are barely covered with soil. Water immediately, then every 10 days until new growth emerges in November.

☐ PERENNIAL COLOR. Plant these fall-bloomers: Desert marigold *(Baileya multiradiata)*, *Gaillardia aristata*, hummingbird trumpet *(Zauschneria arizonica)*, ice plant *(Delosperma cooperi)*, Maximilian sunflower *(Helianthus maximiliani)*, scarlet hedge nettle *(Stachys coccinea)*, Texas hummingbird mint *(Agastache cana)*, and yarrow *(Achillea millefolium)*.

☐ WILDFLOWERS. For a colorful spring show, loosen the soil to a depth of 4 inches, then scatter seeds lightly (mix tiny ones with sand for better coverage). Rake lightly to cover seeds and keep the soil surface moist until they germinate. A good source is Wildseed Farms *(www. wildseedfarms.com or 800/848-0078)*.

—*Kim Nelson*

Gardening for the Northwest

Fall is prime time to plant or revamp your garden

By Jim McCausland

In many ways, the Northwest is one of the best places in the world for gardening. Lakes, rivers, the Pacific Ocean, and Puget Sound moderate the climate. Mountains, pastoral valleys, and waterways often make splendid backdrops. Nurseries offer an amazing variety of shrubs and trees. In spring, rhododendrons bear huge trusses of flowers. In fall, gardens are aflame with maples. All year, evergreens carry the show.

The gardens on these pages show ways to use the right plants in the right places. There's no better time to plant than now. Cooling temperatures and autumn rains will give plants a head start on spring.

A collector's garden in Seattle

Most gardeners favor certain kinds of gardens. Lee Neff is an exception. In her Seattle landscape, she has a vegetable garden, rock garden, woodland garden, perennial garden, mini arboretum, and space devoted to climbers and potted plants. All grow on a site with an interesting horticultural past.

Once, this garden's rich loam supported a holly farm. Then it was cultivated by a notable collector, Loren Grinstead, the plant acquisitions chairwoman for the Washington Park Arboretum during the late 1930s. Grinstead planted such gems as a stately old Himalayan white pine, an immense Camperdown elm, an impressive Sawara false cypress, and a few Exbury azaleas.

After Neff and her husband, John, bought the garden in 1992, she hired Sue Skelly and Kelly Dodson—horticulturists based in Poulsbo, Washington—to help update it. Skelly supervised replacement of a circular driveway with a rock garden, while Dodson focused on introducing Neff to an array

Flanked by a bed of Pacific Coast native iris and a low hedge of *Lonicera nitida* 'Baggesen's Gold', a brick path leads past a brilliant Exbury azalea and *Rhododendron* 'Cunningham's White', and into Lee Neff's tree-shaded lower garden.

Right: 'Claire de Lune' peony blooms beside paperbark maple *(Acer griseum).* Below: In Neff's mixed border, grasses, shrubs, and perennials mingle. Far right: *Enkianthus campanulatus,* with bell-shaped flowers, and a rose pink 'Yachiyo-tsubaki' peony in the distance edge the sitting area. Purple *Aquilegia* 'Hensol Harebell', a row of *Carex comans* 'Frosty Curls', and *Yucca gloriosa* 'Variegata' grow in the foreground.

of unusual plants. Gradually, Neff designed and built the rest of the garden with input from friends, family members, and fellow gardeners.

Her early interests were perennials, but she developed a strong love for shrubs and trees. "Being a gardener," she says, "is going outside and looking. Once you realize what grows in this climate, the next challenge is to try things." That philosophy led her to put in plants like Iigiri tree *(Idesia polycarpa),* which is seldom grown here.

Neff tries to do most of her planting in fall, continuing into winter. By the following summer, the plants have begun to fill in, weaving themselves into a three-dimensional tapestry.

Like Grinstead before her, Neff brings an arboretum connection to her garden. As editor of the *Washington Park Arboretum Bulletin,* she is in close touch with plants and the people who love them.

Design tips

- **Use variegated plants** to brighten the shady places beneath tall trees.

- **Repeat colors.** For each bed, use plants whose colors are either complementary (opposite on the color wheel) or closely related. Group them throughout the planting.

- **Blend colors thoughtfully.** "Once I get a color in my head, I think about what might go with it," says Lee Neff. "When I became interested in the mahogany flowers of *Calycanthus occidentalis,* I realized that I liked a number of other plants with red flowers or dark leaves. So I began putting them together in a bed that featured foliage and flower color in red, black, and white."

- **Repeat textures.** To unify plants in beds and borders, repeat foliage textures. "I work harder at texture than color," says Neff. "In a collector's garden, that's critical."

- **Experiment.** Over time, plants have to prove themselves—both in their ability to compete and to fit in. "I do a lot by trial and error," Neff says. "If something doesn't work, I move it, usually in winter."

Northwest gardening at a glance

EXPOSURE. In much of the region west of the Cascade crest, shade is abundant. To make the most of it, put in woodland plants such as astilbe, azalea, columbine, *Epimedium,* ferns, Japanese anemone, *Kalmia,* rhododendron, sweet woodruff, *Trillium,* and *Vancouveria.*

SOILS. Most are acidic, with a pH level of about 5.5—perfect for rhododendrons, ferns, and most other woodland plants, and acceptable for a fair number of plants from drier climates. If the pH of your soil is lower than 5 and you want to grow plants other than acid-lovers, you'll need to dig in lime at planting time.

WATER. Though most days are cloudy in the Northwest, summers are dry. From May through most of September, gardens here demand plenty of extra water—up to an inch a week when there's no rainfall—to make up for dry weather. Mulch helps, and drip irrigation makes precious water go further.

BEST MULCHES. Regional specialties include composted mint straw, hazelnut shells, and wood chips.

RIGHT: JOHN GRANEN; FAR RIGHT AND ABOVE: JIM McCAUSLAND

Listening to your landscape

When a landscape designer tackles a new project, where does she begin? "In this landscape," Vi Kono told us, "I took my direction from two things: a mature stand of evergreens and a water table that was high in many places." Together, these elements gave her garden in Redmond, Washington, four habitats—wet shade, dry shade, damp sunlight, and dry sunlight—and each one suggested a different set of plants.

Wide beds hold shrubs and perennials, including 140 kinds of hosta. Garden art and several well-placed architectural features nestle among them. "Every garden has to include places to go, things to see," says Kono.

Because of her high water table, Kono avoids using toxic chemicals that would run off into her pond and into a small stream that flows to a nearby salmon creek.

DESIGN: Vi Kono, Creative Designs, Redmond, WA *(425/868-3035)*

Red-flowered Jupiter's beard, green and white–leafed dogwood (far left), *Hosta fortunei* (front right), and other perennials and shrubs line a stone path. Top left: Gunnera leaf sculpted in concrete by Vi Kono is fronted by a real fern. Right: Deeply lobed leaves of *Geranium maderense* and chartreuse foliage of *Helichrysum petiolare* 'Limelight' skirt an urn.

Star performers

FALL COLOR: *Euonymus alatus, Fothergilla,* Japanese maples, katsura tree, liquidambar, *Parrotia persica,* and sour gum. Buy them as soon as their leaves change in autumn so you can see what you're getting.

WINTER-FLOWERING SHRUBS: *Camellia sasanqua,* Chinese witch hazel *(Hamamelis mollis), Corylopsis, Forsythia,* heath *(Erica),* Indian plum, ornamental hazelnut, pussy willow, *Sarcococca,* coast silktassel *(Garrya elliptica), Viburnum* x *bodnantense,* and *V. tinus* 'Spring Bouquet'.

SPRING-BLOOMING BULBS: Bluebells, crocus, daffodils, *Fritillaria,* grape hyacinth, irises, snowdrops, snowflakes, and species tulips. They all naturalize in the garden.

ROCK-GARDEN PLANTS: Sometimes called alpines, these re-create high-elevation flower gardens. Choices include aubrieta, basket-of-gold, *Kalmiopsis, Lewisia,* saxifrages, sedums, and sempervivums. Tuck them between boulders or into stone tubs.

DWARF CONIFERS: They come in a variety of forms (weeping, globular, pyramidal, spreading, and cylindrical) and colors (golden, green, bronze, blue, and silver). Use them singly or in groups.

Dainty white daisies of feverfew edge a shady bed filled with maidenhair fern (left rear), white-flowered *Hosta* 'Blue Angel', and gold-and-green *H. montana* 'Aureomarginata'.

Planting pointers

If you have to plant during warm weather, set the plant's rootball in a water-filled galvanized tub to soak it thoroughly while you prepare the planting hole. Then plant in early evening after temperatures have cooled down. After planting, water well.

Container-grown plants

In fall, most perennials, shrubs, and trees are sold in black plastic containers. To prepare for planting, slide the rootball out of the container and rough up the roots on the sides with gloved hands. Snip off any roots that encircle the outside of the rootball or form a dense mat on the bottom.

1. Dig a planting hole three to four times as wide as the rootball and the same depth (in mild climates, the top of the rootball can sit about an inch above ground level to allow for settling). Set the prepared plant in the hole.

2. If your native soil is loam and drains well, backfill the hole with it. If your soil is extremely sandy or is heavy clay, mix the backfill with an equal part of compost. Add the backfill in stages, firming it around the roots with your hands.

3. Build a berm of soil around the plant to form a watering basin. Irrigate gently. Spread a layer of mulch around the plant, keeping mulch several inches away from the stem or trunk. Don't fertilize until you see new growth emerging in spring.

Balled-and-burlapped shrubs and trees

In the Northwest, some landscape plants (often large specimens) are dug from growing fields with a ball of soil around their roots; the rootball is then wrapped with burlap or similar material and tied with twine. Here's how to plant them.

1. Measure the rootball from top to bottom. In rainy climates, dig the hole a bit shallower than this length so that the top of the rootball is barely above surrounding soil. (In cold climates, the rootball should be level with surrounding soil.)

2. Untie the covering. If it's burlap, it will eventually rot; spread it out to uncover half of the rootball. If it's synthetic material, remove it entirely. On a windy site, drive in a stake upwind of the rootball. Fill the hole with soil to within 4 inches of the top; water gently.

3. Continue to fill the hole, firming the soil as you go. Make a berm of soil to form a watering basin; then thoroughly soak the rootball. If you added a stake, loosely tie it to the plant. ◆

Gardening smart in California

Fall is the best time to plant your low-water landscape

By Kathleen N. Brenzel and Sharon Cohoon • Photographs by Thomas J. Story

Of all the gardens that grow in the Golden State, few can match Mediterranean-inspired landscapes for their toughness, sensual appeal, and suitability to our wet winters and dry summers. Whether their designs spring from the Italian-, Spanish-, or Mission-style architecture of a house or the imaginations of their owners, smart gardens like the two we feature here make sense for our climate. Their plantings don't need much water once established, and maintenance is minimal. If you're planning a new landscape or renovating a forgotten corner of an existing one, these gardens can help inspire your own designs and plant choices. Nurseries are filled with shrubs, perennials, and trees to plant now, and fall's the best time to do it; days are shortening, temperatures are cooling, and autumn rains will soon come to get roots growing.

Creeping thyme grows between flagstone pavers in this entry garden. More thyme fills pots, and lavender and salvias add color. A grafted gardenia ('First Love') near the gate provides a touch of sweetness; a white-flowered geranium fills a pot at far left. The birdhouse on the wall above it—designed to look like a summer hat—houses an active nest.

An herbal haven on the South Coast

Rana Malas wanted a garden that felt like the ones she grew up with near the Mediterranean Sea. That meant aromatic foliage plants like scented geraniums, lavender, rosemary, and thyme. "I was always the granddaughter chosen to help out in the garden," she recalls. "And these are scents I learned to love. To me, they're what a garden should smell like." Malas insisted on a few edibles, such as a fruiting olive tree. "In the Middle East, an olive tree is a lucky plant," she says. "It brings you riches." A grapevine was also a necessity. "Living so

Design notes

Play up details. Pay attention to compact groupings of plants or objects. Such details can enrich a garden—especially a small one.

Use pots as focal points. Fill containers with herbs, such as oregano, trailing rosemary, salvias, or thyme. Display them in prominent places.

Soften hardscape. Plant creeping thyme between pavers, and edge paths with soft-foliaged plants such as hardy geraniums and yarrow.

Include a few workhorses. To add color to a mostly herbal garden, rely on a few shrubs that bloom nearly year-round, such as lavatera and groundcover roses.

DESIGN: Theresa Clark Studio, Capistrano Beach, CA *(949/248-5404)*

Garlic chives and thyme spill from a trio of pots. Below: A private corner.

close to the beach, I knew we might not get much fruit. But I love having the leaves handy to use in cooking."

Malas's ideal garden had to include lots of clay pots in classic shapes. "I can't resist them," she admits. Many contain her favorite herbal plants, but others—especially the large ones—are left empty, to be appreciated for their own beauty.

Fortunately for Malas, her Mediterranean garden vision and Laguna Beach's weather were a perfect match. The plants she wanted all thrive in Southern California's climate. Her herbal garden may not be as colorful as some of the English cottage gardens in the neighborhood, Malas says, but it makes up for that by providing aromatherapy. Take a deep breath on a warm afternoon and all your tensions disappear, she says. "It's very peaceful here, isn't it?"

Lavatera maritima forms a privacy screen near the pool; the plant blooms nearly nonstop. Trailing rosemary, white 'Flower Carpet' roses, and an olive tree topiary complete the picture.

California gardening challenges

SOIL. Depending on where you live, your soil can be heavy clay, alkaline (which plants such as camellias don't like), or salty (especially in the desert). To lighten clay soils, add amendments such as compost. To acidify alkaline soils, mix in peat or acid fertilizer periodically. To leach (wash) salts from the salty soils, water plants' root zones slowly and deeply at least once a year.

WIND. Warm winds that sweep from east to west in late summer can dry out foliage and blow down young trees. Properly stake newly planted trees; prune dead or weak branches from established ones. Deeply irrigate plants.

WATER. Dry summers, recurring drought, and a limited water supply are realities in California. Choose plants that adapt well to aridity, and group them by water needs.

PRIVACY. It's an increasingly valuable commodity in California, especially in urban areas where houses are close together and lots are small. To block unwanted views, use leafy screens of closely spaced, fast-growing shrubs such as purple hop bush.

FIRE. In fire-prone areas (Malibu, Bel Air, Santa Barbara, or the hills behind San Bernardino, Laguna Beach, or Oakland, for example), avoid growing highly flammable plants such as junipers, manzanita, or pines. Create an irrigated greenbelt around your house, and clear out any branches that overhang your roof.

At far left, a sunny yellow sea of Jerusalem sage *(Phlomis fruticosa)* blooms in front of blue pride of Madeira *(Echium candicans)* and golden-flowered *Fremontodendron californicum.* Red-hot poker *(Kniphofia)* glows atop bare stems.

Design notes

Mix the plantings. Many California natives have the same exposure, water, and soil needs as plants from similar Mediterranean climates. In the Schleins' yard, fremontodendron and ceanothus (California natives) pair with plants like lavender (a Mediterranean native) and red-hot poker *(Kniphofia)* from South Africa. Group different plants according to their needs.

Forget lawn. Plant unthirsty groundcovers such as blue fescue, 'Carmel Creeper' ceanothus, dwarf cotoneaster, and gazanias. Mulch spaces between them with fine-textured (¼-inch) fir-bark mulch, and use gravel or pavers for paths and patios.

Pair bold colors. Bright flowers stand up to California's sunlight. Yellows and blues predominate in the Schleins' garden, but other plants splash color around the perimeter—purple asters, orange bird of paradise, ruby-red leptospermum, and red kangaroo paws and penstemons. Bronze-foliaged plants such as hop bush, phormiums, and purple smoke tree are cooling accents.

Add fragrance. Sweet scents from citrus and angel's trumpet mix with herbal aromas like lavender.

DESIGN: Rosemary Wells, Viridian Landscape Architecture, Pacific Grove, CA *(408/656-5829)*

Mediterranean meadow in the Bay Area

When Linda and Ted Schlein moved into their Spanish-style house in Menlo Park, they inherited a totally different landscape than the one they'd known. "We'd just come from a colonial house surrounded by green lawn, shrubbery, and a white picket fence," Linda explains.

By contrast, their new garden had a Mediterranean flavor to complement the house. The building, designed by Richard Elmore and the previous owners, Duane and Michele Maidens, echoes the curves and colors of a sun-washed village.

To enhance this vision, landscape architect Rosemary Wells gave the front yard a Mediterranean meadow look. For bright color year-round, she chose unthirsty bloomers such as scarlet bougainvillea, drifts of yellow Jerusalem sage, and lavender. For shade around the periphery, she planted a locust, a pepper tree, and 'Swan Hill' olive trees. For fragrance, she set an angel's trumpet in the entry courtyard beside

At right, a forged iron gate (designed by Michele Maidens and Francisco Hernandez) is framed by red kangaroo paws. Inside, angel's trumpet (*Brugmansia* 'Charles Grimaldi') dangles fragrant blooms above a trickling fountain. Below: New Zealand tea tree.

a trickling fountain. "Its perfume is intoxicating, especially on balmy evenings when it wafts though the open dining room doors," Michele Maidens recalls.

Linda Schlein quickly got into the garden's sun-country mood. As the landscape grows, she tucks in more perennials that fit its theme—with help from Maureen Decombe of Green Willow Gardens *(www.greenwillowgardens.com)*.

"This garden shows no fear of bright colors or strong architectural shapes," says Decombe.

Getting started

Annuals and groundcovers

1. About two weeks before planting, spread a 3- to 4-inch layer of organic matter such as compost or well-rotted manure over the soil in garden beds.

2. Dig the amendments into the soil, mixing lightly to a depth of 9 to 12 inches. Rake the bed smooth. Water it well, then water again before planting.

 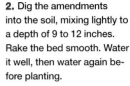

Container trees, shrubs, and perennials

Unless your soil is very sandy or is heavy, poorly draining clay, it's not necessary to add organic amendments before planting native and Mediterranean plants.

1. Dig a planting hole three or four times as wide as the rootball; the hole's sides should taper outward into the soil, as shown. Slip the plant out of its container, loosen roots with your fingers, and set it on the central plateau of firm soil. The top of the rootball should sit just above ground level.

2. If your native soil is loam and drains well, backfill with unamended soil you dug from the hole. If your soil is sandy or is heavy clay, mix the backfill with an equal part of compost. Either way, add the soil in stages, firming it around the roots with your hands as you work.

3. Build a berm of soil around the plant to form a watering basin. Irrigate gently. Spread a layer of mulch around the plant, keeping mulch several inches away from the stem or trunk. Don't fertilize until you see new growth emerging in spring. ◆

ILLUSTRATIONS: TREVOR JOHNSON

High-country

Autumn is prime time to set out permanent plants.
Our tips and selections can help you succeed

By Marcia Tatroe

planting

H ere in the intermountain West, gardeners are routinely challenged by blizzards, blazing summer sun, hailstorms, and, most recently, a drought of historic proportions. Such conditions demand rugged plants (see our list of reliable and water-wise beauties on page 270). But even the most appropriate plants face a struggle until they're established. Spring transplants are exposed to freezing temperatures one day, searing heat the next.

That's why fall planting makes such good sense. Permanent plants—groundcovers, ornamental grasses, perennials, shrubs, and trees—actually have a better survival rate when they're transplanted in fall. To encourage strong root growth, it's best to get plants in at least six weeks before the ground freezes; for the average frost date in your area, check with your county's cooperative extension office.

Fall-planted beauty

This garden in Boulder, Colorado, was started in October. Landscape architect Martin Mosko of Marpa & Associates *(www.marpa.com or 303/442-5220)* has discovered that when the weather stays mild, fall-planted gardens gain a "year's growth" over those planted in spring. Here, a wall frames bright pink peonies, white-striped moss pink *(Phlox subulata)*, cerise dianthus, and purple veronica. Blue-violet hardy geraniums bloom to the right of the steps.

Scenic beds in Colorado Springs

Backed by heavenly views of the Garden of the Gods and Pikes Peak, the 3¹/₂-acre Colorado Springs Utilities Xeriscape Demonstration Garden occupies an exposed site that puts plants to the test. Above, one bed shows how shrubs like burgundy-leafed barberry and small trees like deep green bristlecone pine can be used to reduce turf area. In the foothills zone planting at right, a dry-stacked stone wall creates a warmer microclimate preferred by *Verbascum bombyciferum* 'Arctic Summer', whose powdery white stems carry yellow flowers. At the base of the wall, 'Red Rocks' penstemon blooms near the curled, silvery green leaves of *Marrubium rotundifolia*. This area is watered just twice a month.

Garden open daily, office open 9–5 Mon–Fri. 2855 Mesa Rd., Colorado Springs; www.csu.org or (719) 448-4800.

Intermountain gardening at a glance

GEOGRAPHY. *In lowlands and plains,* aridity is the biggest concern; choose plants with low water needs. *Wooded foothills* offer ideal growing conditions for many shrubs and trees, but wildfires are a threat; choose fire-resistant plants as part of your defensive strategy. *Above 8,000 feet,* the growing season is short; frost and snow are possible any month of the year. Winters are extremely cold, but a reliable snow cover helps protect plants. Cool summers favor many perennials.

SUNSET CLIMATE ZONES. The *Sunset Western Garden Book* assigns climate zones based on a number of factors including temperature, elevation, proximity to mountains, rainfall, and aridity. Find your garden climate among these zones: 1A: Coldest areas (Durango, CO; Laramie, WY). 1B: Coldest areas of eastern Rockies and High Plains (Cheyenne; Helena, MT). 2A: Cold, snowy winter areas (Vail, CO; Missoula, MT). 2B: Chilly winter, hot summer climates (Boise; Denver). 3A: Mild areas (Grand Junction, CO; Salt Lake City).

EXPOSURES. *Colder east- and north-facing sides of structures* are good locations for flowering trees; this siting discourages them from breaking dormancy until later in the season, when their blossoms are less likely to be damaged by late hard frosts. *Warmer southern exposures* and protected areas where soil never freezes are good spots to try slightly tender summer flowers like agapanthus, alstroemeria, and crocosmia.

PAUL BOUSQUET (2)

Cottage style in Idaho

In their mile-high garden in Hailey, Idaho, not far from Sun Valley, Sally and Russ Horn prefer to plant flowering perennials in autumn. Protected by the area's reliable snow cover from mid-December through mid-April, the plants emerge in spring strong enough to withstand the rigors posed by weather. The Horns' cottage-style planting, pictured here in July, shimmers with white Shasta daisies; delphiniums in shades of pink, blue, and white; crimson-flowered clematis (at foot of birdhouse); yellow foxgloves; and purple veronica. Perennials thrive in this area where summer nights are cool and the days are warm but not hot.

Water-wise choices for your garden

GROUNDCOVERS

Dwarf periwinkle (*Vinca minor*): 4–6 in. tall, 3 ft. wide; lavender-blue flowers in spring. Low water; fire resistant. Climate zones 1–3 from the *Sunset Western Garden Book*.

Ice plant (*Delosperma nubigenum*): 1 in. tall, 3 ft. wide; yellow flowers in spring. Moderate water. Zones 2–3.

Rock soapwort (*Saponaria ocymoides*): 6–12 in. tall, 3 ft. wide; pink flowers in spring. Moderate water. Zones 1–3.

Snow-in-summer (*Cerastium tomentosum*): 6–8 in. tall, 3 ft. wide; white flowers in summer. Moderate water. Zones 1–3.

Speedwell (*Veronica pectinata*): 3 in. tall, 1 ft. wide; blue flowers in spring. Low water; fire resistant. Zones 1–3.

Woolly thyme (*Thymus pseudolanuginosus*): 2–3 in. tall, 3 ft. wide; pink flowers in summer. Low water; fire resistant. Zones 1–3.

ORNAMENTAL GRASSES

Blue oat grass (*Helictotrichon sempervirens*): 2–3 ft. tall and wide; fine blue leaves. Low water. Zones 1–3.

Feather reed grass (*Calamagrostis* x *acutiflora*): 4–5 ft. tall, 2 ft. wide; green leaves, burgundy plumes in summer; attractive seed heads. Low water. Zones 2B–3B.

Fescue (*Festuca idahoensis* 'Siskiyou Blue'): 18 in. tall, 15 in. wide; blue-green to silvery blue leaves. Moderate water. Zones 1–3.

Little bluestem (*Schizachyrium scoparium* 'The Blues'): 2–3 ft. tall, 1–2 ft. wide; pale blue leaves turn red in autumn. Low water. Zones 1–3.

Maiden grass (*Miscanthus sinensis* 'Morning Light'): 3–4 ft. tall and wide; white-edged leaves. Moderate water. Zones 2–3.

PERENNIALS

Aster x frikartii 'Mönch': 2 ft. tall and wide; lavender flowers in summer. Moderate water. Zones 2B–3B.

Desert four o'clock (*Mirabilis multiflora*): 1–2 ft. tall, 3–5 ft. wide; magenta flowers all summer. Very low water. Zones 1–3.

English lavender (*Lavandula angustifolia*): 8 in.– 2 ft. tall and wide; fragrant lavender flowers in summer. Low water; fire resistant. Zones 2–3.

Golden columbine (*Aquilegia chrysantha*): 3–4 ft. tall, 1–2 ft. wide; fragrant yellow flowers in spring. Moderate water; fire resistant. Zones 1–3.

Jupiter's beard (*Centranthus ruber*): 3 ft. tall and wide; coral-red flowers in summer. Low water; fire resistant. Zones 2–3.

Mullein (*Verbascum bombyciferum* 'Arctic Summer'): To 6 ft. tall, 2 ft. wide; yellow flowers in summer. Low water. Zones 2–3.

Ozark sundrops (*Oenothera macrocarpa incana* 'Silver Blade'): 6 in. tall, 2 ft. wide; yellow flowers in summer. Low water. Zones 1–3.

Provence broom (*Cytisus purgans* 'Spanish Gold'): 4 ft. tall, 6 ft. wide; yellow flowers in spring. Very low water. Zones 1–3.

Purple prairie clover (*Petalostemon purpureum*): 18 in. tall and wide; purple flowers in summer. Low water. Zones 1–3.

Rocky Mountain penstemon (*P. strictus*): 2–3 ft. tall, 2 ft. wide; blue-violet flowers in summer. Low water. Zones 1–3.

Salvia nemorosa 'East Friesland': 18 in. tall and wide; violet-blue flowers summer through fall. Low water. Zones 2–3.

Statice (*Limonium gmelinii*): 3 ft. tall and wide; purple flowers in summer. Low water. Zones 1–3.

Sundrops (*Calylophus serrulatus*): 18 in. tall and wide; yellow flowers in summer. Very low water. Zones 1–3.

Wine cups (*Callirhoe involucrata*): 6 in. tall, 2–3 ft. wide; magenta flowers all summer. Very low water. Zones 1–3.

Yarrow (*Achillea* 'Moonshine'): 2 ft. tall and wide; silvery leaves and yellow flowers in summer. Low water. Zones 1–3.

SHRUBS

Apache plume (*Fallugia paradoxa*): 3–5 ft. tall and wide; white flowers and feathery seed heads all summer. Very low water; fire resistant. Zones 2A–3B.

Austrian copper rose (*Rosa foetida* 'Bicolor'): 4–5 ft. tall and wide; coppery red flowers in spring. Low water. Zones 1–3.

Blue mist (*Caryopteris* x *clandonensis*): 2 ft. tall and wide; blue flowers in summer. Moderate water. Zones 2B–3B.

Daphne x *burkwoodii* 'Carol Mackie': 3–4 ft. tall and wide; fragrant

NORM PLATE

Eastern redbuds burst into bloom above a pair of *Daphne* x *burkwoodii* 'Carol Mackie'.

pink flowers in spring; gold-edged leaves. Moderate water. Zones 2B–3B.

Dwarf chamisa (*Chrysothamnus nauseosus*): 1–4 ft. tall and wide; yellow flowers in summer. Very low water. Zones 1–3.

False indigo (*Amorpha fruticosa*): 6–8 ft. tall, 15 ft. wide; purple flowers in summer. Low water. Zones 2B–3B.

Fernbush (*Chamaebatiaria millefolium*): 6–8 ft. tall and wide; white flowers in summer. Very low water. Zones 1–3.

Golden currant (*Ribes aureum*): 3–6 ft. tall and wide; yellow flowers in spring; edible fruit; red fall foliage. Low water. Zones 1–3.

Mock orange (*Philadelphus lewisii* 'Cheyenne'): 7 ft. tall, 6 ft. wide; fragrant white flowers in spring. Moderate water. Zones 1–3.

Western sand cherry (*Prunus besseyi*): 3–6 ft. tall and wide; white flowers in spring; edible fruit. Low water. Zones 1–3.

TREES

Crabapple (*Malus* 'Coralburst'): 10–15 ft. tall, 8–10 ft. wide; rose-pink flowers in spring; reddish orange fruit. Moderate water. Zones 1–3.

Eastern redbud (*Cercis canadensis*): 25–35 ft. tall and wide; rosy pink flowers in spring; yellow fall foliage. Moderate water. Zones 1–3.

European mountain ash (*Sorbus aucuparia*): 20–40 ft. tall, 15–25 ft. wide; white flowers in spring; red berries; red fall foliage. Moderate water. Zones 1–3.

Goldenrain tree (*Koelreuteria paniculata*): 20–35 ft. tall, 25–40 ft. wide; yellow flowers in summer; yellow fall foliage. Moderate water. Zones 2–3.

Ornamental pear (*Pyrus calleryana* 'Chanticleer'): 30–35 ft. tall, 12–15 ft. wide; white flowers in spring; red fall foliage. Moderate water. Zones 2B–3B.

Pagoda dogwood (*Cornus alternifolia*): 20 ft. tall and wide; white flowers in spring; blue-black fruit; red fall foliage. Moderate water. Zones 2–3.

'Princess Kay' plum (*Prunus nigra* 'Princess Kay'): 15–20 ft. tall, 15 ft. wide; white flowers in spring; red fall foliage. Moderate water. Zones 1–3.

Russian hawthorn (*Crataegus ambigua*): 15–25 ft. tall and wide; white flowers in spring; red fruit; orange fall foliage. Low water. Zones 1–3.

Serviceberry (*Amelanchier* x *grandiflora* 'Autumn Brilliance'): 15–25 ft. tall, 15–20 ft. wide; white flowers in spring; purplish black edible fruit; orange-red fall foliage. Moderate water. Zones 2–3.

Blue oat grass waves wispy, straw-colored flowers. Below: Golden columbines wear spurs up to 2½ inches long.

Planting pointers

Perennials from 4-inch pots

1. For each plant, dig a hole the same depth as the container and 1 or 2 inches wider.

2. Lightly separate roots. If there's a pad of coiled roots at the rootball's bottom, cut or pull it off.

3. Place each plant in hole so that top of rootball is even with soil surface. Firm soil around roots; water gently and thoroughly.

4. Spread 3- to 4-inch layer of coarse compost or other fine-textured mulch over root zone; don't pile it against crown of plant.

Trees and shrubs from containers

1. Dig a hole at least twice as wide as the rootball; leave a plateau of soil as shown. Make sure the top of the rootball is level with the surrounding soil.

2. Backfill with the un-amended soil you dug from the hole, adding the soil in stages and firming it around the roots with your hands as you work.

3. Make a berm of soil to form a watering basin around the plant's canopy. Irrigate slowly and deeply to soak the entire rootball.

4. Spread a 3- to 4-inch layer of shredded bark or similar mulch over the root zone. Don't pile mulch against the trunk. ◆

Gardening smart in the desert

Fall is the best time to design and plant

By Sharon Cohoon • Photographs by Norm Plate

In the Southwest's deserts, gardeners face tough challenges—extreme temperatures, low rainfall, and poor soils, to name a few. Still, many landscapes here are so exciting that gardens elsewhere seem to pale by comparison. Some are natural, as if plucked from the surrounding desert, while others take the idea of an oasis to fanciful heights.

Either way, consider this: Some of the most interesting plants anywhere are perfectly at home in the Southwest. Cactus and succulents like agave and yucca are the indisputable stars; their bold, architectural shapes are living sculptures. Wispy-leafed shrubs and trees such as brittlebush and palo verde add soft contrast. And wildflowers and perennials—including penstemon and verbena—provide dashes of color.

Fall is the ideal time to plant. Temperatures are beginning to drop, but the soil's still warm enough for roots to take hold. In the Southwest's coldest areas (Flagstaff, AZ; Santa Fe), you'll want to have everything in the ground by early October.

Awash in penstemons

This planting at the home of Daniel and Lisa Dell'Osso in Paradise Valley, Arizona, looks like a natural desert wash. At peak bloom in spring are pink penstemon *(P. parryi and P. pseudospectabilis)* and red firecracker penstemon *(P. eatonii)*. Trees include acacia (middle) and mesquite (left and right). A mulch of decomposed granite covers the soil around them. DESIGN: Greg Trutza, New Directions in Landscape Architecture, Phoenix *(602/264-5202)*

Design tips

• Borrow desert views.
Create a seamless transition between your garden and the wild areas by using some of the same plants that grow there naturally.

• Use plants as sculpture.
Place cactus and succulents where their forms show off to the best advantage—as well as where they'll capture backlighting from the sun or cast shadows across paving. For drama in the evening, light them from beneath. Or cluster bolder plants like saguaros of different heights against a painted wall.

An infinity-edge pool melts into the desert; silhouetted against the evening sky are an ironwood tree and an agave in a pot made by artist Darcy Badiaci for Pearson and Company *(602/840-6447).* Above, water cascades from a canterra-stone scupper.

Desert views in Scottsdale

Simplicity of design gives this Scottsdale, Arizona, garden a Zen-like serenity. The property enjoys views of Black Mountain and a desert panorama. To blur the boundaries between the garden and the surrounding desert, designer-builder Peter Magee of Magee Custom Homes *(480/575-5254)* used a few tricks: A giant "window" in a wall on one side of the patio frames views in that direction; the infinity-edge swimming pool, surfaced with black Pebble Tec *(www.pebbletec.com or 800/937-5058),* drops off to meet the desert.

Sonoran Desert Designs planted the site lightly to enhance—not compete with—these backdrops. A gnarled 150-year-old ironwood tree (brought in with a crane) and a large agave in a stone pot add drama to the hardscape; beyond, mesquite and other native shrubs provide a subtle transition zone between garden and desert.
DESIGN: Sonoran Desert Designs, Cave Creek, AZ *(480/595-6400)*

A wall painted deep eggplant accentuates the dramatic shapes of Argentine saguaros *(Trichocereus terscheckii).* Uplights shining against the wall create dramatic shadows at night. Plants are from Sonoran Desert Designs.

Desert gardening at a glance

GROWING SEASONS. **Low desert** (climate zone 13 from the *Sunset Western Garden Book*; Phoenix): September to May. In early fall, plant hardy ornamentals, bulbs, and cool-season annuals such as Iceland poppy and petunias. By midspring, temperatures soar. **Intermediate desert** (zone 12; Tucson): Mid-March to mid-November. Strong winds in spring can damage tender growth (protect exposed plants with windscreens, walls, or fences); summer rains provide relief. **Medium to high desert** (zone 11; Las Vegas, NV): Mid-March to early November. Temperature extremes (frosty winters, sizzling summers) demand tough, hardy plants. **High desert** (zone 10; Albuquerque; Sedona, AZ): April to October. Cold winters call for spring planting.

SOIL. Generally alkaline, rocky or sandy, and nutrient-poor; contain little organic matter. A cementlike layer of caliche or hardpan often lies on or below the surface, impeding drainage. Natives and other desert-adapted plants work best in such conditions.

WATER. Recently, much of the Southwest has suffered from a severe drought. The lack of precipitation underscores the need to use irrigation water wisely. Choose native and desert-adapted plants with low water needs; place thirstier ones near the house, drought-tolerant ones on your lot's perimeter. Reduce or remove lawns.

Lippia supplants a lawn in the entry courtyard; Mexican grass trees add contrasting texture. Below, angelita daisies skirt an agave in a concrete bowl.

Lush and unthirsty

Richard and Carole Kraemer's garden in Paradise Valley looks almost tropical. But the plants they grow are really quite drought-tolerant.

Beside the front entry, a plush green welcome mat is not thirsty turf but lippia (*Phyla nodiflora*). In the backyard, a snaky plant near the pool's edge with a convincingly aquatic look is lady's slipper *(Pedilanthus macrocarpus),* an unthirsty succulent. Bougainvillea climbs a trellis and grows against the cliff that rises at the back of the garden. And though the space feels quite green, most of the ground is actually covered with hardscape—pavers, a ramada, and a fireplace.

DESIGN: Greg Trutza, New Directions in Landscape Architecture, Phoenix *(602/264-5202)*

Design tips

• **Eliminate turf.** Turf grass demands an enormous amount of water. If you must have lawn, confine it to a small area. (Think of it as a throw rug rather than carpeting.) Better yet, plant a lawn substitute like lippia or another drought-tolerant groundcover.

• **Concentrate greenery.** Create a few lush planting pockets where they'll have the most psychological impact—near the entry, by a patio, edging a path. Less-visible areas can be planted more sparsely, if at all.

• **Celebrate hardscape.** Be lavish in the space you devote to patios, terraces, and pathways and use high-quality materials in colors than echo those found in the desert. Cover bare earth with mineral mulch to further tie the garden to its natural surroundings.

A pergola of salt-preserved cedar leads to the backyard. Pink 'Rosenka' bougainvillea adds a splash of color. The rich colors in the laja negra paving stones echo those of the cliff that forms the garden's backdrop.

Showcase cactus

At this Scottsdale home, cactus and other desert succulents make excellent container plants and serve as sculptural elements in garden beds. They tolerate extreme temperature fluctuations, little water, and tricky northern exposures. Their one demand is fast-draining soil; use a planting mix specially formulated for cactus. For best effects, plant cactus and succulents in big, bold-looking pots, which look best with plants of substance and character. In garden beds, set cactus and succulents among flowering groundcovers, such as purple verbena or a sprinkling of wildflowers, for a soft counterpoint.

DESIGN: Steven Rogers, landscape architect, Sonoran Desert Designs, Cave Creek, AZ *(480/595-6400)*

At the home's front entrance, purple verbena softens structural plants—yucca, golden barrel cactus, and lady's slipper. Above left, a euphorbia is paired with a purple prickly pear in a 27-inch-diameter concrete pot on the patio.

Planting tips for the Southwest

Flower beds and groundcovers

1. About two weeks before planting, spread 3 inches of organic matter such as compost or well-rotted manure over garden beds. 2. Dig amendments into the soil, mixing well to a depth of 8 to 12 inches. Rake the bed smooth. Water it well, then water again just before planting.

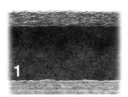

Container-grown trees and shrubs

Unless your soil is very sandy, it's not necessary to add organic amendments. Follow these steps, recommended by the University of Arizona College of Agriculture.

Soil without caliche

1. Dig a hole three to five times the width of the rootball and no deeper than the rootball. The walls of undisturbed soil should be rough and tapered, as shown. 2. Set the plant on undisturbed soil in the center of the hole, with the top of the rootball at or slightly above soil level. 3. For trees that need staking, sink two wood stakes (2 inches in diameter or 2 inches square) at least 6 inches into undisturbed soil on opposite sides of the plant, outside its canopy. 4. Partially backfill the hole, firm the soil, water thoroughly, and finish backfilling. 5. Build a small berm of soil around the rootball and water thoroughly. 6. Mulch with a 3-inch layer of compost or ground bark; mulch should not touch trunk. If you used stakes, loosely tie them to the plant.

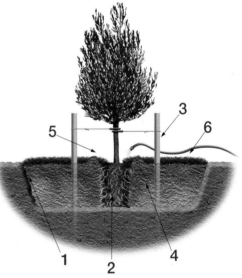

Soil with caliche underneath

Ideally, the workable soil should be 18 to 24 inches deep; if it isn't, you may have to bring in more topsoil. Imported soil should be as similar to your native soil as possible and free of weed seeds, rocks, and debris. If in doubt, consult your nursery, landscape professional, or extension service. 1. Follow step 1 above. 2. Drill or dig through the caliche layer with a soil auger or jackhammer to create two drainage chimneys at opposite ends of the hole as shown. 3. Set the plant in the center of the hole, staking it if necessary. 4. Add backfill as described in step 4 above. 5. Add topsoil as needed to make it level with the rootball. 6. Build a berm as described in step 5 above; soak the plant thoroughly. 7. Apply mulch and tie stakes as described in step 6 above. ◆

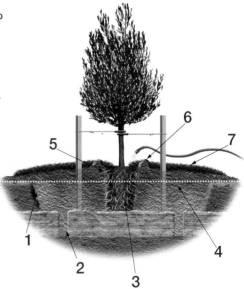

Poppy fever

Choose from a world of colorful beauties

By Jim McCausland

For a quick trip halfway around the globe, consider the common names assigned to a few poppies: California, Flanders, Himalayan, Iceland, Oriental, and Welsh. Some are annual, some are perennial, and a few fall somewhere in between. But they all bear sensuous flowers with rich colors and delicate textures. With so many kinds to choose from, how do you decide which to grow? Here's a guide to the best garden poppies.

One- or two-year wonders

All the poppies in this group can live longer than one season in mild climates and ideal conditions, but they quickly die if they get too cold, hot, or dry. Most people treat them as annuals or biennials, removing plants when flowering declines. These poppies do best in full sun. Most take marginal soil but grow bigger and bear better flowers if grown in good soil and fed occasionally.

California poppy *(Eschscholzia californica)*. In the 1800s, brilliant fields of native California poppies were so dense that sailors could spot them from the coast 30 miles away. The poppies' natural range runs from the Columbia River in the Northwest to Mexico, but they can be grown in all *Sunset* climate zones (from the *Western Garden Book*) except coastal Hawaii.

The most common color of the 2-inch-wide flowers is saffron orange, but yellows and bicolors are common, and breeders have added red, red-orange, rose, pink, cream, and white to the color mix, along with double and fringed blossoms.

PLANTING: Sow seeds in autumn; provide irrigation if rain doesn't fall. Seedlings will emerge in winter in areas where the ground doesn't freeze, in early spring where it does freeze.

Iceland poppy *(Papaver nudicaule)*. Despite its name, this poppy's genetic roots are found in subarctic Asia. In mild parts of California, it's a classic, cool-season bedding plant. In the Pacific Northwest, it's a spring flower. In Alaska and parts of the Rockies, it's a cool-summer flower.

The brightly colored 3-inch-wide flowers have petals that look like crinkled tissue paper. Blooms come in yellow, orange, salmon, rose, pink, cream, and white.

PLANTING: In mild-winter areas, sow seeds or set out seedlings in fall;

Iceland poppies nod on wiry stems that reach 1 to 2 feet tall, depending on the variety.

Opium poppy

Gardeners admire its 4- to 5-inch-wide blossoms in shades of plum, red, pink, and white. Bakers mix its seed into cakes and pastries. But the opium poppy *(Papaver somniferum)* has another side. The sap from its green seed pod yields not only the morphine that physicians have used to ease severe pain but also the opium and heroin that have enslaved addicts for centuries.

The opium poppy presents a legal dichotomy in the United States: Federal law allows the sale and purchase of seeds but makes it a felony to possess the plants. Enforcement is uneven, but the penalties are harsh. Even so, the opium poppy is commonly sold under names like annual poppy, Asian poppy, breadbox poppy, breadseed poppy, Turkish poppy, *Papaver laciniatum, P. paeoniflorum,* and *P. setigerum.*

DAVID CAVAGNARO; ABOVE: ANDREW DRAKE

Himalayan poppy

Shirley poppy

'Thai Silk Fire Bush', a California poppy

Welsh poppy

Sowing tips

Most poppies grow easily from seeds sown in tilled, amended soil. The trick is to sow thinly; do that by mixing the tiny seeds with sand before you scatter. After sowing, rake in the seeds, or cover them with a thin sprinkling of sand. Don't cover Oriental poppy seeds; they need light to germinate.

When seedlings emerge, thin them so there's 1 foot between California, Flanders, Himalayan, Iceland, and Welsh poppies, 2 feet between Oriental poppies.

Fall-sown seeds may lie dormant for months before they germinate. Spring-sown seeds usually germinate as soon as the soil temperature rises into the mid-50s.

in cold-winter areas, sow seeds after the ground thaws in early spring.

Flanders field poppy *(P. rhoeas)*. During World War I, trench-digging soldiers and ground-ripping artillery disturbed the soil of Flanders fields, stimulating a bumper crop of the blood-red poppies now synonymous with Veterans Day. Some of the best single-flowered forms are called Shirley poppies because they were selected by the English Vicar of Shirley in the late 1800s.

The 3-foot plants bear 2-inch or wider flowers with single or double petals. Red is the dominant color, but selections also come in shades of blue, orange, pink, and white.

PLANTING: Sow seeds in fall or early spring, or set out seedlings as soon as they are available in spring.

Varieties that come back for years

In general, perennial poppies do better in cool climates.

Himalayan blue poppy *(Meconopsis betonicifolia, M. × sheldonii)*. In the Himalayas, this poppy is native to elevations of 10,000 to 13,000 feet. Similar climatic conditions in Alaska, the Northwest, and the Rockies make it possible for gardeners in those areas to grow this rare sky blue flower.

Given filtered shade, organically rich acidic soil, and moisture during summer, this poppy can grow 5 or 6 feet tall, but more often the 3- to 4-inch-wide flowers appear on 2- to 3-foot plants.

PLANTING: Sow the freshest seeds you can get in fall, but expect heavy losses. Some nurseries sell seedlings for spring planting.

Oriental poppy *(Papaver orientale)*. Few perennials put on a better spring show. The 4- to 6-inch-wide flowers come in shades of mahogany, plum, red, salmon, pink, and white, but orange is the dominant color. This poppy does not bloom reliably in the mildest parts of the Southern California coast or in the Southwest deserts.

After bloom, the plants decline quickly and look downright ratty. That's why gardeners interplant Oriental poppies with concealing companions such as baby's breath, catmint, globe thistle, *Heliopsis,* purple coneflower, and Russian sage.

PLANTING: Set out seedlings in fall for spring bloom. When established plants go dormant in midsummer, you can divide them.

Welsh poppy *(Meconopsis cambrica)*. Native to Western Europe, this poppy has 2- to 3-inch-wide flowers in shades of lemon yellow and translucent orange. It thrives in filtered sun with regular water.

This poppy grows well in the Northwest, mountain regions, and coastal Northern California. Don't try it in Southern California.

PLANTING: Sow seeds in fall, or set out seedlings in spring.

Sources

Many nurseries and garden centers sell a few kinds of poppies. For a wider selection, purchase seeds by mail.

Heronswood Nursery *(www.heronswood.com or 360/297-4172; $5 catalog)* offers a good selection of *Meconopsis* and Oriental poppy plants.

Seedman.com *(www.seedman.com or 800/336-2064; free online catalog)* offers one of the largest selection of seeds.

Thompson & Morgan *(www.thompson-morgan.com or 800/274-7333; free catalog)* sells seeds of *Meconopsis betonicifolia* and several other varieties. ◆

LEFT, FROM TOP: DENNIS FRATES, JAMIE AND JUDY WILD, ANDREW DRAKE; THOMAS J. STORY

Students water seedlings in a greenhouse; others mix ingredients for compost, below.

Back to school, in the garden

Young thumbs are turning green all over the West

By Steven R. Lorton • Photographs by Shane Young

Excitement runs high on the Saturday after Mother's Day at Mary Woodward Elementary School in Tigard, Oregon. That's the day of the School Carnival and Annual Plant Sale. Parents who attend go home with blooming geraniums or petunias, plus a sense of pride in all that their budding gardeners have grown from scratch.

While many schools and community organizations in Oregon and beyond have started such children's gardening programs, the program at Woodward (kindergarten through fifth grade) is on the cutting edge. Indeed, the school grounds are a living laboratory used by 33 classes. The facilities include an ornamental garden, raised beds, a potting pavilion, a greenhouse, and a composting area. Teacher Jo Barendse coordinates the program, but parents help keep it running by donating more than 16,000 hours of their time each year.

A program like this succeeds for three reasons. First, it enjoys the support of the whole school community, including the faculty, the principal, and parents. Second, the program is woven into the standard science curriculum.

Finally, it is self-supporting; it is funded independently of the school district's budget. To raise money, some schools conduct plant sales or seek private contributions. At Mary Woodward Elementary School, the plant sale raises between $3,000 and $5,000. To get ready for it, students follow the steps listed at right.

A National Gardening Association website, *www.kidsgardening.com,* offers tips to parents and teachers on organizing school programs, plus a directory of 1,400 school gardens. ◆

Summer flower steps

Students at Mary Woodward Elementary School follow this schedule so they'll have plenty of summer flowers to sell in May. You can adapt the steps to propagate bedding plants for your summer garden. You'll need a greenhouse or a bright, warm indoor space.

January. Make stem cuttings of geraniums, dip the cut ends in rooting hormone, and embed them in 4-inch pots filled with sterile soil mix.

February. Sow seeds of summer annuals in "plug" trays filled with sterile soil mix. Sow impatiens first, then lobelia, petunias, dwarf zinnias, marigolds, and sweet alyssum.

March into April. Transplant rooted geranium cuttings into 6- or 8-inch pots. Transplant seedlings from plugs into 4-inch plastic pots.

Late April/early May. Fertilize and groom flowers.

Grow mesclun in patches, by type. Cover the plot with netting to protect it from birds and critters.

Growing tips

1. Thin seedlings when they've reached 1–2 inches tall. Using small, pointed scissors, cut out individual plants (toss thinnings into salads). Or use a chopstick to gently pry up crowded seedlings, then transplant them in bare spots where seeds didn't germinate.

2. Snip leaves of overly vigorous greens (some mustards, for instance) that are overtaking other types in the bed. Cut these plants back to 1–2 inches above the soil. By the time they regrow, the other greens will have caught up in size.

Harvest when leaves are 4–5 inches long; use scissors to shear part or all of the bed, cutting foliage to 1–2 inches above the soil level.

Fertilize plants lightly with fish emulsion solution after cutting them back; continue watering. Plants will put out new leaves, ready to harvest again within one to two weeks.

Mix greens in your garden

Grow mild and spicy blends for salads and stir-fries

By Lauren Bonar Swezey • Photographs by Thomas J. Story

In the Mediterranean region, mesclun is best known as a mix of tasty young lettuces and piquant greens (arugula, chervil, and endive in France; chicory, curly endive, and escarole in Italy). But in the West, the crops now widely sold at farmers' markets and grocery stores as "baby greens" (the term often used for mesclun) can contain any greens you want—from colorful sweet lettuces to a melange of mild or spicy leaves and edible flowers. "Mesclun is about freshness," explains Renee Shepherd of Renee's Garden, which sells seeds for 10 different mixes. That's why the leaves are tastiest when harvested from your own garden.

Mesclun is easy to grow. Start a peppery mix in one bed and a mild lettuce mix in another, and you can blend your salads for every meal. By sowing seed every few weeks during fall and spring in mild-winter climates, or spring into summer in cold-winter climates, you can harvest a bountiful crop over a long season.

Mixes for every taste

Seed catalogs and independent nurseries offer a diverse selection of mesclun combinations, including imports from France and Italy and custom mixes.

Mild lettuces are perfect for everyday salads; to spice them up, add pungent greens such as arugula (also called roquette), chicory, cress, and spicy mustards. Chervil, endive, escarole, kale, mâche (also called corn salad), and mild mustards, such as mizuna, add flavor but not spice.

If you prefer to take the guesswork out of blending your own greens, choose a custom mix; three of our favorites, grown and tasted at *Sunset,* are pictured below.

Planting pointers

In an area that gets full sun, dig compost into the soil; water the bed thoroughly. Sow seeds $\frac{1}{2}$ inch apart. Seeds are small; to help distribute them thinly over soil, mix them with clean sand before broadcasting. Cover seed with $\frac{1}{4}$ inch of fine soil.

Spray the seedbed very lightly with water, then keep the soil evenly moist during growth. Drape a canopy of netting over the seedbed. Extend the season into summer by hanging shadecloth (available at most nurseries) over the bed. ◆

California Spicy Greens

Heirloom Cutting Mix

Paris Market Mix

Our favorite mixes

Letters following the blends listed below indicate seed sources.

SPICY, WITH LETTUCE

California Spicy Greens: Arugula, curly endive, mizuna, and red mustard **(R).**

Italian Misticanza: Italian varieties of chicory, endive, and lettuces **(R).**

Provençal Winter Mix: Arugula, chervil, endive, French lettuces, Italian parsley, mâche, and radicchio **(T).**

Salad Blend Hot Weather: Celtuce, green and red lettuces, and mustard **(N).**

SPICY, NO LETTUCE

French Niçoise Blend: Cress, dandelion, endive, radicchio, and wild onion **(T).**

MILD, WITH LETTUCE

Cook's Cutting Mix: Butterhead, looseleaf, and red and green lettuces **(C).**

Heirloom Cutting Mix: 'Blush Butter Cos', 'Red Devil's Tongue', 'Red Ruffled Oak', 'Sucrine', and 'Troutback' lettuces **(R).**

Mild Mesclun Blend: Kale, green and red lettuces, mâche, mizuna, and mustard **(T).**

Monet's Garden: 'Dutch Redina', 'Little Gem', 'Rouge Grenobloise', 'Red Salad Bowl', and 'Tango' lettuces **(R).**

Nichols Mesclun Mix: Cress, green and red lettuces, mizuna, and 'Red Russian' kale **(N).**

Paris Market Mix: Arugula, chervil, chicory, endive, escarole, and red lettuces **(R).**

Seed sources

(C) The Cook's Garden, *www.cooksgarden. com or (800) 457-9703.*

(N) Nichols Garden Nursery, *www. nicholsgardennursery.com or (800) 422-3985.*

(R) Renee's Garden, *www.reneesgarden.com or on nursery seed racks.*

(T) Territorial Seed Company, *www. territorialseed.com or (541) 942-9547.*

Ruiz and Wynn
created this colorful
terrace garden on
Sixth Avenue.

Beauty in small spaces

Two top botanical designers explain how to beautify
compact urban spaces—or your own backyard

By Steven R. Lorton • Photograph by John Granen

At first Adriana Ruiz and Curtis Wynn seem an unlikely team. She grew up in the high-altitude tropics of Colombia; he comes from Juneau, Alaska. But their divergent backgrounds have been a boon to their gardening careers. The big, stately pots favored by Wynn are on a scale that you might call Alaskan.

Ruiz's love of vivid color combinations and bold leaf shapes seems to be traceable to the natural habitat she knew as a child. The net result of these influences: garden designs that are nothing short of thrilling.

Ruiz and Wynn are the head designers for Botanical Designs *(206/932-3784),* one of a handful of horticulture firms that create, install, and maintain many of Seattle's container gardens. In this garden-obsessed city, beautiful container plantings are just about everywhere you look, providing welcome relief from the hard edges of the urban landscape. Turn any downtown corner and you can expect to see one—if not several—big, bold pots filled with greenery and blooms.

Now that it's time for fall planting, take an urban stroll and gather ideas on how to create innovative pots for your own house and garden. The plants you'll find in nurseries this

long—the sun hits the space where you'll be planting. Pay attention to your routes from the house through the garden and think about what views you want from the inside.

Container. "The simpler, the better," Wynn says. "You want the plants to carry the show." Shop at home and garden stores for solid, heavy pots—when struck with a knuckle, they should make a nice ringing sound.

Soil. "Good soil for containers is like good food for the body," Ruiz says. Potting soil should be dark in color with a clean, woodsy scent. The texture is right when you can pack it into a ball that holds its shape but breaks apart with a tap of the finger. Supplement good soil with a controlled-release fertilizer.

Plants. "Every container has five elements: a centerpiece, fillers, spillers, color, and accents," Ruiz says. The centerpiece plant can stay in place for years; the other plants should be changed three times a year to capitalize on seasonal color and bloom.

Maintenance. Wynn says that to have a respectable green thumb, "you have to be a little fussy, a bit of a control freak." Cut off wilted blossoms and withered foliage daily. If a plant looks straggly, take it out and replace it. Water often, keeping soil evenly moist.

Staging. "One is a solo; two or more are a show," Wynn says. In other words, a single container can be a focal point or dress an entryway, whereas pots in groups of different sizes and shapes become their own environment. Group pots of plants according to height, texture, and color, just as you would stage plants in the ground.

What to put in your pot

Here are some examples of plants to use to create a winning composition.

Centerpiece. To create structure, use a single centerpiece. Dense boxwood, a hardy windmill palm, dracaenas, or a redtwig or yellowtwig dogwood are all fine choices.

Fillers. Place the fillers in groups of three or more, repeating forms to give a sense of harmony. If you buy just

one of each plant, you'll have a crazy-quilt pot. Choices for fillers are infinite: lacy ferns, blood-red heucheras, grassy clumps of Siberian iris.

Edgers and spillers. Use pansies or impatiens pushed close together to sprawl along the sides of the pots, finishing the design like a generous ruffle. Alternatively, use trailing plants, like bacopa or ivy, to cascade dramatically over the sides.

Color. Give careful consideration to how the colors of the plants will blend or contrast with each other. Ruiz and Wynn are fond of strong color punches, such as chartreuse paired with vivid purple, or hot oranges and reds with strong pinks.

Accents. Use seasonal accents, such as a burst of purple tulips or corkscrew willow hovering like a haze over the composition. Or tuck a silver gazing ball into the side of the planting.

Seattle's coolest container gardens

Here are three urban container gardens that were worth going out of your way to see in 2003. All were created by Adriana Ruiz and Curtis Wynn.

Southeast corner of Sixth Avenue and University Street (Park Place Building). Rectangular containers flanking the steps up from the sidewalk burst with seasonal color and richly hued foliage plants. Large shallow pots hold tree fuchsias, begonias, impatiens, and heucheras.

East side of Second Avenue between Seneca and University Streets (Washington Mutual Tower). This is gardening at its most glamorous. The large, exquisitely crafted metal containers are staged on pedestals of granite. Plants erupt from the containers with spiky and full, billowing textures.

East side of Sixth Avenue between University and Union (One and Two Union Square). From the sidewalk all the way up the three levels of plaza surrounding One and Two Union Square, large cast-stone containers are grouped in clusters mixing small-scale deciduous trees, evergreen shrubs, perennials, and annuals. ◆

month can carry a beautiful container show from now through winter.

How to create a container garden

"Look at the shapes and colors of the world around you. That's where design begins," Ruiz says. Here are some points to consider before you start planting.

Location. "A great container planting starts with an understanding of the space," Ruiz says. "What's the light level? The microclimate?" Spend a few days looking at where—and for how

ORNAMENTAL GRASSES help connect this garden in Sonoma County, California, to the meadows that surround it. For details on using grasses in the landscape for striking results, see pages 310–312.

October

Shades of green from shapely conifers, bamboo, and broad-leafed evergreens add serenity beside a raked-gravel pond.

Designing with nature in Mill Valley

Richard Ward discovered Japanese gardens when he moved to Northern California from New York City. "I fell in love with the Japanese way of gardening with nature," he says. So he developed one of his own.

The focal point of the garden is the raked-gravel pond, which Ward built over an old concrete patio. A stream of crushed granite winds to it from the back of the garden. Boulders as large as 500 pounds were carefully positioned and partially buried along its banks and elsewhere in the garden.

Ward planted lippia along the pond edge, adding 50-year-old, bonsai-like cypress (which had been growing in large containers), Japanese maple, and pine trees around the garden. Then he filled in with small-leafed plants such as boxwood, eugenia, and Kurume azaleas. "Using small-leafed plants makes the space seem larger," Ward explains.

Plants get watered by hand so he can interact with them and monitor their growth. And Ward keeps them shapely; "I'm constantly trimming the plants," he says.

DESIGN: Richard Ward, Mill Valley (415/388-9273) —*Lauren Bonar Swezey*

Aster cordifolius 'Little Carlow' bears clusters of inch-wide lavender blooms atop tall stems.

Asters for fall bouquets

Many asters aren't good vase candidates because they wilt too quickly when cut. But there are at least a couple notable exceptions. *Aster cordifolius* 'Little Carlow', which we grew in *Sunset's* test garden last year, has become one of our favorites. It's the plant responsible for the cloud of small lavender flowers pictured above. Another aster we like is *A. cordifolius* 'Cape Cod', which produces long sprays of small, single white flowers. Both grow 3 to 4 feet tall.

These asters make excellent backdrops for larger flowers in bouquets, but we also like letting them shine on their own—toward the fronts of borders or in small, densely planted beds.

Like most asters, 'Cape Cod' and 'Little Carlow' are easy to grow. Both prefer full sun, but 'Little Carlow' tolerates light shade. Both grow in *Sunset* climate zones 1–10, 14–21.

Our asters came from Canyon Creek Nursery in Northern California (www.canyoncreeknursery.com or 530/533-2166). —Sharon Cohoon

Early-blooming cymbidium

Most cymbidiums wait for winter to bloom. But the one pictured here, Autumn Green 'Geyserland', flowers during the warm days of late summer and early fall. It's more compact than standard cymbidiums, reaching about 2½ feet tall (somewhere between dwarfs and standards). And, perhaps best of all, it's fragrant.

'Geyserland' is a descendant of *Cymbidium ensifolium,* whose hybrids come in a wide range of flower colors. The pale yellow-green 'Geyserland' blooms last about three weeks.

C. ensifolium orchids take heat better than more common cymbidiums, setting buds when evenings are in the high 50s or low 60s. Like their cousins, however, these orchids require partial shade, not direct sun. They can live outdoors year-round in areas that get little to no frost (*Sunset* climate zones 15 and 17). Elsewhere, bring them indoors for winter.

A good source for these and other orchids is Santa Barbara Orchid Estate (www.sborchid.com or 800/553-3387).

—David C. Becker

A bulb worth searching for

Other people brake for garage sales; I brake for white watsonia. This South African native looks perfectly fine in shades of pink, rose, red, lavender, and apricot—and all seem more commonly grown than white. But pure white watsonia flowers have a regal presence. The clump pictured at left, in Monetta Smoot's Rancho Santa Fe garden, proves my point.

To grow watsonia, plant the bulbs 4 inches deep and 6 inches apart in a sunny spot. Water regularly during the growing season; watsonia does not need water during summer dormancy, but will accept it if planted in fast-draining soil.

Find white watsonia at Burkard Nursery in Pasadena (626/796-4355); Green Thumb and Green Arrow nurseries (www.supergarden.com for locations); Laguna Hills Nursery in El Toro (949/830-5653); and Walter Anderson Nursery in San Diego (619/224-8217) and Poway (858/513-4900).

—S. C.

Help stop native plant pilfering

The theft of native plants from public and private lands is an ongoing problem in the Southwest. Many species of cactus and other plants command high prices from private collectors seeking prize specimens and from homeowners who unwittingly purchase stolen plants for their landscapes.

Plant plundering is especially prevalent in Arizona. To reduce plant theft, Arizona's Department of Agriculture has implemented a tagging system that requires anyone intending to move and sell a protected plant to obtain a permit and plant tag from the state. The tag, which is attached to the plant and secured with a metal seal, can be legally removed only by the buyer. The tag is imprinted with a permit number.

When buying a protected plant, confirm that it was nursery propagated; or, if it was collected from another location, make sure it has an Arizona Department of Agriculture tag. Also, get a receipt from the seller as proof of purchase.

More than 300 plants are on Arizona's list of protected natives. For a copy of the list, or to verify a plant permit number, call the Arizona Department of Agriculture (602/542-4499).
—Julie Chai

Shadecloth shelters for veggies

In the desert, vegetables need seasonal protection from freezing temperatures, drying winds, and intense sun. To shelter their crops, Master Gardeners Christina and John Grubb of Scottsdale, Arizona, created shadecloth tents over raised beds in their backyard.

On nights when freezing weather is predicted, the heavy shadecloth provides frost protection for their cool-season garden—a colorful mix of herbs, edible nasturtiums, salad greens, and root crops. Later in the season, the same shadecloth will screen warm-season vegetables, such as tomatoes and peppers, from excessive sun and desiccating winds.

The Grubbs form the hoops by bending 10-foot-long sections of $1/2$-inch-diameter PVC pipe into 42-inch-high arcs. They insert the flexible pipe into a bracket on one side of the 4-foot-wide bed, then bend the pipe over the bed and insert the other end into another bracket on the opposite side.

Christina installed plastic grommets along the edges of the shadecloth. To hold the fabric to the hoops, she inserts a plastic locking tie through each grommet hole and secures it loosely around the pipe, allowing her to slide the shadecloth up and down as needed.
—Cathy Cromell

A little bit country in Phoenix

Tera's Garden is located in the Roosevelt Historic District, just a few blocks from downtown Phoenix. But you only notice the skyscrapers looming in the background for a few seconds because everything else about Tera Vessels's nursery is designed to transport you to a country garden.

For starters there's the store itself, a classic bungalow that Tera and husband Gary spent three years restoring to its former charm. The 1914 William Edward Cavness House is listed on the National Register of Historic Places. Potted plants now grace the front porch, and the interior houses garden gifts, books, supplies, and a coffee shop.

The focal point of the grounds is a large lily pond with a convenient ledge that invites you to stop and watch darting fish and the birds that drop in for a drink. All around the pond are plants displayed in vignettes. An arbor provides shade for bedding plants and shoppers. And everywhere you look there's a working fountain or an attractive bench to purchase or simply enjoy.

Tera's Garden: Closed Mon. 606 N. Fourth Ave., Phoenix; www.terasgarden.com or (602) 253-4744. —S. C.

NORM PLATE (2)

Mounding ice plant, *Drosanthemum* 'African Red', and coral spikes of *Aloe striata* brighten cactus planting.

Ice plant heats up a cactus bed

Six years ago, bare dirt and stones flanked the long driveway leading to this contemporary Southwest-style house in Encinitas, California. "I didn't want to work and weed in the front yard, so whatever I planted had to take care of itself," says homeowner Bobbi Hirschkoff. "My goal was to create a low-maintenance landscape that complemented the architecture of my house." The obvious choice, a cactus and succulent garden, has worked out so well, "neighbors tell me drivers slow down to look at it," Hirschkoff says.

In spring, mounds of flowering ice plant (*Drosanthemum* 'African Red') bloom among slender green euphorbias. Blue-gray *Aloe striata* sends up branching flower stalks topped with red-orange bells, and statuesque green- and yellow-striped century plants (*Agave americana*) lend drama year-round. *Aloe ferox* trees bloom in winter, when few other plants do.

Hirschkoff started some of these plants from cuttings and offshoots given to her by friends. She bought others from local nurseries (see "Plant Sources," at right) that specialize in cactus and succulents. As a backdrop, Hirschkoff planted acacia trees, which have dainty, ribbon-like leaves that provide textural contrast.

Cactus and succulents need excellent drainage. If your garden soil is heavy clay, till the soil, then place a 4-inch layer of decomposed granite on top prior to setting out small plants from 4-inch pots. For large plants (2-gal. size and up), add a 1- to 2-foot layer of decomposed granite.

Drip irrigation helped get this garden established, and now the plants survive with two or three hand-waterings during summer and fall.

—*Debra Lee Baldwin*

Plant sources

Cactus King Nursery.
Agaves, aloes.
1534 Crest Dr., Encinitas; www.cactusking.com or (760) 753-6939.

Solana Succulents.
Agaves, aloes, ice plants.
355 N. U.S. 101, Solana Beach; (858) 259-4568.

Tropic World Nursery.
Agaves, aloes, ice plants.
26437 N. Centre City Pkwy., Escondido; (760) 746-6108.

Towering flower stalks of *Agave colorata* flank the entry.

From driveway to cozy courtyard

By relinquishing part of her driveway, Carrie Nimmer solved two problems. The Phoenix landscape designer wanted a private outdoor place to enjoy a cup of coffee or a glass of wine. And she wanted a prettier view from her kitchen window than the strip of concrete driveway and bare wall she was used to seeing. So Nimmer enclosed that section of the driveway with an 8-foot-tall wall and turned the 14- by 14-foot space into an inviting interior courtyard.

Rather than demolishing and removing the driveway, which would have been costly, Nimmer simply covered it. Granite pebbles cover most of the old driveway, transitioning to finer-textured decomposed granite as you near the courtyard. Broad stone slabs placed at the front of the passageway beckon guests to step inside. So do the two imposing Chinese pots planted with silvery blue rosettes of *Agave colorata* and blond Mexican feather grass *(Stipa tenuissima)*.

Nimmer painted the walls with a neutral brown, a perfect foil for the agave but a shade that also works well with greens, pastels, and fiery colors like the red-flowered crown of thorns *(Euphorbia milii)* in the courtyard. Behind this, an ocotillo screen conceals a passage to Nimmer's home office.

DESIGN: Carrie Nimmer *(602/254-0300)*
—*S.C.*

Coordinate a spring flower show

Ellen and Don Scott wanted a cheery "Easter basket" effect at the entry to their Denver home. Landscape designer Rebecca Serratoni fulfilled their wish by mingling Lavender Shades and Ultima Silhouette Mix pansies with soft pink 'Angelique' and white 'Mount Tacoma' tulips. She edged the beds with blue hyacinths (they finished blooming just before this photo was taken in mid-April).

Timing is the key to this coordinated spring bloom. Planting early in fall gives the pansies ample time to send out roots before a hard freeze hits. Before planting, Serratoni tills and amends the soil with bonemeal and compost. The bulbs are planted first, then the pansies.

This south-facing bed gets full sun and is backed by the house's brick wall, which absorbs solar heat by day and radiates it back at night. Consequently, the soil warms even on days when the air temperature hovers below freezing. A 2- to 3-inch layer of cedar mulch helps stabilize the soil temperature and holds in moisture, which the pansies need.

During the winter, Serratoni applies a liquid fertilizer formulated for pansies. After the bulbs emerge, she feeds all of the plants weekly by spraying them with a solution of 1 tablespoon fish emulsion mixed with 1 gallon water.

DESIGN: Rebecca Serratoni, Denver *(720/320-9197)* —*Colleen Smith*

Pink 'Angelique' and white 'Mount Tacoma' tulips poke up through pansies.

Grow a living bouquet from bulbs

Here's a novel way to grow spring-flowering bulbs. This fall, plant a cluster of several kinds with simultaneous or overlapping bloom times. When they flower, they'll form a living bouquet, as shown in this garden. This planting consists of white 2-foot-tall Dutch iris ringed by red sparaxis, blue babiana, and white freesia planted 2 to 4 inches apart. White sweet alyssum, planted from seed, skirts the base.

Most nurseries sell Dutch iris and freesia bulbs in an array of colors. If you can't find babiana and sparaxis at your nursery, try substituting grape hyacinth, anemone, and snowflake *(Leucojum),* or create a bouquet of daffodil hybrids ringed with dainty dwarf varieties.

You can buy babiana, sparaxis, and other South African bulbs from Jim Duggan Flower Nursery *(1452 Santa Fe Dr., Encinitas, CA 92024; www. thebulbman.com or 760/943-1658; $2 catalog).* —*D. L. B.*

BACK TO BASICS

Success with onion seeds

Growing onions from seed gives you a far greater choice of varieties than raising them from sets or transplants. The key is to provide rich, well-drained soil kept evenly moist and weed-free. Sow this month for a winter-into-spring crop. (In coldest climates, wait until spring.)

1. Prepare soil to a depth of 10 to 12 inches; mix in compost. **2. Sow seeds** ½ inch deep and ½ inch apart in rows 18 to 24 inches apart. **3. Water** when top inch of soil is dry. **4. Thin seedlings** to 3 to 4 inches apart. **5. Side-dress,** about four to six weeks after sowing, with a balanced granular fertilizer in a shallow trench alongside plants.

—D. C. B.

Maples in full autumn glory

In the Pacific Northwest, the Japanese maple *(Acer palmatum)* is prized for its ability to provide ornamental interest in every season. One of the most diverse collections you'll find around Puget Sound is at the Evergreen Arboretum & Gardens in Everett, Washington, about 30 miles north of Seattle. Fall is a fine time to see the trees here and imagine which ones might fit into your landscape.

Founded more than 30 years ago, the arboretum occupies 3 acres of Legion Park. Among the first Japanese maples planted here were a pair of *A. p.* 'Osakazuki' (one is shown above). Today, these magnificent trees put on a spectacular show in October. In the same grove are *A. p.* 'Sango Kaku' (coral bark maple), which has apricot gold fall foliage, and *A. p.* 'Shindeshojo', which displays scarlet foliage in spring. Elsewhere on the grounds, you'll find a conifer garden displaying trees and shrubs for residential landscapes.

Evergreen Arboretum & Gardens: dawn to dusk; free. 145 Alverson Blvd.; www.evergreenarboretum. com or (425) 257-8597. —Debra Prinzing

Pair tulips and rhodies

With showy blooms in complementary colors, rhododendrons and tulips make splendid partners. The stunning combination at left graces a bed at Roozengaarde, the display garden of Washington Bulb Company in Mt. Vernon, Washington. The deep pink rhododendrons bloom in April in perfect synchrony with white-edged red 'Leen Van der Mark' tulips (far left) and deep red 'Ile de France' tulips (near left).

When you pick tulips to go with your rhodies, tell the seller when your rhododendrons bloom and ask for help choosing varieties that flower in the same time frame.

Planting tulips couldn't be easier, and fall is the time to do it. For best effect, plant the bulbs in groups of a dozen or more (Roozengaarde plantings include 50 to 75 bulbs of each variety).

You can usually buy tulips like these for about 50 cents each at nurseries and garden centers. Or order directly from Roozengaarde (www.tulips.com or 866/488-5477).
—Jim McCausland

WHAT TO DO IN YOUR GARDEN IN OCTOBER

PLANTING

☐ **BULBS.** All spring-flowering bulbs can go into the ground now. Crocus, *Cyclamen coum,* daffodil, glory-of-the-snow, grape hyacinth, scilla, snowdrop, snowflake, species tulips, and winter aconite are good bets for long-term performance. Hyacinths and hybrid tulips provide one to three years of bloom.

☐ **COVER CROPS.** *Sunset* climate zones 4–7, 17: Sow cover crops like crimson clover and tyfon greens as early in the month as possible. They'll germinate and grow now; till them under in spring to enrich the soil.

☐ **GARLIC.** Separate garlic cloves from "mother" bulbs and plant individual cloves 1 to 2 inches deep. Hardneck types are easiest to peel and have the most intense, refined flavor. Two of the best hardneck varieties, 'Siberian Red' and 'Spanish Roja', are available from Spirit of the Pacific Northwest *(541/929-4532).*

☐ **GROUNDCOVERS.** Zones 4–7, 17: Plant evergreen groundcovers like *Alchemilla mollis, Hypericum calycinum, Lithodora diffusa* 'Grace Ward', and *Vinca minor* now for strong growth next spring. Deciduous and semideciduous groundcovers like *Epimedium* and *Vancouveria* develop strong roots in winter and grow faster in spring.

☐ **LAWNS.** Zones 4–7, 17: It isn't too late to start a lawn from sod, but move fast. Till the seedbed 6 to 8 inches deep, then level the site with a water-filled roller. Keep the site evenly moist until fall rains take over.

☐ **PERENNIALS.** This is the best time of year to plant ferns, grasses, and flowering perennials such as calla, euphorbia, hardy geraniums, hellebore, and Shasta daisy.

☐ **SHRUBS, TREES.** It's the best month to plant shrubs and trees, especially those with fall color. Also look for flowering shrubs such as *Abelia,* azalea, camellia, *Escallonia,* forsythia, hardy fuchsia, and weigela.

MAINTENANCE

☐ **CARE FOR ANNUALS.** Zones 1–3: When frost nips the plants, pull them up, shake the soil off roots, and toss them onto the compost pile. You can leave standing those that have set seed for birds to nibble on during winter. Zones 4–7, 17: Shear off flowers and fertilize one last time early in the month to keep blooms coming until frost.

☐ **CONTROL FUNGUS GNATS.** These gnats, which many gardeners mistake for fruit flies, breed in the organic soil in which potted plants are grown. Stop them by covering potting soil with a layer of sand or gravel.

☐ **IRRIGATE DEEPLY.** Water established plants thoroughly so that they are well hydrated as they go into winter dormancy.

☐ **LET ROSES REST.** Allow some of the spent blossoms to form a few hips, which help ease plants into dormancy.

☐ **MAKE COMPOST.** As you clean out fading annual vegetables, flowers, and perennials, put everything that isn't diseased onto the compost pile. Turn the pile and keep it moist so compost will form over winter. ◆

WHAT TO DO IN YOUR GARDEN IN OCTOBER

SHOPPING

□ **BULBS.** For large quantities of bulbs at a reasonable cost, try John Scheepers *(www.johnscheepers.com or 860/567-0838; $35 minimum order)* or Van Bourgondien *(www.dutchbulbs.com or 800/622-9959).*

□ **SPECIALTY FRUITS.** If you'd like to plant a special variety of fruit this winter—an heirloom apple, a white nectarine, or a pluot, for instance—consider ordering in advance to be certain you get the variety you want. Nurseries like Orchard of Lafayette *(www.orchardnursery.com or 925/284-4474)* take special orders in fall for delivery in winter. You can also order fruit trees by mail from Trees of Antiquity *(www.treesofantiquity.com or 805/467-9909)* and Bay Laurel Nursery *(www.baylaurelnursery.com or 805/466-3449).*

PLANTING

□ **BULBS.** *Sunset* climate zones 7–9, 14–17: To create an informal mass of flowers that look as if they're spreading naturally across the landscape, toss out handfuls of a single kind of bulb over a planting area. Vary the density of each grouping of bulbs—and add a second or third type of bulb if desired—then plant the bulbs where they've fallen. For the best chance of repeat bloom in following years, choose a site in full sun that doesn't get much summer water. Try daffodils, leucojum, muscari, ornamental alliums, scilla, or species tulips, all of which naturalize in mild climates.

Sunset
CLIMATE ZONES

- ☐ Mountain (1–2)
- ☐ Valley (7–9)
- ☐ Inland (14)
- ☐ Coastal (15–17)

□ **COVER CROPS.** Zones 7–9, 14–17: To improve soil texture and nutrient content, plant a fall-to-winter cover crop for tilling into the soil in spring. For maximum benefit, use a mix of cool-season varieties such as Soil Builder Mix from Peaceful Valley Farm Supply *(www.groworganic.com or 888/784-1722),* which contains bell beans (small fava beans), oats, purple vetch, winter peas, and woolypod vetch. Mixes are sold in 5-pound bags; apply 3 to 5 pounds per 1,000 square feet.

□ **GROUNDCOVERS.** Zones 7–9, 14–17: Use wide-spreading groundcovers to blanket banks and large expanses of ground. Try *Arctostaphylos* 'Emerald Carpet' and *A. uva-ursi; Ceanothus* 'Centennial'; coyote brush; varieties of *Juniperus chinensis, J. procumbens,* and *J. horizontalis;* myoporum; and 'Corsican Prostrate' or 'Huntington Blue' trailing rosemary. For fastest coverage, set plants in offset rows (so that groups of four form a diamond). To check spacing for specific plant varieties, look them up in the *Sunset Western Garden Book.*

□ **WILDFLOWERS.** For the best show in spring, sow wildflower seeds now in an area that's been hoed free of weeds and weed seeds. To rid the soil of weed seeds, water the soil well, then hoe out the seedlings. (To figure out which seedlings are wildflowers and which are weeds, sow wildflower seeds in a flat in late winter so you can compare their foliage to what's popping out of the ground.) In zones 1–2, it's too late to use this weeding technique, so you'll need to be diligent about weeding in spring.

MAINTENANCE

□ **CHECK COLE CROPS FOR INSECTS.** Zones 7–9, 14–17: If your broccoli, cabbage, or cauliflower plants have holes in the leaves or the new growth is being chewed, the damage is probably being caused by caterpillars (such as cabbage loopers), snails, or slugs. Check leaves for insects (go out at night with a flashlight to find snails and slugs). If you find caterpillars, pick them off and destroy them or spray plants with Bt *(Bacillus thuringiensis).* For snails and slugs, use an iron phosphate snail bait such as Sluggo. ◆

WHAT TO DO IN YOUR GARDEN IN OCTOBER

PLANTING

☐ **ANNUALS.** Low-desert, inland, and coastal gardeners (*Sunset* climate zones 13, 18–21, 22–24) can set out cool-season annuals. Pansies and violas remain reliable choices for beds, borders, containers, and bulb covers. An interesting newcomer is 'Ultima Morpho', a midsize pansy in a color that one grower describes as "UCLA blue." Also fun is the Whiskers series pansy, with little veined and blotched catlike faces. The Sorbet series viola produces many blooms, and it now comes in a dozen or more colors. Or try Penny Orange Jump-Ups violas, which are orange and mahogany.

☐ **COOL-SEASON CROPS.** In frost-free areas, plant broccoli, brussels sprouts, cabbage, cauliflower, collards, and other cole crops. Before planting, remove a few bottom leaves from seedlings, then plant deeply—up to the leaves—as you would a tomato. This strengthens the stems so they can support heavy heads. Also sow seeds or plant seedlings of beets, carrots, celery, lettuce, parsnips, radishes, spinach, and turnips. Seed potatoes are also available in nurseries now. If you don't have space in the garden, try growing potatoes in a large container, like a whiskey half-barrel.

☐ **ORNAMENTALS.** Plant groundcovers, long-lasting perennials, shrubs, trees, and other permanent plants. You won't see much growth at first, but plants will establish strong root

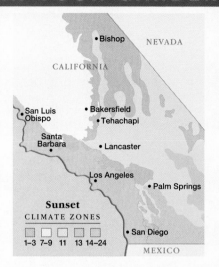

systems over winter and will be ready to explode with new growth in spring. Wait until spring to plant subtropicals, even if you live in a frost-free area.

☐ **SPRING BULBS.** Continue to plant anemone, babiana, daffodil, Dutch iris, freesia, ipheion, ixia, leucojum, ranunculus, sparaxis, and watsonia.

☐ **STRAWBERRIES.** To get lots of fruit rather than foliage, wait until the first half of November to plant strawberries. Professional growers plant then to give fruit the optimum amount of winter chill.

MAINTENANCE

☐ **CARE FOR LAWNS.** To improve water penetration, rake out thatch buildup. Feed fescue and other cool-season turf grasses with a complete lawn fertilizer. Cut Bermuda grass short, then overseed with annual rye if desired. Mulch after seeding with a ¼-inch layer of manure or soil amendment. Keep mulch moist until seeds have sprouted.

☐ **PREPARE FOR SANTA ANAS.** In fire-prone areas, before the onset of winds, cut and remove all dead branches and leaves from trees and shrubs, especially those that grow near the house. Clear leaves from gutters and remove woody vegetation that is growing against structures.

☐ **RECYCLE LEAVES.** Fallen leaves are the start of great compost. Don't trash them. Invest in a mulching mower and let shredded leaves remain where they fall on the lawn. As they decompose, they'll reduce thatch. Or, if your mower has a bag attachment, use the chopped up leaves as mulch in flower beds. No mower? Put raked leaves in a heavy trash bag with a handful of soil and high-nitrogen lawn fertilizer, moisten them lightly, then occasionally toss the bag to mix the contents. In mild climates, you'll have great compost by spring.

PEST CONTROL

☐ **PROTECT CABBAGE CROPS.** Within days after you plant broccoli, cabbage, and mustard greens, cabbage butterflies seem to find the seedlings. To keep them from laying eggs on your crops, cover the seedlings with floating row covers. ◆

WHAT TO DO IN YOUR GARDEN IN OCTOBER

PLANTING

☐ **BULBS.** Get crocus, daffodil, tulip, and other bulbs into the ground before it freezes. If you have many to plant, consider using a bulb-planting auger. This device, which attaches to an electric drill, makes it possible to plant up to 500 bulbs in an hour. Look for bulb augers at local garden centers, or order one from Best Buds Garden Supply Company *(877/777-2837 or www.bestbudsgarden.com).*

☐ **COMPANIONS FOR BULBS.** For a more colorful display, overplant spring-blooming bulbs with early-flowering perennials. Good perennial companions include *Alyssum montanum,* basket-of-gold *(Aurinia saxatilis),* common aubrieta, English primrose *(Primula* X *polyantha),* and wall rock-cress *(Arabis caucasica).*

☐ **HARDY BIENNIALS.** These plants complete their life cycle in two years, growing from seed into leafy plants the first year, then blooming, setting seed, and dying the following year. Good candidates include common foxglove *(Digitalis purpurea),* gopher plant *(Euphorbia lathyris),* hollyhock, horned poppy *(Glaucium corniculatum, G. flavum, G. grandiflorum),* money plant *(Lunaria annua),* mullein *(Verbascum blattaria* and *V. bombyciferum),* skyrocket *(Ipomopsis aggregata),* sweet William *(Dianthus barbatus),* sweet William catchfly *(Silene armeria),* and three-lobed coneflower *(Rudbeckia triloba).* Broadcast seeds where you

Sunset
CLIMATE ZONES
☐ 1–3   ☐ 10–11

want them to grow. Fall rains and winter snows should provide enough moisture to germinate the seeds.

☐ **PANSIES.** It's not too late to plant pansies. In warm areas of *Sunset* climate zones 2A through 3A, pansies will bloom all winter; in colder areas, they'll bloom in early spring when temperatures begin to warm up. Water transplants often enough to keep rootballs from drying out.

MAINTENANCE

☐ **CLEAN OUT BIRDHOUSES.** Wearing rubber gloves, remove and discard nesting material from birdhouses. To help prevent the spread of avian diseases and parasites, rinse birdhouses with a solution of 1 part household bleach to 10 parts water. Allow houses to dry thoroughly, then remount to provide winter shelter for birds.

☐ **LEAVE SEED HEADS FOR WINTER INTEREST.** As you clean up flower beds, leave attractive seed heads of baby's breath, butterfly weed, cone-flower, cupid's dart, datura, globe thistle, goldenrod, ornamental oregano, Russian sage, sedum, Siberian iris, statice, and yarrow.

☐ **MULCH FOR WINTER.** After a hard freeze, spread 2 to 3 inches of compost, weed-free straw, or other organic matter to protect bulbs, perennial flowers, strawberries, and vegetables.

☐ **PREPARE PONDS FOR WINTER.** Move containerized hardy water lilies to the deepest part of the pond, ideally where the water is at least 18 inches deep. Remove tropical water plants such as water lettuce and hyacinth; keep them in a tank indoors or discard them in the trash. To keep the pond from completely icing over, float a de-icer such as Thermo-Pond from Lilypons Water Gardens *(www.lilypons.com or 800/999-5459).*

☐ **PROTECT BULBS FROM RODENTS.** To ward off burrowing squirrels and voles, line a planting hole with wire mesh, plant the bulbs, then fold the mesh over the buried bulbs to form a closed cage. Or treat bulbs before planting by dipping them in the repellent Bulb Guard from Havahart *(order at www.havahart.com, or call 800/800-1819 for retail locations).*
— *M. T.*

WHAT TO DO IN YOUR GARDEN IN OCTOBER

PLANTING

☐ **COOL-SEASON COLOR.** *Sunset* climate zones 1A–3B (Flagstaff, Taos, Santa Fe): Set out transplants of chrysanthemum, dianthus, flowering kale, and Iceland poppy. Sow seeds of baby's breath, larkspur, snapdragon, and sweet alyssum for spring bloom. Zones 10–13 (Albuquerque, Las Vegas, Tucson, Phoenix): Set out transplants of calendula, Iceland poppy, pansy, petunia, scabiosa, snapdragon, and viola. Sow baby's breath, nasturtium, and sweet pea seeds for spring color.

☐ **FALL FOLIAGE COLOR.** Zones 1A–3B: Drought-tolerant choices with reliable autumn color include shrubs like squawbush (*Rhus trilobata*) and staghorn sumac (*Rhus typhina*); trees like amur maple (*Acer tataricum ginnala*) and smoke tree (*Cotinus* 'Grace'); and the vine Virginia creeper (*Parthenocissus quinquefolia*). Zones 10–13: Consider shrubs like heavenly bamboo (*Nandina domestica*), Japanese barberry (*Berberis thunbergii*), Oregon grape (*Mahonia aquifolium*), and purple-leaf winter creeper (*Euonymus fortunei* 'Colorata'); and trees such as Chinese pistache (*Pistacia chinensis*) and the fruiting pomegranate 'Wonderful'.

☐ **GARLIC.** All zones: Separate garlic cloves from "mother" bulbs and plant individual cloves 1 to 2 inches deep. Among the hardneck varieties, which tend to have a hot, spicy flavor, try 'Persian Star', 'Red Rezan',

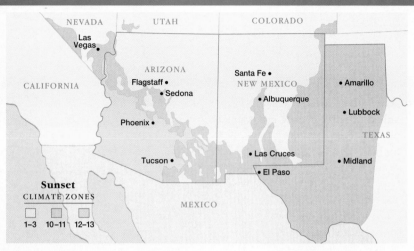

NEVADA · UTAH · COLORADO · Las Vegas · ARIZONA · CALIFORNIA · Flagstaff · · Sedona · Phoenix · Santa Fe · NEW MEXICO · · Albuquerque · · Amarillo · · Lubbock · TEXAS · · Las Cruces · · Midland · Tucson · · El Paso · MEXICO

Sunset CLIMATE ZONES 1–3 10–11 12–13

and 'Shatili'. Softneck kinds with milder flavor include 'Inchelium Red', 'Lorz Italian', 'S&H Silver', and 'Silver White'. One good mail-order source for these is Filaree Farm (*www.filareefarm.com* or *509/422-6940*).

☐ **HERBS.** Zones 10–13: Set out transplants of chives, marjoram, Mexican tarragon, mint, oregano, rosemary, sage, salad burnet, thyme, and winter savory. Sow seeds of borage, cilantro, dill, epazote, and parsley.

☐ **SPRING BULBS.** Zones 1A–3B: Set out crocus, daffodil, hyacinth, ornamental allium, and tulip. Zones 10–11: Plant any of the above, plus freesia and ranunculus. Zones 12–13: Consider amaryllis, anemone, calla, daffodil, grape hyacinth, ornamental allium, ranunculus, and watsonia.

☐ **VEGETABLES.** Zones 10–13: Sow seeds of arugula, beets, bok choy, carrots, fennel, peas, radishes, salad greens, spinach, Swiss chard, and turnips. Set out transplants of artichoke, broccoli, brussels sprouts, cabbage, cauliflower, kale, onions, and shallots.

☐ **WILDFLOWERS.** Zones 10–13: Sow seeds in full sun. Reliable performers include desert bluebells, desert marigold, fleabane, gaillardia, globe mallow, lupine, Mexican poppy, Parry's penstemon, and scarlet flax.

MAINTENANCE

☐ **CUT BACK ON WATER.** As temperatures cool, reduce your frequency of irrigation accordingly.

☐ **MULCH.** Spread a 2- to 4-inch layer of organic or mineral mulch around plants. Both types are effective in slowing evaporation, stabilizing soil temperatures, and reducing weeds.

—Kim Nelson

In Northern California, grapevine foliage is brightly tinged (opposite and above) and a bigleaf maple provides a memento of a country stroll (top).

Autumn joy

Gather fall leaves to decorate your home

By Bud Stuckey and Sharon Cohoon • Photos by Brown Cannon III (locations) and Thomas J. Story (projects)

W hen trees are freshly painted in their burnished fall hues, take advantage of their splendor. Harvest some leaves or branch clippings to create wreaths or swags for hanging on gates, doors, or mantels. Or, for a quick update on your porch, fill a pot or window box with the colors of the season.

Gathering fallen leaves makes a great family activity, and it's a fun thing to do during a Sunday walk with friends or on a picnic in the country. If you grow trees whose foliage colors up in fall you can clip small branches, leaving leaves attached.

Make a window box ▸

Flame-colored foliage adds just the right touch on the mantel of this outdoor fireplace. The arrangement, made of 8- to 12-inch stems of berries and leaves, fills a window box that's 24 inches long, 8 inches wide, and 6½ inches deep. Pin oak, liquidambar, and snowball viburnum clippings are arranged with stem ends in moist florist's foam; clusters of bright red pyracantha berries spill over the box's edges.

HOW-TO: Soak three blocks of florist's foam in a bucket of water, then set them on plastic trays inside the window box. Poke the clippings into the foam. Plastic trays and florist's foam are available at craft stores; window boxes are sold at nurseries and garden centers.

Make a wreath ▸

Bunches of Chinese pistache leaves cover an 8-inch-diameter straw wreath base (about $10 at craft stores) to make this festive wreath. It takes slightly longer to assemble than the other projects, but the method is easy. If you wish, substitute other fall leaves, such as pin oak, or blend together several kinds.

HOW-TO: After you have collected clippings of the leaves you wish to use, gather stems into bunches of four or five. Pin the first bunch to the wreath base with a U-shaped floral pin (available at craft stores) as shown below, with leaf tips facing clockwise. Place a second bunch on the base, overlapping the first slightly to cover the pins. Continue, working counterclockwise, until the base is covered.

Make a swag ▸

This gracefully curving swag creates a leafy half-moon on a garden gate. Japanese maple clippings and liquidambar leaves are tucked into a base of twiggy stems. If you have a birch or similar tree that drops wispy branches, you can gather several into a bunch and tie them in the middle with florist's wire. Otherwise, buy a twiggy swag base at a craft store (about $10 for one 16 inches long).

HOW-TO: Harvest about 12 maple stems, making cuts back to just above a side branch, as you would for usual pruning. Poke the liquidambar leaves into the purchased swag base, working from one end to the other; weave their short stems a bit among the twigs to secure them. Fill in with the Japanese maple clippings, working the stem ends into the swag base to hold everything in place.

Trees for autumn color

Chinese pistache
(Pistacia chinensis).
A garden-scale tree
with a rounded canopy;
narrow leaflets give it
a lacy appearance. In fall,
foliage turns luminous
shades of orange and red to
gold. *Sunset* climate zones
4–16, 18–23.

Japanese maple *(Acer palmatum).*
The most airy and delicate of all
maples. Varieties with colorful
leaves include 'Atropurpu-
reum' (bronzy green); 'Bloodgood' (scarlet); 'Bonfire'
(orange-pink); 'Ever Red' (crimson).
Zones A3, 2–10, 12, 14–24.

Liquidambar. Maplelike
leaves give this stout-
trunked tree a lacy
effect. Fall color varies
by variety. *L. styraciflua*
'Palo Alto' has orange-red to
bright red leaves. *L. styraciflua*
'Festival' turns yellow, peach,
pink, orange, and red. Zones
3–9, 14–24.

Maidenhair tree *(Ginkgo
biloba).* A graceful tree
with fan-shaped leaves
that turn buttery yellow
in fall; they drop all at
once to create a golden
carpet on lawns or paving.
Zones A3, 1–10, 12, 14–24.

Pin oak *(Quercus palustris).*
An open, rounded tree. In brisk
fall weather, the glossy leaves
turn yellow, red, and finally rus-
set brown. Zones 2–10, 14–24.

Japanese persimmon
(Diospyros kaki). In fall,
leaves turn vivid yellow,
orange, or red; after
they drop, brilliant
orange fruits hang on
well into winter. Best in
zones 6–9, 14–16, 18–24, H1. ◆

Wispy, pinkish-plumed *Panicum virgatum* 'Haense Herms' mingles with honey yellow kangaroo paw (left foreground) along the grass walk. On the same side of the path is fountain grass; the clumps of straw-colored grass are Mexican feather grass *(Nassella tenuissima)*. In a row on the far side, *Calamagrostis* x *acutiflora* 'Karl Foerster' has rust-colored flowers.

A garden of grasses

How to use ornamentals in the landscape for striking results

By Lauren Bonar Swezey • Photographs by Saxon Holt

Twelve years ago, Mary and Lew Reid moved north to the rolling grasslands of California's west Sonoma County, where they built their dream home atop an open ridge. Around it, Mary designed a 2-acre garden of ornamental grasses to connect her land to the surrounding meadows. "Ornamental grasses offered the perfect transitional element," she explains. Their restrained height also makes it easy to maintain a view.

Developing the garden became a family affair. Lew's father engineered the layout while Lew started perennials from seed and propagated the grasses by division.

A grass walk at the property's border features spiraling masses of single species (*Miscanthus* 'Gracillimus', for instance) weaving gracefully around others such as *Pennisetum alopecuroides* 'Hameln'. "I designed it like a painting, using sweeps of color and texture," Mary says. For seasonal interest, she adds flowers of a single color—pink *Eupatorium purpureum* 'Gateway' for summer, and yellow *Helianthus angustifolius* along the grass walk for fall.

In the main garden, wide paths covered with gravel in a warm brownish gray weave around large planting beds of various sizes, each designed around a color theme. "I look for perennials that contrast with and complement the colors and textures of the grasses," Mary says. The burgundy of *Pennisetum setaceum* 'Rubrum', for instance,

Giant feather grass (*Stipa gigantea*), left, makes a dramatic focal point when in full bloom. Across the path in the background is pinkish-flowered *Pennisetum orientale* 'Karley Rose'. In the foreground is a bronze-colored sedge. RIGHT: blue oat grass.

Grass uses

FOCAL POINTS

Eulalia grass (*Miscanthus* 'Gracillimus', *M. sinensis* 'Morning Light'); *Sunset* climate zones 2–24.

Feather reed grass (*Calamagrostis* x *acutiflora* 'Karl Foerster'); zones 2B–24.

Fountain grass (*Pennisetum orientale* 'Karley Rose'); zones 3–10, 14–24.

Giant feather grass (*Stipa gigantea)*; zones 4–9, 14–24.

Switch grass (*Panicum virgatum* 'Haense Herms'); zones 1–11, 14–23.

ANCHORS

Blue oat grass (*Helictotrichon sempervirens*); zones 1–24.

Mexican feather grass (*Nassella tenuissima*); 2B–24.

Pennisetum setaceum 'Rubrum'; zones 8–24.

Sedge (*Carex*); zones vary.

BORDER EDGINGS

Festuca idahoensis 'Siskiyou Blue'; zones 1–10, 14–24.

Tufted hair grass (*Deschampsia cespitosa*); zones 2–24.

enriches a hot orange scheme of kangaroo paw, lion's tail, orange cestrum, and orange gloriosa daisy. The blue-gray foliage of blue oat grass pairs well with lavender and salvia.

One of the most beautiful features of ornamental grasses is their winter form—an important criteria. The Reids enjoy the grasses' dormant-season beauty until just before spring, when Mary gets out the power trimmers (see maintenance tips below). Grasses are very forgiving and easy to maintain, she says. "There's only six weeks of downtime before they start popping out again. They truly provide four seasons of interest."

Maintenance tips

To get rid of dead growth, most grasses need to be cut down every year. The exceptions are evergreen grasses, such as sedge *(Carex),* blue oat grass, and some species of feather grass *(Stipa),* which only need renewing every 2 to 3 years (comb out the dead blades with your fingers and cut off old flowers).

1. In late winter or spring (February in the Reids' garden), look for new growth at the base of the old grass blades.

2. After you see new growth, use power trimmers or hedge shears to cut clumps down to 1½ to 3 inches tall for smaller grasses, 3 to 6 inches for taller grasses (depending on the mature height). For instance, cut low-growing tufted hair grass down to 1½ inches, Eulalia grass *(Miscanthus)* to 6 inches.

3. Spread a layer of compost around the base of each plant (Mary uses well-composted turkey manure). ◆

Mahonia, barberry, and maple screen the meadowlike interior of the garden from the sidewalk (below).

Inspired by the forest's edge

Before designing her 40- by 25-foot entry garden in Seattle, Carolyn Temple studied the edges of Northwest forests, noting the plants that thrive in the transition zone between open meadow and deep, dark old-growth forest. In the wild, this fringe provides an ideal habitat for small conifers, deciduous vine maples, evergreen salal, ferns, and wildflowers to form tiers of vegetation that change with the seasons.

Taking her cue from nature, Temple edged the front of her garden with conifers, small-scale deciduous trees, shrubs, and groundcovers. Viewed from the street (see photo at left), the planting forms a foliar screen that masks much of the house. Concealed behind this forest is a private meadow (above), where Temple can relax. Cannas, hostas, and other perennials and shrubs create a colorful fringe around the grass. —*Steven R. Lorton*

Get seeds off to a good start

The annuals listed on the facing page reseed best in soil that is not regularly cultivated. You can give them their own separate bed or tuck them into little pockets of the garden where there's still bare ground.

• Select a site that drains well and gets at least six hours of sun per day. Rake the soil lightly before sowing seeds.

• For a natural look the first year, broadcast half the seeds over the desired area, then sow the remainder in a direction perpendicular to the first. Walk on the soil to make sure the seeds are firmly in contact with the soil.

• Keep the area moist until seedlings emerge—usually 5 to 14 days after sowing. Water with a sprinkler set to a fine spray or a garden hose with a mist nozzle. When seedlings have grown a few inches tall, taper off irrigation. Then water only when plants appear drought stressed.

• After the annuals stop blooming, allow them to set seed. Once most of the seeds have ripened and the foliage has begun to turn brown, pull up the plants and scatter the remaining seeds where you choose. Then let nature take over.

Deep pink corn cockle mingles with plum-colored bracts of *Cerinthe major* 'Purpurascens'.

Many happy returns

Self-sowing spring annuals make great additions to the garden; start them this fall for bloom year after year

By Sharon Cohoon and Debra Lee Baldwin

When visitors stroll through *Sunset's* test garden in May during our annual Celebration Weekend, test garden coordinator Bud Stuckey notices what they pause to admire. The top traffic stopper year after year, he says, is a small patch of annuals near the walkway. It's a mix of corn cockle, godetia, honeywort, and California poppies that came up on its own several years ago and has been self-sowing for repeat performances ever since.

"Wouldn't you know their favorite section of the garden would be the one I didn't create," says Stuckey with amusement—but not much surprise. "I couldn't have planned better combinations. It never ceases to amaze me how beautifully nature does the landscaping."

In our case, nature took over where we left off. We had planted the annuals in a test bed, and when their season was over, Stuckey pulled them up and dragged them to the compost heap nearby. "The next year, their fallen seeds germinated and came up in the same spot," Stuckey says. "They looked so good together, I let them grow."

Something similar happened to Jo Casterline. Twelve years ago, she flanked her rock-lined gravel path in Poway, California, with plants that thrive in fast-draining decomposed granite and require minimal supplemental water. Among them were orange and yellow California poppies; their sunny blooms have returned every year since.

Now Casterline says her poppy-lined walkway "is the best part of my garden, and I don't do anything to make it happen. It just comes back, year after year." And because the poppies and other annuals die back each fall and come up the next spring, Casterline's pathway never looks the same two years in a row. "It's always a surprise," she says of the ever-changing color show.

Think of these kinds of annuals as polite reseeders. If you'd like to introduce some to your own garden, fall is the perfect time to start them in mild-winter climates. (In cold-weather areas, wait until early spring to sow seeds.) Ten of our favorite reseeders are listed below.

Keep in mind that there's a fine line between a well-behaved reseeder and an aggressive pest, and the difference often depends on climate. Our list includes corn cockle, for instance, even though this wispy annual turns up on noxious-weed lists in some areas. It's a pest only in the Southeast; in the West we find it almost too polite—it reseeds rather sparsely.

Seed sources

Renee's Garden: *www.reneesgarden.com or (888) 880-7228.* Corn cockle, honeywort, love-in-a-mist, Shirley poppy, sweet alyssum.

Wild Seed: *(602) 276-3536.* California desert bluebell, California poppy, desert marigold. ◆

California poppies grow in drifts among white Santa Barbara daisies and yellow-centered, hot pink *Senecio elegans* in this Poway, CA, garden.

Godetia

Favorite reseeders

California desert bluebells *(Phacelia campanularia)*. Bell-shaped, dark blue flowers; gray-green, coarse-toothed leaves. Grows 6 to 18 inches tall and wide. *Sunset* climate zones 1–3, 7–24.

California poppy *(Eschscholzia californica)*. Satin-textured, single-petaled flowers, pale yellow to deep orange, on stems 8 to 24 inches long. Zones 1–24; H1.

Corn cockle *(Agrostemma githago)*. Mauve-purple flowers with darker veins. Grows 2 to 3 feet tall and 1 foot wide. Good for cutting. Zones 1–24.

Desert marigold *(Baileya multiradiata)*. Inch-wide, bright yellow flowers; gray-green foliage. Grows 1 to 1½ feet tall. Native to Western deserts. Zones 1–3, 7–23.

Godetia *(Clarkia amoena)*. Single or double flowers in lilac to reddish pink and blotched or streaked with crimson. Grows 18 to 30 inches tall. Good cut flower. Zones 1–24.

Honeywort *(Cerinthe major)*. Upper stems bear sprays of nodding, tubular, violet-blue flowers; fleshy stems and leaves. Grows 2 feet tall and as wide. Attracts bees. Zones 1–24.

Larkspur *(Consolida ajacis)*. Blossom spikes densely set with flowers in shades of white, blue, lilac, and pink above finely cut, ferny leaves. Grows 1 to 4 feet tall. Zones 1–24.

Love-in-a-mist *(Nigella damascena)*. Blue, rose, or white spurred flowers, followed by attractive seedpods (useful in dried arrangements). Grows 1 to 1½ feet tall. All zones.

Shirley poppy *(Papaver rhoeas)*. Single or double cup-shaped flowers in shades of red, pink, orange, and white, including bicolors. Grows 3 feet tall. Zones A1–A3; 1–24 (best in cool-summer areas).

Sweet alyssum *(Lobularia maritima)*. Clusters of tiny, four-petaled white flowers on low mounds that grow 1 foot tall and wide. In mild climates, blooms nearly year-round from self-sown seedlings. Attracts bees. All zones.

Showy beauties

These grow in climate zones 1–24 from the *Sunset Western Garden Book,* except as noted.

Allium caeruleum: 2-inch spheres of denim blue flowers are borne in late spring and early summer on 12- to 18-inch-tall stems.

A. christophii: 6- to 12-inch clusters of starlike lavender flowers appear in late spring and early summer on 12- to 15-inch stems.

A. giganteum: 4- to 8-inch spheres of rose-purple flowers bloom in late spring and early summer on 5-foot or taller stems. *A. aflatunense* has similar but smaller (2- to 4-inch) flowers. Zones 2–24.

A. neapolitanum: 1½- to 3-inch loose clusters of fragrant, pure white flowers open in spring on 1-foot stems. Zones 4–24.

A. oreophilum: 1- to 1½-inch loose clusters of fragrant, deep rose pink flowers appear in late spring on 4- to 8-inch stems.

A. sphaerocephalum: 1- to 1½-inch oval spheres of maroon flowers bloom in midsummer on 2- to 3-foot stems.

Globes of *Allium christophii* bloom above magenta-flowered cranesbill. FAR LEFT: *A. aflatunense.*

Awesome alliums

Ornamental onions are unusually pretty, versatile performers

By Lauren Springer

Who would think an onion could be a garden showstopper? Yet the genus *Allium,* which includes edible onion bulbs, embraces many ornamental species as well. They bear striking spheres of starburst-shaped flowers in shades of blue, purple, rose, pink, yellow, and white. The blossoms make good cut flowers for fresh bouquets and are easily dried for everlasting arrangements.

Plant alliums in fall at the same time you set out other spring-blooming bulbs. Give them a sunny location, except in the hottest regions, where they grow best in partial shade or morning sun. Many alliums tolerate drought and poor soil. They are also rewarding performers in containers. At planting time, space the bulbs of smaller species 4 to 6 inches apart, larger ones 8 to 12 inches apart. Cover the bulbs with 3 to 4 inches of soil. After alliums bloom, their foliage turns yellow and dies back to the ground, which is why they're usually planted among companions. Plant the larger species of alliums among shrubs, roses, perennials, and grasses; tuck the smaller ones into rock gardens or along the edge of plantings.

Sources

These specialists offer a wide selection of alliums: Brent and Becky's Bulbs (www.brentandbeckysbulbs.com or 877/661-2852); McClure & Zimmerman (www.mzbulb.com or 800/883-6998). ◆

How to plant bulbs in pots

October is the perfect time to get these containers started. The bulb pots go together quickly, flower four to seven months after planting, cost no more than a florist's bouquet (about $60, including pot, potting soil, and bulbs), and give three weeks of portable spring color. If you live in a mild-winter climate, refrigerate the bulbs in paper bags (away from ripening fruit) six weeks before planting. Most nurseries sell a variety of bulbs; or check mail-order sources.

1. Start by filling 16- to 24-inch terra-cotta containers with a fast-draining potting mix, to within 5 inches of the rim. (The containers have drainage holes drilled into the bottom.)

2. Plant a solid layer of bulbs shoulder to shoulder (as shown above) in each—the 24-inch container pictured at right holds up to 70 large tulip bulbs. A 16-inch diameter pot holds 40 to 50 bulbs.

3. Cover the bulbs with 4 inches of potting mix; water well.

4. Set the container in shade until stems first emerge, then move it to full sun and water regularly.

Extra-tall white 'Maureen' tulips pack a 24-inch terra-cotta container.

Bulbs for pots

Plant them now for color next spring

By Jim McCausland

Every spring, giant pots of bulbs steal the show in *Sunset's* display gardens in Menlo Park, California. "Nothing could be easier," says head gardener Rick LaFrentz, "since each bulb contains everything it needs to produce perfect spring flowers."

This container is one of a series that LaFrentz uses to stretch the main season of bloom from late February through April. He plants 'Cheerfulness' and 'Earlicheer' daffodils to start the season; 'Delft Blue', 'Kronos', and 'Woodstock' hyacinths to follow the daffodils; 'Maureen' tulips for the early April show; and a selection of parrot tulips and *Allium schubertii* to finish April. He also fills up a few containers with drumstick alliums *(A. sphaerocephalon)* for July and August bloom.

At the end of the season, LaFrentz discards the tulips and hyacinths and transplants daffodils and alliums into perennial beds in the garden. Because he keeps bulbs in pots for only a single season, he doesn't bother to fertilize; the bulbs supply everything the plants and flowers need for the following spring's show. ◆

THOMAS J. STORY. ILLUSTRATION: TREVOR JOHNSON

LATE FALL, WHEN PERSIMMONS ARE AT THEIR MOST GLORIOUS, is the best time to shop for plants. 'Hachiya' persimmons (at the back) are large, with slightly pointed bottoms. 'Fuyu' persimmons are smaller and more golden. For tips on how to grow these pumpkin-colored beauties, see page 325.

November

An all-in-pots garden blends mums in fall colors: rust-colored 'Olivia' (foreground), red mums with ornamental oregano and dwarf nandina (middle), and yellow 'Donna' with cream and pink 'Sweet Stacy' (back).

After-bloom care for potted mums

For all-mum plantings:
In late autumn, after bloom is through, cut back plants, leaving stems about 6 to 8 inches long. (In cold climates, wait until spring, after new growth appears at the base.) Move the pots to a sheltered area protected from frost, and make sure the soil doesn't dry out over winter. When new growth emerges in spring, apply a complete fertilizer, then feed plants weekly with liquid fertilizer through the growing season until buds show color. To keep plants bushy, pinch tips through the summer, nipping the top pair of leaves on every shoot that reaches 5 inches long.

For mixed plantings:
If you want to keep the pot center stage, remove the mum and replace it with a spring bloomer such as Iceland poppy or primrose. You can cut back the mum as above, then plant it in another pot or in the garden.

Fall's richest hues

Orange, rust, ruby red, gold: These are the colors of autumn, forever associated with falling leaves, woodsmoke, and sweater weather. They're also the colors of mum flowers—perfect for brightening patios or porches in fall.

Among the most widely sold perennials, chrysanthemums are easy to find at nurseries and florists, especially in fall. Some are sold as named varieties (Yoder, producer of some of the plants in the pots pictured above, names garden mums after women). Other mums are simply sold by color. Buy them in bloom, then pop a few plants from 6-inch nursery pots into a large (16- or 18-inch) container. For added interest, mix in a couple of low-growing shrubs, perennials, or grasses.

Give mums rich, well-drained soil (add a dose of controlled-release fertilizer at planting time) and protection from dry winter winds; water them often enough so that the soil never completely dries out $1/2$ inch below the surface. Display the container in full sun (light afternoon shade in hot climates). —*Kathleen N. Brenzel*

Denver's bonsai trove

Blending horticulture and art, bonsai was born in China more than 1,000 years ago and developed further in Japan. The term bonsai comes from two Japanese words: *bon,* meaning "tray," and *sai,* meaning "to create." By training plants in trays or shallow containers, bonsai growers create miniature versions of trees and shrubs.

Bonsai became firmly rooted in the Denver area when a Japanese-American couple, Victor and Taeko Tawara, opened the Bonsai Nursery in Englewood, Colorado, in 1960. Twelve years later, Ron Malik began working for the Tawaras, and he purchased the business from them in 1977; he runs its now with help from his wife and siblings.

As the holiday shopping season approaches, the nursery stocks a variety of

Japanese black pine (top left), dwarf juniper (above), and narrow-leaf fig (left).

plants that do well as indoor bonsai, including azalea, bougainvillea, boxwood, pomegranate, and rosemary. The nursery also sells prepared specimens. Prices range from $7 for seedlings in plain 4-inch pots to $295 for a dwarf Japanese juniper in a handsome container.

Bonsai Nursery: 9–5 Mon–Sat, 10–4 Sun. 3750 S. Federal Blvd., Englewood, CO; (303) 761-3066. —Colleen Smith

Mosaic steps in Boise

To add a whimsical touch to their garden path, the Cenell family of Boise covered plain concrete steps with mosaic art panels depicting a wiggling snake, a leaping frog, flowers, ladybugs, and other natural forms. Mary Cenell drew the designs on paper, then used carbon paper to transfer them to the steps. Her daughter, Becca Nielsen, used tile nippers to cut ceramic tiles and old plates into pieces; she then affixed the fragments to the concrete.

After the adhesive was thoroughly dry, they applied tile grout to fill in the gaps between the pieces. Finally, Mary's husband, Ken, framed each panel with redwood 2-by-4s.

—Suzanne Touchette Kelso

PLANT PROFILE

Serviceberry has it all

Native to western North America, Saskatoon serviceberry *(Amelanchier alnifolia)* is a small tree or shrub with year-round interest. In early spring, clusters of white flowers appear on bare branches just as leaves unfurl. The flowers are followed by rosy pink berries that ripen in summer to purplish black; the sweet fruit attracts birds and makes delicious preserves and pie filling. In autumn, the leaves turn golden yellow to fiery red. Winter reveals the plant's upright, arching silhouette.

This serviceberry grows in *Sunset* Northwest climate zones A1–A3 and 1–6. Depending on the variety, it reaches 4 to 15 feet or taller, with an equal spread. It grows in full sun or partial shade and takes any soil with moderate to regular water. Fall is a good time to set out container-grown or balled-and-burlapped plants.

—*Marcia Tatroe*

Small, oval leaves turn from deep green to red or yellow in fall.

Under an oak

Established native oaks can succumb to fungal root diseases if they're watered during the summer months. That's what Cara and Tim Hoxie of Orinda discovered before they relandscaped their front yard. Their coast live oak, underplanted with lawn, was struggling.

The solution: Create a large decomposed granite patio beneath the tree's canopy, then landscape with unthirsty plants nearby. (Since deer regularly grazed on the Hoxie's property, the plants needed to be deer-resistant too.) The garden is mostly green, but perennials and annuals add seasonal color, and a sedge adds beautiful texture—it's backlit by the sun much of the day.

Now, nearly two years after the redesign, the oak is recovering nicely and the resident deer are coexisting with the plants.

Deer-resistant plants

Trees, shrubs, and grasses: African boxwood, *Aster* × *frikartii*, Berkeley sedge *(Carex tumulicola),* breath of heaven, evergreen dogwood (sold as *Cornus omeiense* 'Summer Passion'), and rosemary.

Annuals and perennials: Bacopa, catmint, *Erysimum* 'Bowles Mauve', true geraniums (*Geranium* species), hellebores, Iceland poppy, lobelia, narcissus, Shasta daisy, sweet William.

DESIGN: Shari Bashin-Sullivan and Richard Sullivan of Enchanting Planting, Orinda *(925/258-5500)*

—*Lauren Bonar Swezey*

Rustic trellis made from rebar

Bare garage walls fronted by skinny planting strips cry out for greenery. In such situations, vines are the answer. But instead of supporting them with a conventional wood trellis, consider rebar. Landscape architect Christy Ten Eyck designed the one shown above for Russell and Lynne Kincaid's home at the Anthem development in Maricopa County, Arizona.

Ten Eyck used 7½-foot lengths of ⅝-inch-thick rebar. She evenly spaced the pieces a few inches apart, pounding the bottom of each one 15 inches into the ground. A concrete footing was poured along the trellis to anchor the pieces permanently.

To stabilize the upper part, another segment of rebar was welded horizontally across the vertical pieces (weaving ¼-inch wire would also work).

One Lady Banks' rose was planted on each side of the trellis.

DESIGN: Ten Eyck Landscape Architects, Phoenix *(602/468-0505)*

—*Sharon Cohoon*

Surprising fall color

Most trees that catch your eye this season display colorful leaves or berries. But the red-cap gum (*Eucalyptus erythrocorys*) provides fall color of a different sort. This evergreen lights up the shortest days of the year with scarlet bud caps that drop off to reveal vibrant yellow flowers.

Blooming anytime from November through March, red-cap gum has deep green leaves and white bark. Reaching a modest height of 30 feet, it tolerates drought, withstands considerable heat, and is hardy to 23°, performing well in the intermediate and low deserts (*Sunset* climate zones 12 and 13).

Stake it when young to form a single-trunked tree (growing almost as wide as it does tall), or cut back the main stem to grow it as a large, multitrunked shrub.

Look for red-cap gum at well-stocked nurseries.

—*David C. Becker*

Purple aubrieta is paired with red and pink English daisies in a bed backed by tulips.

Inspiration from Salt Lake City

Some of the West's best orchestrated displays of spring color are found in the gardens at Temple Square in Salt Lake City (above). The beds here feature dazzling combinations of spring bulbs and early perennials that bloom simultaneously, some beneath the canopies of flowering trees. For years these stunning displays were conceived by Temple Square landscape designer Peter Lassig, who recently retired. His horticultural inspiration set the tone for *Temple Square Gardening* (Deseret Book, Salt Lake City, 2003; $27; www. deseretbook.com or 800/453-4532).

Four authors—Diane Erickson, Christena Gates, Larry Sagers, and Shelly Zollinger—teamed up to produce this comprehensive guide to gardening in the Salt Lake City area (*Sunset* climate zone 3A). One chapter tells how to create a spring-blooming garden like the ones at Temple Square. In fall, bulbs are interplanted with pansies and other spring bloomers. This gives the plants a chance to "establish a good root system before winter arrives," reducing the chance that they will be "pushed out of the ground by repeated freezing and thawing— a process known as frost heaving."

Other chapters include "Tricks of the Trade" and "Favorite Lists," which covers perennials, annuals, bulbs, roses, grasses, trees, and shrubs. Among the plants, you'll find early-blooming perennials, such as aubrieta and English daisy, that make great companions for tulips and other spring bulbs. —*Dick Bushnell*

Clockwise from top right: 'Redbor' kale, 'Repens' false cypress, *Heuchera* 'Plum Pudding', and *Euonymus japonicus* 'Aureo-Marginatus'. Below right: 'Rainbow Warrior' phormium and red-berried *Ilex verticillata* accent another pot.

Plant picks

Annuals. Pansies ('Delta Pure Red', 'Skyline Copperfield'), 'Rainbow' chard, 'Redbor' kale, or violas ('Clear Sky Rose', 'Starlet Yellow').

Perennials. *Bergenia cordifolia, Carex hachijoensis* 'Evergold', *Festuca glauca* 'Elijah Blue', *Heuchera* ('Bressingham Bronze', 'Green Spice', 'Plum Pudding'), or *Phormium* ('Amazing Red', 'Duet', 'Maori Queen', 'Rainbow Warrior').

Shrubs. *Aucuba japonica* 'Mr. Goldstrike', *Calluna vulgaris* 'Wickwar Flame', *Camellia sasanqua* 'Yuletide', *Chamaecyparis pisifera* 'True Blue', *Euonymus japonicus* ('Aureo-Marginatus', 'Aureo-Variegatus'), *Ilex verticillata* 'Winter Gold', *Mahonia* x *media* 'Charity', *Nandina domestica* 'Gulf Stream', or *Osmanthus heterophyllus* ('Goshiki', 'Sasaba').

Cool-season color pots

Lisa Freed, co-owner of Wells Medina Nursery in Medina, Washington *(425/454-1853),* has a knack for combining hardy plants in containers that deliver color from fall through winter.

She uses 24-inch plastic containers with a faux terra-cotta finish because they're lightweight and won't crack in freezing weather as ceramic pots do. She fills each one with potting soil, then mixes in a couple handfuls of controlled-release fertilizer to keep growing plants fed.

Freed's pots usually start with a shrub or some other tall accent plant (*Phormium,* for example) transplanted from a 2- or 5-gallon nursery can. Around it, she arranges annuals or perennials from 4-inch pots or 1-gallon cans, pairing plants with contrasting colors and textures. —*Jim McCausland*

'Hachiya' persimmons (at the back) are large, with slightly pointed bottoms; 'Fuyu' persimmons (foreground) are smaller and more golden.

How to grow them

Japanese, or Oriental, persimmon (*Diospyros kaki*) grows and fruits best in *Sunset* climate zones 6–9, 14–16, and 18–24. It reaches 30 feet tall (or more) and has a handsome branch structure. One of the best fruit trees for ornamental use, it sends out light green leaves that turn dark with age; in fall, green foliage turns vivid yellow, orange, or red. After foliage drops, orange fruits hang on for weeks unless harvested. Trees set fruit without pollination.

EXPOSURE: Full sun.

SOIL: Needs good drainage.

WATER: Moderate. Irrigate young trees regularly and feed once in winter or early spring.

BEST VARIETIES: 'Fuyu' (nonastringent, firm-fleshed fruit with flattened bottoms); 'Hachiya' (astringent, large, slightly acorn-shaped fruits).

HARVESTING: To save crops from birds, pick fruit when fully colored but still hard. Eat 'Hachiya' when flesh softens; 'Fuyu' can be eaten when crisp.

Party time for persimmons

With their pumpkin-colored fruit and glowing amber leaves, persimmon trees seem like the very spirit of autumn. Moderately sized and graceful in habit, they're beautiful in the landscape. And late fall, when they're at their most glorious, is the time to shop for plants.

To see what mature persimmon trees look like and to get dozens of ideas for using the ripe fruit, visit the annual Persimmon Party at Pitcher Park in Old Towne Orange. Here, you can sample and buy baked goods as well as jams, jellies, butter, chutneys, and leathers made from persimmons. Buy a persimmon cookbook and some fresh fruit or purée, and you can duplicate the tasty treats at home.

Pitcher Park, once the property of Laurence and Alice Pitcher, was donated to the city in 1992. The Pitchers' extensive home orchard has been preserved—mature 'Hachiya' and 'Fuyu' persimmon trees shade the park—and the family barn now houses antique firefighting and farm equipment. There's also a honey house on the site.

Noon–3 Nov 16 (2003 hours); free. Pitcher Park (corner of E. Almond Ave. and S. Cambridge St.), Orange, CA; (714) 532-5930. —S.C.

STEVEN GUNTHER

Classic Southwest trio

Natural partners

Brittlebush (*Encelia farinosa*), with aromatic silvery foliage and yellow spring flowers, reaches 3 feet tall and 4 feet wide. *Sunset* climate zones 8–16, 18–24, H1.

Bunny ears (*Opuntia microdasys*), with bristly cinnamon-gold pads, grows quickly to 2 to 3 feet tall and 4 to 5 feet wide. Zones 12–24.

Deer grass (*Muhlenbergia rigens*) forms dense clumps 4 feet tall and wide. Zones 4–24.

This planting in Palm Desert, California, was among the first in the area to feature showy drifts of Southwest native species, according to landscape architect Russell Greey of Scottsdale, Arizona. He mixed brittlebush, bunny ears cactus, and deer grass, leaving bare earth between plants. Overhead, mesquite and palo brea trees form an airy canopy.

A decade after planting, the landscape is still thriving, but Greey isn't surprised. After all, these plants are naturally adapted to Southwest deserts, so they're easy to maintain. (For more on natives, see page 332.) Bunny ears are almost self-sustaining. Established plants can survive without supplemental irrigation, though they look fresher when watered periodically in spring and summer. Brittlebush needs only monthly irrigation and hard pruning in the fall (cut it back nearly to the ground to reinvigorate it). Deer grass needs water every few weeks during warm weather; shear it almost to the ground in early spring to stimulate new growth. **DESIGN:** Greey/Pickett Partners, Scottsdale, AZ *(480/609-0009)* —*S.C.*

WHAT TO DO IN YOUR GARDEN IN NOVEMBER

PLANTING

☐ **AMARYLLIS.** Start bulbs or buy leafed-out plants this month for bloom from now through spring. Grow these tender plants indoors where they get plenty of light and regular water.

☐ **CAMELLIAS.** *Sunset* climate zones 4–7: 'Yuletide' is the most popular winter-blooming camellia for good reason: This red-flowered *C. sasanqua* variety starts blooming in November and continues until March, when *C. japonica* varieties carry on the show. Plant both kinds now; mulch roots to protect against hard freezes. Sasanqua types make great espaliers under eaves, where rain can't batter blossoms.

☐ **FALL COLOR.** Shop for trees with colorful fall foliage. Look for ginkgo, katsura tree, many maples, Persian parrotia, sour gum *(Nyssa sylvatica)*, sourwood *(Oxydendrum arboreum)*, and staghorn sumac. Among shrubs, consider *Fothergilla major,* oakleaf hydrangea *(H. quercifolia),* Saskatoon serviceberry (see item on page 321), and winged euonymus *(E. alatus).*

☐ **SPRING-BLOOMING BULBS.** By month's end, many nurseries offer discounts on remaining supplies of spring-flowering bulbs. It's a good time to buy quantities for planting in large drifts under trees. Try anemones, bluebells, crocuses, daffodils, grape hyacinths, hyacinths, ranunculus, and tulips. For forcing indoors, try crocuses, freesias, hyacinths, *Iris reticulata,* and 'Paper White' narcissus.

☐ **WILDFLOWERS.** In all zones, fall-sown wildflower seeds always come up earlier than those sown in spring. Scatter seeds over amended, weeded beds. Tip: Sow 1 tablespoon of seeds in a flat of potting mix so you'll be able to tell the difference between wildflower and weed seedlings after they germinate; then pull the weeds.

MAINTENANCE

☐ **CARE FOR DAHLIAS.** Dig around dahlia tubers, gently lift them out of the ground, shake or hose off the soil, let them dry in a cool spot, then store them for winter in boxes filled with wood shavings. In zones 4–7, if you have fast-draining soil and are willing to mulch dahlia beds with a 4- to 6-inch layer of straw, you can try overwintering tubers in the ground. But if there's a deep freeze, you may lose everything.

☐ **KEEP ON COMPOSTING.** To accelerate its decomposition, run tough, brown, late-season garden waste through a compost grinder or pass a mower over it before putting it on the pile. It also helps to mix shredded leaves with a handful of high-nitrogen lawn fertilizer before tossing them onto the compost heap.

☐ **MOW ONE LAST TIME.** Lawn growth slows down to a snail's pace in winter. Mow one last time on a dry weekend in the middle of the month; you shouldn't have to mow again until spring. If you own a gas mower, run it until all the fuel is gone. If the mower needs service, do it now: Sharpen or replace the blade, change the oil and the air filter, and check the spark plug.

☐ **OVERWINTER GERANIUMS, FUCHSIAS.** Before a hard freeze hits, bring plants into a cool, dark, frost-free place for the winter. An unheated garage is usually sufficient. ◆

WHAT TO DO IN YOUR GARDEN IN NOVEMBER

PLANTING

☐ **AMARYLLIS.** Only 8 to 12 weeks after planting, these gorgeous flowering bulbs produce huge single or double saucer- or trumpet-shaped flowers up to 9 inches wide. Miniature varieties have smaller flowers but may not be as leggy. Colors include coral, pink, red, salmon, white, yellow, and striped and feathered bicolors. Look for them at your local nursery or order from John Scheepers (*www.johnscheepers.com or 860/567-0838*) or Wayside Gardens (*www.waysidegardens.com or 800/845-1124*).

☐ **BUTTERFLY PLANTS.** *Sunset* climate zones 7–9, 14–17: Some of the best plants for attracting butterflies are those that provide nectar and larval food. They include: buckwheat, butterfly bush, coffeeberry, native grasses (*Carex barberae, Festuca californica,* and *F. idahoensis*), mallows (*Lavatera* or *Sidalcea malviflora*), milkweed (*Asclepias incarnata* for moist gardens, *A. speciosa* for dry gardens), native oaks (such as coast live oak), penstemon, pipevine, and willow.

☐ **CRAPE MYRTLE.** Zones 7–9, 14–17: Three of the best crape myrtles for fall color are 'Pecos' and 'Zuni' (both *Lagerstroemia* hybrids) and 'Near East'. If you can't find these trees at your local nursery, ask the staff to order one for you from Monrovia (which is wholesale only).

• Eureka

• Redding

CALIFORNIA

NEVADA

• Mendocino

Santa Rosa

• Sacramento

Sunset
CLIMATE ZONES

• San Francisco
• San Jose

☐ Mountain (1–2)
☐ Valley (7–9)
☐ Inland (14)
☐ Coastal (15–17)

• Fresno

• Monterey

☐ **GARLIC.** Zones 7–9, 14–17: Artichoke (common white) types are easiest to grow. Rocambole has wonderful, intense flavor. Choose a site in full sun with well-drained soil (or plant in raised beds, if your soil is heavy and poorly drained). Mix in plenty of compost. Plant cloves so tips are about 1 to 2 inches beneath the soil surface; elephant garlic isn't a true garlic and is milder in flavor— plant cloves 4 to 6 inches deep. Zones 1–2: Plant in early spring.

☐ **WILDFLOWERS.** For colorful spring blooms, choose a mix that's suited to your climate or buy individual kinds and create your own mixes. You can also buy mixes for specific purposes, such as wildflowers that attract butterflies or beneficial insects. Three regional seed sources are Clyde Robin Seed Company, Castro Valley (*www.clyderobin.com or 510/785-0425*); Larner Seeds, Bolinas (*www.larnerseeds.com or 415/868-9407*); and the Wildflower Seed Company, St. Helena (*www.wildflower-seed.com or 800/456-3359*).

MAINTENANCE

☐ **CARE FOR BEGONIAS.** Zones 7–9, 14–17: Continue watering plants through the mild fall months. When blooms stop developing and leaves begin to yellow with the onset of cool weather, reduce watering. When the leaves fall off, allow the soil to dry out, then lift the tubers, shake off the soil, and let the bulbs dry for a few days. Store them in a cool, dry, dark place.

☐ **CLEAN UP DEBRIS.** To help eliminate overwintering sites for insects and diseases, pull up summer annuals and vegetables that have stopped producing, rake up leaves, and pick up fallen fruit. Add the debris to the compost pile (except weeds that have gone to seed and diseased plants).

WEED WATCH

☐ **INVASIVE PLANTS.** Some plants are either vigorous reseeders or aggressive growers; they can spread far too quickly across the landscape. They include bridal veil broom (*Genista monosperma*), Chinese tallow tree, English ivy, fountain grass (*Pennisetum setaceum*), ice plant (*Carpobrotus edulis*), pampas grass (*Cortaderia selloana* and *C. jubata*), periwinkle (*Vinca major*), Scotch broom (*Cytisus scoparius*), and Spanish broom (*Spartium junceum*). Avoid planting them. ◆

WHAT TO DO IN YOUR GARDEN IN NOVEMBER

PLANTING

☐ **BULBS.** For a constant display of flowers and fragrance indoors during the holidays, start pots of 'Paper White' narcissus every three weeks. Cover bulbs with pebbles and water. Keep in a cool, dark place until growth is well under way, then gradually bring into light.

☐ **CAMELLIAS.** Sasanqua camellias are not as well known as japonicas, but they are extremely useful landscaping plants. They can tolerate more sun than other camellias, and they bloom in autumn when other garden flowers are sparse. Many varieties also espalier well—useful in small yards. Three particularly good sasanquas for training against walls or fences are 'Hana Jiman' and 'Setsugekka' (both white) and 'Showa-No-Sakae' (soft pink).

☐ **NATIVES.** Late fall is an excellent time to plant natives. If you've never grown them before, follow this advice from Valerie Phillips, nursery manager at Las Pilitas *(9–4 Mon–Sat; 8331 Nelson Way, Escondido; 760/749-5930),* a native-plant specialty nursery: Ease into it. Choose two or three species that will coexist with the plants already growing in your garden (for suggestions, see the article on page 332). Once you see how easy natives are, you'll want to grow more of them. Visit *www.bewaterwise.com,* sponsored by the Metropolitan Water District of Southern California, for data on and photos of 1,500 native and California-friendly plants.

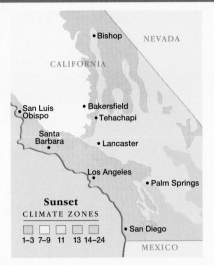

Sunset
CLIMATE ZONES
1–3 7–9 11 13 14–24

☐ **ONIONS AND GARLIC.** Plant onion seeds in early November for a late-spring harvest (or plant bare-root in January). Short-day varieties like 'Crystal Wax', 'Granex', and 'Grano' are best for Southern California. Use copper barriers to protect seedlings from snails and slugs. Separate garlic cloves and plant them base down 1 to 2 inches deep and 3 inches apart.

☐ **SEASONAL COLOR.** Plant African daisy, calendula, columbine, English daisy, foxglove, hollyhock, Iceland poppy, larkspur, linaria, lobelia, nemesia, pansy, *Schizanthus pinnatus,* snapdragon, stock, and viola. To keep blooms going, deadhead often and feed with half-strength liquid fertilizer every other week.

☐ **STRAWBERRIES.** To get lots of fruit rather than lots of foliage, plant strawberries during the first half of November; that's when professional growers plant. This time period gives fruit the optimum amount of winter chill. Plant strawberries a foot apart in rich, sandy soil and in full sun.

☐ **WILDFLOWERS.** Broadcast seeds of baby blue eyes, blue flax, California poppies, godetia, *Phacelia campanularia,* and other native wildflowers. Rake lightly to cover them slightly with soil, or walk over seed to press into ground. Keep soil moist until seeds germinate. Water with a sprinkler set on fine spray or use a garden hose with a mist nozzle.

MAINTENANCE

☐ **LIFT DAHLIAS.** Withhold water to let the plants go dormant. When foliage is mostly brown, cut off the stalks. If your soil drains well, you can leave tubers in the ground. Otherwise, lift them out carefully with a spade, brush off soil, and store them in vermiculite, sand, or shredded newspapers in a dry place. Tag them with variety names before storing.

☐ **PULL WEEDS.** Pull out annual bluegrass, chickweed, spurge, and other young weeds as they emerge. If not allowed to set seed, next year's weeding will be easier. To prevent weed seeds from germinating in lawns, apply a preemergence weed killer now. ◆

WHAT TO DO IN YOUR GARDEN IN NOVEMBER

PLANTING

☐ **FORCE BULBS.** When bulbs go on clearance, buy a few dozen extra crocuses, daffodils, grape hyacinths, hyacinths, or tulips for forcing. Choose containers that can spend the winter outside—recycled plastic nursery pots are ideal. Fill containers with potting soil and plant the bulbs with pointed sides up so the tips are just above the soil surface. Water and place the containers out of direct sunlight, in a dark, cold (33°–40°) location; water whenever the soil dries out. After 12 weeks, or when the bulbs begin to sprout, bring them into a cool, brightly lit room to bloom.

☐ **MAKE A CACTUS AND SUCCU-LENT DISH GARDEN.** Choose a low, wide container with a drainage hole, such as those sold for bonsai. Fill the container with a couple inches of potting soil formulated for succulents. Remove the plants from their containers (use kitchen tongs for cactus) and arrange them so rootballs are touching. Fill in around the rootballs with more soil. Mulch the surface between the plants with gravel, stone, or marbles. Place the dish in a sunny window and water once or twice a month.

☐ **START WILDFLOWERS FROM SEED.** Seeds of many perennial wildflowers need a period of moist chilling (called stratification) before they will germinate. Begin this process outdoors now. Following the directions

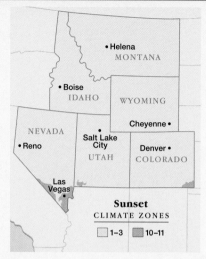

Sunset
CLIMATE ZONES

☐ 1–3   ☐ 10–11

on the package, sow seeds in plastic containers (with drainage holes) filled with potting soil. Place containers outside where they are open to the elements. Keep the soil moist; whenever snow is available, pile it on the pots. When seeds germinate in spring and true leaves emerge, transplant seedlings into individual containers and continue growing them outdoors until large enough to plant in the garden. A good source for wildflowers is Western Native Seed *(www.westernnativeseed. com or 719/942-3935).*

MAINTENANCE

☐ **MAKE A LATE-SEASON GARDEN ARRANGEMENT OUTDOORS.** As you clean up flower beds, save attractive stems with dried foliage and seed heads and arrange them in frostproof containers like half-barrels. Push branches of dried material into the soil. Good candidates include allium, coneflower, globe thistle, goldenrod, ornamental grasses, Joe Pye weed, sea holly, sedum, and Siberian iris. Add twigs of birch, rabbitbrush, and redtwig dogwood. For color, add rose canes with hips attached.

☐ **PREPARE PLANTING BEDS.** Before the ground freezes, till a 2- to 3-inch layer of composted manure or compost into beds so they'll be ready to plant when the soil warms in spring.

☐ **PROTECT PLANTS FROM DEER.** To prevent deer from damaging young trees and shrubs, surround them with cages formed from chicken wire or hardware mesh. Use stakes to hold cages in place.

☐ **PROTECT YOUNG TREES FROM SUNSCALD.** Trees with trunks less than 4 inches in diameter are vulnerable to sunscald, a damaging form of sunburn caused when the low winter sun shines on tender bark. Paint the trunks with white latex, or cover them with a commercial tree wrap.

☐ **RECYCLE POTTING SOIL.** As you clean out containers, toss dead annuals on the compost pile but dump the soil and any roots into a large plastic garbage can (drill a few small holes in the bottom for drainage). Leave can outside without a lid over the winter. The organic matter will compost and the soil will be ready to reuse next spring. —*Marcia Tatroe*

WHAT TO DO IN YOUR GARDEN IN NOVEMBER

PLANTING

☐ **COOL-SEASON FLOWERS.** *Sunset* climate zones 10–13 (Albuquerque, Las Vegas, Tucson, Phoenix): Set out transplants of ageratum, calendula, candytuft, coreopsis, dianthus, hollyhock, pansy, petunia, snapdragon, stock, and sweet alyssum. There's still time to sow seeds of nasturtium and sweet peas.

☐ **COOL-SEASON VEGGIES.** Zones 10–13: Sow seeds of beets, carrots, leeks, peas, radishes, rutabagas, salad greens, spinach, Swiss chard, and turnips. Set out transplants of artichoke, broccoli, brussels sprouts, cabbage, and cauliflower.

☐ **LANDSCAPE PLANTS.** Zones 10–13: Through midmonth, set out perennial color, including autumn sage *(Salvia greggii),* globe mallow *(Sphaeralcea* species), Mexican evening primrose *(Oenothera speciosa),* Mexican honeysuckle *(Justicia spicigera),* and penstemon. It's also an ideal time to plant woody shrubs and trees like acacia, carob *(Ceratonia siliqua),* creosote bush, mesquite, myrtle, rosewood *(Dalbergia sissoo), Senna (Cassia)* species, Texas olive *(Cordia boissieri),* and Texas ranger *(Leucophyllum* species).

☐ **SPRING-BLOOMING BULBS.** Consider bulbs that don't need deep winter chill to bloom well year after year. Try Afghani iris *(I. cycloglossa),* glory-of-the-snow *(Chionodoxa lucilae* 'Alba'), *Iris reticulata,* spring star

flower *(Ipheion uniflorum* 'Wisley Blue'), and species tulips *(Tulipa bakeri* 'Lilac Wonder', *T. clusiana, T. sylvestris).* All are available from High Country Gardens in Santa Fe *(www.highcountrygardens.com or 800/925-9387).*

MAINTENANCE

☐ **CARE FOR ROSES.** Zones 10–13: Remove faded flowers and feed with a complete fertilizer for the last time this year; water well. Spread a 4-inch layer of compost beneath the bushes.

☐ **CONTROL PESTS.** Blast aphids off plants and vegetables with a jet of water from the hose, or spray with insecticidal soap. Watch for beetles, cabbage loopers, and harlequin bugs (half-inch, brick red to yellowish with black masklike markings); remove them by hand.

☐ **PREPARE FOR FIRST FROST.** When frost is forecast in your area, move container plants to protected locations, such as under trees or overhanging structures. Cover the tips of exotic cactus and succulents with frost blanket or triple-layered paper bags tied on with twine. For warmth, hang a light bulb or a string of Christmas lights in the center of young citrus trees and cover the canopy with old sheets. Protect the tender trunks of newly planted trees by wrapping them loosely with several layers of burlap, cardboard, or newspaper. Cover recent transplants with row covers.

☐ **PRUNE WOODY HERBS.** Zones 11–13: Cut back marjoram, oregano, rosemary, sage, and thyme to reduce woodiness and stimulate fresh, green growth. Prune down to the lowest new growth and remove all dead wood. Dry the cut foliage and store in airtight containers for culinary use.
—*Kim Nelson*

MAP: DEBRA LAMBERT

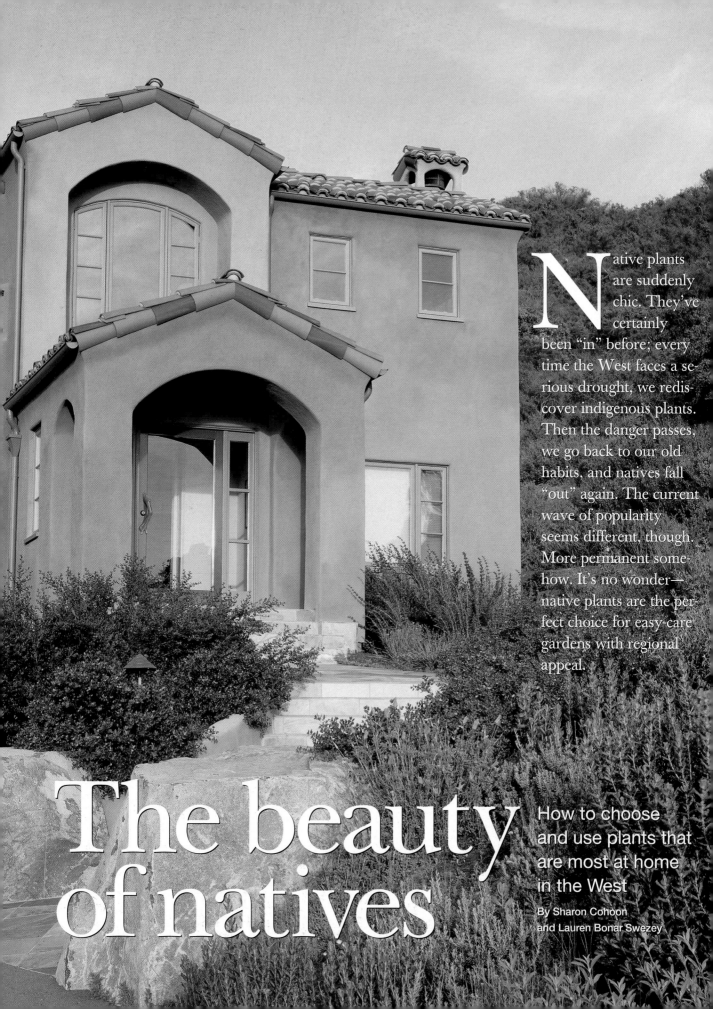

Native plants are suddenly chic. They've certainly been "in" before; every time the West faces a serious drought, we rediscover indigenous plants. Then the danger passes, we go back to our old habits, and natives fall "out" again. The current wave of popularity seems different, though. More permanent somehow. It's no wonder—native plants are the perfect choice for easy-care gardens with regional appeal.

The beauty of natives

How to choose and use plants that are most at home in the West

By Sharon Cohoon and Lauren Bonar Swezey

Golden blooms cover flannel bush *(Fremontodendron)*, a native California shrub, in spring. A front garden in Vista, CA (left), mixes native shrubs such as mimulus, woolly blue curls, and *Arctostaphylos* 'Sunset'. **DESIGN:** Greg Rubin, Escondido, CA *(760/746-6870)*.

A Paradise Valley, AZ,
garden mixes agaves and
cactus with desert marigold
and a palo verde tree.
DESIGN: Marcus Bollinger,
Phoenix (602/619-5245)

Growing natives doesn't have to be an all-or-nothing proposition; you can have sagebrush and a patch of lawn too, just not side by side. Here are ways to incorporate natives into your landscape. Consult the *Sunset Western Garden Book* for climate zones and more ideas suited to your area.

PERIMETER PLANTS. Plant natives that have low irrigation needs, like brittlebush or ceanothus, on the edges of your property, then spend your water on a more oasis-like planting closer to the house. Or, if you have a wilderness view, use some of the same plants that grow naturally nearby on your property's borders.

PROBLEM-SOLVERS. Some natives solve common landscape problems. To help stabilize slopes, try mahonia, manzanita, *Ribes,* or sumac. For dry shade, consider bush anemone, Pacific Coast iris, or Western sword fern. Where resistance to oak root fungus is needed, try bush anemone, Catalina cherry, or spice bush. Near windy coasts, where salt spray is a problem, use coyote brush or lemonade berry.

WATER-TOLERANT NATIVES. Some natives will not tolerate summer water at all (flannel bush is notorious for this). But many others happily adapt to a regular garden irrigation regime: coral bells, monkey flowers, wild strawberry, Western columbine, and wild ginger are examples. Match the plant's water needs to the conditions in each part of your garden.

MEDITERRANEAN MATES. Western natives and Mediterranean plants like similar growing conditions, but many Mediterraneans tend to bloom later than natives—late spring and summer. Combining the two gives you a longer season of interest.

Vine maple, native to moist Northwest woods, glows like embers in fall.

Why natives?

They look Western. Many people in the West have grown up with hikes in the hills and summer camp-outs, and we want our gardens to be extensions of those adventures. Instead of copying English cottage gardens, we want our own little bit of wilderness.

Many natives smell like the Wild West. Cleveland and white sage, creosote bush and brittlebush, pine and redwood, for instance, are filled with resins and release their scents on warm afternoons. Think of it as free aromatherapy.

They can attract wildlife. Birds and butterflies are at home in native plant gardens because many of the plants are rich in nectar or seed. Homeowners who grow these plants are used to hearing comments like "Why does your garden get all the birds in the neighborhood?" Children who grow up in these gardens learn to be curious about insects and lizards instead of fearful. It's like having a life-science lab in your backyard.

They're low-maintenance. Don't bother amending the soil—natives are adapted to it. Forget fertilizer; they rarely need it.

Planting tips

Follow these guidelines to ensure that native plants will thrive.

Plant at the right time. *In mild-winter climates:* You can plant natives any time of the year, but the best time is fall through early spring, when cool and rainy weather allows plants to establish themselves more easily. *In cold-winter climates:* Plant in early fall, stopping six weeks before the ground freezes, or in spring after the ground thaws (after last frost for tender plants).

Check soil drainage. Many natives need well-drained soil. Before planting, test the soil by digging a hole (ideally 2 ft. deep) and filling it with water. After it drains, fill it again; if the soil drains slowly the second time (taking an hour or more), plant in raised beds or use plants suitable for heavy soil.

Forget soil amendments. In most areas, there's no need to add amendments such as compost to the soil at planting time. Set the plant in a planting hole and backfill with native soil. If the topsoil has been scraped off or the soil is compacted, replace ⅓ of the native soil with well-composted organic matter.

Water carefully. All native plants need regular water the first season. If rain is sparse, water deeply once a week (less often on the coast, more often in the desert or in sandy soil) to encourage deep rooting. Slowly reduce watering frequency as plants become established. ◆

Desert beard tongue *(Penstemon pseudospectabilis),* a shrubby, upright plant to 4 feet tall with rosy pink flowers, is one of many penstemons native to various parts of the West.

Pacific Northwest natives to plant

Native plants are wise additions to Northwest gardens. The eight examples pictured on this page are naturally suited to the climate; all bear showy blooms or lush and lovely foliage. And when water is scarce, many kinds can survive on little more than rainfall. Just give them what they need—the right exposure, and well-drained soil—and they'll thrive. If you start with nursery-raised plants, remember that even drought-tolerant natives need to be watered during the dry season for a year or two until they're established.

Lewisia
(Lewisia cotyledon)
1 foot tall, 10 inches wide. Clusters of white or pink flowers often striped rose or red. Plant where drainage is perfect (as in a rockery or wall); little or no extra water. Climate zones 1–7, 17.

Mahonia
Two evergreen species spread by underground stems; both have early-spring flowers followed by berries loved by birds. *M. aquifolium* grows 6 feet tall. Zones 2–7, 17. *M. nervosa* grows 2 feet tall. Shade; little or no extra water. Zones 2B–7, 17.

Pacific Coast iris
(Iris douglasiana and others). 1 to 2 feet tall. Many hybrids with spring-blooming flowers in various colors, including blue, copper, pink, and white. Partial shade (sun on coast); little to moderate water. Zones 4–7, 17.

Redtwig dogwood
(Cornus stolonifera)
Deciduous shrub; 7 to 9 feet tall, 12 feet wide. Red fall foliage and winter stems. Spreads by creeping underground stems. Partial shade; regular water. Zones A1–A3; 1–7, 17.

Vine maple
(Acer circinatum)
5 to 35 feet tall. One or multiple trunks; leaves start turning red tinged with orange or yellow as early as midsummer. Partial shade (can take full sun with regular water). Zones A3; 2B–6, 17.

Western azalea
(Rhododendron occidentale)
6 to 10 feet tall. In late spring, the plant is covered with fragrant white or pinkish white flowers with yellow blotch. Moderate water helps bloom, but sparing summer water is fine. Zones 4–7, 17.

Western columbine
(Aquilegia formosa)
Perennial; $1^{1}/_{2}$ to 3 feet tall, $1^{1}/_{2}$ feet wide. 2-inch red and yellow flowers. Seeds relished by many small songbirds. Partial shade; regular water. Zones A1–A3; 1–7, 17.

Western sword fern
(Polystichum munitum)
2 to 4 feet tall. Classic mounds of sword-shaped, dark green fronds. Partial to full shade; little water. Zones A3; 2–7, 17.

—*Jim McCausland*

California natives to plant

Native plants are wise additions to California gardens. The nine beauties pictured here are naturally suited to our rainy-winter, dry-summer climate. And where water is scarce, they're especially appropriate; most of them can thrive on rainfall alone. Some attract butter- flies or hummingbirds. Just give the plants what they need—the right exposure and well-drained soil. If you start with nursery-raised plants, remember that even drought-tolerant natives need to be watered during the dry season for a year or two until they're established.

Bush anemone
(Carpenteria californica)
Evergreen; 4 to 6 feet tall. Clusters of scented white flowers with yellow centers in late spring and summer; dark green leaves. Shade to sun; little to moderate water. Climate zones 7–9, 14–24.

California fuchsia
(Zauschneria californica)
1 to 2 feet tall. Orange- red flowers in late sum- mer and fall; grayish leaves. *Z. c. latifolia* 'Everett's Choice' has broad green leaves. Partial shade to sun; little water. Zones 2, 3, 7–9, 11, 14–24.

Ceanothus
Many kinds, from groundcovers to small trees. Blue or white flowers in winter or spring. Most prefer sun. Little to no water. Zones 7–9, 14–24 (with some exceptions). *C.* 'Blue Jeans', tolerates summer watering.

Cleveland sage
(Salvia clevelandii)
Evergreen; 3 to 5 feet tall. Whorls of 1-inch- long flowers in sum- mer; gray-green leaves. 'Winnifred Gilman' has dark blue flowers. Sun; little water. Zones 8, 9, 12–24.

Coral bells
(Heuchera). 1 to 2 feet tall. Small white or pink flowers on 1$\frac{1}{2}$- to 3- foot-tall stems in spring. *H. micrantha* 'Palace Purple' has purple leaves; *H. maxima* makes a good ground- cover. Partial to full shade; moderate to reg- ular water. Zones vary.

Matilija poppy
(Romneya coulteri)
6 to 8 feet tall. 9-inch- wide white flowers with yellow centers appear late spring into summer. Spread by underground runners; dig and discard unwanted clumps. Little to no water. Zones 7–9, 14–24; H1.

Scarlet monkey flower
(Mimulus cardinalis)
2$\frac{1}{2}$ feet tall. 1$\frac{1}{2}$- to 2-inch-long tubular, scarlet flowers in summer; sticky green leaves. Sun or shade; regular water. Zones 2, 3, 7–9, 11, 13–24.

Woolly blue curls
(Trichostema lanatum)
Evergreen; 3 to 5 feet tall. Blue flowers on long stalks appear in spring to early fall; narrow green leaves. Little to no water. Zones 14–24.

Rocky Mountain natives to plant

Native plants are wise additions to gardens in the Rocky Mountain region. The eight species pictured on this page are naturally suited to the cold-winter, short-summer climates in Colorado, Idaho, Montana, Utah, and Wyoming. Many of their flowers attract butter-flies or hummingbirds—or both. Many of them thrive on rainfall alone. Plant them in spring; if you start with nursery-raised plants, remember that even drought-tolerant natives need to be watered during the dry season for a year or two until they're established.

Blue flax
(Linum lewisii)
1½ feet tall and wide. Blue flowers in spring. Sun to partial shade; little water. Climate zones 1–3.

Butterfly weed
(Asclepias tuberosa)
1½ to 3 feet tall, 2 feet wide. Orange flowers in summer. Attracts masses of butterflies. Needs good drainage. Sun; moderate water. Zones 1–3, 10, 11.

Dotted gayfeather
(Liatris punctata)
6 inches to 3 feet tall and equally wide. Pur-plish pink flower spikes in late summer. Sun; little water. Zones 1–3.

Mountain spray
(Holodiscus dumosus)
Deciduous shrub; 3 to 6 feet tall and as wide. Creamy white flowers in summer. Partial shade; little to regular water. Zones 1–3, 10.

Prairie smoke
(Geum triflorum)
Mounding perennial; 20 inches tall and wide. Maroon flowers in spring. Sun to partial shade; little water. Zones 1–3.

Rocky Mountain columbine
(Aquilegia caerulea)
1½ to 3 feet tall, 2 feet wide. Blue and white flowers in spring. Sun to partial shade; regular water. Zones 1–3, 10, 11.

Small-flowered penstemon
(P. procerus)
1 foot tall and wide. Bluish purple flowers in late spring. Partial shade; moderate water. Zones 1–3.

Tufted evening primrose
(Oenothera caespitosa)
8 to 12 inches tall, 2 feet wide. Fragrant white flowers all sum-mer. Sun; little water. Zones 1–3, 10, 11.

—*Marcia Tatroe*

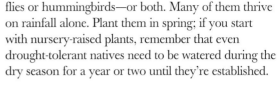

Southwest natives to plant

Native plants are wise additions to Southwest gardens. The nine species pictured on these pages are naturally suited to the desert climate, where heat and aridity prevail. Most bear showy blooms. And when water is scarce, all are appropriate (and thrifty) choices, since they survive on nothing more than rainfall. Just give them what they need—sun and well-drained soil—and they'll thrive. If you start with nursery-raised plants, remember that even drought-tolerant natives need to be watered during the dry season for a year or two until they're established.

Angelita daisy
(Tetraneuris acaulis)
8 inches tall, 1 foot wide. Yellow flowers during warm months. Sun; little to moderate water. Climate zones 1–3, 10–13.

Blackfoot daisy
(Melampodium leucanthum)
1 foot tall and wide. Fragrant white daisies during winter in mild climates, spring and summer in cold areas. Sun; little water. Zones 2, 3, 10–13.

Brittlebush
(Encelia farinosa)
Deciduous shrub; 3 feet tall, 4 feet wide. Has silvery, woolly leaves; yellow daisies with brown centers in spring. Sun; little or no water. Zones 10–13.

Desert marigold
(Baileya multiradiata)
$1\frac{1}{2}$ feet tall, 2 feet wide. Bright yellow flowers appear spring through fall or longer. Annual or perennial. Sun; moderate water. Zones 1–3, 10–13.

Mexican hat
(Ratibida columnifera)
$2\frac{1}{2}$ feet tall, 1 foot wide. Flowers resemble sombreros with drooping yellow rays around conical centers all summer. Sun; little to moderate water. All zones.

Verbena gooddingii
$1\frac{1}{2}$ to 2 feet tall, 3 to 4 feet wide. Pinkish lavender flowers in summer. Sun; little water. Zones 10–13.

Woolly butterfly bush
(Buddleja marrubiifolia)
Evergreen shrub; 5 feet tall and wide. Has soft, silvery foliage; orange flower clusters appear in spring and summer. Sun; little water. Zones 10–13.

Yellow bells
(Tecoma stans angustata)
4 to 10 feet tall, 3 to 8 feet wide. Deciduous shrub has bright green, finely divided leaves; trumpet-shaped, yellow flowers from midspring to late fall. Sun; little to moderate water. Zones 12, 13. —*Dick Bushnell*

Girl power

An all-female gardening team shares secrets for keeping plantings beautiful year-round

By Debra Lee Baldwin
Photographs by Claire Curran

Sisters Brenda Gousha and Barbara McFadden founded their landscaping business six years ago with the mission to create and maintain flower gardens in Southern California's Rancho Santa Fe area. Gousha, who has a degree in ornamental horticulture, and McFadden, a Master Gardener, pooled their talents to select their clients' plants, position them, and keep the beds and borders looking beautiful. They called their business Sisters Specialty Gardens.

Making the rounds of high-end homes is nothing new to the sisters; as kids, they tagged along with their father, who cofounded San Diego's Weir Bros Custom Homes. As demand for Gousha and McFadden's services increased, they sought additional help, recruiting Patrice Longmire, an honorary sister with a great eye for floral design.

Most of their clients want year-round flower color, lush greenery, and

Pansies, nemesias in white, pink, and blue, and red penstemons border the path. Star jasmine climbs the wall.

Cloaking the dry slope are lavender, pride of Madeira, salvias, and pink society garlic. Below: Gardening sisters Barbara McFadden (left), Brenda Gousha (right), and Patrice Longmire.

Grooming and tools

Groom plants often. When cutting back perennials and annuals to clear sidewalks or paths, trim the plants at a 45° angle (cutting downward toward the path's edge), rather than perpendicular to the ground. "It looks better," Longmire says.

Use the right tools. Matching the tool to the job eases garden chores. Each woman has her preference.

Longmire: "A small hand rake from Smith & Hawken. It lets you maneuver under shrubs to clear leaves and debris." *(Gardena Hand Rake: 800/981-9888 or www.smithandhawken.com)*

McFadden: "A French pruning knife for weeding. It has a hooked blade—perfect for getting at roots." *(Bahco P20 pruning knife: Rittenhouse, www.rittenhouse.ca or 877/488-1914)*

Gousha: "Joyce Chen garden scissors [pictured above]. They have long, tapered blades, which make cutting flowers quick and easy." *("Unlimited" Garden Scissors: www.joycechen. com or 812/238-5000)*

no bare spots or dead blooms. Such perfection takes time, effort, and gardening savvy, so it's not surprising that the women learned to streamline their techniques for garden design and maintenance. Follow their guidelines in your own garden and you can't go wrong.

Design tips for gardeners

Use perennials as backbones, annuals as fillers. Sisters Specialty Gardens uses flowering shrubs and perennials as mainstays in beds and borders, filling in around them with annuals for quick and easy color. The pathway pictured on the previous page, for example, is accented by flowering shrubs such as *Westringia fruticosa* 'Morning Light' and deep purple butterfly bush *(Buddleja davidii)*. There are also white 'Iceberg' roses, penstemons *(P. x gloxinioides),* and dwarf *Agapanthus* 'Peter Pan'. Annual nemesias in white, pink, and blue border the path, where they can be easily reached and swapped out. "Annuals bloom for six months and can be replaced at minimal cost," Gousha explains. Low, mounding chamomile and creeping thymes grow between the nemesias.

Choose easy-care plants wherever possible. For the hot, dry slope pictured above, Sisters mixes

tough, unthirsty perennials, mostly in purples, pinks, and grays. Among them: *Armeria maritima,* with globular pink flowers; *Artemisia* 'Powis Castle', with silvery foliage; purple bearded iris; lavender *(Lavandula dentata, L. x intermedia);* pride of Madeira *(Echium candicans),* with blue-purple flower spikes; salvias; Santa Barbara daisy *(Erigeron karvinskianus),* with white, daisylike flowers; *Santolina chamaecyparissus,* with yellow, buttonlike blooms; society garlic *(Tulbaghia violacea),* with pale lavender-pink blooms; and yarrow *(Achillea millefolium).* Horizontal pathways and rock walls help hold the slope.

Tuck in flowers for cutting. To bring the beauty of the garden indoors, Sisters finds places to

Scotch moss covers bare soil around these violas. The wire container is lined with sphagnum moss and filled with soil; cinerarias surround it.

add cutting flowers for use in bouquets. Against a trellis beside a driveway in one garden, the women planted sweet peas that bloom from mid-January or early February into May, depending on the weather. "In spring, we harvest often," Longmire says. "The more you pick and deadhead, the longer the plants produce flowers." McFadden adds: "A simple jar or white earthenware pitcher is perfect for displaying them." Sisters starts sweet peas in midfall, sowing seeds about 2 inches apart in well-prepared soil.

Plant seasonal color in pots. To brighten entries and soften hardscapes such as patios and poolsides, the women fill pots and bowls with annuals twice a year: in October for fall through spring color, and in May for summer color.

They combine two or three different types of plants per pot ("Less is more," Gousha says). Johnny jump-ups, pansies, and violas in shades of purple and violet might fill pots during the cool season. In May, they're replaced with warm-season bloomers such as white African daisies (*Osteospermum* Symphony Series), lavender bacopa, pale pink geraniums, hot pink million bells (*Calibrachoa* hybrids), and blue and white nemesias.

Before planting, Sisters fills pots with four parts potting soil to one part worm castings (available at nurseries). To achieve fullness fast, they pack the pots with plants—a flat of 4-inch annuals (16 plants total) for a 2-foot-diameter pot, for instance. Plants get water as needed (about once a week in winter, twice weekly in summer) and are fed every two weeks with liquid fertilizer.

Cover bare soil. Nothing makes a planting look unfinished or immature like bare soil around it. Sisters lays lime-colored Scotch moss (*Sagina subulata*) over the soil beneath potted topiaries or other plants in containers (such as the violas pictured above). A blanket of moss lends a weathered, Old World appeal to pots. Use a knife to cut pieces of moss from nursery flats, trimming them to fit your container. Moss needs regular watering and occasional feeding with liquid fertilizer.

Sisters Specialty Gardens: (760) 473-0234. ◆

2 easy ideas

Raise pots on posts. Place bowls filled with cascading plants on stone pedestals. The pot pictured at top contains lime green sweet potato vine (*Ipomoea batatas* 'Marguerite') and *Helichrysum petiolare* 'Variegatum'.

Train vines on walls. Star jasmine, trained into a diamond pattern, spreads a green tapestry across an 8-foot-tall, 10-foot-long stucco wall above a trickling fountain in the garden pictured above. The vines grow from planting pockets on either side of the fountain and spread along stainless steel wire attached to eye screws in the wall.

Green ash shows off its golden fall canopy in a Colorado yard.

Really fast trees

These 15 speedsters sprout 2 to 4 feet in a single year

By Jim McCausland
Illustrations by Mimi Osborne

At *Sunset's* annual Celebration Weekend, visitors often ask our garden staff: "Can you recommend a tree that grows really fast?" With that in mind, we figured there were many readers who might have the same question. So we talked with arborists and horticulturists to learn about the pros and cons of fast-growing trees for each region in the West. The chart on the facing page can help you find a good tree for your garden. Most

trees grow fastest when they're young, then slow down as they mature. In mild areas of the West, plant early this month; in cold-winter areas, wait until the ground thaws in early spring.

Throughout the year, nurseries offer balled-and-burlapped or container-grown stock. In late winter or early spring, they may offer bare-root stock (trees without any soil around the roots); these are cheaper and usually adapt faster to native soil.

15 trees for rapid results

These trees are deciduous unless noted. Expect them to grow about 2 feet per year or more as noted. However, growth rates can vary from zone to zone and garden to garden. Zones (below) refer to *Sunset* climate zones, which are detailed in the *Western Garden Book*.

Common name (Botanical name)	Height/width	Zones	Characteristics
'Accolade' elm (*Ulmus* x 'Accolade')	70 ft./45 ft.	2A–9, 14–21	Dark, shiny leaves. Can grow 3 ft. per year. Shows resistance to Dutch elm disease and elm scale.
Beefwood, or she-oak (*Casuarina stricta*)	20–35 ft./20–35 ft.	8, 9, 12–24; H1, H2	Evergreen. Attractive silhouette, with fine-textured branches like pine needles. *C. cunninghamiana* (often sold as *C. stricta*) reaches 70 ft. tall, 30 ft. wide.
Cajeput tree, or paperbark tree (*Melaleuca quinquenervia*)	20–40 ft./15–25 ft.	9, 12, 13, 15–17, 20–24	Evergreen. Yellowish, pink, or purple flowers in summer and fall. White or tan bark peels off in sheets. Needs little water. Not invasive in California or Arizona.
Catalpa (*C. speciosa*)	40–60 ft./20–40 ft.	2–24	White, trumpet-shaped flowers come in late spring and summer over big, heart-shaped leaves. Grows fastest in mild climates. Brittle wood; aggressive roots.
Chitalpa (x *C. tashkentensis*)	20–30 ft./20–30 ft.	3–24	Pink, lavender, or white flowers appear from spring to fall. Susceptible to verticillium wilt in cool climates.
Desert willow (*Chilopsis linearis*)	15–30 ft./10–20 ft.	3B, 7–14, 18–23	Orchidlike burgundy to white flowers appear all summer among willowy leaves. Grows 3 ft. per year. Seedpods hang on through winter and can look messy.
Empress tree (*Paulownia tomentosa*)	50 ft./40 ft.	4–9, 11–24	Fragrant, trumpet-shaped purple flowers appear in spring, followed by large, heart-shaped leaves. Can grow 4 ft. per year with good soil, water, plenty of sun.
Gold medallion tree (*Cassia leptophylla*)	20–25 ft./30 ft.	15, 16, 20–24; H1, H2	Nearly evergreen. Fast, shapely growth if pruned to a single trunk; otherwise low, spreading form. Deep yellow flower spikes bloom heavily in summer.
Green ash (*Fraxinus pennsylvanica*)	30–40 ft./30–40 ft.	A2, A3; 1–6	'Marshall', 'Patmore', 'Prairie Spire' are best bets for intermountain zones. Good leafy shade trees; some have yellow or bronze fall color. Needs regular water.
Honey locust (*Gleditsia triacanthos*)	35–70 ft./25–35 ft.	1–16, 18–20	Airy, fernlike foliage, but trunk is thorny and seedpods are messy. Choose the pyramidal 'Skyline' or upright 'Shademaster', both of which grow 3–4 ft. per year.
Nichol's willow-leafed peppermint (*Eucalyptus nicholii*)	36–48 ft./15–36 ft.	5, 6, 8–24; H1, H2	Evergreen. Graceful, open form with reddish brown bark. Narrow leaves that exude peppermint scent when crushed. Hardy enough for coastal Northwest.
Peppermint tree (*Agonis flexuosa*)	25–35 ft./15–30 ft.	15–17, 20–24	Evergreen. Willowy leaves smell like peppermint when crushed. Abundant white flowers come in late spring. Spreading form; prune to maintain pleasing look.
Plains cottonwood (*Populus sargentii*)	80 ft./50–60 ft.	1–4, 6, 7, 10	Can grow 3 ft. per year in youth. Pyramidal when young, rounded with age. Keep its invasive roots away from sewage and water lines.
Purple-leaf acacia (*A. baileyana* 'Purpurea')	20–30 ft./20–30 ft.	8, 9, 13–24	Feathery leaves turn from purplish to blue-gray as they age. A profusion of yellow flowers appears from early to midwinter. Needs little water.
Silk tree, or mimosa (*Albizia julibrissin*)	40 ft./80 ft.	4–23	Pink powder-puff flowers appear in summer among finely cut leaves. Brittle branches break in snow. Needs regular water for fast growth.

MINIATURE WHITE LIGHTS sparkle on the venerable olive trees at *Sunset*'s Menlo Park, California, headquarters. For ideas on how to make a splash with holiday lights in your garden, see pages 362–364.

December

Hydrangea basics

Exposure: Full sun on the coast; partial shade where afternoons are hot.

Soil: Rich, porous soil; lighten heavy clay soils by mixing in compost or peat moss.

Water: Irrigate plants regularly during the growing season; established plants can get by on less water in coastal areas.

Pruning: To control plant size and shape, prune in winter in mild climates. Cut stems back to the strongest pair of new shoots.

To air-dry the blooms: Cut off several whole flower heads when blossoms are fully open and still fresh. Put the stems in a small vase with about 2 inches of water in the bottom. As the water evaporates, flowers will begin to dry, turning a pale lime green in the process. When they have fully dried (in several weeks), snip individual blossoms from flower heads to cluster in small vases.

A new star for the tabletop

Forced into flower for the holidays, snow-white hydrangeas make perfect companions for red poinsettias and evergreens. Now a new lace cap variety offers a dainty alternative to hydrangeas with solid clusters of blossoms. 'Shooting Star' bears double flowers, each shaped like a star within a star. They keep their white color four to six weeks before maturing to a greenish hue, and you'll be glad to know that their sterile flowers won't sprinkle pollen on your furniture or the floor.

Look for 'Shooting Star' hydrangeas in bloom (mostly in 6-inch pots) at supermarkets and garden centers around the West. During the holidays, keep plants in a cool spot where they'll get plenty of light. Water whenever the top $1/2$ inch of soil dries out. As flowers fade, snip them off.

You can save these hydrangeas to grow outdoors in *Sunset* climate zones 3B–7 and 17. After frost danger is past, transplant them to rich, porous soil in a location that gets partial shade. Water plants regularly and fertilize when new growth emerges. In the garden, these deciduous shrubs can reach 5 to 6 feet tall and wide.

—Jim McCausland

Creamy centers are backed by solid dark pink bracts up to 12 inches across.

A poinsettia with a splash of cream

An astounding 80 percent of the poinsettias sold around the world are grown in the greenhouses of Paul Ecke Ranch in Encinitas, California. The late Paul Ecke Jr., the firm's second president, is the man responsible for turning this Mexican native flower into a global gift plant. Most recently, Ecke was the champion of a new selection called 'Strawberries and Cream' (shown here). Ecke, who passed away last year, loved this hybrid and was sure consumers would too, despite misgivings from some of his staff.

People either loved or hated this plant, says Laurie Scullin, the firm's director of marketing. The hybrid's strong coloring—dark pink outer bracts with a sharply contrasting cream interior—provoked the equally strong reactions.

Customer reaction has validated Ecke's faith. 'Strawberries and Cream' sold well in trial markets last year, so it will be widely available in nurseries and floral sections of supermarkets this year. Ecke would have been pleased, says Scullin, "but he wouldn't have been surprised." —*Sharon Cohoon*

Global guide to plants

Reflecting the fact that horticulture has become a global industry, an Australian publisher recently teamed up with regional publishers in Canada, the United States, and other countries to produce the most comprehensive pictorial encyclopedia of plants from around the world. *Flora: A Gardener's Encyclopedia* (Timber Press, Portland, 2003; $100; www.timberpress.com or 800/327-5680), a 1,584-page two-volume set, lists more than 20,000 plants and is copiously illustrated with more than 12,000 color photographs.

Flora benefits from the input of its chief consultant, Sean Hogan, a Portland-based horticulturist who brought his expertise to bear on the plant listings, which include a strong selection of Western natives.

The first edition of *Flora* comes with a CD-ROM that lets you search for plants by USDA hardiness zone, height, uses, exposure, flower color, and bloom season. —*J. M.*

Deck the wall with fresh-cut greens

Giving outdoor walls a festive look for the holidays is just as easy as gathering greens from your own garden. Here we show a striking arrangement made with prunings from golden juniper, deodar cedar, and cotoneaster.

To hold the display, we used a flat-backed terra-cotta wall planter (8 inches deep and 16 inches wide) that cost about $25. The planter is securely mounted to a stucco wall with masonry screws. The greens are simply tucked in the empty planter. For a strong vertical punch, we placed several 18- to 24-inch-long stems of gold-tipped juniper in the upright position at the rear. As a horizontal accent, we added a few 14- to 18-inch-long boughs of deodar cedar. We finished off with sprigs of berry-laden cotoneaster.

Even without water, the prunings lasted well over a week.

—*Julie Chai*

Light-draped boulders form a cool stream that glows at night.

Top-rated perennials for the Rockies

A new publication provides valuable guidance for mountain gardeners. *Best Perennials for the Rocky Mountains and High Plains,* by Celia Tannehill and James E. Klett (Colorado State University Cooperative Extension, Bulletin 573A, Fort Collins, CO, 2002; $20; www.cerc. colostate.edu or 877/692-9358), is an encyclopedic list of more than 100 perennials and 10 ornamental grasses that have excelled in the test gardens of Colorado State University at Fort Collins.

The authors detail each plant's uses, growth habit, and cultural needs. You'll find some uncommon but gardenworthy perennials among them, such as crested gentian (*Gentiana septemfida*), a blue, midsummer bloomer. Color photographs illustrate many of the plants (but many of the images could be sharper and brighter). An appendix charts the bloom time and color of the flowering plants. —*Marcia Tatroe*

A river of lights in Tucson

The secret to illuminating a garden for the holidays is letting the landscape dictate the lighting design, says Sean Danks of Desert Custom Lighting. Elizabeth and Marty Ryan's Tucson yard, shown above, illustrates his technique beautifully.

A "stream" of boulders runs from the house to the driveway's end. Danks simply draped the rocks with strands of blue outdoor lights to create the effect of flowing water at night.

The stream sweeps past a mature palo verde. Danks trimmed it with green lights to remind viewers of the tree's greenish bark. Nearby, he wrapped a pair of barrel cactus with plenty of lights so viewers can "see the shape of the whole plant." Atop each cactus, he created the effect of night-blooming flowers by bundling clusters of white lights with twist ties.
DESIGN: Desert Custom Lighting, Tucson *(520/400-7835)* —*S.C.*

Terra-cotta pots come in many shapes and sizes at Dig.

Dig it in Del Mar

Antique olive jars from Turkey. Stone urns and terra-cotta pots from Italy. Handblown hummingbird feeders. You'll find all this and more at Dig—John and Kim Kelly's garden boutique in Del Mar. "We sell houseplants, but we're not a nursery," John says. "We sell our own line of English-made tools, but we're not a garden supply store." Southern Californians who see a garden as yet another room to accessorize will find plenty of items from which to choose, ranging from potpourri sold in bulk ($2 per ounce) to a 20-inch-diameter stone urn from England ($2,000). Some inventory changes seasonally—from furniture and patio umbrellas in summer to bulbs and wreaths of dried materials (made to order) in fall and garlands in winter. Pottery is available year-round. *In Flower Hill Mall, 2690 Via de la Valle, Del Mar; (858) 481-3478.* —*Debra Lee Baldwin*

Fresno's festival of lights

The soft light of 3,000 luminarias (candles set in paper bags with sand in the bottom), Christmas carols around the campfire, hot cider, and winter's best flowers and vegetables combine for a magical evening at the Garden of the Sun and Discovery Center's Noche de las Luminarias in early December.

During the event, you can stroll along candlelit paths through the 1½-acre Garden of the Sun, which includes an All-America Selections demonstration garden, an orchard, an herb garden, and a perennial garden, all maintained by UC Cooperative Extension Master Gardeners. Next door at the Discovery Center—a hands-on children's science and discovery museum—visitors can meander through the 5½-acre landscape, which includes a cactus garden set aglow by dozens of luminarias. There are activities for kids as well.

Noche de las Luminarias benefits the Discovery Center and the Master Gardeners. 6–9:30 P.M.; $6 for adults, $3 ages 12 and under (2003 information). 1944 N. Winery Ave.; http://mgfresno.ucdavis.edu or (559) 456-7285.—Lance Walheim

Bookshelf

Award-winning books. Any of these books, which have won awards from the Garden Writers Association, would make a fine holiday gift for a gardening friend. *Amaryllis,* by Starr Ockenga (Clarkson Potter/Publishers, New York, 2002; $20; 866/726-3661), was named Best Book of the Year in 2002 and includes the history and care of amaryllis, plus gorgeous photography by the author. *Gardens for the Soul,* written by Pamela Woods and photographed by John Glover (Rizzoli, New York, 2002; $35; 800/522-6657), shows how to create a garden that reflects your spiritual beliefs. *The Grape Grower: A Guide to Organic Viticulture,* by Lon Rombough (Chelsea Green Publishing, White River Junction, Vermont, 2002; $35; www. chelseagreen.com or 800/ 639-4099), is a must for anyone interested in growing grapes organically. *Melons for the Passionate Grower,* by Amy Goldman (Artisan, New York, 2002; $25; 800/722-7202), focuses on heirloom varieties and how to grow them. Victor Schrager's photographs are stunning.

Clipping

FREE TREES. If you are a Los Angeles Department of Water and Power customer, you are eligible to receive up to seven free 5-gallon shade trees for your home through the LADWP's Trees for a Green L.A. program *(www.greenla.com or 800/473-3652).*

BACK TO BASICS

Prune for swags and boughs

When you cut winter greens for decorating, keep proper pruning principles in mind so you won't harm or disfigure plants. Use sharp shears, and make each cut just beyond a side branch and just outside the branch bark ridges; don't leave stubs. Starting at the bottom of the plant, trim off branches from the inside out, so you don't destroy its overall shape.

Some good choices for decorating: Douglas fir, evergreen magnolia, fir, holly, holly-leaf osmanthus, juniper, pine, and redwood. —*J. M. and Lauren Bonar Swezey*

Control moss and algae

Brick, concrete, and other paved surfaces in moist, shady areas are often susceptible to moss or algae growth, which can be very slippery. The best cure is prevention: Improve air circulation and light above the paved surface by pruning up overhanging branches. If moss or algae is already established, rent a pressure washer from an equipment rental yard and blast off the growth. Or apply an environmentally safe product *(such as Safer Moss & Algae Killer & Surface Cleaner, $15; available from garden centers or Biocontrol Network, www.biconet.com or 800/441-2847)* to eliminate the problem. —*L. B. S.*

'Fanny'

'Fire Cracker'

'Fool's Gold'

'Bandera'

Bromeliads sizzle with color

Intensely colored bromeliads are ideal houseplants—they thrive on neglect, yet their blooms typically last 8 to 12 weeks. Plus, their leaves provide year-round appeal. These variegated *Guzmania* bromeliads, which grow from 1½ to 2 feet tall, can be found at nurseries and at home and garden stores.

'Bandera': White and green leaves; orange-red flower. **'Candycane'** (not shown): White and green leaves that turn pink toward the center; red flower. **'Fanny'**: White and green leaves with a pinkish tinge; reddish purple flower. **'Fire Cracker'**: White, green, and red leaves; dark red flower. **'Fool's Gold'**: Creamy white and green leaves; yellow and orange flower.

Display plants indoors in bright, indirect light. Water them when the top inch of soil feels almost dry to the touch—about every two weeks. Also add water to the cupped leaf bases.

—*L.B.S.*

WHAT TO DO IN YOUR GARDEN IN DECEMBER

PLANTING

☐ **AMARYLLIS.** Among the most spectacular flowers you can grow indoors, amaryllis are available as bulbs and leafed-out plants this month. Buy budded plants for Christmas bloom. Plant bulbs now for March bloom. Amaryllis need plenty of light and regular water.

☐ **CAMELLIAS.** *Sunset* climate zones 4–7, 17: Winter-flowering *Camellia sasanqua* are in bloom now, so it's a good time to choose varieties with the colors you like. *C. sasanqua* are not susceptible to camellia petal blight as are spring-blooming *C. japonica* varieties. Mulch to protect roots from freezing. Fertilize when new growth starts in spring. Shop for plants at local nurseries, or order by mail from Nuccio's Nurseries *(626/794-3383)*.

☐ **CONIFERS.** It's a perfect time to shop for conifers. If you're looking for a living Christmas tree, consider alpine fir, Douglas fir, noble fir, or white fir. For landscape plants, see the story on page 358.

☐ **DECIDUOUS TREES, SHRUBS.** Zones 4–7: Set out container-grown plants now, or wait until next month to plant bare-root stock.

MAINTENANCE

☐ **CARE FOR LIVING CHRISTMAS TREES.** If you buy a living Christmas tree, leave it in its nursery container and try to limit its time indoors to 10

days. Water regularly; one way is to dump ice cubes on top of the soil daily. After its indoor stay, move the tree to a cool, bright porch where its rootball won't freeze. When the soil is workable, transplant the tree into the garden; you can also leave it in the container for another year.

☐ **GLEAN FRAGRANT GREENS.** Cut snippets of fresh foliage to scent your house. Try pungent cedars, firs, pines, and rosemary, plus native Oregon myrtle *(Umbellularia californica)*.

☐ **INSULATE ROSES.** Zones A1–A3, 1–3: Mound soil over the plant's base; if it's a grafted rose, be sure the soil covers the bud union from which canes emerge. Set a cylinder of chicken wire or a tomato cage around each plant and fill with a mulch of leaves, pine boughs, or straw. Postpone pruning until spring.

☐ **PROPAGATE EVERGREENS.** Zones 4–7, 17: You can easily multiply many kinds of evergreen shrubs, including azalea, camellia, daphne, mahonia, and rhododendron, by a

process called layering. First, scrape a fingernail-size patch of bark off the bottom of a low branch, then dust the wound with rooting hormone. Press the scraped area into a shallow depression in the soil below, firm a little soil over the branch, and anchor it in the ground with a brick or rock. The branch will form roots where it contacts the soil. Next fall, you can cut the new plant free from the parent and plant it elsewhere.

☐ **TRIM A TREE FOR WILD BIRDS.** Decorate a small conifer or other evergreen tree with garlands of unsalted popcorn, cranberries, and grapes strung on heavy-duty thread. Add ornaments of oranges and grapefruits sliced into wedges, dried corn on the cob, and pinecones slathered with a mixture of $1/2$ cup peanut butter and $2^{1}/_{2}$ cups cornmeal or oatmeal. Tie ornaments to the tree with heavy-duty thread. ◆

WHAT TO DO IN YOUR GARDEN IN DECEMBER

GIFT SHOPPING

☐ **FAVORITE TOOLS.** Every gardener on your gift list can use a new tool. Here are some of our favorites: the **Classic English Garden Fork** *($49)* or the **Heirloom Hand Trowel** *($12),* both from Smith & Hawken *(www. smithandhawken.com or 800/981-9888);* and the **Felco #8 Pruners** *($39)* or the **Traditional Japanese Farmer's Knife** *($19),* used for dividing plants, planting, transplanting, weeding, and other chores, both from Lee Valley Tools *(www.leevalley.com or 800/871-8158).*

PLANTING

☐ **ESPALIERED CAMELLIAS.** *Sunset* climate zones 7–9, 14–17: 'Yuletide' sasanqua camellia is the perfect choice for espaliering against a bare wall. The compact, upright grower is easy to train up a trellis, and the abundant red blooms come just in time for the holidays. Do most pruning right after bloom (next season's flower buds develop in late spring), but you can prune off some outward growth during the growing season to keep the plant flat.

☐ **LIVING BOUQUETS.** Zones 7–9, 14–17: Most nurseries have a good supply of 4-inch pots of color that you can cluster in large containers. Choose azaleas, calendulas, cinerarias, cyclamen, kalanchoe, pansies, English primroses, fairy primroses, *Primula obconica,* and snapdragons. Mix in foliage plants such as dusty miller, ferns, liriope, or dwarf nandina. Protect kalanchoe from frost.

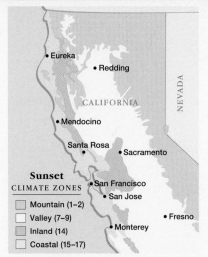

Sunset
CLIMATE ZONES

☐ Mountain (1–2)
☐ Valley (7–9)
☐ Inland (14)
☐ Coastal (15–17)

☐ **ROSES.** Zones 7–9, 14–17: Set your garden ablaze with color in spring by planting one or several of these tried-and-true roses soon: 'Bonica' (pink shrub rose), 'Brandy' (apricot hybrid tea), 'Double Delight' (red and white bicolor hybrid tea), 'Iceberg' (white floribunda or climber), 'Just Joey' (apricot hybrid tea), 'Kaleidoscope' (orange-tan to lavender shrub rose), 'Knock Out' (cerise shrub rose), 'Marmalade Skies' (tangerine floribunda), 'Mister Lincoln' (red hybrid tea), or 'Peace' (yellow and pink blend hybrid tea). Good supplies of bare-root plants should be available at nurseries starting this month.

MAINTENANCE

☐ **ADJUST IRRIGATION SYSTEMS.** Zones 7–9, 14–17: In winter, soil dries out more slowly. If rain is spotty, adjust your automatic irrigation system to operate less often (test soil moisture between irrigations to determine frequency). But continue to water deeply. If rains are consis-

tent, set the controller on rain delay (or turn it off) or install a rain shutoff to do this automatically.

☐ **KEEP CUT CHRISTMAS TREES FRESH.** To find the freshest tree, look for one that has been stored in water at a Christmas-tree lot. After bringing it home, prolong your tree's freshness by sawing an inch off the bottom of the trunk. Then stand the tree in a bucket of water and store it outdoors in a shady area until you're ready to bring it indoors for decorating. Before setting it in a stand, saw another inch off the trunk's bottom (you may need to remove some branches if they start low on the trunk). Use a stand that holds water, and keep the reservoir full (check daily the first week). Keep the tree away from heaters.

PEST CONTROL

☐ **SPRAY FOR PEACH DISEASES.** Zones 7–9, 14–17: To control peach blight and peach leaf curl, spray with lime sulfur mixed with dormant oil after leaves have dropped; repeat in January or early February. Spray on a dry day and follow label directions carefully. To avoid leaf burn, never use lime sulfur when temperatures are above 85°. ◆

WHAT TO DO IN YOUR GARDEN IN DECEMBER

PLANTING

☐ **BARE-ROOT PLANTS.** Coastal, inland, and low-desert gardeners (*Sunset* climate zones 22–24, 18–21, and 13, respectively) can plant artichokes, asparagus, cane berries, deciduous fruit trees, grapevines, and roses bare-root this month. If soil is too wet for immediate planting, cover roots with soil or plant temporarily in containers.

☐ **NATIVES.** California's native plants love being planted just before winter rains. Good choices for novices are buckwheat (*Eriogonum*), Cleveland sage and other salvias, coral bells, galvezia, lemonade berry, and mimulus.

☐ **ORNAMENTAL BERRY PLANTS.** Brighten the winter garden with berry-producing shrubs such as beautyberry (*Callicarpa*), cotoneaster, holly, pyracantha, snowberry (*Symphoricarpos*), and toyon. Most of these shrubs attract birds to the garden.

☐ **SPRING BULBS.** Coastal, inland, and low-desert gardeners can still plant spring-flowering bulbs. Crocuses, hyacinths, and tulips that have been chilled for at least six weeks can go into the ground now too.

☐ **WINTER VEGETABLES.** As you harvest winter crops, replace them with other winter vegetables. Beets, carrots, chard, kale, lettuce, peas, radishes, and spinach can go in from seed. If you've had difficulty with carrots before because of heavy soil,

Sunset
CLIMATE ZONES
1–3 7–9 11 13 14–24

try 'Romeo' from Renee's Garden (*www.reneesgarden.com* or *888/880-7228*). It's a short, round baby carrot. If you want to add broccoli, brussels sprouts, cabbage, and cauliflower, start them from seedlings.

MAINTENANCE

☐ **CARE FOR INDOOR PLANTS.** To counteract the dry air from heating systems, place potted plants on trays of moistened pebbles. Grouping plants close together and misting them frequently also helps increase humidity.

☐ **FEED CYMBIDIUMS.** To encourage flowers, feed cymbidiums with a fertilizer containing a high percentage of phosphorus (middle number on label), such as 15-30-15, until buds open.

☐ **PREPARE FOR FROST.** Move tender container plants under house eaves or indoors when cold weather is predicted. Cover plants in the ground with perforated plastic or

burlap supported by a frame—such as four tall stakes—that will keep the cover from touching the foliage.

☐ **PREPARE FOR RAIN.** Apply mulch 3 inches deep on garden beds to keep soil from becoming compacted in the rain. Set aside a protected area, away from rain and wind, for potted plants. Assemble plastic garbage cans to collect rainwater for houseplants and potted plants. Use concrete edging to redirect water away from areas where soil does not drain.

☐ **PRUNE RASPBERRIES.** To keep low-chill raspberries under control, cut back all canes to within a few inches of the ground this month. New growth will emerge in the spring.

DISEASE CONTROL

☐ **APPLY DORMANT SPRAY.** To prevent peach leaf curl next summer, spray peach and nectarine trees with lime sulfur or fixed copper now. If a few leaves remain on trees, shake them down first. Then spray branches, twigs, trunk, and ground beneath trees out to drip line. Repeat treatment when trees reach their peak dormancy around New Year's Day, and again at first bud swell around Valentine's Day. If it rains within 48 hours of spraying, repeat treatment. ◆

WHAT TO DO IN YOUR GARDEN IN DECEMBER

SHOPPING

☐ **FLOWERING CACTUS.** Just in time for the holidays, Christmas cactus *(Schlumbergera × buckleyi)* bears abundant blossoms in shades of orange, pink, purple, red, white, and yellow. This long-living houseplant does best when grown in bright, indirect light and fed weekly during bloom.

☐ **LIVING CHRISTMAS TREES.** Good choices include alpine fir *(Abies lasiocarpa)*, Colorado blue spruce *(Picea pungens glauca)*, Engelmann spruce *(P. engelmanii)*, and white fir *(A. concolor)*. Keep the tree in its nursery container, and try to limit its indoor stay to 10 days. Water it regularly; one easy way to do this is to dump two trays of ice cubes on top of the soil daily. If you don't have space to transplant the tree in your garden, consider buying a subtropical Norfolk Island pine *(Araucaria heterophylla)*, which can be grown indoors after the holidays.

MAINTENANCE

☐ **GIVE WILD BIRDS A TREAT.** To attract chickadees, jays, and woodpeckers, put out suet cakes. Many birds are also attracted to chunks of apple, banana, and orange impaled on tree branches. For tips on attracting and feeding specific birds, visit the website of the National Bird Feeding Society *(www.birdfeeding.org)*.

Sunset
CLIMATE ZONES

☐ 1–3   ☐ 10–11

☐ **IDENTIFY MICROCLIMATES.** When the snow from a recent storm has mostly melted, walk through your garden and make note of areas where the snow lingers longest. In these locations, snow provides good insulation from extreme cold, making them ideal microclimates to grow broadleaf evergreens like *Arctostaphylos*, boxwood, heavenly bamboo; conifers such as arborvitae, false cypress *(Chamaecyparis)*, and yews; and perennials that need extra protection.

☐ **INSULATE ROSES.** After temperatures have been below freezing for a few weeks, mound soil over the plant's base. If it's a grafted rose, be sure the soil covers the bud union (the enlarged knob from which canes emerge). Once the soil surface freezes, set a cylinder of chicken wire or a tomato cage wrapped in burlap around each plant, and fill it with a mulch of leaves, pine needles, or straw. Postpone pruning until spring. Spray exposed canes with an anti-transpirant.

☐ **MULCH WITH SNOW.** Snow insulates and protects the roots of shrubs, roses, and perennials from freezing and thawing cycles. Shovel snow off walks and driveways and onto borders and the bare areas beneath conifers. When the snow melts, it helps replenish soil moisture, which plants will draw from next spring.

☐ **PROPAGATE HOUSEPLANTS.** It's easy to start new plants by propagating them from existing parents. **For ivy,** snip tip cuttings from the parent plant, dip cut ends in rooting hormone, and place them in moist potting soil. **For pothos,** snip off elongated stems and immerse cut ends in water until roots form, then transplant into potting soil. **For spider plant,** snip off baby plants and place them in potting soil.

☐ **SPRAY ANTI-TRANSPIRANT.** Dwarf conifers and broadleaf evergreens such as holly and rhododendrons are susceptible to dehydration and windburn in winter. To protect them, spray the foliage with an anti-transpirant such as Wilt-Pruf Plant Protector *(www.wiltpruf.com or 800/972-0726 for store locations)*, following label instructions. One application lasts for several months. You can also use these types of products to prolong the life of cut greens in holiday arrangements. —*Marcia Tatroe*

WHAT TO DO IN YOUR GARDEN IN DECEMBER

SHOPPING

☐ **FLOWERFUL INDOOR CACTUS.** Just in time for the holidays, Christmas cactus *(Schlumbergera* x *buckleyi)* bears abundant blossoms in shades of orange, pink, purple, red, white, or yellow. This long-living houseplant does best when grown in bright, indirect light and fed weekly during bloom with liquid fertilizer.

☐ **LIVING CHRISTMAS TREES.** *Sunset* climate zones 1A–3B (Flagstaff, Taos, Santa Fe): Consider Colorado spruce *(Picea pungens)* or Douglas fir *(Pseudotsuga menziesii)*. Zone 10 (Albuquerque): Choose from Arizona cypress *(Cupressus arizonica),* Colorado spruce, Douglas fir, or piñon *(Pinus edulis).* Zones 11–13 (Las Vegas, Tucson, Phoenix): Try Afghan, or eldarica, pine *(Pinus eldarica),* bristlecone pine *(P. aristata),* or Italian stone pine *(P. pinea).* Keep the tree in its nursery container, trim it with cool-burning lights, keep the soil moist, and limit its indoor stay to two weeks or less. Afterward, transplant the tree into the garden or a generous container.

PLANTING

☐ **COOL-SEASON FLOWERS.** Zones 10–13: Set out transplants of chrysanthemum, dianthus, Iceland poppy, Johnny-jump-up, pansy, petunia, primrose, snapdragon, stock, sweet alyssum, and sweet pea.

☐ **COOL-SEASON VEGETABLES.** Zones 10–13: Set out transplants of artichoke, broccoli, cabbage, cauli-

Sunset CLIMATE ZONES
☐ 1–3 ☐ 10–11 ☐ 12–13

flower, kohlrabi, peas, salad greens, and onion seedlings. Zones 12, 13: Sow seeds of beets, bok choy, carrots, chives, green onions, lettuce, radishes, spinach, and turnips.

☐ **DISH GARDEN.** Choose a broad, shallow container with a drainage hole. Select an assortment of 2- or 3-inch potted specimens of cactus and succulents such as *Crassula, Lithops,* or sedums. Fill the container with 2 inches of potting mix formulated for cactus and succulents. Arrange the plants so their rootballs touch, placing taller ones in the center and shorter or trailing kinds at the edges. Fill in with more potting mix as needed, then mulch the surface with coarse sand or gravel. Place the dish in bright, indirect light; water every 10 to 14 days.

DECORATING

☐ **ASSEMBLE LUMINARIAS.** Also called *farolitos,* or little lanterns, luminarias are easy to make. Fold down the top 2 inches of a paper lunch bag, pour in 2 inches of sand, then place a votive candle or tea light in the middle of the bag, tapping it into the sand. Set the open bags 2 feet apart along paths, driveways, or patios. Use a long-necked butane lighter to light each candle.

☐ **GATHER NATURAL ORNAMENTS.** Collect materials from your garden or purchase them from a local craft store to make Southwest-style wreaths and arrangements. Good plants to incorporate include desert spoon petals, devil's claws *(Proboscidea),* mesquite beans, pomegranates, prickly pear pads, and yucca pods. Use dried chilies, cornhusks, and grasses as accents.

—Kim Nelson

Every garden evergreens

These beautiful conifers work wonders

By Steven R. Lorton

During the holidays, we tend to associate conifers with Christmas trees as we select the prettiest cut firs and spruces to decorate. But conifers are also beautiful landscape plants that serve many uses. You can plant them this month.

Conifers come in all sizes, textures, and colors—dark and light greens, sparkling blues and golds, and even variegated color combinations. And they do many jobs in the garden. The deodar cedar stretches out its long, horizontal limbs to do a graceful hula each time a stiff breeze blows through them, adding motion to the garden; its cousin, weeping Atlas cedar, makes a sculptural accent above lower-growing plants. And leave it to ground-hugging junipers to sprawl happily over a hot, dry bank through a rainless summer.

Thirteen of our favorite conifers are listed on the following pages according to their role in the garden. They represent just a fraction of the hundreds of conifer species, but this should give you an idea of what you can try in your own garden. Most are sold in 1-, 5-, and 15-gallon containers. All can take full sun and require regular water unless noted.

CLAIRE CURRAN

A curving row of Monterey cypress 'Gold Crest' trees creates a green backdrop for a garden bench. DESIGN: Brenda Gousha, Escondido, CA (760/473-0234)

◄ Conifers for hedges, screens

Dwarf Alberta spruce (*Picea glauca albertiana* 'Conica'). Compact, bushy shrub to 8 feet tall with short, soft, gray-green needles. Needs protection from drying winds and strong, reflected sunlight. Little to moderate water once established. *Sunset Western Garden Book* climate zones A2, A3; 1–7, 14–17.

Irish yew (*Taxus baccata* 'Stricta'). A glistening, dark green column, 15 to 30 feet tall and 3 to 10 feet wide. Sun or shade. Zones A3; 3–9, 14–24.

Italian cypress (*Cupressus sempervirens*). This dark green pillar reaches 60 feet when fully grown, 5 to 10 feet wide. *C. s.* 'Glauca' has blue-green needles. Zones 4–24; H1, H2. *C. arizonica,* a related species, grows to 40 feet tall and 20 feet wide. Zones 7–24. Both need little to moderate water once established.

Leyland cypress (x *Cupressocyparis leylandii*). Needs regular pruning to stay shapely. Can grow as much as 4 feet a year to 60 or 70 feet tall with a 15-foot spread. *C. l.* 'Castlewellan' has golden new growth. *C. l.* 'Naylor's Blue' has grayish blue foliage. Zones 3B–24.

Conifers
for accents ▸

Hollywood juniper
(*Juniperus chinensis*
'Torulosa'). This Western
standby makes great gar-
den sculpture, zigzagging
its way up to 15 feet tall
with dark, rugged-looking
limbs and rich green fo-
liage. Sun or light shade;
low to moderate water
once established. Zones
1–24; H1, H2.

Japanese cryptomeria
(*Cryptomeria japonica*
'Yoshino'). Nearly as colorful as the regular species,
but grows to only 30 or 40
feet tall (versus 100 feet).
Zones 4–9, 14–24.

Mugho pine *(Pinus mugo
pumilio).* Shrubby, sym-
metrical pine with deep
green foliage. Grows
slowly to 4 feet tall; good
in rock gardens (with little
to moderate water) and
containers. Zones A1, A3;
1–11, 14–24.

Shore pine *(Pinus contorta contorta).* A Western
native, this pine grows
relatively quickly to 20 to
35 feet tall and wide, with
rich green needles. Nurs-
ery trees are pyramidal
(along the coast, trees are
often contorted by winds).
Equally useful in groups as
an informal screen or singly
in a mixed shrub border.
Zones A3; 4–9, 14–24; H1.

Weeping Atlas cedar
(*Cedrus atlantica* 'Glauca
Pendula'). This handsome
conifer arches up slightly
and fountains down. Ex-
cellent for planting above
walls or to spill over rocks.
Moderate water once es-
tablished. Zones 3B–10,
14–24.

Weeping blue Atlas cedar spreads sculptural branches behind a water basin in Sherwood, OR. Right: Colorful conifers in Washington's Skagit Valley include golden *Thuja occidentalis* 'Rheingold', deep green mugho pine, and blue Spanish fir (*Abies pinsapo* 'Glauca'). Bottom right: Shore juniper spills from a raised bed.

Conifers for color ▲

Chamaecyparis pisifera 'Boulevard'. A dense, slow-growing bush with soft, silvery blue-green foliage on reddish branches. To 8 feet tall. Zones A3; 2B–6,15–17.

Thuja occidentalis 'Rheingold'. Forms a vibrant golden cone with a mixture of scale and needle foliage. To 6 feet tall and wide. Zones A2, A3; 1–9, 15–17, 21–24; H1, H2.

◄ Conifers that spill and drip

Sargent weeping hemlock (*Tsuga canadensis* 'Pendula'). Dark green needles cover arching branches (about 5 feet long) that spill down to the ground or, if planted atop a wall, even farther. *T. c.* 'Gentsch White' is smaller (to 2 feet) with white-tipped new growth. Sun or light shade. Zones A3; 2–7, 17.

Shore juniper *(Juniperus conferta)*. Blue-green needles on multiple stems that cascade 3 to 4 feet; 1 foot tall. Sun or light shade; little to moderate water once established. Zones 3–9, 14–24; H1, H2. ◆

White lights, attached to the ceiling with hooks, shimmer over this porch in Bellingham, WA.

All aglow

How to make a splash with holiday lights, beside an entry or in your garden

By Kathleen N. Brenzel

As twilight arrives earlier and earlier on cold December days, something magical happens at homes around the West: Holiday lights flicker to life. They create glittering galaxies on porch ceilings, bathe eaves and gables in a warm glow, and turn stately saguaros, gnarled olive trees, or stout-trunked palms into shimmering sculptures. Some dangle in bundles beneath patio arbors like luminescent grape or wisteria clusters, or poke through rhododendron foliage in brilliant bursts. Others are draped along the edges of boat docks in places like Lake Washington and California's Newport Beach, their reflections dancing across dark waters.

Let holiday lights spark your imagination. When creating your own display, be sure to use lights approved for outdoor

Tree lighting, *Sunset*-style

Colored lights once flecked the olive-tree canopies at *Sunset's* headquarters in Menlo Park, California. But two years ago, head gardener Rick LaFrentz decided to wrap the trees' trunks and branches with miniature white lights instead. "I'll do anything to keep from climbing those trees," he says. Each tree requires twelve 150-bulb strands of lights (connected in four ropes of three strands each), plugged into four outlets near the trunk's base. To keep the lights from tangling while he works, LaFrentz wraps each strand around an 8½- by 11-inch piece of corrugated cardboard (pictured below). He secures the end of each rope to the tree's bottom with a U-shaped staple, then wraps the tree from the bottom up, turning the cardboard slowly as he goes. LaFrentz spaces the lights as evenly as possible, sometimes doubling back on an area. Finally, to keep out moisture, he covers each joint between two plugs with electrical tape (bottom).

Miniature white lights sparkle on *Sunset's* venerable olive trees; white cyclamen grow below. The lights glow each night from dusk until 11 P.M., December 1 through January 2.

Miniature white lights, wrapped around ⅜ inch-diameter black rope, create wisteria "branches" at Bellevue Botanical Garden. Flower clusters are bunches of purple lights bound together with cable ties and attached to individual extension cords above the arbor.

Top: Miniature white lights and blossoms made from red lights brighten climbing roses outside Sharp's Cabin at Bellevue Botanical Garden in Bellevue, WA. Above: Pink, purple, and white lights, gathered in bunches and secured with cable ties, poke through rhododendron foliage to mimic flower trusses.

use according to label directions; cool-burning miniatures are best for plants. And, of course, wear sturdy leather gloves when stringing lights around cactus or roses. A strand of miniature white lights typically costs $4–$10; these and other lights are available at most drug stores and discount stores such as Target.

Use lights to ...

Highlight your home's architectural features. Run white lights along the edges of structural elements such as bay windows and chimneys.

Enhance your garden. String white lights around trellises or gazebos.

Brighten sculptural plants. Plants with interesting curves or angles can be more beautiful still when illuminated against the night sky: Try *Arbutus* 'Marina', cactus such as saguaro and opuntia, Harry Lauder's walking stick (*Corylus avellana* 'Contorta'), and Mediterranean fan palm *(Chamaerops humilis)*.

For more ideas, design advice, lighting sources, and tips on good lights for specific situations, pick up *Holiday Lights! Brilliant Displays to Inspire Your Christmas Celebration,* by David Seidman (Storey Publishing, North Adams, MA, 2003; $17; 800/441-5700). ◆

Pint-size citrus

Gardeners everywhere can find room for these dwarf trees

By Lauren Bonar Swezey
Photographs by Thomas J. Story

For nearly 300 years, the mild-winter West has had a love affair with citrus. Orchards carpet the land in parts of California, and oranges, lemons, limes, and other citrus are familiar trees in home gardens.

Until fairly recently, most of these trees were robust growers, reaching 20 to 30 feet tall and as wide—too big for small gardens and certainly too big for most pots. Even semidwarf trees, introduced in the mid-1900s, grow 10 to 15 feet tall.

Now dwarf citrus trees that grow slower than standards—reaching 5 to 7 feet tall in 13 years in the ground and staying even shorter in containers—are becoming more widely available. What makes them so compact are their roots. Sold as "dwarf" or "genetic dwarf," these citrus trees are grafted onto a

This mandarin thrives in a 28-inch-wide, 11-inch-tall container on a front porch.

Dwarf lime displays fruits in various stages of growth.

rootstock called Flying Dragon—a naturally dwarf, contorted form of trifoliate orange *(Poncirus trifoliata)*—which reduces their height by 75 percent. But fruits are standard size, all within easy reach at harvest time.

Nurseries now offer an array of citrus trees on this dwarfing rootstock, from 'Washington' navel orange and 'Lisbon' lemon to 'Pixie' mandarin and 'Oroblanco' grapefruit-pummelo hybrid. In the mildest climates, shop for trees this month; in slightly colder climates, your best selection is in spring. In *Sunset Western Garden Book* climate zones 1–7, which are outside the citrus-growing range, you can buy a tree by mail and keep it indoors until after last frost. A good mail-order source is Clifton's Nursery (www.buyplantsonline.com or 888/209-4356; does not deliver to Arizona).

Is it really a dwarf?

Nursery labels can be confusing. Some trees marked "true dwarf" are actually semidwarfs. But citrus grown on Flying Dragon rootstock are labeled as such by Monrovia and C & M wholesale nurseries; Willits & Newcomb wholesale nursery identifies its Flying Dragon citrus with a sticker on the label that just says "dwarf." If in doubt, ask your nursery whether the plant is growing on Flying Dragon.

Citrus care

Location: Choose a site that gets at least six hours of full sun per day and is pro-

Tree height

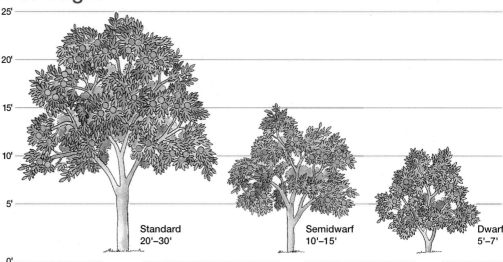

25'

20'

15'

10'

5'

0'

Standard
20'–30'

Semidwarf
10'–15'

Dwarf
5'–7'

Planting in containers

Pot size: Choose a container at least 18 inches in diameter. Or start with a smaller pot (at least 12 inches wide) and transplant the tree into a larger pot in a year or two.

Soil: Use a high-quality potting mix. If the pot won't be watered by an automatically controlled drip-irrigation system, add soil polymers (such as Broadleaf P4) to the potting mix. As the soil dries out, polymers offer an extra supply of moisture to the roots, helping to prevent the tree from becoming moisture stressed between waterings.

Repotting: If the soil starts drying out quickly and the roots are compacted, you'll need to pull the plant from its container, prune the roots, and repot the tree. Vigorous trees such as 'Lisbon' lemon or 'Oroblanco' may need repotting after 3 to 5 years; very small trees (kumquats, for instance) may go twice as long.

tected from wind. In cool or foggy climates, locate the tree where it gets reflected heat from a sunny south-facing wall or driveway.

Drainage: Before planting citrus in the ground, make sure the soil is well drained. If your soil is compacted or of heavy clay and drains slowly, plant citrus in raised beds or containers. To improve water retention in sandy soils, dig in a 4- to 6- inch layer of compost to a depth of about 1 foot.

Mulch: Citrus tend to have shallow roots; adding a layer of mulch on top of the soil helps keep them cooler and reduces moisture loss from the soil. Apply a 2- to 3-inch layer of compost or other organic amendment under the tree's canopy, keeping it away from the trunk.

Fertilizer: Citrus grown on Flying Dragon rootstock are sensitive to highly alkaline soils (pH 7 and above). As long as the tree is fed regularly, such soils shouldn't be a problem. Use a fertilizer labeled for citrus; besides nitrogen, phosphorous, and potassium, it should contain the minor nutrients iron, manganese, and zinc. Follow package directions for application rate. If the foliage turns chlorotic (indicated by yellow leaves with green veins), spray it with a foliar food containing chelated iron and the minor nutrients listed above. Withhold fertilizer from fall through midwinter.

Watering: Drip irrigation is the most reliable way to keep citrus watered, particularly if it's growing in a container. Run the system often enough to keep the soil moist but not soggy. (For plants in the ground, water when the soil is starting to dry out 5 to 6 inches below the

surface; in containers, when it's starting to dry 1 to 2 inches down.) Whether you water by drip or by hose, water long enough to moisten the entire root area. Consistent irrigation is key; fluctuating soil moisture can cause fruit splitting, especially of navel oranges.

Frost protection: When frost is predicted, make sure trees are well watered ahead of time. Wrap the tree with a string of Christmas lights, then cover it with a frost blanket or floating row cover (available from Harmony Farm Supply & Nursery, *www.harmonyfarm.com* or *707/823-9125*).

Pruning: Prune in late spring or summer to shape trees. Remove suckers that form below the graft union (denoted by a scar on the lower trunk). In the desert, fruit and trunks are susceptible to sunburn; allow tree canopies to grow low and full to provide shade.

Harvest: Most citrus fruits ripen from late fall into winter; exceptions are 'Valencia' orange, which ripens into spring and summer, and lemons and limes, which can bear year-round. Allow fruits to ripen on the tree. To determine whether sweet fruits like oranges are ready to harvest, pluck, slice, and taste one first. Pick lemons and other tart fruits before they become puffy.

Pest control: Aphids, scale, or spider mites may infest a tree, especially if it's weak from poor growing conditions. To control them, spray thoroughly (including cracks and crevices) with horticultural oil or insecticidal soap. (Scale are most susceptible to pesticides at the crawler stage, in midspring and mid- to late summer.)

Choose the right citrus for your climate

Cool-summer areas (*Sunset* climate zone 17) and **cold-winter areas** (zones 1–7): Sour types of citrus, which need less heat to ripen than sweet kinds, are good choices along the coast, as well as in cold-winter areas, where indoor-outdoor container culture is a must. These include 'Bearss' lime, calamondin, kumquat, kumquat hybrids, lemon, and 'Rangpur' lime (sour mandarin). 'Improved Meyer' lemon is a particularly good choice indoors.

Mild-summer areas (zones 15, 16, and 24): You can grow all of the sour types of citrus listed at left, plus 'Oroblanco' grapefruit-pummelo hybrid and 'Valencia' orange (although the fruit won't be as sweet as that grown in inland areas). Protect fruit from frost.

Hot-summer, mild-winter areas (zones 8, 9, 12–14, 18–23): All citrus thrive in these climates (protect fruit from frost). Deserts produce the sweetest grapefruit. ◆

Citrus type		Characteristics	Zones	Uses
	'Moro' blood orange	Orange-red flesh darkens to deep red as fruit hangs on the tree. Orange flavor with raspberry overtones.	8, 9, 12–14, 15 (warmest areas), 18–23	Easy to peel; makes beautiful reddish juice.
'Improved Meyer' lemon		A lemon-orange hybrid. Dark yellow flesh tastes sweeter, less acidic than other lemons; flavor has floral overtones.	8, 9, 12–24; H1, H2; indoors	Best in desserts (sorbet, tarts, lemon soufflé) and sweet spreads (lemon curd).
'Nagami' kumquat		Small oval fruit has sweet rind and tart-tasting flesh. Fruiting tree is very ornamental.	8, 9, 12–24; H1, H2; indoors	Eat fresh (unpeeled) or use in sauces, candies, and marmalade.
'Pixie' mandarin		Seedless, late-ripening variety with sweet, mild flesh and a bumpy rind. Pick fruits as soon as they ripen.	8, 9, 12–14, 18–23	Good to eat fresh (it's easy to peel); tasty in salads.
'Oroblanco'		Grapefruit-pummelo hybrid with sweet, juicy flesh and few to no seeds. Better flavor than other grapefruit-pummelo hybrids. Thick rind.	8, 9, 12–24; H1, H2	Cut in half to eat fresh with a spoon grapefruit-style (avoid bitter membranes); great for juice.
	'Star Ruby' grapefruit	Smallish fruit has thinner rinds than many other grapefruits and few to no seeds; tastes less acidic than other grapefruit. Flesh is the deepest red in hot-summer climates.	8, 9, 12–14, 18–23	Halve to eat fresh with a spoon; makes excellent pinkish juice.
	'Washington' navel orange	Large fruit with moderately thick rind; navel at one end. Moderately juicy, seedless.	8, 9, 14, 15 (warmest areas), 18–23; H1, H2	Tastes best fresh (it's easy to peel and segment) but can be juiced if used right away (juice turns bitter soon after squeezing); 'Valencia' orange is best for juicing.

Growing citrus in cold climates

You'll get the best fruit production if the tree is grown outdoors in summer and brought indoors before the first frost in fall. Move the tree to a greenhouse or cool, bright location, such as a sunroom.

Supply humidity: Place the pot on a tray of wet pebbles or run a small humidifier nearby.

Watering: Be careful not to overwater the soil. Don't allow the pot to stand in water.

Holiday blooms

Narcissus bulbs planted in a paint can will brighten someone's life for weeks.

1. Cover a **1-quart paint can** (about $1 at hardware stores) with **wrapping paper**, securing the seam with **double-stick tape**.

SIMPLE GIFT

2. Guided by the depression in the can's lid, trace and cut out a paper label, write your message, and attach to lid with double-stick tape. **3.** Fill can halfway with **sand**. **4.** Place two or three **paperwhite** (shown) or other narcissus **bulbs** (about $5 for a 10-pack) in the sand (roots down, points up). **5.** On a paper slip, offer advice for the giftee: *To force bulbs, set aside lid and add water until sand is just moist. Place in sunny spot and keep moist; blooms in about seven weeks.* **6.** Tuck instructions in can, and, covering lid with a **dishcloth**, gently tap into place with a **hammer**. —*Jil Peters*

Forced paperwhites rise from a gift container.

happy holidays from jil

THOMAS J. STORY

Article Titles Index

A

Abundant gardening, 116
Acres of hardy perennials, 186
After-bloom care for potted mums, 320
Agave stars in this pot, 9
All aglow, 362–364
All-America Selections for 2003, 8
All-star gerberas, 172–175
As savory as its name, 231
Asters for fall bouquets, 293
Autumn joy, 304–310
Avocado for small yards, 190
Awesome alliums, 316

Aquilegia caerulea

B

Back to school, in the garden, 285
Bali chair grows tropicals, 190
Beauty in small spaces, 288–289
Beauty of natives, 332–340
Benefits of fall planting, 241
Best tools, 11
Bewitching hazel, 23
Big ideas, tiny trees, 80–81
Blanket flower, 123
Bougainvillea for a slope, 217
Bromeliads sizzle with color, 352
Bulbs for pots, 317
Bulb worth searching for, 293

C

Cactus plus poppies, 32
Cactus reigns supreme, 88
Camass: A true Northwest beauty, 238
Carefree & colorful, 98–105
Casual, colorful city garden, 236
Cinderella makeover, 198–201
Classic Southwest trio, 326
Classy combo, 10
Clematis columns accent a fence, 188
Compact, colorful, carefree entry, 155
Compact lavenders, 146
Conservatory blooms again, 237
Containers for all seasons, 142–143
Control moss and algae, 351
Cool-season color pots, 324
Cool-toned plants bask in the sun, 242
Coordinate a spring flower show, 297
Costa Rican butterfly vine, 185
Crops that thrive in pots, 118

D

Deck the wall with fresh-cut greens, 349
Delicious potager in Denver, 243
Denver's bonsai trove, 321
Designing with nature in Mill Valley, 292
Devil's claw, a summer surprise, 156
Devoted to topiary in Colorado, 62
Dig it in Del Mar, 350
Dog tunnel, 192
Dripless in Denver, 216
Drought-proof color in Colorado Springs, 189

E

Early-bird bulbs, 241
Early-blooming cymbidium, 293
Echeveria on ice, 211
Edelweiss grows high in the Rockies, 189
Every garden evergreens, 358–361
Exotic nights, 208–209

F

Fall's richest hues, 320
Family garden, 76–77
Feeding tulips, 62
Few seeds, a lot of lupines, 159
Firecracker penstemon, 155
Flower-bed cymbidiums, 30
Flowering tepee, 36
Flowers make good neighbors, 214
Flowers thrive on gray water, 126
Flying colors, 228–230
Focus on flowers, 87
Fresh ideas at Seattle's big show, 35
Fresh Southwest spirit in Phoenix, 240
Fresno's festival of lights, 351
From driveway to cozy courtyard, 296
From driveway to sun garden, 184
Front-yard design, 106–110
Front-yard facelift, 33

G

Garden art, 11
Garden checklists, Mountain
January, 16
February, 41
March, 66
April, 96
May, 132
June, 166
July, 196
August, 226
September, 248
October, 302
November, 330
December, 356
Garden checklists, Northern California
January, 14
February, 39
March, 64
April, 94
May, 130
June, 164
July, 194
August, 224
September, 246
October, 300
November, 328
December, 354
Garden checklists, Pacific Northwest
January, 13
February, 38
March, 63
April, 93
May, 129
June, 163
July, 193
August, 223
September, 245
October, 299
November, 327
December, 353
Garden checklists, Southern California
January, 15

Fremontodendron

General Subject Index

Aquilegia formosa

Asclepias tuberosa

Acer circinatum

Beech, weeping, 201
Beefsteak plant, 242
Beefwood, 345
Begonia, 142, 177
Beneficials, 36
Berberis thunbergii, 201
Bergenia cordifolia, 324
Berms
    designing with, 33, 110, 200
    irrigation, 150, 192, 257, 265, 273
Bird-friendly gardening, 12, 51, 103, 137
Bird of paradise, 160, 263
Bird's nest fern, 190
Bismarckia nobilis, 205
Black-eyed Susan, 8
Blackfoot daisy, 340
Blanket flower, 123

Baileya multiradiata

Bloodleaf, 180
Bluebell, 256
Blue fescue, 44–45, 263
Blue flax, 339
Blue grama, 241
Blue mist, 59, 270
Blue oat grass, 161, 270, 273, 312
Blue star creeper, 100, 107, 108
Bonsai, 80–81, 321
Borders. *See* Beds and borders
Bottlebrush, lemon, 160
Bougainvillea, 46, 109, 122, 123, 160, 209, 217, 263, 278
Bouquets. *See* Floral arrangements and bouquets

Buddleja marrubiifolia

Bouteloua gracilis 'Hachita', 241
Bouvardia longiflora, 79, 180
Boxwood, 292
Brachyscome, 21
Brahea armata, 204
Breath of heaven, 100, 322
Breynia nivosa 'Roseopicta', 220
Bristlecone pine, 268
Brittlebush, 33, 89, 217, 275, 326, 334, 335, 340
Broccoli, 74, 136
Bromeliads, 34, 180, 190, 352
Broom
    Provence, 270
    Scotch, 59
Brugmansia, 191, 264
Buddleja
    davidii, 342
    marrubiifolia, 340
Bulbs
    combinations of, 297
    companions for, 238, 297, 298, 323
    early-blooming, 241
    fertilizing, 62
    massing, 149
    for Pacific Northwest, 256
    in pots, 317, 368
    uncommon, 238, 293
Bunny ears, 326
Bush anemone, 334, 338
Bush morning glory, 222

Butia capitata, 204
Butterflies, attracting, 78, 158, 186
Butterfly bush, 342
Butterfly weed, 339

C

Cabbage, 74–75, 139, 230, 243
Cactus, 32, 51, 88, 128, 217, 280, 295, 334
Caesalpinia pulcherrima, 187
Cajeput tree, 345
Caladium, 216
Calamagrostis x *acutiflora*, 270, 310, 312
Calathea, 180
Calibrachoa, 110, 216, 238, 343
Caliche soils, 281
California desert bluebells, 315
California fuchsia, 338
California poppy, 105, 161, 282, 315
Calla, 53
Callirhoe involucrata, 147, 216, 270
Callisia elegans, 180
Callistemon citrinus, 160
Calluna vulgaris 'Wickwar Flame', 324
Calocedrus decurrens, 201
Calycanthus occidentalis, 253
Calylophus serrulatus, 270
Camassia, 238
Camellia, 177, 261
    sasanqua, 256, 324
Campanula, 21
    new double, 61
    persicifolia, 188
Canary Island date palm, 205
Candytuft, 21
Canna, 21, 113, 180, 313
Carambola, 156
Cardinal flower, 185
Cardoon, 113, 219
Carex, 51, 312
    buchananii, 201
    comans 'Frosty Curls', 252

Carex (cont'd)
    hachijoensis 'Evergold', 324
    morrowii, 77
    tumulicola, 322
Carpenteria californica, 338
Carrots, 75, 118, 136
Caryopteris x *clandonensis*, 59, 270
Cassia leptophylla, 345
Casuarina stricta, 345
Catalina cherry, 334
Catalpa speciosa, 345
Catmint, 21, 51, 104, 171, 322
Cedar
    golden deodar, 198, 201
    incense, 201
    Port Orford, 10
    weeping, 35, 142, 185, 238, 360, 361
Ceanothus, 100, 263, 334, 338
    'Victoria', 101

Carpenteria californica

Cedrus
    atlantica 'Glauca Pendula', 142, 238, 360
    deodara 'Aurea', 201
Celosia spicata, 116
Centaurea dealbata, 188
Centranthus ruber, 270
Cerastium tomentosum, 31, 270
Cercidium
    floridum, 187
    praecox, 33, 217
Cercis canadensis, 37, 272
Cerinthe major, 314, 315

Desert willow, 345
Design
    awards, 43–53
    focal points in, 46, 48, 103, 207, 260
    tips, 253, 260, 263, 276, 278, 342–343
    of vegetable plots, 68–71, 73, 185, 186, 243
Devil's claw, 156
Dianthus, 21, 267
    'Corona Cherry Magic', 8
    deltoides 'Brilliancy', 188
    nardiformis, 147
    'Zing Rose', 136
Diascia, 87, 179
Dieffenbachia, 180
Digitalis, 185
Diospyros kaki, 309
Diseases, plant
    fungal root, 322, 334
    powdery mildew, 92
    See also specific plants
Dogwood, 200, 255
    pagoda, 272
    redtwig, 154, 337
    Tatarian, 77
Donkey tail, 244
Doritaenopsis, 218
Dracaena fragrans, 180
Drainage problems, land-scaping to solve, 47, 255
Driveways, borrowing from, 179, 184, 296
Drosanthemum 'African Red', 295
Drought-tolerant plants. *See* Water-wise gar-dening, plants for
Dry streambeds, 47, 158, 201, 350
Duckweed, 25
Dusty miller, 21
Dypsis decaryi, 204

E

Echeveria, 160, 184, 211, 244
Echium candicans, 60, 263, 342
Edelweiss, 189

Edgings, 76, 77, 240, 243
Eggplants, 118, 138, 139, 215
Elephant's ear, 113
Elm, 345
Empress tree, 345
Encelia
    californica, 78
    farinosa, 33, 89, 217, 326, 340

Encelia farinosa

English daisy, 323
English laurel, 219
Enkianthus campanulatus, 252
Ensete, 113
Entertaining in the garden, 79, 90, 168–171, 192, 208–209
Entryway ideas, 31, 89, 155, 296, 313
Epimedium, 254
Eranthis hyemalis, 241
Erica, 10, 256
Erigeron, 21, 51
    karvinskianus, 342
    speciosus 'Azure Fairy', 188
Eriogonum umbellatum, 186
Erysimum
    'Bowles Mauve', 236, 322
    linifolium 'Variegatum', 101
Eschscholzia
    californica, 105, 282, 315
    mexicana, 32

Espaliers, 177, 343
Eucalyptus
    erythrocorys, 322
    nicholii, 345
Eugenia, 292
Eulalia grass, 312
Euonymus, 77
    alatus, 256
    japonicus, 324
    radicans 'Kewensis', 124
Eupatorium
    purpureum, 12, 185, 243, 311
    rugosum 'Chocolate', 98
Euphorbia, 101, 280
    biglandulosa, 162
    characias wulfenii, 37, 184
    marginata 'Summer Icicle', 180
    x *martinii,* 77
    milii, 296
    tirucalli, 109
Euryops pectinatus, 160
Evening primrose
    tufted, 339
    white, 147, 240
Evergreens, 89, 142, 239, 244, 358–361
Everlasting flowers, 123, 316, 348

F

Fabric panels, 46, 228–230
Fagus sylvatica 'Pendula', 201
Fall color, plants for, 221, 256, 309, 310, 322, 325
Fall planting, 239, 241, 251, 259, 267, 275
Fallugia paradoxa, 59, 270
False cypress
    Hinoki, 201
    'Repens', 324
False indigo, 272
Fatsia japonica, 142
Feather reed grass, 142, 270, 312
Fences, ideas for, 53, 210
Fennel, 12
Fernbush, 272
Ferns, 47, 157, 177, 180, 219, 254, 255, 256

Ferns (*cont'd*)
    sword, 49, 76, 201, 334, 337
Fescue, 44, 51, 76, 185, 236, 270
Festuca
    glauca 'Elijah Blue', 31, 324
    idahoensis 'Siskiyou Blue', 270, 312
Feverfew, 21, 256
Ficus pumila, 143, 187
Fig, edible, 177
Fir, 35
    blue Spanish, 361
Fireplaces, ideas for out-door, 51, 71
Fire, protection from, 261, 269
Flannel bush, 333, 334
Floating row covers, 117, 136, 140
Floral arrangements and bouquets
    cutting tips for, 175, 293
    Easter egg baskets for, 84
    fall foliage for, 306–309
    fresh-cut greens for, 349, 351
    for winter holidays, 348, 349, 368
Focal points, ideas for, 46, 48, 103, 207, 260
Foeniculum vulgare, 12
Foliage interest, 86, 112, 149, 180, 200, 239, 253, 259, 304–310
Forsythia, 256
Fothergilla, 256
Fountain grass, 310
Fountains, ideas for, 46, 47, 85, 171, 179, 201, 206, 218
Fouquieria splendens, 187
Four o'clock, desert, 270
Foxglove, 100, 105, 136, 185, 214, 270
Foxtail palm, 204
Fragrance, planting for, 23, 57, 79, 180, 258–260, 335
Fraxinus pennsylvanica, 345
Freesia, 142, 297
Fremontodendron californicum, 263, 333
Fritillaria, 256

High-elevation gardening. *See* Harsh-climate gardening
Hillsides. *See* Slopes
Holiday gift ideas, 84, 351, 368
Holodiscus dumosus, 339

Holodiscus dumosus

Hollyhock, 100, 136, 162
Honeywort, 315
Hop vine, 90
Hosta, 113, 157, 198, 313
  'Blue Angel', 256
  fortunei, 255
  'Francee', 77
  montana 'Aureomarginata', 256
  'Patriot', 201
Houseplants. *See* Indoor gardening
Houttuynia cordata 'Variegata', 189
Howea forsteriana, 205
Hummingbirds, 72, 78, 155, 158
Humulus lupulus, 90
Hyacinth, 297, 317
Hyacinth bean, 243
Hydrangea, 141, 238
  'Pia' dwarf, 110
  quercifolia 'Snowflake', 162
  'Shooting Star', 348
Hypoestes phyllostachya, 180
Hyssop, 72

I

Iceland poppy, 214, 322
Ice plant, 147, 270, 295
Idesia polycarpa, 252
ligiri tree, 252
Ilex verticillata, 324
Impatiens, 110, 190, 216
  New Guinea hybrids of, 180, 189
Inch plant, 180
Indian plum, 256
Indigo bush, 33
Indoor gardening, 24–27, 180, 222, 352
Insects, new book about, 36
International plant resource, 349
Ipomoea, 111, 142
  batatas, 343
Iresine, 180
Iris, 256
  bearded, 21, 122, 136, 159, 342
  Dutch, 297
  Japanese, 157
  miniature, 31
  Pacific Coast, 49, 78, 89, 251, 334, 337
  pseudacorus, 219
  spuria, 114

Iris douglasiana

Irish moss, 24, 27
Ironwood tree, 276
Irrigation. *See* Watering tips

J

Jade plant, 160
Japanese aralia, 142
Japanese cryptomeria, 360

Lewisia cotyledon

Japanese maple, 107, 110, 198, 219, 256, 292, 298, 308, 309
Japanese snowdrop tree, 201
Japanese style and influence, 49, 292
Jasmine, 62, 79, 180
  star, 341, 343
Jerusalem sage, 191, 263
Joe Pye weed, 12, 185, 243
Johnny jump-up, 137, 343
Juniper, 90
  'Broadmoor', 59
  Hollywood, 360
  shore, 361
Juniperus
  chinensis 'Torulosa', 360
  conferta, 361
  squamata 'Blue Star', 239
Jupiter's beard, 155, 255, 270

K

Kalanchoe, 102, 109, 244
Kale, 143, 324
Kalmia, 254
Kalmiopsis, 256

Kangaroo paw, 47, 264, 310
Katsura tree, 256
Kentia palm, 205
King palm, 205
Knautia macedonica Melton Pastels, 188
Kniphofia, 263
Koelreuteria paniculata, 272

L

Laburnum watereri, 177
Lady's-mantle, 155
Lady's slipper, 278, 280
Lamb's ears, 21, 158
Lamium, 180
  'Aureum', 142
  maculatum 'White Nancy', 87, 177
Landscape fabric, using, 85, 117
Lantana, 9, 128, 187
Larkspur, 315
Lavandula angustifolia, 270

Linum lewisii

Lavatera, 100, 261
Lavender, 21, 50, 51, 60, 98, 109, 127, 158, 161, 169, 259, 263, 312, 342
  compact varieties of, 146
  English, 146, 270
  'Hidcote', 189
  'Provence', 136
  Spanish, 105, 146

Mimulus cardinalis

N

Oenothera caespitosa

O

P

Prickly poppy, 78
Pride of Madeira, 263, 342
Primrose, 143, 157
Primula obconica, 142
Princess flower, 142
Privacy, designing for, 46, 53, 76, 79, 90, 179, 261, 313
Proboscidea, 156
Projects
    construction, 79, 85, 192, 210, 215, 294, 322
    craft, 306–308, 368
    culinary, 178, 231
    planting, 12, 85, 186, 190, 211

Ratibida columnifera

Propagation methods, 89, 141
Protea, 102
Pruning, 159, 351
Prunus
    besseyi, 272
    nigra 'Princess Kay', 272
Pumpkins, 74
Purple coneflower, 136
Purple fountain grass, 126, 216, 242
Purple hop bush, 47, 263
Purple passion vine, 180
Purple prairie clover, 270
Pussy willow, 256
Pygmy date palm, 202, 204, 205
Pyracantha, 177, 306
Pyrus calleryana 'Chanticleer', 272

Q

Queen palm, 205
Quercus palustris, 309

R

Rabbitbrush, 221
Rabbit's foot, 180
Radishes, 118
Raised beds, 31, 48, 53, 73, 85, 86, 138, 174
Ramadas, 278
Ranunculus, 58
Ratibida columnifera, 340
Recipes. See Projects, culinary
Recycled materials, using, 53, 85, 103
Red bird of paradise, 187
Redbud, eastern, 37, 272
Red-hot poker, 263
Redwood, 335
Reed grass, 53
Renovation, garden, 33, 48, 60, 198–201
Reseeding, plants prone to, 32, 86, 161, 314–315
Retreats, garden, 89, 179, 232
    book about, 351
Rheum palmatum, 113
Rhododendron, 77, 200, 201, 251, 254, 298, 337. *See also* Azalea
Rhopalostylis sapida, 204
Rhubarb, ornamental, 112
Ribes, 334
    aureum, 154, 272
Rock gardens, 31, 147, 189
    plants for, 256
Rockrose, 60, 184
Rock soapwort, 270
Romneya coulteri, 338
Rooftop gardening, 90, 104
Rosemary, 51, 56, 62, 261, 322
Roses
    Austrian Copper, 270
    'Ballerina', 104
    banksiae 'Lutea' (Lady Banks'), 58, 322
    bare-root planting of, 12
    'Bonica', 59

Roses *(cont'd)*
    Canadian Explorer Series, 137
    care of, 20, 159
    climbing, 11, 58, 177
    companion plants for, 21
    in containers, 104
    'Don Juan', 22
    'Eden', 21
    for every climate, 22
    'Eye Paint', 104
    'Flower Carpet', 236, 261

Rhododendron occidentale

    fragrant antique, 11
    'Gold Medal', 159
    Harison's yellow, 156
    'Iceberg', 101, 236, 342
    landscaping with, 18–22
    'Mme. Alfred Carrière', 11
    'Mary Rose', 20
    'Polka', 19
    raised bed for, 31
    'Royal Sunset', 19
    'Sally Holmes', 20
    'Simplicity', 104
    'What a Peach', 135
Rosmarinus officinalis, 56
Ruby grass, 216
Rudbeckia, 189
    'Cherokee Sunset', 116
    hirta 'Prairie Sun', 8
    Rustic Colors Mix, 136
Russian sage, 12, 21, 59

S

Sage
    Cleveland, 334, 338
    culinary, 56
    golden, 56
    Mexican bush, 51
    purple, 98
    Russian, 12, 59
    white, 334
Sagina subulata, 343
Sago palm, 142, 143
Saguaro, 88, 277
Salix integra 'Hakuro Nishiki', 86
Salvia, 109, 216, 259, 342
    clevelandii, 78, 338
    'Dara's Choice', 78
    greggii, 78
    nemorosa 'East Friesland', 77, 270
    officinalis, 56
    x *superba,* 155, 179
    x *sylvestris* 'Mainacht', 147
Sansevieria, 45
Santa Barbara daisy, 50, 315, 342
Santolina chamaecyparissus, 21, 109, 342

Romneya coulteri

Saponaria ocymoides, 270
Sarcococca, 256
Satureja hortensis, 231
Saxifrages, 256
Scabiosa, 21, 98, 136
Schizachyrium scoparium 'The Blues', 270

Strawberries
  edible, 135, 136
  as groundcover, 334
Strelitzia reginae, 160
Styrax japonicus, 201
Succulents, 88, 109, 211,
  215, 244, 280
  book about, 217
Sulfur flower, 186
Sumac, 334

Tetraneuris acaulis

Summer savory, 231
Sundrops, 270
Sunflower, 138, 162
Sunken garden areas, 46,
  49, 186
Sun, protecting plants from,
  85, 117, 220, 294
Supports for plants, 36,
  115, 124, 140, 189,
  215
Sweet alyssum, 9, 21, 73,
  85, 297, 315
Sweet pea, 243, 343
Sweet potato vine, 87, 126,
  216
Sweet William, 136, 214,
  322
Sweet woodruff, 254
Swimming pools and spas,
  49, 51, 170, 276
Swiss chard, 75, 118
Switch grass, 312
Sword fern, 49, 76
  Western, 201, 334, 337
Syagrus romanzoffianum,
  205
Symphoricarpos
  albus, 154
  mollis, 78

Symphytum, 56
Syngonium, 180

T

Tanacetum densum amanii,
  189
Taxus baccata 'Stricta',
  359
Tecoma stans angustata,
  340
Tetraneuris acaulis, 33, 240,
  340
Texas mountain laurel, 57,
  177
Thuja
  occidentalis, 185, 201,
    361
  orientalis, 239
Thyme
  for culinary use, 56
  as ground cover, 21,
    100, 108, 136, 158,
    241, 259, 270, 342
  as topiary, 62
Thymus pseudo-
  lanuginosus, 270
Tibouchina urvilleana, 142
Tiling. *See* Garden art, mosaic
Tomatoes
  growing, 115, 215
  types of, 74, 118, 136,
    139, 237
Tools and products
  Axe & Tool Sharpener, 9
  Beckett's Ceramic Wa-
    tering Vase, 218
  to control moss and al-
    gae, 351
  Diggit2 weeder, 36
  electric trimmers, 181
  experts' favorite, 342
  Interlocken detachable-
    head tools, 237
  Japanese blades, 11
  landscape fabrics,
    117
  Microfleur Microwave
    Flower Press, 123
  Root Irrigator, 151
  Soaker Ring, 151
  soil sampling tube,
    150
  water-wise hanging
    pots, 216

Tools and products *(cont'd)*
  wireless weather sta-
    tions, 9
Topiary, 62, 261
Trachycarpus fortunei, 204
Trees
  for espalier, 177
  for fall color, 309, 321,
    322
  fastest-growing,
    344–345
  free, in Los Angeles,
    351
  holiday lights on, 363
  irrigating, 192
  mature, for privacy, 60,
    71
  pruning, 159
  patio-size, 86
  planting, 241
  protection of, during re-
    modeling, 144–145
  use for stumps of, 185
  value of, 145, 148

Trichostema lanatum

Trellises, 110, 137, 140,
  176–177, 179, 215,
  322
Triangle palm, 204
Trichocereus, 128, 277
Trichostema lanatum, 89,
  338
Trillium, 254
Tropical
  plants, 47, 180, 190
  style, 202–205, 219,
    278
Tsuga canadensis
  'Gentsch White', 239
  'Pendula', 361

Tuberose, 180
Tufted hair grass, 312
Tulbaghia violacea, 342
Tulip, 84, 297, 298, 317,
  323
  care, 62
  species, 256
Tulip tree, 44

U

Ulmus x 'Accolade', 345
Unthirsty plants. *See*
  Water-wise gardening,
  plants for

V

Vancouveria, 254
Vegetables
  for containers, best, 118
  garden design with,
    68–71, 73, 185, 186,
    243
  healthiest, 73–75
  for high elevations, 136
  for high temperatures,
    138–140
  mixed with ornamentals,
    86, 135, 162, 243
  organically grown, 116
  protecting, 85, 117, 140,
    294
  seeds for unusual vari-
    eties of, 35
  sunken beds for, 186
  when to pick, 215
  See also specific plants
Verbascum, 12
  bombyciferum 'Arctic
    Summer', 268, 270
Verbena, 21, 87, 216, 236,
  275, 280
  bonariensis, 21
  gooddingii, 340
Veronica, 267
  'Georgia Blue', 84
  pectinata, 270
  spicata 'Red Fox', 147
  'Sunny Border Blue', 21
Vertical-space gardening,
  177, 322
Viburnum, 77, 110, 256,
  306

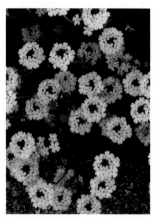

Verbena gooddingii

Y

Zauschneria californica

Z